Living Gluten-Free For Dummies®

Naturally Gluten-Free Foods

These are just a few of the nutritious foods you can eat when you're enjoying a gluten-free lifestyle; the list assumes these foods are fresh and unseasoned, because some flavorings and seasonings can contain gluten:

- Meat
- Poultry
- Fish
- Seafood
- Tofu
- Fruits
- Vegetables
- Nuts
- Seeds
- Berries
- Eggs

Grains and Starches You Can Eat Instead of Wheat

- Beans
- Legumes
- Flax
- Corn
- Potatoes
- Rice (any kind)
- Sorghum
- Soy
- Sago
- Tapioca (manioc, cassava)
- Millet
- Montina
- Mesquite
- Quinoa
- Buckwheat
- Amaranth
- Arrowroot
- Teff

Restaurant Card

When dining out, you can show this card to a server or chef. It explains the basics of the gluten-free dietary guidelines.

> I have a **severe** reaction to gluten and am on a strict gluten-free diet. Thank you for working with me to prepare a meal I can enjoy safely.
>
> I **cannot** eat these items: Wheat, rye, barley, or their derivatives, which include kamut, spelt, duram, semolina, bulgar, triticale, or malt.
>
> I need to **avoid** these foods and ingredients: oats, croutons, bread, breadings, flour, soy sauce, orzo, buns, rolls, and malt vinegar.
>
> I **can** eat rice, corn, potato, tapioca, soy, beans, amaranth, arrowroot, buckwheat, quinoa, millet, teff, and nut flours. I can also eat vinegar (except malt vinegar) and distilled alcohols.
>
> If you have any questions, please ask me. Thank you for working with me on this! Know that you have given me the opportunity to relax and enjoy my meal, and I appreciate it very much.

Living Gluten-Free For Dummies®

The Main Foods to Avoid

Gluten is in many ingredients, but here are the main ones you need to avoid. You should make sure you have a complete and accurate list of gluten-containing ingredients (like the one in this book) before assuming a product is or isn't gluten-free. Anything derived from these foods, or anything with these foods in the name, contains gluten:

- Wheat (durum, kamut, semolina, spelt, farina, bulgur, cake flour, matzo, matzah, couscous, and so on)
- Rye
- Barley
- Triticale

Ingredients to Question

You need to dig deeper and find out more about the source of these ingredients before you can eat them:

- Malt (usually contains gluten; okay if derived from corn rather than barley)
- Soy sauce (usually contains wheat)
- Modified food starch (usually gluten-free)
- Starch (in medications)
- Dextrin (usually gluten-free, as is maltodextrin)
- Flavorings
- Seasonings
- Oats (may be contaminated during harvesting or processing)
- Brown rice syrup
- Enzymes (which are sometimes made from barley)

Gluten-Free Indulgences

If you're in the mood for some decadent snacks, you can choose from plenty of gluten-free indulgences. You still have to check the labels, but many varieties of these foods are gluten-free:

- Tortilla chips
- Potato chips
- Ice cream
- Popsicles
- Chocolates
- Candy
- Gum
- Soda

Healthy Gluten-Free Snacks

You still need to read the labels, but here are some nutritious gluten-free snacks to get you started.

- Fruit and veggies (with dip)
- Dried fruit and nuts
- String cheese
- Hummus
- Rice or nut crackers
- Cream cheese
- Yogurt
- Deli meats
- Popcorn
- Juice

For Dummies: Bestselling Book Series for Beginners

Living Gluten-Free

FOR

DUMMIES®

by **Danna Korn**

Foreword by Alessio Fasano, M.D.

WILEY

Wiley Publishing, Inc.

Living Gluten-Free For Dummies®

Published by
Wiley Publishing, Inc.
111 River St.
Hoboken, NJ 07030-5774
www.wiley.com

For general information on our other products and services, please contact our Customer Care Department within the U.S. at 800-762-2974, outside the U.S. at 317-572-3993, or fax 317-572-4002.

For technical support, please visit www.wiley.com/techsupport.

Wiley also publishes its books in a variety of electronic formats. Some content that appears in print may not be available in electronic books.

Library of Congress Control Number: 2005939200

ISBN 978-0-471-77383-2

Manufactured in the United States of America

10 9 8 7

1O/RV/QT/QY/IN

WILEY

About the Author

Danna Korn is also the author *of Wheat-Free, Worry-Free: The Art of Happy, Healthy, Gluten-Free Living* and *Kids with Celiac Disease: A Family Guide to Raising Happy, Healthy Gluten-Free Children*. Respected as one of the leading authorities on the gluten-free diet and the medical conditions that benefit from it, she speaks frequently to health care professionals, celiacs, parents of celiacs, parents of autistic kids involved in a gluten-free/casein-free dietary intervention program, and others on or considering a gluten-free diet. She has been invited twice to be a presenter at the International Symposium on Celiac Disease.

Danna has been researching celiac disease since her son, Tyler, was diagnosed with the condition in 1991. That same year, she founded R.O.C.K. (Raising Our Celiac Kids), a support group for families of children on a gluten-free diet. Today, Danna leads more than 100 chapters of R.O.C.K. worldwide. She is a consultant to retailers, manufacturers, testing companies, dietitians, nutritionists, and people newly diagnosed with gluten intolerance and celiac disease. She also coordinates the International Walk/Run for Celiac Disease each May in San Diego.

Dedication

This book is dedicated to the people who have patiently supported my sometimes-over-zealous-and-usually-over-the-top efforts as The Glutenator, singing the praises of a gluten-free lifestyle throughout the land. Most importantly, to my family and friends, who encourage, inspire, and energize me. Your support means more to me than you could ever know, and I couldn't have written a word without you. And to those of you who embrace or are planning to embrace the gluten-free lifestyle, I hope I can make a difference, if only a small one, in your lives by inspiring you to love the gluten-free way of life.

Author's Acknowledgments

A huge thank-you to the hard-working team at Wiley Publishing. First, thank you to Mikal Belicove, the acquisitions editor who came up with and promoted the idea of doing a *For Dummies* book about the gluten-free lifestyle, and then held my hand as I learned the ropes of writing in the *For Dummies* format. To senior project editor Tim Gallan, thank you for keeping me on track and for your attention to organization and detail. To both Tim and copy editor Danielle Voirol, thank you for tolerating my sometimes quirky sense of humor and my many made-up words. It must have driven your spell-checker crazy. Danielle, your speedy grasp of the subject, in-depth research, and clever questions were amazing. Can't get anything by you, that's for sure!

I'd like to thank Emily Nolan for testing all of the recipes, and for her tactful and humorous comments when the dishes I had invented were outrageous flops (don't worry, we fixed 'em!). And thank you to Patty Santelli for nutritional analysis of the recipes.

I'm extremely grateful to my friends and colleagues, Michelle Pietzak, M.D. and Cynthia Kupper, R.D., for their careful technical review of the book. Both of you go far and above the "call of duty" in helping the gluten-free community each and every day.

A huge thank you to my friend and hero, Alessio Fasano, M.D., who is one of the biggest fish in the celiac sea. I'm honored that you wrote the foreword for this book, and am grateful for your phenomenal work in the celiac world.

To the entire gluten-free community, thank you for your steadfast encouragement. You motivate me to be passionate.

And last, but by no means least, I'm incredibly grateful to my family and friends. After I finished the book before this one, I asked you to slip cyanide in my coffee if I ever thought about writing another book. Thanks for not doing that. Seriously, without your patience, encouragement, support, optimism, love and inspiration, I couldn't have written a word.

Publisher's Acknowledgments

We're proud of this book; please send us your comments through our Dummies online registration form located at www.dummies.com/register/.

Some of the people who helped bring this book to market include the following:

Acquisitions, Editorial, and Media Development

Senior Project Editor: Tim Gallan

Acquisitions Editor: Michael Lewis

Copy Editor: Danielle Voirol

Editorial Program Coordinator: Hanna K. Scott

Technical Editors: Michelle Maria Pietzak, MD; Cynthia R. Kupper, CRD

Recipe Tester: Emily Nolan

Nutritional Analyst: Patricia Santelli

Editorial Manager: Christine Meloy Beck

Editorial Assistants: David Lutton, Nadine Bell, Erin Calligan

Cartoons: Rich Tennant (www.the5thwave.com)

Composition Services

Project Coordinator: Ryan Steffen

Layout and Graphics: Stephanie D. Jumper, Barbara Moore, Heather Ryan, Julie Trippetti, Erin Zeltner

Proofreaders: Leeann Harney, Jessica Kramer, Aptara

Indexer: Aptara

Publishing and Editorial for Consumer Dummies

Diane Graves Steele, Vice President and Publisher, Consumer Dummies

Joyce Pepple, Acquisitions Director, Consumer Dummies

Kristin A. Cocks, Product Development Director, Consumer Dummies

Michael Spring, Vice President and Publisher, Travel

Kelly Regan, Editorial Director, Travel

Publishing for Technology Dummies

Andy Cummings, Vice President and Publisher, Dummies Technology/General User

Composition Services

Gerry Fahey, Vice President of Production Services

Debbie Stailey, Director of Composition Services

Contents at a Glance

Recipes at a Glance

Entrées

Pizza, Pasta, and Bread

Desserts

Table of Contents

Foreword

● ●

Celiac disease is an immune mediated disease characterized by damage of the small intestinal mucosa caused by the gliadin and glutenin fractions of wheat gluten and similar proteins of barley and rye in genetically susceptible subjects. The presence of gluten in these subjects leads to a self-perpetuating intestinal damage, while the elimination of gluten results in a full mucosal recovery.

The clinical manifestations of celiac disease are protean in nature and vary markedly with the age of the patient, the duration and extent of disease, and the presence of extra-intestinal pathology. In addition to the classical gastrointestinal form, a variety of other clinical manifestations of the disease have been described, including atypical and asymptomatic forms.

While in the past celiac disease was typically considered a pediatric condition, we are now aware that the disease may become clinically manifest after years of silent intestinal damage following exposure to gluten. Therefore, the diagnosis of celiac disease can be extremely challenging and currently relies on a sensitive and specific algorithm that allows the identification of different manifestations of the disease. Serological tests developed in the last decade provide a non-invasive tool to screen both individuals at risk for the disease and the general population. However, the current gold standard for the diagnosis of celiac disease remains the histological confirmation of the intestinal damage in serologically positive individuals.

The keystone treatment of celiac disease patients is a life-long elimination diet in which food products containing gluten are avoided. While in principle the treatment appears simple and straightforward, embracing a gluten-free diet is not an easy enterprise. There are things in life that we do automatically without paying too much attention to them. How many times do we drive home from work thinking about something else and find ourselves at the garage door without recalling how we got there? How often do we perform routine tasks such as tying our shoes, brushing our teeth, or listening to sounds of nature, and yet, we don't have any distinct memory of these acts? For the vast majority of human beings, eating is another automatic activity, but not for those affected by celiac disease, for which eating is a very engaging task of their daily routine. A fair amount of mental, physical, and social energy is devoted to what should be one of the most natural and enjoyable activities. In the United States, this task has been aggravated in the past by the limited alternatives to gluten-containing food. All this translates to a monumental undertaking, particularly for those that have to please the taste of celiac children. To make the story even more challenging, the "fast lane" life style typical of our society, including our food habit (that is, fast food), cannot be applied to the celiac cuisine.

With this book, Danna is sharing her personal experience as a mother of a celiac child with her navigated expertise in managing the emotional, social, personal, and practical aspects of the disease. Her enthusiasm in teaching how to live with celiac disease in a normal and joyful way makes her the best "cheerleader" of the celiac community.

Celiac disease is now becoming a problem of the masses rather than the uncommon disease of a few. We are experiencing an exponential increase in the number of people diagnosed with celiac disease. Given the complexity of the disease and of the proper diet to manage it, we have also witnessed confusion on what a gluten-free diet consists of. While the professional literature is abundant on this topic, simple "hands-on" guidelines accessible to everyone are limited. Danna's book represents a terrific vehicle to explain in a simple and practical way how to deal with celiac disease with a smile on the face. The book is direct, easy to read, and extremely informative for the newly diagnosed as well as the experienced patient.

Alessio Fasano, M.D.
Professor of Pediatrics, Medicine, and Physiology
Director, Mucosal Biology Research Center
University of Maryland School of Medicine

Introduction

● ●

*N*ot so many years ago, the gluten-free lifestyle was reserved for an obscure cluster of people who were forced to settle for wannabe foods that resembled sawdust but didn't taste as good.

Today, the gluten-free lifestyle is sweeping the world with the force of a really big blowtorch, and the ramifications are enormous. Gluten-free products abound (and are a far cry from the foods we used to choke down), labels are far less ambiguous, and people no longer look at you like you have four heads when you ask for a burger without the bun.

Being gluten-free isn't about being on a diet. It's about living a lifestyle. Whether you've been gluten-free for decades or are only considering the idea of giving up gluten, this book is loaded with information that can impact every aspect of your life, from the obvious — your health and how you shop, cook, and eat — to more subtle facets, like finances, socializing, dealing with friends and family, and managing various emotional ups and downs.

I live a gluten-free lifestyle, and I have for years. I have no ulterior motives, other than some quirky desire to don a cape, call myself the Glutenator, and travel far and wide to extol the virtues of a gluten-free diet. Whether you go gluten-free really doesn't matter to me. I have no supplements to sell you, no gluten-free food products that I endorse — I don't even get paid for running the world's largest support organization for gluten-free kids!

What *does* matter to me is that I do my best to tell you everything you need to know about living a gluten-free lifestyle so you can make healthy decisions. This book is the reference guide you need to help you with all those aspects. It's your reference for living — and loving — a gluten-free lifestyle.

About This Book

Living Gluten-Free For Dummies, like all *For Dummies* books, is divided up so you don't have to read it all at once, or even front to back, if you don't want to. You can skip from B to R to A and even reread B if you want to. You can read it sideways and standing on your head if you'd like; all you have to do is find a section you're interested in and dig in (how's *that* for liberating?).

I suggest you peruse the Table of Contents and see whether any particular chapter or subject really floats your boat, and start there. Or you can flip through the book and see whether any of the headings catch your interest.

If you're new to the gluten-free lifestyle and have tons of questions, you're probably best off starting at Chapter 1 and working your way through most of the book in order.

If you've been gluten-free for years, do yourself a favor and take a look at Chapter 4. You may be surprised at some of the foods that are allowed on the gluten-free diet that used to be considered no-nos. You may find this chapter opens a lot of cupboard doors that you once thought were closed!

Conventions Used in This Book

To keep things consistent and easy to follow, here are some of the basic ground rules and conventions this book uses:

- ✔ I make words up, but they're pretty easy to figure out. For instance, *glutenated* means a product's been contaminated with gluten. *Glutenous* means it has gluten in it, *glutenivore* is something that eats gluten, *Glutenator* is one who battles the evils of gluten, and so on. It's fun! Before you know it, I'll bet you'll be making up your own *glutenologisms*.

- ✔ All Web addresses appear in monofont, which looks like `this`.

- ✔ When this book was printed, some Web addresses may have needed to break across two lines of text. If that happened, rest assured that I haven't put in any extra characters (such as hyphens) to indicate the break. So when using one of these Web addresses, just type in exactly what you see in this book, pretending as though the line break doesn't exist.

- ✔ Feel free to tinker with the recipes. If you don't have an ingredient a recipe calls for, don't worry — make a substitution. You may find your swap is a huge improvement. And don't worry if you don't want to measure. I estimated the measurements, anyway, because I'm not sure I even own measuring spoons and cups!

- ☼ If you want a vegetarian recipe, just look for the tomato icons.

Here are some conventions for the ingredients themselves:

- ✔ If an ingredient appears in a recipe, it's assumed to be gluten-free. For instance, I don't specify "gluten-free vanilla," because all vanilla is gluten-free. And soy sauce usually has gluten, but when I call for soy sauce in a recipe, I'm assuming you'll use a gluten-free version.

✔ Baking with gluten-free flours works best if you use a mixture of flours. Chapter 9 goes into detail about how to mix gluten-free flours to get the best results.

✔ Milk substitutes can be used in place of milk in most recipes.

✔ Eggs are large.

✔ Butter and margarine are interchangeable.

✔ All temperatures are Fahrenheit.

What You're Not to Read

You won't get in trouble if you *do* read everything, but if you're a skimmer, you can skip some stuff and not miss anything important. In other words, there won't be a pop quiz on the following:

✔ **Anything that has a Technical Stuff icon:** The Technical Stuff icon represents information that's interesting (downright fascinating sometimes!) but not crucial to your understanding of the subject matter.

✔ **Sidebars:** These are the stories and tidbits of information in shaded boxes scattered throughout the chapters. Just like the Technical Stuff, you may find the information interesting, but you won't be missing critical information if you skip them.

✔ **Recipes:** Unless you're actually using them to cook or to decide what to make for dinner, recipes aren't the best late-night reading material. Feel free to skip them until you're ready to whip up some gluten-free goodies.

What I Assume about You

You spent your hard-earned cashola on this book, and that means either you want to learn more about the gluten-free lifestyle or you're related to me. Because my family members already hear way more about this stuff than any human should have to endure, I've written this book with you in mind — and I've taken the liberty of making a few assumptions about you. One or more of the following should apply:

✔ You're considering going gluten-free and will use this book to determine whether to take the plunge.

✔ You love someone who's gluten-free, and you're so cool that you want to learn about the lifestyle so you can be supportive.

  ✔ You're new to the diet and are looking for the "manual" that can tell you how to live a gluten-free lifestyle.

  ✔ You've been gluten-free for years and want the latest, greatest information about dietary guidelines and state-of-the-art research.

  ✔ You're a professional who has gluten-free clients, customers, or patients, and you want to learn more about the gluten-free lifestyle and the medical conditions that benefit from it.

At the same time, you can make a few assumptions about me and what I tell you in this book:

  ✔ I generally know what I'm talking about. I *do* live a gluten-free lifestyle and have been immersed in it since 1991. My experience is worth noting, because some people who write about gluten-free living aren't gluten-free themselves. I assure you, I wasn't brought on to write this book because I was bored and looking for a project: I really do live — and love — the gluten-free lifestyle (and I have way too many projects, thank you very much!).

  ✔ To the best of my knowledge, the information in this book is correct. This book has been reviewed by two experts who are extremely knowledgeable in their fields. Michelle Pietzak, M.D., is an expert in celiac disease and has reviewed this book for medical accuracy. Cynthia Kupper, R.D., is a dietitian and executive director for the Gluten Intolerance Group and has reviewed it to make sure I'm in line on the dietary and lifestyle topics.

  ✔ This book is not intended to provide medical advice, so you're not allowed to sue me for anything. Please see your physician for further follow-up if you feel you need it; void where prohibited; all rights reserved; good only while offer valid; only while supplies last; till death do us part; and all other legal disclaimers heretofore. There. My hiney is covered!

How This Book Is Organized

Living Gluten-Free For Dummies is organized so that all the "like" material goes together. So I don't repeat too much information, I sometimes include cross-references to related topics. This book has five parts. Each part has several chapters, and each chapter is divided into sections. In the following sections, I explain how the parts are divided up.

Part I: Going Gluten-Free: Who, What, Why, and How

As the name implies, this part dives into the big-picture basics of being gluten-free. Chapter 1 is an overview. If you read nothing else in this book, read Chapter 1, because then you'll at least sound like you know what you're talking about. The rest of this part talks about who may want to consider going gluten-free and why, what you can and can't eat on the gluten-free diet, and how to dig a little deeper so you're *sure* the foods you're eating are really safe for you.

Part II: Planning and Preparing: The Preludes to Cooking

Part II takes you to the next level: getting ready to eat. It starts with some guidance on choosing the most nutritious approach to the gluten-free lifestyle and then helps you with preparing your kitchen, planning menus, shopping, and developing the techniques unique to gluten-free cooking that you'll want to know before you cook.

Part III: From Menus to Meals: Recipes for the Gluten-Free Gastronome

You can find 65 recipes in this part submitted by a not-a-cookbook author: me. Okay, I admit I made 'em up. And I admit I don't measure, nor is any one recipe ever the same the second time around. But my publisher has a real-live tester on hand to make sure the recipes work, and much to my surprise, they do! So stop snickering, and start stewing — or baking — or whatever it is you want to do in the kitchen. Whether you're a culinary fledgling or a Martha Stewart protégé, you'll find these recipes to be simple, delicious, sometimes impressive, and most definitely gluten-free.

Part IV: Living — and Loving — the Gluten-Free Lifestyle 24/7

For some people, the gluten-free lifestyle presents unique social, practical, and emotional challenges. In this part, I help you figure out ways to handle some of the practical issues like attending social events; eating at restaurants;

traveling; talking with friends and loved ones about your lifestyle; and raising happy, healthy, gluten-free kids. I also help you deal with some of the emotional challenges that sometimes come up so you can truly learn to love the gluten-free lifestyle.

Part V: The Part of Tens

What would a *For Dummies* book be without a Part of Tens? Incomplete, that's what, because nearly all *For Dummies* books have them, and this one's no exception. The Part of Tens is a few short chapters, each with (cleverly enough) *ten* tips, questions and answers, factoids, and tidbits of information about the gluten-free lifestyle.

Icons Used in This Book

Some people are more visual than others. That's why icons are cool. This book uses several icons, and each has a little tidbit of information associated with it. Here's what each icon means:

Cleverly designated as Tips, these are, well, *tips* that can help you live (and love!) the gluten-free lifestyle. They include info to help you save time or cut down on frustration.

Everyone can use a friendly little reminder. The Remember icon is a quick and easy way to identify some of the more important points that you may want to make note of throughout the book.

Text flagged with the Warning icon can keep you out of trouble.

Sometimes I get really into the juicy, technical, and scientific stuff. Some of you will love it; others will be bored to tears. That's why I put it in its own area, marked by a Technical Stuff icon, so you can skip it (if you want to) without missing the gist of what's going on in that chapter or section.

Where to Go from Here

What I suggest you do at this point is curl up in your comfiest chair and dive into the book. If you find the section you start with to be boring (puh-lease!) or for whatever reason it doesn't pop your cork, then skip it and move on.

If you're feeling a little down about going gluten-free, I hope my sincere passion for the gluten-free lifestyle and the healthy benefits that go along with it touches you by offering comfort, optimism, and inspiration.

Part I

Going Gluten-Free: Who, What, Why, and How

The 5th Wave   By Rich Tennant

"It's the gluten-free edition."

In this part . . .

1 cover the basics to help get you off and running on the gluten-free lifestyle. I start by taking a look at the many medical and psychological conditions that improve on a gluten-free diet so you can decide whether this lifestyle can benefit you and can set realistic expectations for how your health may improve. Then I spell out the basics of the gluten-free diet and introduce you to foods you may never have even heard of before, some of which are far more nutritious than gluten ever wished it could be. Finally, I tell you how to think outside the ingredients box so you know what hidden sources of gluten to look for and how to make *sure* products are, in fact, gluten-free. So what are you waiting for? Today may be the first day of the rest of your new lifestyle.

Chapter 1

Gluten-Free from A to Z: The Basics of Being Gluten-Free

• •

In This Chapter

▶ Getting a grip on gluten

▶ Discovering the advantages of the gluten-free lifestyle

▶ Making the most of meals

▶ Going from gluten-gorger to gluten-free forager — and loving it

• •

I figured the doctor had made a mistake. "You mean *glucose*," I corrected him with a tinge of exasperation at his clumsy blunder. "You must mean my son can't eat *glucose*." Geesh. This was going to be tough. No more gummi bears.

"No, I mean *gluten*," he insisted. "And to be honest, I really don't know much about the gluten-free diet. You can see our hospital dietitian, but she won't have much on the diet, either. You're going to have to do some homework on your own."

All I could muster was a blank stare. What the heck was *gluten?* Keep in mind this was 1991, when I knew as much about gluten as I know about piezoelectric polymers. Approximately nothing.

Stranded on some figurative island located somewhere between Terror Bay and the Dread Sea, I figured I had two options: Tyler could starve to death, or I could get busy trying to figure out what the heck gluten was all about. People probably frown on mommies who let kids starve to death.

Al Gore hadn't invented the Internet yet, and I couldn't find any books or support groups; it was time to get resourceful and creative. I was determined to find out everything I could — and then share it with the world (at least the other six people on the planet who were gluten-free at the time).

Little did I know that gluten-free-ness would explode into what it is today — one of the fastest-growing nutritional movements in the world — and this mission of mine would become all-consuming. This chapter gives you a basic rundown of what living gluten-free is all about.

What Is Gluten, Anyway?

Gluten has a couple of definitions; one is technically correct but not commonly used, and the other is commonly used but not technically correct. I give you more details on both definitions in Chapter 4, but to get you started and for the purposes of most of this book, here's the common definition: *Gluten* is a mixture of proteins in wheat, rye, and barley. Oats don't have gluten but may be contaminated, so they're forbidden, too.

Common foods that contain gluten

You can find lots of information about what you can and can't eat in Chapter 4, as well as a detailed listing of safe and forbidden ingredients at www.celiac.com or other Web sites. But you need to have a general idea of what kinds of foods have gluten in them so you know what to avoid. Things with flour in them (white or wheat) are the most common culprits when you're avoiding gluten. The following are obvious gluten-glomming foods:

- Bagels
- Beer
- Bread
- Cookies, cakes, and most other baked goods
- Crackers
- Pasta
- Pizza
- Pretzels

But there are not-so-obvious suspects, too, like licorice, cereals, and natural flavorings. When you're gluten-free, you get used to reading labels, calling manufacturers, and digging a little deeper to know for sure what you can and can't eat (more on that in Chapter 5).

You have to do without those foods, but you really don't have to do *without*. Food manufacturers make delicious gluten-free versions of just about every food imaginable these days. I talk more about those and where to buy them in Chapter 8.

Wheat-free doesn't mean gluten-free

You may see lots of labels proudly declaring a product to be wheat-free (some of which, like spelt and kamut, aren't really wheat-free at all). That doesn't mean the food's gluten-free.

Gluten is in wheat, but it's also in rye and barley — and most people don't eat oats on the gluten-free diet, either. So something can be wheat-free but still have other gluten-containing ingredients, like malt, which is usually derived from barley. In that case, the product's wheat-free, but it's not gluten-free.

Discovering the Benefits of a Gluten-Free Lifestyle

The gluten-free lifestyle isn't about your diet. Oh, sure, this book talks about food, but the diet itself takes up only a few pages. Being gluten-free involves a lot more than just cutting gluten out of your diet. It affects every aspect of your life, from how you communicate and with whom, to how you handle ordering at restaurants, attending social functions, and dealing with emotional challenges.

I believe it's important to take control of the diet, or if it's your kids who are gluten-free, help them gain control. Going gluten-free also gives you an opportunity to reach out and help others who may be embarking upon the wonderful world of gluten freedom, as well as a chance to discover more about nutrition and what you're actually putting in your body on a daily basis. If that sounds like a lot of work, relax. I guide you through it. And not only can you feel better, but you can also feel better about yourself!

You have lots of company. The gluten-free movement is sweeping the nation for lots of reasons, but the one that stands out is that when people give up gluten, they often feel better. This section tells you what the gluten-free diet can do for your body — the benefits you can enjoy in addition to all the emotional perks of the lifestyle.

People today live in a quick-fix, panacea-pursuing, pill-popping, make-me-better-fast society, and if they see promise of a quick way to fix what's ailin' them, they're buyin' it. Changing both your diet and lifestyle is neither quick nor easy, but the benefits of going gluten-free can be fantastic — no surgery or medication required!

Abstinence makes the gut grow stronger

When gluten is what's making you sick, what your symptoms are doesn't matter; even if your symptoms don't seem to be related to your gastrointestinal tract, nasty battles are going on inside your gut.

Hairlike structures called villi are on the lining of your small intestine. The job of the villi is to increase the surface area of the small intestine so it can absorb more nutrients.

For people who have gluten intolerance, the body sees gluten as a bad guy or toxin and attacks it. In doing so, it also accidentally attacks the villi, and those villi get blunted and shortened, sometimes to the extreme of becoming completely flat.

Flat villi can't absorb stuff, so those good-for-ya nutrients just slide right by and you don't get enough of the important vitamins, minerals, and other things that are vital for good physical and emotional health. You develop what's called *malabsorption* and become poorly nourished.

Don't worry! This story has a happy ending. Your villi are tenacious little things, and when you quit eating gluten, they begin to heal right away. Before you know it, your villi grow back and absorb nutrients again, and your health is fully restored. That's why I say abstinence makes the gut grow stronger.

By the way, lactase, which is the enzyme that breaks down the sugar lactose, is produced in the tip of the villi. When the villi get blunted, sometimes your ability to digest lactose decreases and you become lactose intolerant. When you quit eating gluten and the villi heal, you're usually able to tolerate dairy foods again.

Eating isn't supposed to hurt

Food is supposed to give you energy and make you feel good, not make you hurt. But when you eat things that your body doesn't like for one reason or another, it has a sometimes not-so-subtle way of telling you to knock it off. Food that your body objects to can cause gas, bloating, diarrhea, constipation, and nausea — and even things that don't seem to be associated with the gastrointestinal tract, like headaches, fatigue, depression, joint pain, and respiratory distress.

The cool thing about all this is that when you figure out which food or foods your body doesn't approve of, you can stop eating them, and then your body stops being so pouty. In fact, feed it right, and it can make you feel great in lots of different ways.

Making nutrition your mission: Head-to-toe health benefits

The 12th-century physician Maimonides said, "Man should strive to have his intestines relaxed all the days of his life." No doubt! When your intestines aren't relaxed — or when they're downright edgy or uptight — they affect all your other parts, too. It's kind of like when you're in a really good mood and your best friend is grumpy — the situation can make you grumpy, too; one cantankerous intestine can be a buzz-kill for the entire body.

In a way, the body's reaction to gluten doesn't compute. In some people, eating gluten can cause headaches, fatigue, joint pain, depression, or infertility; at first those types of symptoms may seem unrelated to something going on in your gut, much less something you eat — much less something as common in your diet as wheat.

But those — and about 250 others — are symptoms of celiac disease and gluten sensitivity. People with celiac disease or gluten sensitivity do sometimes have gastrointestinal symptoms, but more often the symptoms are *extraintestinal,* meaning they take place outside the intestinal tract.

If your body has problems with gluten, the gluten-free diet may help relieve lots of symptoms, such as

- Fatigue
- Gastrointestinal distress (gas, bloating, diarrhea, constipation, vomiting, heartburn, and acid reflux)
- Headaches (including migraines)
- Inability to concentrate
- Weight gain or weight loss
- Infertility
- Joint, bone, or muscle pain
- Depression
- Respiratory problems

The list's impressive, isn't it? The idea that eliminating one thing from your diet — gluten — could improve so many different conditions is almost hard to believe. Yet it's true — and it really makes sense when you realize that if the food you're eating is toxic to your body, your body's going to scream in lots of different ways.

In people with gluten intolerance, eating gluten may make the symptoms of some psychiatric conditions worse. (I talk more about that in Chapter 2, and you can also find out more at www.gfcfdiet.com or www.autismndi.com.) Some researchers think removing gluten from the diet can improve the behaviors of people with

- ✔ Autism
- ✔ Schizophrenia and other mood disorders
- ✔ Attention-deficit (hyperactivity) disorder (ADD/ADHD)

Millions of people have wheat *allergies,* which are different from gluten sensitivity or celiac disease — and they, too, improve dramatically on a wheat-free/gluten-free diet.

But beyond the obvious improvement you enjoy if you have an intolerance, other conditions and symptoms can improve on a wheat-free diet: PMS and menopausal symptoms, for instance. Eliminating wheat may even slow or even reverse the signs of aging, reducing wrinkles and improving the tone and texture of skin.

But I thought wheat was good for me!

Of course you did. Anyone who's spent more than a day on planet Earth has been barraged with messages hailing the virtues of wheat — especially in its whole form! It and other grains hog most of the food pyramid(s), suggesting you should eat gobs of it, and it's touted as a good source of fiber and nutrients. Wheat does provide some health benefits, but you can find them in other food sources, too. So how can wheat be at the root of so many health problems? Here are some reasons wheat may not be the key to perfect dietary health.

Wheat was invented yesterday

Wheat wasn't introduced until the Agricultural Revolution, about 10,000 years ago — that's yesterday, evolutionarily speaking. Before that, people ate lean meats, fish, seafood, nonstarchy vegetables, and fruits.

When wheat came on the scene, it was completely foreign. Human bodies have to adapt in order to tolerate it, and lots of people don't tolerate it well at all.

Humans don't fully digest wheat

Most humans have only one stomach — and one just isn't enough to digest wheat. Cows have four stomachs (actually, four chambers within one stomach). That's why Bessie the Bovine does okay with wheat. It goes from one stomach to another and another and — well, you get the picture. By the time it reaches tummy number four, it's fully digested, and Bessie's feeling fine.

Wheat contributes to leaky gut ("Z" is for zonulin)

When people eat wheat, they produce extra amounts of a protein called *zonulin.*

The lining of the small intestine is basically a solid wall of cells that most materials can't pass through on their own. On the lining of the small intestine, zonulin waits for nutrients to come along. When important vitamins and minerals are present, zonulin tells the passageways in the intestinal wall to open so those nutrients can pass into the bloodstream. The blood then carries the nutrients to other parts of the body.

But when some people eat wheat, they produce too much zonulin, and the gates open too wide. All sorts of stuff gets in the bloodstream, some of which shouldn't be there, like toxins. This increased permeability of the lining of the small intestine, or *leaky gut syndrome,* can cause lots of different health issues.

Mastering the Meals

This book is about a lifestyle, not a diet. But no matter where that lifestyle takes you — eating in, eating out, social events, choosing, planning, shopping, preparing — being gluten-free all comes down to one thing: food.

If you're a culinary hacker and you're afraid you'll have to wake up at 4 a.m. to bake gluten-free bread and make pasta from scratch, turn off the alarm and go back to sleep. There are plenty of gluten-free specialty foods available to take the place of all your old favorites.

Whether you're a kitchenphobe or a foodie, living a gluten-free lifestyle offers you an enormous selection of foods and ingredients to choose from.

Planning and preparing

Putting together smart and healthful gluten-free meals is a lot easier if you plan ahead. Walking through a store, perusing restaurant menus, or (gasp!) sitting in a bakery with a growling tummy isn't exactly conducive to making good food choices.

Give yourself a healthy advantage by planning and even preparing meals in advance, especially if your busy schedule has you eating away from home frequently. If you know you're pressed for time at breakfast or lunch, make your meals the night before, and bring healthful gluten-free snacks in resealable plastic bags.

One of the coolest things about adopting a new dietary lifestyle is exploring new and sometimes unusual or unique foods. You may never have heard of lots of gluten-free foods and ingredients, many of which not only are gluten-free and delicious but are also nutritional powerhouses. With the new perspective on food that the gluten-free lifestyle can offer you, you may find yourself inspired to think outside the typical menu plan, exploring unique and nutritious alternatives.

Shopping shrewdly

The healthiest way to enjoy a gluten-free lifestyle is to eat things you can find at any grocery store or even a farmer's market: meat, fish, seafood, fruits, and nonstarchy vegetables (see Chapter 6). If you want to add canned, processed, and even junk foods to your shopping list, you can still do most of your shopping at a regular grocery store, and you can even buy generics.

If you hope to enjoy the delicious gluten-free specialty products that are available these days, you can find them in health food aisles or at health food stores or specialty shops. Or you can shop in your jammies on one of the many Internet sites specializing in gluten-free products (if you're using your library's Internet or an Internet café to shop online, I suggest you change out of your jammies).

Some people worry about the cost of the gluten-free lifestyle, but it doesn't have to be more expensive. I talk about eating gluten-free affordably in Chapter 8.

Kitchen considerations

For the most part, a gluten-free kitchen looks the same as any other kitchen — without the gluten, of course. You don't need to go out and buy special gadgets and tools, and with only a couple of exceptions, which I cover in Chapter 9, you don't need two sets of pots, pans, utensils, or storage containers, either.

If you're sharing a kitchen with gluten, you need to be aware of some contamination issues so you don't inadvertently glutenate (contaminate with gluten) a perfectly good gluten-free meal. Keeping your crumbs to yourself isn't just a matter of hygiene but can mean the difference between a meal you can eat and one you can't.

Some people find having separate areas in the pantry or cupboards for their gluten-free products helpful. This is an especially good idea if you have gluten-free kids in the house, because they can see that there are always lots of things for them to eat and can quickly grab their favorite gluten-free goodies from their special area.

Cooking outside the recipe box

I believe if you give someone a recipe, you feed 'em for a meal. Show them how to make *anything* gluten-free, and you feed 'em for a lifetime. The point is, you can make anything gluten-free, and you're not constrained by recipes or the fact that you can't use regular flour or breadcrumbs. All you need is a little creativity and some basic guidelines for using gluten-free substitutions, which you can find in Chapter 9.

If you're a die-hard recipe fan, never fear — I give you recipes in Chapters 10 through 15. Most of them are super simple to follow but leave your guests with the impression that you spent all day in the kitchen (and being thus indebted, they may volunteer to do the dishes).

Getting Excited about the Gluten-Free Lifestyle

Most people who embark on a gluten-free lifestyle are doing so because of health issues — and that means they have little or no choice in the matter. When people are forced to make changes in their routine, especially changes that affect what they can and can't eat, they're not always so quick to see the joy in the adjustments.

If you're a little gloomy about going from gluten-glommer to gluten-freebie, I understand. But prepare yourself to read about the scores of reasons to be excited about the gluten-free lifestyle (for you impatient types like me, feel free to skip to Chapters 19 and 20 for a jump-start on the Kumbayah side of being gluten-free).

"A" is for adapting your perspective on food

If you've been eating gluten (I believe that would make you a *glutenivore*) for a long time — say, for most of your life — then giving up foods as you know them may seem like a tough transition at first. Besides the obvious practical challenges of learning to ferret out gluten where it may be hidden, you have to deal with emotional, physical, social, and even financial challenges.

You have to do only one thing in order to learn to love the gluten-free lifestyle, and that's to adjust your perspective on food just a tinge. You really don't have to give anything up; you just have to make some modifications. The foods that used to be your favorites can still be your favorites if you want them to be, just in a slightly different form.

Or you may want to consider what may be a new and super-healthful approach for you: eating lean meats, fresh fruits, and nonstarchy vegetables. Again, you may have to tweak your perspective a bit before the diet feels natural to you, but it is, in fact, natural, nutritious, and naturally nutritious. I talk more about this approach in Chapter 6.

Savoring gluten-free flavors

People who are new to the concept of being gluten-free sometimes comment that the diet is boring. When I ask what they're eating, their cuisine routine usually centers on carrots and rice cakes. Who wouldn't be bored with that? That type of a diet is appalling, not appealing.

I *love* food. I love the flavor, the feeling of being full, the nutritional value it provides. Most of all, I love to explore foods I've never tried before — as long as they're gluten-free, of course. I'd never encourage you to endure a diet of blandiose foods that could double as packing materials.

A healthful, gluten-free diet doesn't have to be boring or restrictive. You're not constrained to eating 32 individual portions of fruits and vegetables each day, like a rabbit nibbling nervously on carrots. If you enjoy bland foods, snaps for you. But if you think gluten-free has to be flavor-free, you're in for a pleasant surprise.

Getting out and about

You don't have to let the gluten-free lifestyle hold you back from doing anything you want to do. Well, okay, there are some things you can't do — like eat a pizza from the place around the corner or devour a stack of gluten-laden donuts. But as far as your activities and lifestyle are concerned, you can — and should — get out and about as you always have.

For the most part, ordering out isn't as easy as walking into a restaurant and asking for a gluten-free menu (a girl can dream). But eating at restaurants is definitely doable; you just need to learn to special order and tune in to contamination concerns. Traveling is a breeze after you master eating at restaurants (and get a handle on language considerations if you're traveling abroad). Going to social events just requires a little advance planning, and holidays may barely faze you — after you get the hang of getting out and about gluten-free style. Chapter 16 gives you more information on this.

Raising kids to love the lifestyle

When we heard that Tyler would have to be gluten-free for the rest of his life, we were flooded with a bunch of emotions, most of which weren't very pleasant. At first, we felt burdened and overcome with grief and frustration, and we longed for the perfectly healthy little baby we thought we were entitled to. It was easy to focus on what we had lost and all that we'd have to change in our lives. But making adjustments didn't take long, and soon we'd learned not just to live the gluten-free lifestyle — but to *love* the gluten-free lifestyle.

Most importantly, we wanted Tyler to love the lifestyle. After all, it was his diet, his life, and his future that would be most impacted. Thankfully, Tyler does love the gluten-free lifestyle, and your kids can, too.

Lots of ideas are key in raising happy, healthy, gluten-free kids. Some of the highlights include giving them control of their diet from day one; always having yummy gluten-free treats on hand; reinforcing the benefits of the gluten-free lifestyle (if you need some crib notes, see Chapter 19); and always remembering that they're learning how to feel about the lifestyle from *you*. Promoting an optimistic outlook can instill a positive approach in them. Chapter 17 deals in detail with raising kids to love the gluten-free lifestyle, and for even more inspiration and practical advice, see *Kids with Celiac Disease: A Family Guide to Raising Happy, Healthy, Gluten-Free Children,* by yours truly.

Kids are flexible and resilient. Adopting a new lifestyle is usually harder for the parents than for the child.

Setting realistic expectations

Some people call me PollyDanna because they think I have an unrealistically optimistic view of the gluten-free lifestyle. It may be optimistic, but it's not unrealistic.

Setting reasonable expectations for what things will be like when you adopt a gluten-free lifestyle is important, because you *will* encounter challenges, and you need to prepare to handle them well. Friends, family, and loved ones may not understand. They may not accommodate your diet when you hope or expect they will. You may find social events to be overwhelming at first; or you may get confused or frustrated and feel like giving up on the diet. You can overcome these trials and come out stronger for them.

How the gluten-free lifestyle saved my son

I didn't aspire to do any of this. I was deeply involved in a successful career, and was a mommy first and foremost. But today I'm an accidental author, researcher, and support group founder who was pushed into the deep end of the gluten-free pool and realized I needed to learn to swim. Fast.

Until 1991, my family and I ate a fairly typical American diet. I tried to keep it nutritious (extra cheese on the spaghetti to add protein), and I was aware of the need to limit fat and calories (scratch the extra cheese), but we didn't spend a lot of time worrying about what we ate or the long-term effects food may have on our bodies. We pretty much took eating for granted.

All that changed when my first child, Tyler, was about 9 months old and developed what seemed to be chronic diarrhea. The pediatrician chalked it up to the antibiotics Ty was taking for ear infections and told me to call if it hadn't cleared up in a few weeks. Three weeks later, I was back in the pediatrician's office. "Yep, he still has diarrhea," the doctor declared with confidence. "Yeah, I know. That's why I'm here," I mumbled with self-restraint worthy of the Nobel Peace Prize. "Give him foods that will plug him up like crackers and bread — and call me if it hasn't cleared up in a few weeks."

I waited. Not patiently (patience isn't my greatest strength), but I waited. Three weeks later, after another perfunctory examination of Tyler's ears, nose, and throat, the doctor made that "mmhhhmmm" noise that doctors make when they figure out the problem. Yay! We were finally going to get some answers! "Yep. He still has diarrhea." All those years of medical school had really paid off. "Don't worry about it. He's not dehydrated, and he's in the 75th percentile for height and weight. It's nothing to be concerned about." Gee, could the fact that I practically infuse him with liquids have anything to do with the fact that he's not dehydrated? And does the fact that he started off in the 99th percentile

and has *dropped* to the 75th mean anything? Apparently not. I was instructed not to bring him back for diarrhea because there was nothing to be concerned about. If I was going to insist on bringing him back, I'd be kicked out of that pediatric office. I guess they meant it.

Doctor number two agreed with doctor number one. After a quick look in the ears, nose, and throat, he declared that we had a healthy baby boy. "But what about the diarrhea?" I eeked. "Really, it's nothing to worry about. He's a healthy height and weight, he's not dehydrated, and he looks fine to me," he chirped as he raced to his next four-minute appointment. I considered offering to give Doctor Do-Nothing a close look at the 22 diarrhea diapers a day that I was changing but somehow managed to control myself.

In desperation, we changed doctors again, and — long story short — a quick look in the ears, nose, and throat turned up — you guessed it — nothing. By this time, Tyler's belly had grown hugely distended, his arms and legs had wasted to skinny little limbs, his hiney had disappeared completely, and his personality had changed. He had transformed from a lively, energetic toddler to a listless, irritable, clingy, and quiet little boy. It had been nearly a year since the diarrhea first started, and we figured we were just neurotic first-time parents with a mellow kid who pooped a lot.

Eventually, we ended up in the hands of doctor number four. By this time, "realizing" there was nothing wrong with Tyler, I thought nothing of dragging a lifeless baby with a Biafra belly into the pediatrician's office for a routine visit. After looking in Tyler's ears, nose, and throat, he laid Tyler down on his back and thumped on his belly like you might thump a honeydew melon to see whether it's ripe. "My goodness," he said with that I'm-alarmed-but-I'm-a-doctor-and-don't-want-to-freak-you-out tone. "What's going on with his belly? It's very distended." I couldn't answer through the tears of relief.

After testing for cystic fibrosis, blood diseases, and cancer, we finally got the bittersweet diagnosis. "Your son has celiac disease." *Huh?* Is that anything like the flu? Surely a few weeks of antibiotics will wipe it out. "He'll need to be on a gluten-free diet for the rest of his life."

I don't have room here to give the details of the rest of the story, but you can read it in my other books or on my Web sites. Suffice to say that the words "for the rest of his life" had a huge impact, and we realized it was time to step up to the plate and do some research and lifestyle and attitude adjustments to help ourselves — and others.

When we heard that Tyler would have to lead a gluten-free lifestyle, we had come to a fork in the road. At first, we were devastated, confused, frustrated, and grief-stricken. But we knew there was another path we could choose — a path that would have a more positive effect on Tyler's life. As we found out how to live with the diet and its ramifications, we worked hard to find a way to turn the adversity into a positive force in our lives. More than a decade later, I realize that what we once interpreted as misfortune has actually been a huge blessing in our lives — and most importantly, Tyler agrees.

This book is the resource you need — wade your way through it, and dog-ear the pages you want to come back to when you need some practical or emotional reminders for how to deal with difficult issues. If you have an optimistic but realistic approach, you'll encounter fewer obstacles along the way.

Arming yourself with good information

The good news is that because the gluten-free diet is exploding in popularity, there's lots of information about it. The bad news is that not all of it's accurate.

Be leery of what you hear and read, and check the reliability of the source on everything. If you find conflicting information — and you will — dig deeper until you find out which source is right.

I cite a few good sources of information in Chapter 5, and I'm sure you can find more on your own. Just remember to keep a skeptical eye out for the good, the bad, and the completely ludicrous.

Chapter 2

Going Gluten-Free: Who's Doing It and Why

So you've given up — or are considering giving up — gluten. If you're like most people, you're doing so for one of the following reasons:

✔ A medical professional told you that you have to; your health will improve if you do.

✔ You haven't been to any doctors, but you suspect you'll feel better on a gluten-free diet.

✔ You or your child has behavioral issues, and you believe a gluten-free diet will help.

✔ You think it's chic.

Which group you fall into doesn't matter — you're probably right on all counts. (Except maybe that chic thing, but whatever floats your boat.)

And you're definitely not alone. Millions of people are going gluten-free for a variety of reasons, and most of these individuals are seeing dramatic improvements in their health. The bottom line is that gluten doesn't sit well with a lot of people.

That's because many (some even say *most*) people have some form of gluten sensitivity. So you're thinking, "What exactly does that mean, and can I or can't I eat pizza?" Ah, you want to cut to the chase! There's not always an easy answer to either one of those questions.

This chapter explains what gluten sensitivity is, how gluten can affect your body and your behavior, and what tests can help you decide whether you need to go gluten-free.

Shedding Light on the Gluten-Sensitivity Spectrum

Gluten sensitivity is a physical sensitivity to gluten — hence the clever name. It's not easy to define, because these sensitivities come in a variety of forms. Think of gluten sensitivities as falling somewhere on a spectrum, ranging from allergy to disease (see Figure 2-1).

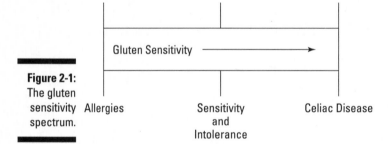

Figure 2-1:
The gluten
sensitivity
spectrum.

Gluten Sensitivity ⟶

Allergies   Sensitivity   Celiac Disease
               and
               Intolerance

At one end: Allergies

There's no such a thing as an allergy to gluten, but someone can have allergies to the things that contain gluten: wheat, rye, and barley. In fact, wheat is one of the most common allergens, affecting millions of people.

These allergies are just like other typical food allergies — the same as an allergy to strawberries or shellfish, for example. They're all responses to a food allergen, and the reaction that someone has to those foods varies from person to person and from one food to another.

Many food allergies are called *IgE-mediated responses* to foods. Basically, all that means is that the immune system is overreacting to a food, treating it as a foreign "invader." IgE just designates a class of immunoglobulin. *Immunoglobulins* are proteins that the body makes to help fight against things it perceives to be threats. IgE's main evolutionary role has been to protect the body against parasites, but it also fights other "bad guys," which is what it's doing when you have an allergic reaction to food. The body creates a specific variation of IgE antibody for each allergen it encounters.

Allergic symptoms can be respiratory, causing coughing, nasal congestion, sneezing, throat tightness, and even asthma.

Acute allergic reactions to food usually start in the mouth, with tingling, itching, a metallic taste, and swelling of the tongue and throat. Sometimes symptoms are farther down the intestinal tract, causing abdominal pain, muscle spasms, vomiting, and diarrhea.

Any severe and acute allergic reaction also has the potential to be life threatening, causing anaphylaxis. *Anaphylaxis* — or *anaphylactic shock* — affects different organs, and symptoms can include a tingling sensation, swelling in the mouth or throat, and a metallic taste. Other symptoms can include a feeling of agitation, hives, breathing problems, a drop in blood pressure, and fainting. Anaphylaxis can sometimes be fatal unless the person having the allergic reaction receives an epinephrine (adrenaline) injection.

Somewhere in the middle: Gluten sensitivity and intolerance

Moving across the spectrum of gluten sensitivity, you go from allergies into an ambiguous area that a lot of people call sensitivity or intolerance. Often used interchangeably, the terms *sensitivity* and *intolerance* basically mean that your body doesn't react well to a particular food and you should avoid it. Notice I said *should,* not *must.*

What *is* clear is that people who fall in this area have a response to gluten very similar to a celiac response (which I talk about in the "Identifying Symptoms of Gluten Sensitivity and Celiac Disease" section in this chapter). So do they have celiac disease? Maybe. Here's where things get fuzzy:

✔ Some people who are diagnosed with gluten sensitivity actually have celiac disease, but their testing was done improperly or was insufficient to yield conclusive results.

> ✔ Others may not have celiac disease — yet — but if they continue to eat gluten, they may develop it (a condition in its early stages like this is sometimes referred to as *subclinical* celiac disease).
>
> ✔ And still others may not have celiac disease and may never get it. But they do have a sensitivity to gluten, and their health improves on a gluten-free diet.

Symptoms of gluten sensitivity are usually the same as those of celiac disease, and as with celiac disease, they usually go away on a gluten-free diet.

Testing can help clarify whether you have celiac disease or gluten sensitivity. If you test positive for celiac disease, then that's what you have. But if you're negative for celiac disease, yet your symptoms go away on a gluten-free diet, you probably have some form of gluten sensitivity. (And to further complicate the issue, you may have celiac disease, with a false negative test result. I talk more about this situation in "Getting Tested for Gluten Sensitivity and Celiac Disease".)

Sadly, because protocol for defining and diagnosing gluten sensitivity isn't yet established and there's very little agreement or awareness of gluten sensitivity in the medical community, patients are often told to ignore "inconclusive" or confusing test results and to go back to eating their bagels and pizza.

Crossing the line: Celiac disease

Somewhere along the way on this gluten-sensitivity spectrum, the ambiguous sensitivity is no longer ambiguous: You have celiac disease. Unlike gluten sensitivity, celiac disease is well-defined.

Celiac disease is a common (yet often misdiagnosed) genetic intolerance to gluten. Triggered by eating gluten, the immune system responds by attacking the gluten molecule, and in so doing, it also attacks your body cells. This is called an *autoimmune response*. The disease can develop at any age, in people of any ethnicity, and it results in damage to the small intestine, which can cause poor absorption of nutrients. Although the damage occurs in the gastrointestinal tract, not all symptoms are gastrointestinal in nature. In fact, symptoms are vast and varied, and they sometimes come and go, which makes diagnosis difficult.

Identifying Symptoms of Gluten Sensitivity and Celiac Disease

The symptoms that I describe in this section are accepted as symptoms of celiac disease, but they're also symptoms of gluten sensitivity. Notice that the symptoms affect all different parts of the body. That's because celiac disease is *multisystemic;* although the actual damage is occurring in the gastrointestinal tract — specifically in the small intestine — the symptoms manifest in many different ways.

Gluten sensitivity and celiac disease have hundreds of symptoms, so I can't list them all. The following sections give some of the more common ones, starting with the symptoms that are gastrointestinal in nature.

Going for the gut: Gastrointestinal symptoms

Most people think the most common symptoms of celiac disease are gastrointestinal in nature — diarrhea, constipation, gas, bloating, reflux, and even vomiting. These are some of the "classic" — though not the most common — symptoms of celiac disease:

✔ Abdominal pain and distension

✔ Acid reflux

✔ Bloating

✔ Constipation

✔ Diarrhea

✔ Gas and flatulence

✔ Greasy, foul-smelling, floating stools

✔ Nausea

✔ Vomiting

✔ Weight loss or weight gain

Flatulence factoids

Farts. Tooties. Butt burps. Trouser coughs. Flatus. Ask any boy between the ages of 2 and 102, and he'll tell you that there's absolutely no subject on this entire planet that's funnier than farts. So what's the deal with farts, anyway? Everyone does it (except me), yet some people deny it (I don't need to); others, usually those with a Y chromosome, proudly publicize their impending arrival ("Fire in the hole!"). The average person cuts the cheese 14 times a day (I wonder who counted?), each boasting a distinct sound effect (or lack thereof) and fragrance.

Farts — all bodily gas emissions, for that matter — are caused by the air you swallow and the fermentation of certain foods by the bacteria in your digestive system. People generally make about one to three pints of gas every day, and less than 1 percent of it smells (I know some people who are skewing the average). Speaking of skewing the averages, if you're doing more than your fair share of the 14 times per day and suspect you have gluten sensitivity or celiac disease, you may find that the gluten-free lifestyle significantly diminishes the flagrant (and not-so-fragrant) farting problem. So go ahead. Pull my finger.

Identifying nongastrointestinal symptoms

Interestingly, although gluten sensitivity and celiac disease affect the gut, most people's symptoms are not gastrointestinal in nature. People more commonly have what are called *extraintestinal* symptoms, and the list of those is extensive, topping over 250. This is only a partial listing that includes some of the more common symptoms:

- Fatigue and weakness (due to iron-deficiency anemia)
- Vitamin and/or mineral deficiencies
- Headaches (including migraines)
- Joint/bone pain
- Depression, irritability, listlessness, and mood disorders
- "Fuzzy brain" or an inability to concentrate
- Infertility
- Abnormal menstrual cycles
- Dental enamel deficiencies and irregularities
- Seizures
- Ataxia (bad balance)
- Nerve damage (peripheral neuropathy)
- Respiratory problems

- Canker sores (apthous ulcers)
- Lactose intolerance
- Eczema/psoriasis (skin conditions; not to be confused with dermatitis herpetiformis, which I talk about in Chapter 3)
- Rosacea (a skin disorder)
- Acne
- Hashimoto's disease, Sjögren's syndrome, lupus erythematosus, and other autoimmune disorders
- Early onset osteoporosis
- Hair loss (alopecia)
- Bruising easily
- Low blood sugar (hypoglycemia)
- Muscle cramping
- Nosebleeds
- Swelling and inflammation
- Night blindness

Celiac disease is related to infertility, spontaneous abortions, menstrual problems, and *intrauterine growth retardation* (abnormally slow growth of the fetus). The incidence of celiac disease in women with unexplained infertility has been estimated to be as high as 10 percent. In many of those cases, a gluten-free diet restores fertility. Furthermore, some research shows that women with fertility issues test positive for celiac disease-related antibodies at a rate ten times higher than the general population. If you've had fertility problems and you're pregnant or trying to become pregnant, find out whether you have celiac disease or gluten sensitivity; if you do, get on a gluten-free diet right away.

When no symptoms are a symptom

Some people have no noticeable symptoms whatsoever — these people are called *asymptomatic.* (Truly, though, if they read the list of 250+ symptoms, I'm wondering whether they could honestly say they have *none* of them!) Even though they don't feel any symptoms, though, gluten is damaging their small intestine, which can result in nutritional deficiencies and associated conditions. These people have it tough, in terms of both diagnosis and treatment. They usually get diagnosed because they have a relative who has celiac disease and they're smart enough to know that means they should be tested, too. As for treatment, they need to be gluten-free in order to be healthy. But it's tough to stay motivated to give up some of your favorite foods when those foods don't seem to make you feel bad!

Spotting symptoms in kids

Kids who have celiac disease tend to have the "classic" gastrointestinal symptoms of diarrhea or constipation. They may also have some of these symptoms:

- ✔ Inability to concentrate

- ✔ Irritability

- ✔ ADD/ADHD or autistic-type behaviors (I go into more detail on these behaviors and their connection to gluten later in this chapter)

- ✔ Failure to thrive (in infants and toddlers)

- ✔ Short stature or delayed growth

- ✔ Delayed onset of puberty

- ✔ Weak bones or bone pain

- ✔ Abdominal pain and distension

- ✔ Nosebleeds

Discovering misdiagnoses and the missed diagnoses

In Europe, the average time between the onset of symptoms and a diagnosis of celiac disease is six months. In the U.S., if the diagnosis ever comes, it takes an average of 11 years after symptoms develop.

A *Reader's Digest* article titled "10 Diseases Doctors Miss," cited celiac disease as one of the top ten misdiagnosed diseases. For every person diagnosed with celiac disease, 140 go undiagnosed. And that doesn't even account for the population that has gluten sensitivity (not celiac disease) and may never know it.

Thankfully, as awareness of celiac disease and gluten sensitivity is increasing, diagnoses are on the rise, and people are discovering improved health on a gluten-free diet.

Why the diagnosis is missed

Gluten sensitivity and celiac disease are common. They can cause severe problems if undiagnosed. Yet most people with gluten sensitivity or celiac disease go undiagnosed or misdiagnosed. Why are doctors missing the diagnosis of this common condition? Michelle Pietzak, M.D., one of the foremost experts on celiac disease, offers some ideas:

✔ **Physicians aren't exposed to it enough in medical school and residency training.** These are critical periods when doctors' opinions and future practices are molded. If they don't hear enough about it during medical school and training, they're not likely to look for it after they graduate.

✔ **Some doctors get "continuing medical information" from drug reps, journal articles, and conferences.** Right now, there aren't any drugs for celiac disease, so there aren't drug reps strolling into the doctors' offices and chatting it up. Nor are there many conferences and journal articles to bring celiac disease to the forefront, where it would be more likely to get top-of-mind awareness during the testing procedures.

✔ **Symptoms are vast and sometimes even absent.** Symptoms of gluten sensitivity and celiac disease are often quite varied, affecting many different parts of the body, sometimes all at once. Some people don't seem to have any symptoms. That makes pinpointing a cause difficult.

✔ **Physicians may think the patients are exaggerating or just plain "crazy."** More than one person with celiac disease has been called neurotic or a hypochondriac because of the many and sometimes dramatic symptoms involved. The long laundry list of symptoms may come across as being exaggeration or hysteria.

✔ **Physicians may be uncomfortable if they feel ignorant.** Not knowing what's wrong with you is difficult for doctors, and if you come in armed with information about celiac disease and they don't know much about it, they may feel defensive and may disregard your views and opinions as a result.

✔ **Routine blood tests don't pick it up.** Complete blood count (CBC) and chemistry panels don't test specifically for celiac disease or gluten sensitivity. So although a physician is likely to order CBC and chemistry panels for patients with celiac symptoms, those panels don't offer any hints that a patient may have celiac disease. An astute physician, though, will see signs in these panels: Anemia; low potassium, bicarbonate, and protein levels; and high liver enzymes are red flags for gluten sensitivity and celiac disease.

✔ **Routine endoscopies and poorly done biopsies don't detect celiac disease.** Some patients think they've been tested for celiac disease because their doctor did an endoscopy. But an endoscopy without a biopsy doesn't detect celiac disease (although a perceptive physician will see red-flag warning signs). Even if doctors do a biopsy, they may miss the diagnosis if they do the biopsy poorly, or if they don't take enough samples, or if the results are read by someone not knowledgeable about current diagnostic procedures.

✔ **Cost-containment in the medical field may limit testing.** Unfortunately, physicians are limited in some of the testing they can do because of cost-containment measures in the health care industry. This limit may result in insufficient testing or no testing whatsoever.

But in the meantime, underdiagnosis is still a big problem. Patients are often misdiagnosed with a variety of maladies before finding out that they really have celiac disease — easily cured by diet. Common misdiagnoses include

- ✔ Irritable bowel syndrome (IBS) or spastic colon
- ✔ Chronic fatigue syndrome (CFS) or fibromyalgia
- ✔ Lupus (an autoimmune disease)
- ✔ Unexplained anemia
- ✔ Migraines or unexplained headaches
- ✔ Unexplained infertility
- ✔ Psychological issues (hypochondria, depression, anxiety, or neurosis)
- ✔ Inflammatory bowel disease (IBD), such as Crohn's disease and colitis
- ✔ Cancer
- ✔ Viral infections (viral gastroenteritis)
- ✔ Food allergies or lactose intolerance
- ✔ Parasites or other infection
- ✔ Gallbladder disease
- ✔ Thyroid disease
- ✔ Cystic fibrosis (a respiratory disorder)
- ✔ Acid reflux
- ✔ Diverticulosis (small pouches in the colon where food gets trapped)
- ✔ Diabetes
- ✔ Eczema or psoriasis (skin conditions)

Blaming the Bread: How Gluten Affects Behavior

Rarely considered a culprit in behavioral issues, gluten is sometimes behind the scenes wreaking havoc on behavior and moods.

"Sorry I haven't been productive at work lately; I've been eating too much bread," sounds a bit ridiculous. But really, that's a valid excuse because bread — gluten — can affect your behavior in lots of different ways, including "fuzzy brain" or an inability to concentrate. Some behavioral manifestations of gluten sensitivity and celiac disease can include

 ✔ Inability to concentrate or focus

 ✔ Attention deficit disorder (ADD) and attention deficit hyperactive disorder (ADHD) type behaviors

 ✔ Autism

 ✔ Depression, bipolar disorder, schizophrenia, and mood disorders

 ✔ Irritability

 ✔ Lack of motivation

Exploring dietary treatment for autism

I think this is one of the most intriguing areas of research concerning the gluten-free diet. Evidence shows that some people with autism show extraordinary improvement on a gluten-free (and casein-free) diet.

Several well-designed randomized, controlled studies are currently underway at reputable institutions to offer more-substantive data, but years of anecdotal evidence supports the concept, and I've personally met hundreds of people who have experienced amazing results on the diet.

Although celiac disease and autism may actually be associated, in many cases, an entirely different mechanism's at work. Some people with autism may metabolize gluten and casein (the protein found in milk) into the form of an opiate — much like heroin. Basically, when they eat gluten and casein, they're getting a high off it — and they're becoming addicted.

TECHNICAL STUFF

Why food affects mood

Food can affect your mood for lots of reasons, including the fact that the hormones and *neurotransmitters* (the chemicals that relay messages between nerves) in your gut are almost identical to those in your brain. Some interesting studies apply specifically to people with gluten sensitivity or celiac disease, shedding light on why behavioral disorders may be a symptom of difficulties with gluten.

People who have problems with absorbing nutrients (like people with gluten sensitivity or celiac disease who are still eating gluten) often have high levels of adrenocorticotropic hormone (ACTH) and acetylcholine (Ach). These are referred to as *stress hormones*. High levels of ACTH and Ach interfere with learning and create anxiety, the desire to escape, a fear of new or unfamiliar things, and a poor ability to learn from experiences.

Also, experimental evidence suggests that people with malabsorption act similarly to people who have lesions in certain parts of the brain, like the hypothalamus (which regulates body processes) and the hippocampus (part of the limbic system, which affects mood and motivation).

This "high" they experience is similar to the high that an opiate user experiences, and it may account for traits typical in autistic kids, such as monotonous body movements (for instance, finger-flicking in front of their eyes, spinning, and head-banging), as well as being withdrawn and having a fascination with parts of objects (like fixating on one part of a toy rather than the toy itself). Also typical of opiate users and autistic kids is the distress they feel when there are small changes in their environment or routine.

Results on the gluten-free, casein-free diet vary. Some see improvement within a week — others within a year. Others see no improvement at all. Of those who report changes in behavior, the changes themselves vary, too. Some people with autism reflect an ability to sleep through the night; others become more verbal and interactive; and some are completely "normalized" on the diet.

There's definitely some connection between celiac disease and autism, although exactly what that connection is isn't clear yet. It's well-documented that autistic kids often have gastrointestinal problems, and the frequency of celiac disease is higher in autistic people than in the general public. Some researchers have presented alternate hypotheses, including the idea that the malabsorption that takes place with celiac disease results in a deficiency of neurotransmitters; with the nerves unable to properly transfer information, these people may experience autistic behaviors. Several studies are underway to determine the relationship between the two conditions.

Autistic kids tend to like a small selection of foods — usually those that are loaded with gluten and casein. A therapist may be able to help you develop a plan for introducing new (gluten-free) foods into the diet of an autistic child. You can search www.autismndi.com to find out more about autism and diet.

Diminishing depression and other mood disorders

Clinical depression, bipolar disorder, schizophrenia, and a variety of mood disorders can sometimes be associated with or exacerbated by gluten sensitivity and celiac disease. Some journal articles even list these mood disorders as "symptoms" of celiac disease. These conditions sometimes improve on a gluten-free diet.

Schizophrenia has been associated with celiac disease since the 1960s, when it was first noted that a gluten- (and dairy-) restricted diet led to improvement in some institutionalized patients. Interestingly, the same opiate-like chemicals found in the urine of autistic people are often found in schizophrenics.

Some investigators have noted that the incidence of schizophrenia is higher in places where wheat is the staple grain than where they normally eat non-gluten-containing grains. In one study done in the highlands of Papua, New Guinea, where little or no grain is consumed, only two people out of 65,000 adults could be identified as overtly insane, chronic schizophrenics. In the coastal area, where wheat is consumed more, the prevalence of schizophrenia was about three times higher.

Getting Tested for Gluten Sensitivity and Celiac Disease

Testing for gluten sensitivity and celiac disease isn't an exact science — nor do "exact scientists" agree on protocol for some of the testing procedures available today. The most widely accepted testing protocol for celiac disease includes a blood test followed by an intestinal biopsy.

Blood tests

Blood tests — also called *serological* tests — look for antibodies that the body produces when someone with a sensitivity or celiac disease eats gluten.

You have to be eating gluten for an extended length of time before blood testing. If you don't eat gluten, or haven't eaten it for long enough, your body may not produce enough antibodies to show up on the tests, and the results will seem to show that you're "normal" — or "negative" for gluten sensitivity or celiac disease. No one knows for sure exactly how much gluten you need to be eating, but if you eat the equivalent of about one or two pieces of gluten-containing bread a day for at least three months, you should have enough gluten in your system to provide a measurable response. If you have severe symptoms during that time, consult your physician to see whether you should continue to eat gluten.

The most comprehensive panel of blood tests that you can get for gluten sensitivity and celiac disease includes five tests for antibodies:

- ✔ **tTG (anti-tissue transglutaminase)-IgA:** This test is very specific to celiac disease, meaning that if you have a positive tTG, it's very likely that you have celiac disease and not another condition.

- ✔ **EMA (anti-endomysial antibodies)-IgA:** This test is also specific to celiac disease. When it's positive, especially if tTG is positive too, it's extremely likely that you have celiac disease.

✔ **AGA (antigliadin antibodies)-IgA:** The antigliadin tests are less specific for celiac disease, and these antibodies sometimes show up in other diseases (including gluten sensitivity). AGA-IgA is useful when testing young symptomatic children, who don't always produce enough tTG or EMA for diagnostic purposes.

AGA-IgA is also useful for monitoring compliance on the gluten-free diet (if it's still elevated after you've been gluten-free for several months, gluten may be sneaking into your diet). Some people feel that a positive AGA-IgA indicates gluten sensitivity.

✔ **AGA (antigliadin antibodies)-IgG:** This is another antigliadin test (like the preceding one) and is less specific to celiac disease, but it may be useful in detecting gluten sensitivity or leaky gut syndrome. Also, if the IgG levels are highly positive and all the other tests are negative, that may signal that the patient is IgA-deficient (see the next point for more information on this), in which case the results of the other tests are erroneous.

✔ **Total serum IgA (total serum, immunoglobulin A):** A significant portion of the population is IgA-deficient, meaning their IgA production is always lower than normal. Three of the four tests above are IgA-based (the only one that isn't IgA-based is antigliadin IgG), so in someone who's IgA-deficient, results of those three tests would be falsely low. By measuring total serum IgA, doctors can determine whether a patient is IgA-deficient and can compensate when reading the results of the three IgA-based tests.

Any lab can draw the blood, as long as you have an order from a doctor, registered nurse, chiropractor, or other health care practitioner allowed to order blood draws.

The lab technicians can get the blood they need for all five of the tests with a single blood draw. They just have to insert the needle once to fill the vials. Your results are sent to the doctor who ordered the blood draw, and although each lab takes a different amount of time to process the results, most take about two weeks.

Your doctor may order a Reticulin (anti-reticulin antibodies — ARA) test. This test isn't nearly as specific as the others mentioned in this section and isn't used much anymore for diagnostic purposes.

If one or more of these tests are positive, the results may indicate celiac disease. Your doctor will probably want to do an intestinal biopsy to confirm the diagnosis (you can find more information on biopsies in the next section).

Testing for allergies

The RAST test is a blood test that can detect immunoglobulin E (IgE), which mediates wheat allergies. But many people have food allergies that can't be detected by the RAST test, which limits its usefulness.

You may have been tested for allergies by what's called a "scratch test." Some people don't consider scratch tests reliable in the diagnosis of a food allergy. For one thing, some people who have apparent allergy symptoms in response to foods they eat don't react to those same foods in scratch tests. Another point is that through the digestion process, your body changes the food dramatically. Doing the scratch test with basically "whole" food on your skin isn't the same as presenting digested food to your gut.

You could have the blood test for gluten sensitivity and celiac disease done at the same time as you have your RAST test done, even though they're completely different tests. Ask your doctor about doing all the tests at once.

Your doctor may do some other blood tests to evaluate the severity of the disease and the extent of your malnutrition, malabsorption, and organ involvement. Doctors may test for

- ✔ CBC (complete blood count) to look for anemia and other vitamin/mineral/enzyme deficiencies
- ✔ ESR (erythrocyte sedimentation rate) to evaluate inflammation
- ✔ CRP (C-reactive protein) to evaluate inflammation
- ✔ CMP (complete metabolic panel) to determine electrolyte, protein, and calcium levels, as well as to verify the status of the kidney and liver
- ✔ Vitamins D, E, and B12 to measure for vitamin deficiencies
- ✔ Stool fat levels, to help evaluate malabsorption

Biopsies

In the olden days, the only way to diagnose celiac disease was to do not one, not two, but three biopsies of the small intestine. Today, biopsies are still considered the "gold standard" for diagnosing celiac disease, but thanks to the accuracy of blood tests, the number of biopsies required is far less, and usually only one is required.

When doctors do a biopsy, they do it by way of an endoscopy: They put a tube down your throat to the small intestine and then clip samples of the *villi,* hairlike structures on the lining of the small intestine. Earlier in this chapter, I explain that when people with celiac disease eat gluten, the body launches an attack and ends up attacking itself, blunting the villi. The biopsy determines how much blunting, if any, has occurred.

The endoscopy itself and the clipping of the villi aren't painful. The doctor, a gastroenterologist, sprays your throat with some numbing medication and gives you pain-killing medications and a sedative that makes most people tired enough that they sleep through the procedure. Then he or she inserts a tube through the mouth into the esophagus, to the stomach, and finally to the small intestine. Some people have some mild discomfort when the tube is inserted into their throat, and sometimes people have a mild sore throat after the procedure.

Like the blood test, you have to be eating gluten for an extended length of time in order for the biopsies to be accurate.

Here are a few important things to know about a biopsy:

- ✔ It's an invasive procedure, so some risks are involved. Adults are usually sedated with drugs like Versed (midazolam) and Demerol (meperidine); children usually require a general anesthetic.

- ✔ The doctor should take several biopsy samples. Celiac disease can be patchy, sometimes affecting one area but not affecting the area right next to it. Taking several samples maximizes the chance that at least one will be from an affected area, if there is one.

- ✔ Even mild blunting can indicate damage. People used to think that in order to diagnose celiac disease, there had to be *total villous atrophy,* or completely flattened or blunted villi. Today, different degrees of damage are measured by the Marsh rating system, and even partial blunting indicates damage.

- ✔ For the most part, doctors can't make a diagnosis by doing an endoscopy alone. Although visual clues can indicate damage due to celiac disease, biopsies give more definitive answers.

The biopsy samples are sent to a pathologist, who then gives the results to the gastroenterologist. You should hear back from the gastroenterologist with the results of your biopsy within three to four days.

Urine tests

The *urine peptide test* may be valuable in determining whether people with autism or schizophrenia may benefit from a gluten-free, casein-free diet. The test looks for peptides in the urine, which are evidence that the body isn't properly breaking down proteins like gluten.

Peptides are chains of amino acids, and proteins are a type of large peptide. Everyone metabolizes the proteins gluten and casein into peptides called *gliadinomorphin* and *casomorphin,* respectively. In most people, the body further breaks down these peptides into amino acids, but in autistic or schizophrenic people, the peptides sometimes remain intact. These peptides, which can function much like opiate drugs, are usually excreted in the urine. Doctors look for elevated levels of peptides in the urine peptide test.

The only way these relatively large peptides can get into the bloodstream is if the gut is extra permeable — as in *leaky gut syndrome,* a component of celiac disease that I discuss in Chapter 3. A gluten-free diet discourages the peptides from entering the blood.

Stool tests

At least one lab does home stool-testing for gluten sensitivity, microscopic colitis, genetic susceptibility, and several other gastrointestinal conditions. Like the blood test, the stool test looks for the immune system's reactions to gluten by detecting the presence of AGA and tTG antibodies.

The lab sends you a convenient container, and then you just do your business in it and send it back by overnight mail.

The most established lab doing this testing in the United States is EnteroLab, and it claims the stool test is more sensitive than the blood test. It asserts that the immune response to food in gluten-sensitive individuals takes place in the intestine, and therefore antibodies are easily detectable in the stool, even before they're detectable in the blood. Therefore, people with slight sensitivities or people in the early phases of gluten sensitivity would show an antibody response in stool testing, even if they don't show a response in blood tests.

This lab claims these advantages:

- ✔ The test is noninvasive.
- ✔ You don't need a doctor's involvement.
- ✔ The test is more sensitive than a blood test.
- ✔ You don't need to have eaten gluten recently for the test to be accurate.

Although stool testing certainly has some exciting and promising implications and offers some logistical advantages over the other testing methods, it is not yet considered a standard diagnostic tool for celiac disease.

Genetic tests

Genetic testing can be done by blood or stool. Doctors look to see whether someone has the genes associated with celiac disease.

Genetic testing is valuable for ruling out celiac disease, because if your body doesn't produce either the protein HLA-DQ2 or HLA-DQ8, there's a 99 percent chance you don't have celiac disease. The test isn't valuable for predicting who will get celiac disease, though, because lots of people have these genes and never develop it. There's more information about the genetics of celiac disease in Chapter 3.

Interpreting your test results

Sometimes interpretation of your test results is straightforward — and other times it's not even close.

For one thing, there are false negatives and occasionally false positives. False negatives can be due to several factors:

- ✔ Testing is somewhat subjective, and not all labs do it well. Many lab technicians rarely, if ever, see celiac panels and don't always do them properly.

- ✔ Different pathologists read biopsies differently. Some, for instance, believe that mild blunting of the villi indicates celiac disease; others think celiac disease is a possible diagnosis only if the villi are completely blunted. Most pathologists today agree that partial villous blunting can indicate celiac disease.

- ✔ Not eating enough gluten prior to testing can affect the amount of antibodies you produce.

- ✔ Testing that doesn't include all five blood tests may leave an antibody unnoticed.

- ✔ IgA deficiency makes the tests come out "normal" or negative, when if there were no IgA deficiency, they would have been positive.

- ✔ About 5 to 10 percent of people don't produce the antibodies tTG and EMA.

- ✔ Young children don't always produce enough antibodies to show a response. This is especially true for tTG and EMA.

- ✔ A compromised immune system may weaken the antibody response. Although people with celiac disease do not have a compromised immune system as a result of their condition, illness can weaken their immune systems. This can produce lower-than-normal test results on the IgA-based tests.

✔ In the very initial stages of sensitivity or disease, you may not have produced enough antibodies or experienced enough villous blunting — *yet.*

Celiac disease and gluten sensitivity can be triggered at any age, so just because you tested negative once doesn't mean you're "out of the woods" forever.

I realize there are endless iterations of the chart I've put together for you in Table 2-1, but I couldn't possibly include all the various combinations. So for the most part, tests can be interpreted like this (this chart assumes you're not IgA deficient, so IgA-based tests are conclusive):

Table 2-1	Interpreting Your Test Results
Test Result	*Likely Diagnosis*
Positive EMA, tTG, or biopsy (regardless of AGA-IgA and IgG results)	Celiac disease likely; step away from the pizza
Negative EMA, tTG, and biopsy Positive AGA-IgA and IgG	Most likely not celiac disease but could be gluten sensitivity; forget the donuts
Positive AGA-IgG All other tests negative	Could be gluten sensitivity or another leaky gut syndrome
All tests negative	You don't seem to have any problem with gluten; enjoy all the pizza and donuts you like (but don't blame me when your pants don't fit!)

Some people test negative on some or all the tests, yet they find that they don't feel right when they eat gluten. Perhaps you got false negatives — or maybe gluten just doesn't sit right with you. Bottom line: If it makes you feel bad, don't eat it!

I've tested positive! Now what?

If you've tested positive, your next step depends on what you tested positive for. It also depends on whether you had the complete testing panels done. Read on.

You're positive for gluten sensitivity

If you actually have gluten sensitivity and not celiac disease, you may be able to get away with eating gluten from time to time. I can hear you now: *Yeah, I'm thinkin' I have a gluten sensitivity, not celiac disease. Pass the pizza and beer, wouldja?* You may want to rethink that strategy unless you know for sure that you're really negative for celiac disease, because sometimes people are told they're gluten sensitive when, in fact, they have celiac disease. If that's the case and you do go back to eating gluten, you could be doing some hefty damage every time you indulge. Ask yourself and your doctor:

- ✔ **Were all of the tests for celiac disease done?** Sometimes doctors don't do any of the tests that are specific to celiac disease; they just test for sensitivity. Other times, they do only one test for celiac disease, which may not be enough.

- ✔ **If a child's being tested, is the child old enough to show an antibody response?** Some of the tests that are specific to celiac disease may not show accurate results in children 2 and under because their immune systems aren't strong enough to produce antibodies. In that case, a child may appear to be positive for gluten sensitivity but not celiac disease — when in fact, he or she actually has celiac disease.

- ✔ **Were the results "iffy" or "inconclusive," or were they definitive?** Sometimes someone's celiac-specific antibodies are considered "iffy" because the results aren't off-the-charts high. Sometimes these people are told they don't have celiac disease, but they do have gluten sensitivity.

If you aren't sure you can trust your test results, you may want to be tested again somewhere down the line.

You're positive for celiac disease

If you've been diagnosed with celiac disease, you're lucky! You know the key to your better health: A gluten-free lifestyle. Going gluten-free right away is important. You may make mistakes at first, and that's okay. Learn from them, and move on.

Celiac disease is a genetic condition. If you've been diagnosed, your family members need to be tested, too.

You're positive for wheat allergies

Although the conditions are different, you could have an allergy *and* a gluten sensitivity or celiac disease. So if you're diagnosed with wheat allergies, make sure you're also tested for the more global conditions, gluten sensitivity and celiac disease, to know just what dietary guidelines you need to follow.

If you're not positive for those but have only a wheat allergy, then you need to avoid wheat but can still eat rye and barley. If you suspect you may have an anaphylactic response, you should consider carrying an EpiPen or other brand of epinephrine shot that allows you to inject yourself, in case you accidentally eat wheat.

Considering the Risks If You Don't Give Up Gluten

Invariably, at least four groups of people decide they're going to continue to eat gluten even if they have problems with it:

- ✔ Those who feel like the diet is too restrictive, so they're not going to bother trying
- ✔ People who don't feel symptoms or were never properly diagnosed and figure that cheating from time to time is okay
- ✔ People who feel symptoms but figure the discomfort is worth the chance to enjoy a few beers (or other glutenous favorite) from time to time
- ✔ Relatives who refuse to hear anything about gluten

If you fall into one of these categories and refuse to give up gluten even though you have or suspect you may have gluten sensitivity or celiac disease, there's not much anyone can do. But before you finish your donut, at least read the next two sections, which talk about the conditions that are associated with celiac disease — and the serious complications that can arise if you continue to eat gluten.

Looking at associated conditions

Certain conditions are associated with celiac disease, meaning that someone who has one is more likely to have the other. It's not always clear which one developed first (except, for instance, Down syndrome, which people are born with), but if you don't give up gluten, your chances of developing some of these conditions may increase.

Also, if you have one of these conditions but haven't been tested for gluten sensitivity or celiac disease, you should be tested, because the two go hand in hand; the fact that you have one of these diseases is a red flag that you may also have gluten sensitivity or celiac disease.

Autoimmune diseases

Several autoimmune diseases are associated with celiac disease, including

- ✔ Addison's disease (hypoadrenocorticism)
- ✔ Autoimmune chronic active hepatitis
- ✔ Crohn's disease
- ✔ Insulin-dependent diabetes mellitus (Type 1)
- ✔ Myesthenia gravis
- ✔ Raynaud's phenomenon
- ✔ Scleroderma
- ✔ Sjögren's syndrome
- ✔ Systemic lupus erythematosus
- ✔ Thyroid disease (Graves' disease and Hashimoto's disease)
- ✔ Ulcerative colitis

Mood disorders

Some of the mood disorders that are associated with gluten sensitivity and celiac disease include

- ✔ ADD/ADHD
- ✔ Autism
- ✔ Depression and bipolar disease

Nutritional deficiencies

Because gluten sensitivity and celiac disease affect the small intestine, nutritional deficiencies are associated. In addition to specific vitamin and mineral deficiencies, people may have

- ✔ Anemia
- ✔ Osteoporosis, osteopenia, or osteomalacia

Neurological conditions

Some neurological conditions are associated with gluten sensitivity and celiac disease, including

- ✔ Epilepsy and cerebral calcifications
- ✔ Brain and spinal cord defects (in newborns born to mothers with celiac disease who are eating gluten)
- ✔ Neurological problems, such as ataxia, neuropathy, tingling, seizures, and optic myopathy

Other conditions

Several other conditions are commonly associated with celiac disease, including

- ✔ Cancer (especially intestinal lymphoma)
- ✔ Down syndrome
- ✔ Internal hemorrhaging
- ✔ Organ disorders (of the gallbladder, liver, spleen, or pancreas)
- ✔ Tooth enamel defects
- ✔ Cystic fibrosis

Type 1 diabetes and celiac disease often go hand in hand. About 6 percent of people with Type 1 diabetes have celiac disease, but many don't know it. People with celiac disease and Type 1 diabetes often find managing blood-sugar levels is much easier on the gluten-free diet.

The earlier in life you go on a gluten-free diet, the lower your risk of developing associated conditions. And sometimes symptoms of other autoimmune diseases, like multiple sclerosis, improve on a gluten-free diet.

Living with compromised health

You may feel perfectly healthy. You may be *asymptomatic* (have no apparent symptoms) or have mild symptoms that you barely notice. But if you have gluten sensitivity or celiac disease and you continue to eat gluten, you're doubtlessly compromising your health. Your body is being robbed of important nutrients that it needs to function properly and stay strong.

Many people say that they didn't realize how bad they felt until they went gluten-free. Then they enjoy such improved and even optimal health that they realize that eating gluten compromised their health, and they didn't even know it.

Healing Begins on Day One

One of the coolest things about going gluten-free when you have gluten sensitivity or celiac disease is that you start healing the minute you start on the diet.

Most people begin feeling better immediately; some take months to improve; and some feel better initially but then take a nosedive a few months into the diet. All these are normal responses to your body's healing process, and in the long run, you can look forward to improved health in ways you may not have even expected.

Although most, if not all, of the intestinal damage caused by gluten is reversible, some of the prolonged malnutrition and malabsorption issues, such as short stature and weakened bones, may have long-lasting, if not permanent effects. That's one of the reasons catching gluten sensitivity or celiac disease early is important — so you can start skipping down the road to recovery.

Chapter 3

A Closer Look at Celiac Disease

*G*luten sensitivity and celiac disease are similar in many ways: symptoms, treatment, and maybe even some of the testing methods. But because gluten sensitivity hasn't been well-defined and celiac disease has, I focus on celiac disease in this chapter.

Celiac disease has a bunch of names that all mean the same thing, including *sprue, celiac sprue, non-tropical sprue* (not to be confused with tropical sprue), *gluten-sensitive enteropathy, Gee-Herter disease,* and *coeliac disease* (the European spelling).

Three aspects of celiac disease make it uniquely contradictory and intriguing. These factors interrelate, beckoning a closer look at this complex condition:

✔ Celiac disease is extremely common but rarely diagnosed.

✔ If undiagnosed, it can severely compromise your health.

✔ It's fully treatable by diet alone.

So just how common is it? Well, since you asked . . .

Exposing One of the Most Common Genetic Diseases of Mankind

Occurring in nearly 1 percent of the population, celiac disease is one of the most common genetic diseases of mankind. According to the Center for Celiac Research, the numbers break down like this:

✔ As many as 1 in 133 people has celiac disease (most don't know it). (Remember, this doesn't even take into account those who have non-celiac gluten sensitivity.)

✔ For people with "classic" symptoms, the incidence is 1 in 40.

✔ For people with parents or siblings with celiac disease, the incidence is 1 in 20.

✔ For people who have an aunt, uncle, grandparent, or first cousin with celiac disease, the incidence is 1 in 40.

To put these numbers in perspective, celiac disease is more common than Crohn's disease, ulcerative colitis, multiple sclerosis, Parkinson's disease, and cystic fibrosis combined. Check out Table 3-1 to see how celiac disease measures up.

Table 3-1	Incidence of Common Genetic Diseases in the U.S.
Disease	*Estimated Number of People*
Celiac disease	3 million (www.celiaccenter.org)
Epilepsy	2.7 million (www.epilepsyfoundation.org)
Parkinson's disease	1 million (Parkinson's Disease Foundation)
Alzheimer's disease	4.5 million (Alzheimer's Association)
Ulcerative colitis	500,000 (Crohn's and Colitis Foundation of America)
Crohn's disease	500,000 (Crohn's and Colitis Foundation of America)
Multiple sclerosis	300,000 (National Center for Health Statistics)
Cystic fibrosis	30,000 (National Institute of Diabetes & Digestive & Kidney Diseases)

People often wonder: If celiac disease is so common, why don't more people have it? They do! They just don't know it yet (and may never know it).

Myths and misconceptions

Some of the things I hear about celiac disease have about as much truth as the Loch Ness Monster legend, but without even a grainy photograph to back it up (no, you don't "catch it" from potatoes). Here are some of the more common myths:

Myth: Celiac disease is rare.

Fact: Celiac disease is one of the world's most common genetic diseases, affecting about 1 percent of the population. On top of that, a huge percentage has gluten sensitivity, which can produce the same symptoms and possibly have the same serious repercussions as celiac disease.

Myth: Celiac disease is a pediatric condition.

Fact: Actually, celiac disease can be "triggered" at any point in life and more often appears in the later years.

Myth: Severe gastrointestinal problems, like diarrhea, are the most common symptoms.

Fact: Most people with celiac disease don't have any gastrointestinal symptoms, much less severe ones — their symptoms are extraintestinal, like headaches, fatigue, joint pain, depression, and feeling overall crummy.

Pinpointing Who Develops Celiac Disease and Why

There's no way to know who will develop celiac disease. What doctors *do* know is that you need at least three things in order to develop the condition:

- ✓ The genetic predisposition
- ✓ A diet that includes gluten
- ✓ An environmental trigger

Even if you have all three, you may never develop celiac disease. You *can* say, though, that if you're missing one of these three things, you won't develop celiac disease (but you could still have gluten sensitivity).

Celiac disease is a nondiscriminatory condition, found in all races and nationalities. It's commonly thought to be more prevalent in people with Northern European ancestry, but that distinction is diminishing as people are becoming more diverse and intermingled.

Some people think that civilizations that developed between the Tigris and Euphrates in the Middle East, where grain was first cultivated, have had longer to evolve to cope successfully with gluten-containing grains; that's why the prevalence of gluten sensitivity among these people is lower. Other groups, like the Germans, Scandinavians, and Celts of England, Scotland, and Ireland, began cultivating wheat only in limited amounts in the post-Roman era. They were mostly hunter-gatherers until the Middle Ages, so those populations have had less time to adjust to gluten-containing grains.

It's in the genes

No one knows all the genes that are involved in developing celiac disease, but researchers do know of two key players: HLA DQ2 and HLA DQ8. You don't have to have both — just one will do — and DQ2 is the one seen most often in people with celiac disease.

But about one-third of the general population has these genes and doesn't develop celiac disease — so knowing whether you have these genes is most valuable if you want to rule out celiac disease. In other words, if you have the genes, you may or may not develop celiac disease. But if you don't have either gene, there's a 99 percent chance you won't develop celiac disease (which has always left me wondering about that 1 percent!). Keep in mind also that if you don't have these genes, you can still have non-celiac gluten sensitivity.

Celiac disease isn't dominant or recessive — it's *multifactorial* or *multigenic*, meaning several different types of genes play a part in the development of the condition.

Triggering celiac disease: What turns it on

People use the word *trigger* in two ways when they talk about celiac disease. The first refers to gluten being the "trigger" for initiating a response of the body's immune system (you can delve into that more deeply in the next section). The type of trigger I'm talking about here is an environmental trigger that "flips a switch," so to speak, launching celiac disease into an active mode.

Most people have a pretty clear idea of when their celiac disease got triggered, because in many cases they're relatively healthy, and then *boom!* Their symptoms appear "out of the blue," and they have no idea why.

Common triggers include

- ✔ Pregnancy
- ✔ Surgery
- ✔ Car accident or other physical injury
- ✔ Divorce, job loss, a death in the family, or emotional trauma
- ✔ Illness

Understanding Celiac Disease and What It Does to the Body

Celiac disease is an *autoimmune disease* (a disease in which the immune system attacks the body) that gets activated when someone eats gluten. To help you understand exactly what damage is being done, I review just a tinge of basic human anatomy, specifically focusing on the gastrointestinal tract. I keep it brief and easy to understand, and I promise there won't be a pop quiz.

Some people think that because celiac disease is an autoimmune disease, someone with celiac disease has a compromised immune system. Not at all! In fact, the opposite is true — the immune system in people with celiac disease is working overtime to fight what it perceives to be bad guys — like gluten.

How your guts are supposed to work

You got guts, but do you know how they work? I can help here. Skipping approximately dozens of important steps, I start my explanation in the upper part of the small intestine. The food has already been chewed, swallowed, passed through the stomach, and broken down by enzymes into nutrients that the body can use to nourish itself.

The small intestine is lined with hairlike projections called *villi*. The purpose of the villi, shown in Figure 3-1, is to increase the surface area of the intestine so they have more room to absorb important nutrients.

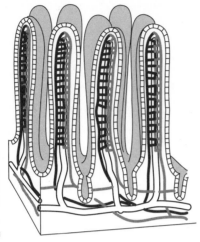

Figure 3-1:
The villi of
your small
intestine.

The lining of the small intestine is basically a solid wall. All the cells on the lining are joined together by *tight junctions*. When the body is ready to absorb the nutrients, these tight junctions open the space between cells and let the good stuff in — but keep the bigger bad stuff, like toxins, out.

How do the tight junctions know how far to open? They have a comrade-in-arms named *zonulin*. Zonulin is a protein — its job is to be a gatekeeper, opening the tight junctions just enough to let the good stuff in but keep the bad stuff out.

How your guts work with celiac disease

When someone with celiac disease eats gluten, everything's going along just fine until the gluten reaches the small intestine.

The first thing that goes wrong at this point is that wheat causes the body — in all humans, not just celiacs — to produce too much of the protein *zonulin*. This excess of zonulin causes the junctions between cells in the small intestine to open too much, and next thing you know, there's a party in the blood-stream and all sorts of things can get into the bloodstream that shouldn't be there — things like toxins and gluten fragments.

When stuff leaks through the intestinal wall that normally shouldn't be able to, the condition's called *leaky gut syndrome*.

So now, thanks to the excess of zonulin that was released because you ate gluten, the gluten fragment has made its way into the bloodstream. In people with celiac disease, the body sees gluten fragments an invaders — toxins that shouldn't be there. So it launches an all-out attack against these invaders, but — and here's why celiac disease is called an *autoimmune response* — the body also attacks itself.

Reducing the chance that your baby develops celiac disease

New studies show that you may be able to protect a baby from developing celiac disease later in life. University of Colorado scientists have published information indicating that exposing babies to gluten in the first three months of a baby's life increases the risk of celiac disease fivefold. Their studies indicate that waiting until the baby is at least six months old decreases the risk but that waiting beyond seven months increases the risk again. In other words, the best time to introduce gluten, according to this study, is between four and six months old.

Another factor that seems to have an effect on the development of celiac disease is breastfeeding. Studies show that breastfeeding longer than three months may delay the onset of celiac symptoms and decrease the risk of developing celiac disease. Gradual introduction of gluten-containing foods and continuing to breastfeed while those foods are introduced seem to reduce the risk of developing celiac disease, as well.

An *autoimmune disease* is one in which the body's immune system produces antibodies that react against normal, healthy tissue (rather than against bacteria or viruses), causing inflammation and damage. Celiac disease is unique, because it's the only autoimmune disease for which people know the trigger that sets off the response. A survey from the American Autoimmune Related Diseases Association found that 45 percent of people eventually diagnosed with an autoimmune disease were initially labeled as hypochondriacs because doctors thought they were imagining their symptoms.

Specifically, the body attacks the villi on the lining of the small intestine. As the villi get chopped down — *blunted* is the technical term — they can no longer be as effective in absorbing nutrients. That's why you see *malabsorption* (poor nutrient absorption) and nutritional deficiencies in people with celiac disease who still eat gluten.

Because the food is just passing through without being absorbed the way it's supposed to be, you sometimes see diarrhea. But think about this: The small intestine is nearly 22 feet long, and damage from celiac disease starts at the upper part — so there's *lots* of small intestine to compensate for the damaged part that's not able to do its job. That means by the time you have diarrhea, you're usually a very sick puppy.

And now for the pop quiz. Ha! I'm kidding! Really, that little lesson wasn't so bad, now, was it? And just think of what a hit you'll be at cocktail parties now that you can enrapture your friends with discussions of your villi, zonulin, and leaky gut syndrome.

Scratching the Surface of Dermatitis Herpetiformis

Okay, that heading was funny only to me, I'm sure. *Dermatitis herpetiformis* (I refer to it as *DH* from now on) is a severe, itchy, blistering skin condition often referred to as a "sister" to celiac disease. Everyone with DH has celiac disease (but not the other way around). Their symptoms are usually just external — on the skin — but about 20 percent of people with DH also have intestinal symptoms. A gluten-free diet improves and sometimes completely clears up the condition.

Usually, the rash starts as groups of red bumps with tiny blisters on top, but they itch so intensely that people usually scratch them to the point of opening the blisters, which then crust over. They occur commonly on the elbows, knees, butt, back of the neck, and scalp but can also be on the face, trunk, and other parts of the arms and legs.

To diagnose DH, doctors take a biopsy of the skin *near* (but not in) the lesion. The process isn't painful, because doctors can use a local anesthetic to numb the site. They're looking for an antibody called IgA (I talk more about IgA in Chapter 2), and if they see it, they make a diagnosis of DH. Blood screenings can confirm the diagnosis and help doctors monitor progress on a gluten-free diet, but an intestinal biopsy usually isn't necessary.

Treatment is a strict gluten-free diet. Sometimes doctors put DH patients on sulfa-based medications such as dapsone or sulfapyridine, but doctors must first test for enzymes to avoid toxicity problems from taking the drug. Ideally, patients can decrease their use of medications as they heal on the gluten-free diet. If the gluten-free diet isn't helping, you may need to avoid other foods and chemicals as well. Iodine can present a problem, and it's found in shellfish and table salt. Kelp (found in some toothpastes and in some oriental foods) and potassium iodide (used as an expectorant in cough medications) may present a problem, as may nonsteroidal anti-inflammatory agents (NSAIDS), found in over-the-counter pain and fever medications.

The name for DH comes from *dermatitis,* meaning inflammation of the skin, and *herpetiformis,* because it looks similar to herpes, which involves clusters of lesions. Some people have made the erroneous assumption that DH is caused by the herpes virus, but there's actually no relationship to the herpes virus at all.

Chapter 4

Grasping the Ground Rules
of the Gluten-Free Diet

In This Chapter

▶ Understanding what gluten is

▶ Knowing what you generally can and can't eat

▶ Introducing superfoods and other stuff you may not have heard of

▶ Uncovering gluten in nonfood items

*W*hether you're brand new to the wonderful world of gluten-freedom or an old pro who's been gluten-free for years, this chapter tells you things about the gluten-free diet that may surprise you.

The diet seems like it should be so easy: Gluten is in wheat, rye, and barley — so just avoid those foods, right? If the diet were that simple, I'd be signing off with "The End" or "Love, Danna" right about now, and the book would be finished. No, the diet's not quite that straightforward, thanks to additives, flavorings, derivatives, fillers, binders, and other fancy terms that are really just euphemisms for "stuff that may have gluten in it."

The good news is that the list of things you can eat is a lot longer than the list of things you can't. Sure, you're going to have to kiss your pizza goodbye (but wipe the crumbs off your lips — those crumbs are loaded with gluten), along with your bagels, bread, cookies, brownies, cakes, and — yep — beer (at least the kinds of those things that you're probably used to).

But you'll realize the amazing world of incredible gluten-free foods that can take the place of your old favorites — some of which you may never have heard of before, like *quinoa*, (if you read the rest of this chapter, you may even know how to pronounce it). You'll know that *Job's Tears* are not a religious icon but that they are gluten-free. And if you think *ragi* is a spaghetti sauce and *sorghum* is what you get when you have your teeth cleaned, now's the time to learn more about some of the unique grains and starches available to you on a gluten-free diet.

Don't be discouraged if you feel like the guidelines are a little overwhelming at first. For some people, learning what's allowed and what isn't on a gluten-free diet requires an entirely different mindset. For others, it's less dramatic of a change. And for still others, it's a welcome skew from their everyday fare.

Whether you're a one or a ten on the I'm-overwhelmed-by-this-diet scale, this chapter is key because it establishes basic gluten-free guidelines. I outline what is and isn't gluten-free and why you sometimes have to question a product. I introduce you to gluten-free alternatives that you may never have heard of. I also talk about nonfood items that you may or may not need to be concerned about, such as dental products, alcoholic beverages, medications, and external products like lotions and shampoos.

When In Doubt, Leave It Out

I can say unequivocally that at some point, you will have occasion to wonder whether a product is gluten-free; you're at a restaurant or party and you have no idea what's in the food, the labeling isn't clear, no labels are in sight, or you don't know half the words on the label. And if you don't have your handy-dandy copy of *Living Gluten-Free For Dummies* nearby, you may be tempted to make assumptions that could get you in trouble.

This assumptive process in these situations usually goes something like this:

> I don't know this is gluten-free, but it looks really yummy. It doesn't look like it has gluten in it. Therefore, because I don't *know* that it's *not* okay, I'll assume that it's safe for me to eat. Mmmm. That was delicious. It didn't taste like it had gluten in it. . . . Excuse me, where's your restroom?

Don't do it. If you need a reminder of what you're doing to your body when you eat gluten, take a look at Chapter 2, which talks about associated conditions and serious complications that can develop if you have gluten sensitivity or celiac disease and eat gluten, even from time to time.

Even if your symptoms are mild or absent, the damage gluten causes — even small amounts of gluten — can be severe.

You're a lot better off being safe instead of sorry, so follow this common-sense commandment: When in doubt, leave it out.

Defining Gluten So You Can Avoid It

You have to know what gluten is — and not just so you can be the life of the party, sparking tantalizing conversations that begin with audacious lines like, "So, which do you find harder to avoid? Gliadin, hordein, or secalin?" (Yeah, that'll get the party started, Smooth Talker.) No, you need to know about gluten so you can avoid it (gluten, not the pickup line). The definition of this term is so convoluted that it's hard to offer a technically correct definition of gluten at this point, but I'll try.

Gluten is what scientists call a storage protein, what bakers call the dough-forming elastic ingredient in wheat, and what some newbies to the gluten-free diet pine away for. Gluten is a group of proteins that technically comes from wheat and only wheat.

At some point in our not-so-distant history, someone made the association between wheat (specifically gluten) and celiac disease. People widely accepted that gluten makes celiacs sick, which is true. Soon, physicians realized that barley and rye make celiacs sick, too, and people started saying, "Celiacs can't eat gluten. They can't eat wheat, barley, and rye, either; therefore, wheat, barley, and rye all have gluten." Right? Kind of, but not really. One of the types of proteins in gluten is also in barley and rye.

Prolamins are a class of proteins present in a variety of grains, and they're what cause problems for people who can't eat "gluten." Technically, gluten is made up of the proteins glutenin and *gliadin,* a specific type of prolamin in wheat. However, gluten has become a general term for any kind of potentially harmful prolamin. The prolamins that cause damage to people with gluten sensitivity and celiac disease include *gliadin* (in wheat), *secalin* (in rye), and *hordein* (in barley). Other grains have prolamins, too (corn's prolamin is called *zein,* and rice's prolamin is *orzenin*), but their prolamins aren't toxic to people with gluten sensitivity or celiac disease.

The "wheat, barley, and rye (and maybe oats) all have gluten" idea stuck, and even though it isn't technically correct, it *is* widely accepted today. For the purposes of this book, I stick with it, too.

Wheat-free doesn't mean *gluten-free.* Something can be wheat-free and still have, for instance, malt (derived from barley), so then it's not gluten-free.

Recognizing Gluten-Free Foods at a Glance

Keep in mind that you have to become familiar with lots of ingredients when you're learning the intricacies of the gluten-free diet.

The reason the gluten-free diet can seem cumbersome at first is that "derivatives" of gluten-containing grains may contain gluten. Then, of course, processed foods — which contain seasonings, additives, and flavorings — can contain ingredients that raise questions, too.

But breaking foods down into those that usually have gluten and those that don't isn't too tough. Keep in mind that these lists vary and that they're only to get you started. You can find up-to-date lists of foods that are safe, forbidden, and questionable at www.celiac.com.

Forbidden grains

I'm not starting with the forbidden grains to be negative — I'm starting with them because the list is a lot shorter than the list of grains you can eat. Here are the grains you need to avoid on a gluten-free diet:

  ✔ Barley

  ✔ Oats (because of contamination issues)

  ✔ Triticale (a hybrid of wheat and rye)

  ✔ Rye

  ✔ Wheat

You need to avoid (or at least question) anything with the word wheat in it. This includes hydrolyzed wheat protein, wheat starch, wheat germ, and so on. Wheat grass, however, like all grasses, is gluten-free. (But see the upcoming sidebar "Grasses, sprouted grains, berries, and bran" to make sure you're not dealing with contamination from sprouts. Hey, I know it's confusing; I'm just the messenger.) Here are a few additional details to keep in mind:

  ✔ Wheat starch is actually wheat that's had the gluten washed out. In some countries, a special type of wheat starch called Codex Alimentarius wheat starch is allowed on the gluten-free diet — but it's not allowed in North America, because some people question whether the washing process completely removes all residual gluten.

  ✔ Triticale is a made-up grain — a hybrid of wheat and rye. Inventors developed it to combine the productivity of wheat with the ruggedness of rye, not just to add another grain to your list of forbidden foods. And relatively speaking, it's fairly nutritious for people who can eat gluten (but wait till you hear about "alternative grains" in the next section!).

✔ Wheat has several names and varieties. Beware of aliases like *flour, bulgur, semolina, spelt, frumento, durum* (also spelled *duram*), *kamut, graham, einkorn, farina, couscous, seitan, matzoh, matzah, matzo,* and *cake flour.* Often marketed as a "wheat alternative," spelt is as much of a wheat alternative as I am a human alternative. It's not even remotely gluten-free.

✔ Wheat just isn't what it used to be. In fact, in an effort to bring down the cost of commercial baked goods and make wheat slightly more nutritious for the countries the U.S. ships to, ambitious farmers are actually finding ways to hybridize wheat to make it have more gluten than ever before.

✔ Derivatives of gluten-containing grains aren't allowed on the gluten-free diet, either. You can find a complete listing at www.celiac.com, but the most common derivative that you have to avoid is malt, which usually comes from barley. Avoid malt, malt flavoring, and malt vinegar. If malt is derived from another source, such as corn, that fact usually appears on the label. If not specified, though, don't eat it.

So you want to sow your oats . . .

I know that people desperately want to include oats in their gluten-free diet. Know how I know? Because here's a typical excerpt from many of my talks:

Danna: For now, commercially available oats aren't usually guaranteed to be pure, so they're still on the "forbidden" or "questionable" list because of contamination issues.

Hand-raiser No. 1: But what about Irish oats?

Danna: Yep, those, too, because they're still manufactured commercially and can be contaminated.

Hand-raiser No. 2: Can you talk about rolled oats?

Danna: Yeah, I could, but I just did. Off limits.

Hand-raiser No. 3: What if you cook 'em?

Danna: Even cooked, most oats are still forbidden on the gluten-free diet.

Hand-raiser No. 4: Steel-cut?

Danna: Steel-cut, uncut, shortcut, crinkle-cut, buzz-cut, bikini-cut, price-cut, Connecticut. No go.

Hand-raiser No. 5: So are you saying we can or can't have oats?

There's no clear-cut (or steel-cut) answer on oats — yet. In and of themselves, most people agree that oats are gluten-free (although at least one study showed otherwise), but when processed commercially, they can become contaminated during the manufacturing process. Some people argue that the risk of contamination is extremely low — but you need to assess whether you're willing to take that risk. If you can find pure, uncontaminated oats, they may not present a problem.

Grasses, sprouted grains, berries, and bran

Grasses like wheat grass and barley grass, frequently sold in health food stores and at juice bars, are gluten-free. The grass hasn't yet formed the gluten-containing proteins that cause problems in people with gluten sensitivity and celiac disease. When you can watch someone cut the grass so you know it's fresh and hasn't sprouted yet, you're safe. Be careful, though, of grasses that are an ingredient in a product. These grasses could be contaminated with seeds, and since you don't know for sure, you could risk getting gluten.

You should avoid sprouted grains because you don't know where in the sprouting process the grain is. Eating the sprouts could be okay, but it may not be. Berries are the seed kernels and are definitely not safe. The jury's still out on bran, so until nutritionists do more research, remember the common-sense commandment I refer to in this chapter: *When in doubt, leave it out.*

Grains and starches you can safely eat

You have lots of choices for gluten-free grains and starches. Even if you're an old pro who's been gluten-free for years, I'm guessing some of these may be new to you:

Amaranth

Arrowroot

Beans

Buckwheat/groats/kasha

Chickpeas (garbanzo beans, besan, cici, chana, or gram — not to be confused with graham, which does have gluten)

Corn

Garfava

Job's Tears

Mesquite (pinole)

Millet

Montina (Indian ricegrass)

Oats (but they may be contaminated with wheat and other grains)

Potato

Quinoa (hie)

Ragi

Rice

Sorghum

Soy

Tapioca (gari, cassava, casaba, manioc, yucca)

Taro root

Teff

Corny tales

Maize (Indian corn) dates back thousands of years, and its cultivation was a remarkable feat. Native Americans developed as many as 24 different kinds of corn to accommodate the length of growing season, altitude, rain, sunlight, and soil type. To ensure a full season's yield, the people grew both early and late ripeners, and all the corn came in a variety of colors.

Corn has played an important role socially, as well. A Hopi bride-to-be would grind corn for three days at her future husband's house to prove she had "wifely skills." When a Hopi child was born, he or she received a special blanket and a perfect ear of corn as a welcome into the world (who needs binkies?). And early American settlers learned quickly to depend on corn, which is easy to grow and store and needs little maintenance. Corn-based dishes became a backbone of early frontier dining for rugged settlers who were busy fending off grumpy Indians (undoubtedly more than a tad cranky that their cornfields were being taken over) and cantankerous outlaws.

Glutinous rice does not contain gluten! Manufacturers make glutinous rice, or *sweet rice* or *mochi,* by grinding high-starch, short-grain rice. Glutinous rice thickens sauces and desserts in Asian cooking and is often the rice used in sushi.

You may run across different names or forms of corn that are gluten-free in addition to plain ol' corn. They include grits, hominy, masa, masa harina, harinilla (blue corn), atole, maize, polenta, corn gluten, and of course, cornstarch, corn flour, corn bran, and cornmeal.

Gums, such as xanthan and guar gum, contain no gluten. People use them frequently in gluten-free baked goods because gums help give the spongy, elastic texture that gluten-containing flours usually provide. For some people, gums — especially guar gum — may have a laxative effect.

Other foods that are usually gluten-free

In general, these foods are usually gluten-free (these refer to plain, unseasoned foods without additives and processed products):

Beans	Fish
Dairy products	Fruit
Eggs	Legumes

Meat	Seafood
Nuts	Vegetables
Poultry	

The foods listed here are naturally gluten-free. You can buy specialty products such as cookies, cakes, brownies, breads, crackers, pretzels, and other products that have been made with gluten-free ingredients. I talk more about those products and where to buy them in Chapter 8, which covers shopping.

Foods that usually contain gluten

Companies offer special gluten-free varieties of some foods, and those gluten-free varieties obviously don't have gluten in them. But unless you're buying specialty products, you can assume the following foods contain gluten:

Beer	Imitation seafood (for example, imitation crab)
Bread, breadcrumbs, biscuits	
	Licorice
Cereal	
	Marinades (such as teriyaki)
Communion wafers	
	Pasta
Cookies, cakes, cupcakes, donuts, muffins, pastries, pie crusts, brownies, and other baked goods	Pizza crust
	Pretzels
Cornbread	
	Soy sauce
Crackers	
	Stuffing
Croutons	
Gravies, sauces, and roux	

Exploring Alternative Grains and Superfoods

When it comes to grains beyond corn, wheat, and rice, most people don't know barley from bulgur. Actually, there's a great big world of grains out there to be explored, many of which are gluten-free, delicious, and loaded with nutritional value.

Don't eat the wheat meat

Seitan, pronounced say-*tahn,* is a chewy food made from gluten that resembles meat in texture. Also called *wheat meat,* people make seitan by making dough out of wheat flour and water, kneading it to develop the gluten, and rinsing away the starch and bran, leaving only the gluten. They then simmer it in water or vegetable broth that's been seasoned with soy sauce, resulting in a chewy, firm, meatlike food . . . food that not only is *loaded* with gluten but *is* gluten. Loosely translated, the Japanese word seitan means "is protein"; it's called *kofu* in China.

They're called "alternative grains," yet many aren't grains at all. Instead, they're grasses, seeds, or flowers. People also call them *superfoods* because they're foods that are *super*-nutritious. Take a look at some of these alternative grains and discover an entirely new world of gluten-free superfoods (where *is* that cape?!?).

For years, rumors have spread that some of these alternative grains aren't safe for people with gluten sensitivity or celiac disease. These foods are, in fact, gluten-free. Some people may have had reactions to these grains (as they would to corn, soy, or other allergens or foods to which they may have a sensitivity), but it's not a gluten reaction. But regardless of whether a food contains gluten, if it makes you sick, don't eat it!

Amaranth

Loaded with fiber, iron, calcium, and other vitamins and minerals, amaranth is also high in the amino acids lysine, methionine, and cysteine, and it's an excellent source of protein. A small beadlike grain, amaranth is not only nutritious but also delicious, with a pleasant peppery and hearty nutty flavor.

Amaranth isn't a true cereal grain at all, but it's a relative of the pigweeds and ornamental flowers called *cockscomb.* People grow it not only for its seed but for its leaves, which you can cook and eat as greens. Amaranth can be milled or toasted, which gives it extra flavor. You can even pop some varieties like popcorn, boil and eat them like cereal, or use them in soups and granolas or as a side dish. You should always cook amaranth before eating it, because like some other edible seeds, it contains compounds that can inhibit the proper absorption of certain nutrients.

For centuries, the Aztec culture depended on amaranth and believed it had mystical powers that could bring strength and power even to the weakest of men. The name means "not withering," or more literally, "immortal." Although amaranth may not make you immortal, it is extremely nutritious — and gluten-free.

Arrowroot

Once revered by the ancient Mayans and other inhabitants of Central America as an antidote to poison arrows, arrowroot is now used as an herb thought to soothe the stomach and have antidiarrheal effects. People use it in cooking as a thickener for soups, sauces, and confections.

An easily digested and nutritious starch, arrowroot is a fine, white powder with a look and texture similar to that of cornstarch. The translucent paste has no flavor and sets to an almost clear gel. You can use arrowroot in gluten-free cooking or as a thickening agent to replace cornstarch, although it thickens at a lower temperature than either cornstarch or wheat and its consistency doesn't hold as long after cooking. The superfine grains are easy to digest, making arrowroot a perfect "invalid" food. In fact, arrowroot biscuits are one of the first solid foods babies can safely eat (but beware — manufacturers usually add wheat flour to arrowroot biscuits, so they're not gluten-free).

Buckwheat (soba)

The fact that buckwheat is gluten-free often confuses people; after all, buckwheat has the word "wheat" right in the name. But buckwheat isn't even related to wheat; in fact, it's not even a true cereal grain. It's a fruit, a distant cousin of garden-variety rhubarb. The buckwheat seed has a three-cornered shell that contains a pale kernel known as a *groat*. In one form or another, groats have been around since the tenth century B.C.

High in lysine, which is an amino acid lacking in many traditional grains, buckwheat contains several other amino acids — in fact, this grain has a high proportion of all eight essential amino acids, which the body doesn't make but still needs to keep functioning. In that way, buckwheat is closer to being a complete protein than many other plant sources. It's also high in many of the B vitamins, as well as the minerals phosphorus, magnesium, iron, copper, manganese, and zinc. And buckwheat's a good source of linoleic acid, an essential fatty acid.

Whole white buckwheat is naturally dried and has a delicate flavor that makes it a good stand-in for rice or pasta. When the hulled buckwheat kernels are roasted, they're called *kasha*, which has a deep tan color, nutty flavor, and a slightly scorched smell. Cooks often use buckwheat in pancakes, biscuits, and muffins — but be aware that manufacturers often combine buckwheat with wheat in those products, so you have to read the labels carefully before buying buckwheat products. In Japan, people often make buckwheat into *soba*, or noodles, which sometimes — but not always — have wheat flour as well.

Mesquite (pinole)

Most people know of mesquite as an on-the-grill flavoring that makes foods taste smoky and sweet. But mesquite has been a staple for Native Americans for thousands of years. Its sweet, fragrant flowers make a honeylike substance, and the pod produces a ground meal called *pinole*. Mesquite flour is a low-glycemic-index flour (it's a 25 — see Chapter 6 for what that kind of rating means), making it helpful in controlling blood sugar levels. Furthermore, soluble fibers in the seeds and pods slow the absorption of nutrients, which also helps in managing blood sugar.

The sweet pods and seeds are a good source of fiber, calcium, manganese, iron, and zinc. They're also high in protein, and they contain the amino acid lysine, which isn't present in many traditional grains. Not only does mesquite flour stabilize blood sugar, but it tastes great, with a sweet, slightly nutty flavor that bears a hint of molasses.

Mixes that combine mesquite with other gluten-free flours are now available, making creating gluten-free goodies with this unique flour a snap.

Millet

Not a grain at all, millet is actually a grass with small, round, ivory and yellow kernels that swell when you cook them. Millet supplies more servings per pound than any other grain.

Millet is packed with vitamins, minerals, and other nutrients. High in iron, magnesium, phosphorus, and potassium, it's also loaded with fiber and protein as well as the B-complex vitamins, including niacin, thiamin, and riboflavin. Millet is more alkaline (it has a higher pH — I talk more about acidic and alkaline foods in Chapter 6) than many traditional grains, and digesting it is very easy.

Millet has been a staple food in Africa and India for thousands of years, and people grew it as early as 2,700 B.C. in China, where it was the prevalent grain before rice became the dominant staple. Today, millet is still a significant part of the diet in northern China, Japan, Manchuria, and various areas of the former Soviet Union, Africa, India, and Egypt. Grown today in Western countries mostly for cattle and bird feed, millet's gaining popularity as a nutritious, delicious part of the human diet as well.

Montina (Indian ricegrass)

Montina is actually Amazing Grains's trademarked name for Indian ricegrass. Indian ricegrass was a dietary staple of Native American cultures from the Southwest U.S. to Canada more than 7,000 years ago. Extremely hearty, Indian ricegrass was a good substitute during years when maize crops failed or game was in short supply. It has a bold flavor and is loaded with fiber and protein.

Quinoa (hie)

Quinoa (pronounced *keen*-wa) — and also called *hie* (pronounced *he*-uh) — is yet another of the grains that isn't really a grain; it's actually a fruit and a relative of the common weed lambsquarter. The National Academy of Science describes quinoa as "the most nearly perfect source of protein from the vegetable kingdom."

Like other superfoods and alternative grains, quinoa is packed with lysine and other amino acids that make it a complete protein. It's also high in phosphorus, calcium, iron, vitamin E, and assorted B vitamins, as well as fiber. Quinoa is usually pale yellow in color, but it also comes in pink, orange, red, purple, and black.

Because the uncooked grains are coated with *saponins* — sticky, bitter-tasting stuff that acts as a natural insect repellent — you should rinse quinoa thoroughly before cooking. Most quinoa that you buy in the store has already been rinsed.

Although new to North Americans, people in the South American Andes have cultivated quinoa since at least 3,000 B.C. Ancient Incas called this annual plant "the mother grain" because it was self-perpetuating and ever-bearing. They honored it as a sacred food product, because a steady diet appeared to ensure a full, long life; and the Inca ruler himself planted the first row of quinoa each season with a golden spade.

Sorghum (milo, jowar, jowari, cholam)

Sorghum is another of the oldest known grains (that isn't a true cereal grain), and it's been a major source of nutrition in Africa and India for centuries. Now also grown in the United States, sorghum is generating excitement as a gluten-free insoluble fiber and is probably best known for the syrup that comes from one of its varieties.

Because sorghum's protein and starch are more slowly digested than that of other cereals, it may be beneficial to diabetics (and healthful for anyone). It's high in iron, calcium, and potassium, and doctors actually used to prescribe it as a supplement for people low in these nutrients.

Sorghum fans boast of its bland flavor and light color, which don't alter the taste or look of foods when you use sorghum in place of wheat flour. Many cooks suggest combining sorghum with soybean flour. Sorghum is also fermented and used in alcoholic beverages.

Sorghum and millet are both rich in a group of compounds called nitrilosides. Some people notice a correlation between high nitriloside intake and low cancer rates, leading some to speculate that nitrilosides may actually help fight or prevent cancer. For instance, in Africa, where as much as 80 percent of the diet consists of high-nitriloside-yielding foods, the cancer incidence is very low.

Teff (tef)

It's tiny, but teff's a nutritional powerhouse. Teff is the smallest of the grains that aren't true cereal grains, and in fact the name itself means "lost," because if you drop it on the ground, you probably won't find it. A staple grain in Ethiopia for nearly 5,000 years, teff packs a protein content of nearly 12 percent and is five times richer in calcium, iron, and potassium than any other grain. Teff, which has a sweet, nutty flavor, grows in many different varieties and colors, but the most common are ivory, brown, and reddish-tan varieties.

You can cook the whole grain and serve it with sliced fruit or as a breakfast cereal with butter and brown sugar on top. Or you can add teff flour to baked goods to add a unique flavor and beef up the nutritional value.

If you've heard of teff, it's probably in reference to *injera,* a traditional fermented bread with a spongy texture and yeasty taste. Treated as an edible utensil, injera is used to soak up juices and soups and even to grab meat and eat it. Beware, though; traditional injera has wheat flour added to it.

Checking Up on Questionable Ingredients

The diet gets a little trickier when you don't know that a food is almost always gluten-free or gluten-loaded. In this section, I go over what items you need to question, and I discuss some of the foods people used to question but now know are gluten-free.

The facts on flavorings

Flavorings have been considered a questionable ingredient on the gluten-free diet for years. But according to Shelley Case, one of the leading authorities on the gluten-free diet, there's little or no need to question flavorings anymore. She points out that there are only two instances when gluten can be used in flavorings. One is in hydrolyzed proteins, but with current labeling laws, wheat would have to be declared on the label if it were used. The other is in barley malt extract or syrup, but Case points out that it's almost always listed on the label as "barley malt," "barley malt extract," or "barley malt flavoring." She notes that some companies may list it as "flavor (contains barley malt)", but very rarely is it listed as only "flavor" or "natural flavor." So why do I still leave it on the "to be questioned" list? Because "very rarely" leaves room for the possibility, however slight, that barley malt may have been used and listed only as a "flavoring."

Knowing which foods to research

Of course, to be safe, you need to question everything. Tea, for instance — I never saw a tea with gluten in it until recently, when I happened to read the label and there it was: barley malt.

Discovering the malt was easy because the label clearly listed what contained the gluten. But some ingredients aren't so clear, because sometimes these ingredients are gluten-free and sometimes they're not. For these ingredients, you have to look deeper into the question of "is it or isn't it?" I talk at length about how to do that in Chapter 5.

Ingredients you need to question include

- ✔ Brown rice syrup
- ✔ Fillers
- ✔ Flavors and natural flavorings
- ✔ Seasonings and spice blends
- ✔ Stabilizers
- ✔ Starch (in pharmaceuticals)

These ingredients don't always have gluten. In fact, they rarely do. But according to the U.S. Food and Drug Administration Code of Federal Regulations, they *can* contain gluten, so to be safe, you need to check.

Thanks to new labeling laws, there are far fewer "questionable" ingredients. Now manufacturers have to clearly indicate if a product has wheat in it. See Chapter 5 for more details on the new laws.

Putting an end to the controversy over certain foods

People used to question certain ingredients, and they were on the have-to-dig-deeper-to-make-sure-this-is-gluten-free list. These people questioned ingredients because of rumors, bad information, and misunderstandings. They questioned because of ambiguous labeling laws. But today, thanks to new labeling laws and more definitive research, the following ingredients are no longer in question:

Alcohol (distilled)	Modified food starch
Caramel color	Mono- and diglycerides
Citric acid	Starch (in food)
Dextrin	Vanilla and vanilla extract
Flavoring extracts	Vinegar (except malt vinegar)
Hydrolyzed plant protein (HPP)	Wheat grass
Hydrolyzed vegetable protein (HVP)	Yeast (except brewer's yeast)
Maltodextrin (except in pharmaceuticals)	

The gluten-free status of these ingredients applies to ingredients produced in the U.S. and Canada. Other countries may have different manufacturing processes.

The Buzz on Booze: Choosing Alcoholic Beverages

At nearly every talk I give, I'm about five minutes into explaining the diet when someone shoots his hand up Arnold Horseshack–style, with a please-tell-me-it-ain't-so look on his face, and I can predict the question: "Beer doesn't have gluten in it . . . does it?" Yeah, it does.

But lots of alcoholic beverages are gluten-free — and if you try, you can even find gluten-free beer. What follows is the buzz on booze.

Booze you can use

The list of gluten-free alcoholic beverages is way longer than the list of bevies that are off-limits. Other forms of alcoholic beverages may be gluten-free in addition to these, but this list covers the basics of the booze you can use:

- ✔ Bourbon
- ✔ Brandy
- ✔ Cider (occasionally contains barley, so be careful)
- ✔ Cognac
- ✔ Gin
- ✔ Rum
- ✔ Schnapps
- ✔ Tequila
- ✔ Vodka
- ✔ Whiskey (such as Crown Royal and Jack Daniels)
- ✔ Wine (and sparkling wine or Champagne)

Knowing what kinds of liquor you can consume can be confusing, because some alcoholic beverages are distilled from gluten-containing grains. However, as long as the drinks are distilled and the grains aren't added back into the gluten-containing mash, the drinks remain gluten-free.

Step away from the bottle

Just a few types of alcoholic beverages aren't allowed on the gluten-free diet. They include (but may not be limited to)

- ✔ Beer (with a few exceptions, as listed above)
- ✔ Distilled spirits that are added back to the mash
- ✔ Malt beverages

The distillation process completely eliminates any traces of gluten, which is why you can safely eat distilled vinegar, vanilla made with distilled extracts, and many alcoholic beverages made from distilled alcohol. If you're not sure that your favorite bevy is gluten-free, check the gluten-free alcoholic beverages list in this chapter and confirm with the manufacturer.

Three cheers for gluten-free beers!

Most beer has gluten and is off-limits. But a few gluten-free specialty beers are available, including Bard's Tale Beer (www.bards beer.com), which has several varieties and distributes widely. Ramapo Valley Brewery (www.ramapovalleybrewery.com) in New York offers gluten-free beer at its brewery in New York and distributes throughout the United States as well. You can also check out La Messagere, made by New France Beers of Quebec; Green's Discovery in the U.K.; Bi-Aglut in Italy; and beers from O'Brien Brewery in Australia. If you like to make your own home brew, lots of good recipes are available on the Internet. A quick search should turn up several options.

Making Sure Your Medications and Supplements Are Safe

Remember, anything you ingest can cause problems if it's not gluten-free — even a tiny little pill. Be sure to check the label first, because some products actually say "gluten-free" right on the label.

Starch and modified food starch in pharmaceuticals may come from wheat. If you see either of these on the label, you need to call the manufacturer and find out more about where the starch is from.

If you're wondering about a prescription drug, ask the pharmacist if he or she knows whether the product is gluten-free. If the pharmacist doesn't know, ask for the package insert and use the pharmacy's *Physician's Desk Reference* (PDR) to look up the name and phone number of the manufacturer. Then you can just call the manufacturer and find out. (See Chapter 5 for more on calling manufacturers.)

Here are a few tips to keep in mind:

✔ Have your pharmacist make a notation in the computer, either under your personal records or under the record for that drug, indicating whether the product is gluten-free. That way you'll know for the future, as will others who ask.

✔ If the product is over-the-counter, call the manufacturer to ensure the drug's gluten-free status. Usually, the drug company sends you a list of all the gluten-free products it makes and you can keep the list on hand.

I recommend that you figure out now which of the over-the-counter products you commonly use are gluten-free. Painkillers, fever-reducers, cold medications, and anti-inflammatories, for instance, are often gluten-free — but you sure don't want to be wondering about it at 1 a.m. when your child's earache is keeping him — and you — up at night.

> ✔ Write "GF" in permanent marker on the medication container. That way you don't wonder whether the drug's safe when you need to take it.
>
> ✔ See www.glutenfreedrugs.com for more information, or take a look at some of the product guides and downloadable databases commercially available.

Using Nonfood Products: What You Need to Know

You may get lots of conflicting information about nonfood products and whether you need to be concerned. You may hear that you need to beware of plastic storage containers, pots and pans, lotions, shampoos, envelopes, stamps, glues . . . what's a gluten-freebie supposed to do?!?

The biggest question is if you're not eating it, does it really matter? The answer is sometimes yes and sometimes no (you expected something more concrete?).

Play-Doh has gluten in it. I know you're not supposed to eat Play-Doh, but really — who can resist a nibble or two? Lots of recipes for gluten-free play-doughs are available.

You don't have to worry about plastic storage containers, pots and pans, envelopes, or stamps. The following sections let you know what to check out and what you can let slide.

Make-up matters

Well, sometimes it matters. And sometimes it doesn't. The make-up that matters most is make-up you're likely to get in your mouth (or someone else's), like lipstick, lip gloss, lip balm, and anything else that goes on or near your lips. Foundation, eye make-up, powder, and other make-up products shouldn't matter unless you get them close to your mouth and could possibly ingest them.

Lotions and potions

The experts assert that the gluten molecule is too large to pass through skin, so lotions, shampoos, conditioners, and other external products shouldn't be a problem unless you have open sores, rashes, or dermatitis herpetiformis, also know as DH. (See Chapter 3 for more information on DH.)

Sometimes lotion from your hands or arms can get on the food you're eating or preparing, and that can cause a problem. Be sure to wash your hands well (along with any other area that may touch food) so you don't end up eating your lotion.

In spite of the scientific evidence suggesting external products shouldn't pose a problem, I've heard from hundreds of people that they do have a reaction to external products that contain gluten. Who am I to argue? If it bothers you, don't use it.

Deciding on dental products

You're really not supposed to swallow your toothpaste, mouthwash, or other dental products — but you're undoubtedly going to get a swallow or two from time to time, and if it contains gluten, that can potentially cause a problem. I've never found a toothpaste or mouthwash that does contain gluten, but remember to read labels just in case.

Most products used in the dental office such as polish, fluoride, and other dental agents are gluten-free. But call your dentist in advance and ask him or her to check for you.

Chapter 5

Making Sure It's Gluten-Free: Digging a Little Deeper

· ·

· ·

A product is either gluten-free or it isn't, right? End of story? Well, no.

Personally, I like things simple and straightforward, so I can understand if this is-it-gluten-free-and-why-isn't-there-a-simple-answer issue is driving you nuts. The good news is that there's a lot less ambiguity than there used to be, and clarity is improving all the time. The bad news is that sometimes you still have to take an extra step (or four) before you know for sure whether a product is truly gluten-free.

In this chapter, I show you how to do everything you can to ensure the food you're eating is as gluten-free as it can be. I take you through the art of reading labels, explain why 100 percent gluten-free may not really mean 100 percent gluten-free, and offer a crash course in calling manufacturers.

Gluten-Free Ambiguously: Why It Isn't So Straightforward

You: Does your product contain gluten?

Polite Lady on Phone: We don't add any gluten to our products.

You: (heavy sigh of relief) Oh, terrific. Then it's gluten-free, right?

Polite Lady on Phone: Oh, no, I didn't say that. Thank you for calling!

You may feel like you're being toyed with. Customer service reps seem to specialize in obfuscation, euphemism, and other forms of double-speak when you ask the seemingly simple question "Is it gluten-free?"

Truth is, they're not messing with you to get their jollies. Questions arise for a variety of reasons. The most common causes involve ambiguous labeling, uncertainty about the origin of ingredients, and contamination concerns.

Loose labeling terminology

It would be great if you could just read a label and know what ingredients are in a product. Isn't that the point of having ingredient listings? But unfortunately, some ingredients aren't consistent; sometimes they have gluten, and sometimes they don't.

A fairly new food labeling law has helped — a lot. The Food Allergen Labeling and Consumer Protection Act requires clear labeling of all foods that contain any of the top-eight allergens — wheat, milk, eggs, fish, shellfish, tree nuts, peanuts, and soybeans. This means manufacturers must now clearly identify wheat and all of its derivatives on food labels. For more info on this new law, see the upcoming sidebar "New labeling law answers some questions but raises others."

With the law in place, knowing which foods are definitely off-limits because they contain wheat is much easier. Reading labels and knowing what's in a product is much more definitive, because wheat is really the bulk of what you're avoiding on a gluten-free diet.

Although wheat and its derivatives are now called out on all labels, you still need to watch for other gluten-containing grains (barley, rye, and cross-contaminated oats) and their derivatives, and realize that they can be (but aren't often) hidden in flavorings and additives.

New labeling law answers some questions but raises others

The Food Allergen Labeling and Consumer Protection Act, which requires manufacturers to clearly identify wheat and its derivatives on ingredient labels, is amazing progress for people avoiding wheat. Getting this labeling law passed was huge, and the celiac community was super influential in getting it done. The law even requires that by the year 2008, the U.S. Food and Drug Administration has to define exactly what *gluten-free* on a label means and how it'll be used.

Until some of the kinks get worked out, be prepared for a little confusion among people who need to know for sure what is and isn't gluten-free. The biggest areas of concern include

✔ **How much wheat must be in the product to be subject to labeling requirements:** One hundred percent gluten-free is not only unrealistic but untestable, though you can test for 100 percent wheat-free. The new law calls for "zero tolerance," meaning a product must have absolutely no allergen (in this case, wheat) in it — so even ingredients with the offending protein gluten removed have to be labeled as being allergenic.

✔ **Overlabeling:** Sometimes manufacturers may label food as having wheat in it even if it doesn't. That's because some interpretations of the new law say that wheat should be on the label if an ingredient's original source was wheat — even if that wheat is completely gone by the time the product's processed.

Some foods from gluten-containing grains — like citric acid, glucose syrup, and distilled vinegar (not malt) — are so highly processed that what grain they were derived from doesn't matter. They are, and always have been, gluten-free after processing (most of the time these foods come from gluten-free sources, anyway). But some interpretations of the new labeling law may require that companies put wheat on the label if those products were made from wheat; this would lead the consumer to believe the product contains gluten when it actually doesn't.

Manufacturers can ask for an exemption if they can prove that the ingredient doesn't cause a harmful allergenic response or if they can provide scientific evidence that the ingredient doesn't contain allergenic proteins. This may be a challenge, because proving that white bread causes damage for people with various forms of gluten sensitivity, autism, autoimmune diseases, and other conditions can be tough enough. Proving the opposite is even harder.

Malt is often from barley, and products that use malt as a flavoring don't necessarily call it out on the label. Natural flavorings, for instance, may contain barley malt.

"Gluten-free" may not mean 100 percent

I unequivocally advocate a strict gluten-free diet. I even go so far as to use the term *100 percent gluten-free,* but in reality, something that's gluten-free isn't necessarily 100 percent gluten-free.

The reality is that food may actually have minute traces of gluten, but as long as those traces are truly small, the product may sometimes still be called gluten-free and be safe for everyone — regardless of sensitivities or disease.

For a variety of reasons usually concerning cross-contamination, even foods that are inherently gluten-free sometimes turn out to contain gluten. Of course, this does not mean you should cheat, figuring you're going to get glutenated anyway. Quite the opposite. You need to be even more diligent to make sure you're doing everything you can to be safely gluten-free — as gluten-free as you can be.

Contamination risks

One of the most common reasons a product that is technically gluten-free may have trace amounts of gluten is contamination. Even if a product is made without any gluten-containing ingredients, contamination can occur at several points during processing. (Contamination is a risk when you're preparing and cooking your own foods, and manufacturers are dealing with food on a much larger scale. You can see more about how to avoid contamination in the kitchen in Chapter 7.)

Grain processing

Commercially grown grains can contain trace amounts of other grains, because preventing cross-contamination is nearly impossible. The cross-contamination starts at the farm, where crops are often rotated between fields each year, and volunteer crops from previous years can pop up where they're least expected. Contamination can also occur in grain storage, transportation, and during milling.

So if the product you're eating contains a grain — even a non-gluten-containing grain — there's a risk of contamination. Usually, the amount of contamination is miniscule and doesn't pose a health threat. The only time you know there's no cross-contamination is when the grains are from suppliers who grow, harvest, mill, and package only one (gluten-free) grain.

Oats are a good example of a grain that often undergoes cross-contamination. Frequently rotated with fields where wheat is grown, oats — gluten-free in and of themselves — can be contaminated in the fields as well as in the transportation and milling processes. Oats are more likely to be contaminated (and at greater levels) than other grains, which is why oats land on the forbidden list but other grains are still considered safe.

Shared equipment or facilities

Many companies produce several different products on one production line. For instance, a company that produces several types of cereal may run them all on the same equipment. Although the United States and many other countries have strict laws about cleaning lines between products, sometimes traces of gluten remain on the lines — or in the facility — and contaminate the gluten-free products that are made there. Some people eat only products made in dedicated gluten-free facilities.

Mysterious ingredient sources

Sometimes the gluten-free status of a product is questionable because tracking the source of its ingredients is tough. Most product manufacturers get their ingredients from a variety of suppliers. Sometimes a supplier can't guarantee the gluten-free status of the ingredients it's supplying or an ingredient's source can't be traced.

Some suppliers may not really understand what gluten-free is and yet still may claim that their ingredient is safely gluten-free when, in fact, it may not be.

Defining Safe Amounts of Gluten

At every talk I give, I proselytize about being 100 percent gluten-free — I admonish you for even thinking about smelling the donuts, lest some crumbs jump off and pry their way into your mouth. So I realize that by using the term *safe amounts of gluten,* I may appear to be contradicting myself.

Yet the truth is that there's a threshold of gluten that's safe for everyone, even on a daily basis. The amount that's safe is equal to about a fraction of a crumb. A teensy-weensy fraction of a teensy-weensy crumb.

People measure gluten in *parts per million (ppm).* There aren't any consistent standards for determining what's gluten-free. Some countries use 20 ppm as a current limit, meaning anything that has less than 20 ppm of gluten can be considered gluten-free. But the standards vary from country to country, and the U.S. doesn't currently have any limits in place.

How much is a part per million, anyway? For easier math, take bread that contains 200 ppm of gluten as an example. Cut that slice of bread into 5,000 pieces, and you have 5,000 crumbs. One of those crumbs is equivalent to 200 out of a million parts — equal to the amount of gluten in that piece of bread. That fraction of the bread weighs about 0.006 grams, or about 0.0002 ounces.

Certified Gluten-Free: "GF" marks the spot

A new certification program with an easy-to-recognize logo is making an impressive and helpful mark on the gluten-free community. The *Certified Gluten-Free* logo indicates that a food contains less than 10 ppm of gluten. The Gluten-Free Certification Organization checks ingredient lists, tests foods, and inspects manufacturing plants — giving shoppers the assurance that a product is gluten-free and the manufacturing facility is free of contaminants.

The Codex Alimentarius Commission is a committee set up to ensure consumer protection as it pertains to food safety and quality by developing internationally agreed-upon standards and regulations. These standards are based on scientific principles and fair-trade practices. For gluten content, the International Codex safe threshold is 200 ppm. But safe thresholds for gluten content vary around the world (not everyone follows Codex standards, including the United States). In Finland, 100 ppm is considered safely gluten-free.

Testing for Gluten in Foods

With so many questions about what does and doesn't have gluten, there should be a test you can do to know for sure. And there is!

Several types of gluten tests are available; some are used commercially, and some are designed for consumer use. Some of the commercial tests are so sensitive they can detect as little as 5 ppm (parts per million); several manufacturers of gluten-free products use them to ensure the purity of their foods.

Gluten home tests usually work a lot like a home pregnancy test: A series of lines appear on a small wand to give you a reading. To dissolve the gluten, you mix the food with some fluid in a tube; you then use a small comb to place the liquid in the wand, which is about the size of a large, flat pen. The liquid flows through a test "window," and within about five minutes, lines appear to indicate whether the food contains gluten.

The home test can detect wheat, triticale, rye, and some amounts of barley. Sensitivity of the home kit is 75–100 ppm for most samples, and kits of the future will likely detect even lower levels.

Deciphering Label Lingo

The good news — and the bad news — is that you don't have to look for "gluten-free" on the label. In other words, there's a big, bold world of gluten-free goodness that doesn't say "gluten-free" on it but is nonetheless gluten-free. The first step to finding out whether a food is gluten-free is reading labels.

Reading ingredient labels on food products can be informative, enlightening, question-provoking, emotion-evoking, confusing, frustrating, timesaving, and time-consuming — all in one. Sometimes seeing what's in the foods you eat is downright scary. But for people who are serious about being gluten-free, label-reading is not optional.

Reading labels is almost an art, beginning with the label flip-scan. If you've been reading labels for a while, you know what I mean — you grab a product, and with a fancy twist of the wrist, you flip to the list of ingredients and scan for forbidden items. Spot one, and the product goes back on the shelf. This becomes such a habit that you may find yourself doing the label flip-scan with products you don't even eat.

Reading labels can be intimidating at first, because many processed foods contain all sorts of multisyllabic ingredients that you've probably never heard of (most of those are chemicals, and many of them are on the safe ingredients list). But you get used to the many (sometimes scary) ingredients you actually eat, and before you know it, you've mastered the label flip-scan — all while you make mental calculations of how much you can save with your double coupons.

Reading Glutenese: Knowing what to look for

The key to efficient label-reading is knowing what to look for. Of course, if you happen to spot the words "gluten-free" on the label, you may find yourself wanting to do a touchdown dance. Go ahead. Seeing "gluten-free" on a label is worthy of celebration.

But usually, label-reading is far more complex than that, and you're relegated to poring over lengthy lists of ingredients.

 For ingredients other than wheat, or to check ingredients you've never heard of, the safe and forbidden ingredients and additives lists at www.celiac.com are a good guide. (Click on Safe & Forbidden Gluten-Free Foods and Ingredients to find the lists.) I suggest you print out a copy of the lists and take it with you when you shop. When you encounter ingredients you've never heard of, you can check your lists and decide whether the product goes back on the shelf or in the cart.

You need to check labels often. Ingredients change, and a product that may have been gluten-free at one time may not necessarily still be gluten-free.

Avoiding tempting marketing come-ons

Labels are cluttered with tempting enticements touting tempting benefits like *organic, all-natural, no GMOs, healthy, nutritious,* and the forever-to-be-dreaded *new and improved.* Few of these claims are substantive, and none of them say anything about the gluten-free status of a product. In fact, "new and improved" is actually a euphemism for "now you definitely have to check ingredients — again — because we've changed our formula."

People sometimes make the erroneous assumption that if a product is healthful, it's more likely to be gluten-free. Not true. In fact, if you see the words *whole grain* emblazoned on a label, step away from the product. Chances are it's not gluten-free.

Even if a product says *wheat-free* on the label, that doesn't mean it's gluten-free. You still need to watch for barley, rye, and oats — as well as their derivatives.

Checking with Food Manufacturers

After you've read the label and you've determined that the product doesn't include any obvious sources of gluten, you may want to check with the manufacturer to make sure your food doesn't have any hidden sources.

These days, checking is pretty easy. Most products have a toll-free phone number listed right on the package. When you call that number, you often get connected with someone who actually knows what you're talking about, and the company usually sends you a whole bunch of coupons for its products. In fact, the manufacturer will sometimes send you a long list of its gluten-free items.

Sometimes, though, you get the friendly customer service rep, the coupons, and the list but confusing answers to your questions.

Take a cell phone into the store with you. That way, when you find a food you have questions about, you can call right then and there.

For the most part, all you have to say when you call is, "I'd like to find out whether your product is gluten-free," and the friendly customer service reps know exactly what you're talking about. Occasionally, though, being specific is helpful and even necessary. Say, "I'm calling to see whether this product is gluten-free, which means it doesn't contain wheat, rye, barley, or oats." You may educate one more person about gluten.

Some manufacturers have voluntarily adopted a policy to declare all gluten-containing ingredients and their derivatives, so if you don't see anything on their labels, you don't have to contact the company. When you contact a company and find out that this is its policy, make note of it. Before long, you'll have a list of companies that declare their gluten-containing ingredients and you won't have to spend so much time checking the status of products.

Interpreting company responses

When you call a company to find out whether its product is gluten-free, you get one of a few responses. Interpreting these responses sometimes requires a little inference, deduction, and conjecture on your part. If you can't get a straight answer, play it safe and leave the product out of the cart. These are the most common responses you get and the possible interpretations.

"We can't guarantee our product is gluten-free."

This doesn't necessarily mean, "Our product may not be gluten-free." It usually translates to, "Yes, our product is gluten-free, but our legal department asks that we cover our tushies by telling you we can't guarantee it."

Aside from legal considerations, the "we can't guarantee our product is gluten-free" reply — the most common you'll hear — may be for other reasons, as well:

- ✔ The product has ingredients that may be derived from a gluten-containing source.

- ✔ The company gets ingredients from other suppliers and doesn't know for sure that they're gluten-free.

- ✔ The company suspects that other products produced in the facility could cause contamination.

- ✔ The company doesn't test for gluten, so even though the company's certain the products are gluten-free, it doesn't want to guarantee that.

- ✔ The company suspects its products are gluten-free but doesn't completely understand the concept, so it defers to this reply.

If you're told "we can't guarantee our product is gluten-free," ask questions and find out why they won't vouch for the product's gluten-free status. With more information, you can decide for yourself whether the product is safe to eat.

"Our product is not gluten-free."

Sometimes the "no, our product is not gluten-free" response is really what the customer service rep means, and gluten that isn't clearly indicated on the label is in the product.

But don't make the mistake of interpreting this one as always being "our product is not gluten-free." You need to probe a little deeper. One time, when I told the customer service rep that I didn't see anything in the ingredients that appeared to contain gluten, I was told it was the whey. I pointed out that whey doesn't contain gluten. She quickly replied, "Well, then, it must be the canola oil." Strike two. I was quickly losing faith in this woman's credibility.

"Yes, our product is gluten-free."

You have to judge for yourself whether the person on the other end of the phone truly understands the concept. Did Sally Jo really understand what you were talking about? Or did she then say, "Of course we don't put gluten in our products. Sugar isn't good for you, anyway"?

Sometimes the rep follows up the gluten-free claim with, "There are no sources of wheat, rye, barley, or oats, and there are no questionable additives. Therefore it's safe for someone with wheat allergies, gluten intolerance, or celiac disease." Feel the love, baby. Feel the love.

Other times when the rep gives this response, she gets a little squirmy if you push her. For instance, if you reply, "Terrific! Then I can assume the brown rice syrup is from a non-gluten-containing source, right?" she asks you to hold. For a really long time. You may want to probe a little more before trusting her final answer.

"We won't tell."

Seriously, folks, I'm not trying to steal the special sauce formula (I know it's just ketchup and mayo, anyway). I just need to know whether the product is going to cause severe intestinal trauma.

Company representatives who won't tell you anything about the ingredients probably don't have a good idea of what's in the product themselves, so avoiding those foods is a good idea.

"Huh?"

Hey, at least you know where you stand with these people — no fakers or know-it-alls in this bunch. They don't have a clue what you're talking about, and that's okay!

Fortunately, this isn't a common response anymore, but it does happen. Politely try to explain what types of ingredients may be in the product you're calling about, and if it still doesn't click, ask to speak to a quality control supervisor or nutrition expert.

Getting the most out of your calls to manufacturers

If you're going to take the time to contact manufacturers to learn more about the products you're eating, you may as well get the most out of the calls. Here are a few things to keep in mind:

- **Tune in.** Really listen to the person on the other end of the phone. Does he get it, or is he faking it? Is he giving you conflicting information or taking wild guesses? Does he sound confident and knowledgeable? You need to assess these things before you know for sure that you can trust what he says.

- **Don't be afraid to take it up a notch.** Asking to speak to a supervisor is not offensive or rude. If you feel the person you're talking to isn't giving you credible answers, ask to speak with a supervisor or the director of quality control or nutritional services.

- **Learn from the answers.** If you see an ingredient on a package you've never heard of before, call the manufacturer about it. If the customer service rep tells you that product is gluten-free, take note. That means the ingredient is gluten-free, too. Feel free to question the specific ingredient to make sure, and you may find the customer service rep is especially knowledgeable and can tell you the exact source.

- **Acknowledge the rep's knowledge.** You need customer service reps, and the fact that they're becoming more knowledgeable about the gluten-free status of the company's products is immensely helpful. If they're friendly and knowledgeable, let them know how much you appreciate it. Maybe even take the time to write a letter to the company thanking it for supporting the gluten-free community by having knowledgeable customer service reps and gluten-free products.

- **Speak up.** Being a squeaky wheel is not only okay but important — you should call frequently. One reason to call often is that ingredients change and you need to continually verify that a product is still gluten-free. But calling is also beneficial for everyone, because it sends a message to the company that the gluten-free community is important. Calling encourages better labeling, and maybe company leaders will think twice before adding malt flavoring to their products!

- **Take note.** You may want to keep a folder of the products you use the most and make note of when you called the manufacturer and what response you got. You may even want to share your homemade product list with others.

Mark it up for safety! After you've called a manufacturer about a product you have in your pantry, use a permanent marker to write "GF" all over it, so you remember that it's gluten-free.

Getting product listings from a company

Food manufacturers, restaurants, stores, and distributors are usually happy to send you lists of their gluten-free products, and sometimes they ice the (gluten-free) cake with a few coupons.

Keep in mind that if a product isn't on the list, that doesn't mean it's not gluten-free. Recently, someone on a chat site I participate in received a listing of gluten-free items from a fast-food chain. She quickly posted an announcement that the broiled chicken was not gluten-free, sending shockwaves through guilt-ridden mommies who had stuffed their kids full of the chicken patties for weeks. I made a few calls and found out the chicken was, in fact, gluten-free but hadn't made the list due to publication deadlines.

Also remember that just because a product is on the list doesn't mean it's always gluten-free. An item could be gluten-free one day, make it onto the list, and next thing you know, cruel gluten-spiking chefs somewhere take a vote and decide to add malt flavoring.

If you want to buy product listings, you have a few choices. Product guides are available from some support groups, and they're very helpful, but realize that they may not include regional brands and that they're up-to-date only at the time of printing. Software and databases are more current. You can purchase Clan Thompson's Celiac/Gluten-Free SmartLists at www.clanthompson.com or www.celiac.com in the products and store sections of those sites.

Searching for Information: The Good, The Bad, and the Completely Ludicrous

The good news is that tons of information on gluten, gluten sensitivity, celiac disease, related disorders, and the gluten-free diet is available. The bad news is that lots of it is garbage.

No matter what the source, always question the credibility of the authors, and remember that even seemingly credible sources can perpetuate bad information.

You may find that a lot of the information is conflicting. One source says vinegar is safe, another says it's forbidden. Here are a few tips to help sort out the reality from the ridiculous:

✔ **Check the publication date.** Information on the Internet and in books and magazines can all become outdated the minute it's published, so make sure what you're reading is current.

✔ **Look for credentials.** Are the authors knowledgeable, or are they just sharing personal experiences and opinions? Where do they get their information? Not all writers are reliable: You don't need a license to publish, nor do you have to let the facts get in the way of a good story.

✔ **Compare the information to what you find from other sources.** A lot of the information out there is conflicting, so compare all the sources and figure out which source stands up to closer scrutiny. The sources of information that I cite in this chapter are reputable and reliable.

The Internet, for better and for worse

The Internet's awfully convenient. You can be in your jammies, cup of coffee in hand, before the sun even rises and find out more about gluten than you ever knew you didn't know. The problem is that you can't always trust what you read online, and checking credibility is difficult. Furthermore, people publish information to the Web and sometimes forget about it or don't take the time to update it. What you're looking at could be several years old — and lots has changed in the past several years.

Some sites are excellent, and at the risk of omitting some good ones that should be included here, I give you a starter list (Also remember to check out the sites I list in the "Magazines and newsletters" and "Support groups" sections.):

✔ **www.glutenfreedom.net:** An informative and inspirational site that helps people live and learn to love a gluten-free lifestyle.

✔ **www.celiac.com:** A celiac disease and gluten-free diet support site that includes general information, research, products, a message board, a calendar of events, news, and dietary resources.

✔ **www.celiackids.com:** An informative site for families of kids on a gluten-free diet.

✔ **www.glutenfreeresources.com:** A site with links to manufacturers of gluten-free foods and items related to the gluten-free diet.

✔ **www.glutensolutions.com:** An online shopping site with hundreds of gluten-free products from all over the world; it allows you to sort products by allergens.

✔ **www.clanthompson.com:** An informative site with general information and links to resources.

✔ **www.glutenfreemd.com:** An educational site to address the medical issues associated with gluten sensitivity and celiac disease.

Why is there so much conflicting information?

Good question. (Thanks, I thought of it myself.) For one thing, a lot has changed in the gluten-free world in the last few years. Ingredients that were once questionable because they *could* contain gluten were found rarely, if ever, to actually contain gluten. Modified food starch is a good example of that. The new labeling laws that require manufacturers to call out wheat on the labels mean just about all of the once-questioned "questionable" ingredients are no longer questionable at all, yet on many lists you still see these ingredients listed as iffy.

Another reason for conflicting information is that old rumors are hard to kill. The best example of that is vinegar, which has always been gluten-free (except malt vinegar), regardless of its origin. Yet information has been published for years (and continues to be published) claiming that vinegar may contain gluten — so the misinformation lives on.

Canola oil fell victim to rumor a few years ago when someone said canola oil made him feel bad and naively concluded that canola oil has gluten in it (it doesn't). People began spreading the "fact" that canola oil has gluten in it (it doesn't), and soon enough, canola oil was listed as a questionable ingredient, even by some very reputable sources. You can still find canola oil on many "to be questioned" lists.

A nonprofit group called Information Center for Online Resources and Services, Inc. (ICORS) (`www.listname.icors.org`) runs a celiac *listserv*, which is a list specifically targeted to the celiac community. You subscribe to the list (make sure you do so from the e-mail you want to use each time), and then you receive postings from other people — questions, comments, product recommendations, recipes, and similar topics. You can post your questions and comments, too. You receive the posts as e-mail, and they also appear in a threaded discussion on a Web page.

Keep in mind that this list is open to anyone and that you have to carefully scrutinize any information for accuracy. To subscribe, send an e-mail to `listserv@listserv.icors.org` and write "SUBSCRIBE CELIAC" in the body, followed by your first and last name.

A quick Internet search should also turn up several chat sites for people living a gluten-free lifestyle.

Magazines and newsletters

Some outstanding magazines and newsletters are targeted to the gluten-free community. They're one of the best places to find current, accurate information about gluten-free products, guidelines, and the medical conditions that benefit from a gluten-free diet. In particular, I recommend

✔ *Gluten-Free Living* (www.glutenfreeliving.com)

✔ *Living Without* (www.livingwithout.com)

✔ *ScottFree* (www.celiac.com)

The major support groups (discussed in a following section) have excellent newsletters as well.

Books

Several superb gluten-free cookbooks are available online or at most bookstores.

An excellent resource for the dietary guidelines of the gluten-free diet is *Gluten-Free Diet,* by Shelley Case, R.D. (www.glutenfreediet.ca). And for a scientific look at gluten's effects on health, you can read *Dangerous Grains,* by James Braly, M.D., and Ron Hoggan, M.A.

Wheat-Free, Worry-Free: The Art of Happy, Healthy, Gluten-Free Living, by yours truly, is an informative and inspirational guide to living and loving the gluten-free lifestyle. *Kids with Celiac Disease: A Family Guide to Raising Happy, Healthy, Gluten-Free Children,* also by me, is just what the title says — a guide for raising happy, healthy, gluten-free kids.

Support groups

Australia, Ireland, Spain, the United Kingdom, Finland, and many other countries have their own support groups that meet the needs of the celiac and gluten-free communities. You can find them with a quick Internet search. The national support groups in the United States include

✔ Gluten Intolerance Group (www.gluten.net)

✔ Celiac Disease Foundation (www.celiac.org)

✔ Celiac Sprue Association (www.csaceliacs.org)

✔ Raising Our Celiac Kids (R.O.C.K.) (www.celiackids.com)

✔ GFCF Diet Support Group Information Website (www.gfcfdiet.com)

Check the Web sites to see which group most adequately meets your needs and has a chapter near you. These support groups meet regularly and offer a variety of programs.

Chapter 6

Gluten-Free ... Nutritiously

● ●

In This Chapter

▶ Recognizing what food has to offer

▶ Getting to know the glycemic index and load

▶ Trying the clever caveman approach

▶ Making sure you get enough nutrients

▶ Controlling your weight with the gluten-free diet

▶ Going gluten-free — athletically!

● ●

*W*hether you're a salad-dodger or suffering from orthorexia (an extreme desire to eat only health foods), eating gluten-free nutritiously is simple but not plain. You don't have to balance any food blocks (and turn them upside down every few years), weigh portions, keep a food log, or count calories — and you're not limited to deprivation dining.

I have more than just a passing passion for nutrition, and my interest extends far beyond whether something is gluten-free or not. I love to eat, and I believe food is to be respected and revered — partly for the diversity of flavors, textures, and consistencies; partly for the buzz you get from enjoying a delicious, nutritious meal; partly for the energy it gives you; and most definitely for the big-picture way it nourishes your body with ramifications that affect every element of your being.

In this chapter, I hope to share with you my fervor for food as being more than just something that satisfies your hunger pangs. I explain why gluten-free doesn't always mean guilt-free and why paying attention to the glycemic load is crucial to a healthful lifestyle. And with a few gentle nudges, I hope to help steer you — oh-so-gently — down the path of eating gluten-free nutritiously.

If the subject of nutrition seems intimidating or overly complex, don't worry. I boil it down to the raw ingredients and make this a lesson in nutrition that's easy to digest.

Appreciating Your Food

I may be preaching to the choir here, because most of you definitely pay attention to what you eat, whether you want to or not — faithfully reading labels and scrutinizing the ingredients, acutely aware of where gluten could be lurking, and avoiding it like vampires avoiding garlic. But if you want to be healthy, you should really pay attention, tuning in to your food and what it offers, way beyond whether it's gluten-free.

People tend to think that *gluten-free* means *healthful.* After all, gluten-free foods are usually available only at "health food" stores, and they cost four times what "normal" foods cost. More importantly, they don't have the evil villain gluten in them, so they have to be nutritious, right? Nope.

The way most people approach the gluten-free diet really isn't all that nutritious, but it *is* gluten-free, so they get points for that.

Another way to approach the diet, though, is ultra-nutritious. It can fuel your body, help prevent disease, improve your skin's appearance, help you manage your weight, reverse the signs of aging, decrease symptoms of PMS and menopause, and increase longevity. It's gluten-free — nutritiously! (For a quick rundown of the health benefits of being gluten-free, check out Chapter 19.)

Food is obviously essential — without it, you'd starve. But the *type* of food you eat has powerful effects on preventing disease and on maintaining proper organ function, energy levels, moods, appearance, athleticism, and even your longevity and how you age. Almost everything about how you look and feel is directly related to the food you eat.

Good Carbs, Bad Carbs: Tuning In to the Glycemic Index and Glycemic Load

Hey! Put down that remote control! I know you're tempted to skip this section because this sounds complicated, tedious, boring, or all of the above. Please don't! It's a really important section, and it's the basis for a lot of what I talk about in this chapter, so hang in there.

To start, here's a pop quiz: True or false — a potato is worse for you than a candy bar. The answer is *true,* at least if you're talking about how each food affects your blood-sugar levels. Now are you interested? Read on.

Perusing the glycemic index (GI)

All carbs are not created equal. When you eat carbohydrates, the digestive process breaks them down into the sugar glucose, which is what gives your body the energy it needs to function. Because glucose is a sugar, it raises your blood-sugar levels when it enters your bloodstream.

The *glycemic index* (GI) is just a measurement of how much your blood sugar increases in the two hours after you eat. Foods high in fat and protein don't really affect your blood-sugar levels that much (if anything, they stabilize it), so the glycemic index really only concerns foods high in carbohydrates.

To measure the glycemic index of food, you need a reference point. To determine that reference point, someone had to find a food that had a super-high glycemic index — one of the nastiest foods you can eat in terms of turning to sugar the minute you eat it. And the winner was . . . white bread! The glycemic index of white bread was set at 100, and all foods are compared to it.

A food's glycemic index is how much that food increases your blood sugar level compared to how much that same amount of white bread would increase it. (The amount of food is measured in grams of carbohydrates, not by the weight or volume of the food.)

Some charts use pure glucose as the reference point instead of white bread. In the white bread index, glucose has a glycemic index of 140, so different charts have different glycemic indices for a particular food, depending on whether they use the white bread or the glucose scale. To convert to a white bread scale, multiply the score on the glucose scale by 1.4.

The lower the glycemic index, the less effect that food has on blood-glucose levels. Obviously, the higher a food's glycemic index, the more it causes a spike in blood sugar.

The glycemic effect of foods depends on a bunch of things, including the type of starch that's in it, whether that starch is cooked, how much fat is present, and the acidity. For example, adding vinegar or lemon juice (acidic) to a food actually lowers the glycemic index. And fat or dietary fiber can help inhibit the absorption of the carbohydrates, which also lowers the glycemic index. That, by the way, is why a candy bar — which has fat in it — has a lower glycemic index than a potato. Processing affects the glycemic index of a food, too. The more highly processed a grain such as rice, corn, or wheat is, the higher its glycemic index and the more quickly your blood sugar rises.

People with diabetes used to think they had to avoid sugar — as in table sugar. But simple sugar (like table sugar) doesn't make your blood-glucose level rise any faster than complex carbohydrates do. That's why using the glycemic index is a more valuable tool in controlling blood-sugar levels than cutting down on sugar is.

Comparing the glycemic indices

Take a look at the glycemic indices of some grains and starches. Remember, lower is "better," because a lower score means the food doesn't cause a rapid rise in your blood sugar.

You may find variations from one chart to another. This glycemic index is based on the glucose scale, where glucose = 100.

Food	Average Glycemic Index	Food	Average Glycemic Index
Rice (white)	88	Refined flour	70
Potato (baked)	85	Rice (brown)	57
Corn	75	Buckwheat	54
Millet	75	Quinoa	51
White bread	73	Whole wheat	45
Whole wheat bread	72		

The glycemic index value tells you how fast a carbohydrate turns into glucose, but it doesn't tell you how much of that carbohydrate is in a particular food. That's where the glycemic load comes in. And as luck would have it, that's what I discuss in the next section.

Hauling the glycemic load (GL)

Using the glycemic index alone can be misleading. Watermelon, for example, has a high glycemic index, but because watermelon's mostly water, you'd have to eat a lot of it to raise your blood sugar much. The glycemic load (GL) measurement is actually a little more valuable. *Glycemic load* looks at how many grams of available carbs a food provides. The *available carbohydrates* are the ones that provide energy, like starch and sugar but not fiber.

The key is that glycemic load is measured by serving size, which not only standardizes the numbers so you can compare one food to another but also allows you to add up your total glycemic load for each meal. Less than 80 glycemic load units per day is a low-glycemic-load diet; more than 120 is high.

The only hitch with glycemic load and the reason I don't include a chart of foods and their glycemic loads is that the portion size is subjective. So a small portion of white bread, for instance, may end up with a lower glycemic load than a large portion of buckwheat. Then you'd see a run on white bread, and the world would never be the same.

Here's an example of how serving size affects glycemic load. A baked Russet Burbank potato has a glycemic index of 85 (that's high!) and a glycemic load of 26 for a 150-gram serving. A 120-gram serving of banana has a glycemic index of 52 and a glycemic load of 12. The banana's better for you. But if you're mainly concerned about blood sugar and your choice is between eating that baked potato or two large bananas (130 grams each), you can splurge on the potato — your blood-sugar level rises about the same amount no matter which you eat.

To calculate the glycemic load, multiply the glycemic index percentage (glycemic index divided by 100) times the grams of *total carbohydrates* per serving. Of course, you also can go online and do a search for glycemic-load charts that use standard serving sizes.

For each food, glycemic index and glycemic load numbers are ranked this way:

	Glycemic Index	*Glycemic Load*
Low	Below 56	Below 11
Medium	56 to 69	11 to 19
High	70 and up	20 and up

What do blood sugar levels have to do with anything?

Lots. Your blood-sugar levels can have profound effects on your health in many ways: disease cause and prevention, weight loss and weight gain, moods, energy levels, and even how quickly you age.

The underlying principle is simple: What goes up must come down. When you eat high-glycemic-load foods — such as bread, pasta, bagels, pizza, cookies, and cakes (gluten-free or not) — your blood sugar spikes. And chasing that spike in blood sugar is your friend *insulin,* a hormone produced by the pancreas. Insulin's job is to get nutrients from the blood and make them available to various tissues in the body.

Glucose is the fuel that your body uses. Insulin is in charge of getting the glucose into the cells where they can use it for energy. Think of insulin as the delivery guy — bringing glucose to the cells, opening the door, and tossing the glucose inside.

When insulin shuttles the glucose from the bloodstream into the cells, insulin *lowers* your blood sugar level (the sugar isn't in the blood anymore; it's in the cells).

When your blood sugar level is high, your body makes a bunch of insulin to try to bring that level down. The problem is that insulin is sometimes a little *too* good at its job.

The high cost of high insulin

When you eat a lot of high-glycemic-load foods (see "Hauling the glycemic load [GL]"), your blood sugar spikes and the pancreas has to work really hard to pump out a bunch of insulin to bring the blood-sugar level down. And it works — blood sugar drops fast. You crash. You get fatigued, sometimes a little dizzy — and hungry.

When high-glycemic-load foods cause your blood sugar levels to spike and then drop quickly, your hormones are strapped in the front seat on this roller-coaster ride, wreaking havoc on your energy levels and even moods.

People who eat high-glycemic-load foods for years can develop a condition called insulin resistance. *Insulin resistance* is when the body has so much insulin all the time that it doesn't respond like it should anymore. Usually, just a little bit of insulin can bring blood sugar down, but in someone who's insulin resistant, this doesn't happen. So in an effort to lower blood-sugar levels, the body keeps producing insulin and has elevated levels of it all the time. This can be very hard on the body.

Syndrome X, or *metabolic syndrome,* is a cluster of diseases caused by insulin resistance. These conditions include

- ✔ Adult-onset diabetes (Type 2)
- ✔ High blood pressure
- ✔ Hardening of the arteries and damage to arterial walls
- ✔ High ratio of bad cholesterol to good
- ✔ Elevated blood uric acid levels (which can cause gout or kidney stones)
- ✔ Weight gain and obesity
- ✔ An excess of triglycerides (fat in the bloodstream)

Excess insulin is also blamed for nutrient deficiencies, including deficiencies in calcium, magnesium, zinc, vitamin E, vitamin C, B complex vitamins, and essential fatty acids.

Insulin also increases the amount of cortisol in the body. *Cortisol* is a stress hormone that can accelerate aging and cause other health problems.

Taking a Healthful Approach to Gluten-Free Living

Being gluten-free is a great start! Rice, corn, potatoes, and other high-glycemic-load foods are gluten-free, but they offer relatively little in the way of nutritional value, and can, as I discuss in the preceding section, cause some serious problems. Some awesome gluten-free specialty foods are available today, but loading up on those, as yummy as they are, isn't doing your body any favors, either.

Over the last 500 generations or so, individual human bodies have had to adapt to foods like cereal grains, sugar, and dairy, because they've become dietary staples. But in forcing their bodies to adapt, people have messed with Mother Nature. The result is disease, discomfort, and overall physical and emotional infirmity.

A healthier approach to the gluten-free lifestyle — or *any* lifestyle, for that matter — is to eat what your body was designed to eat: meats, fish, seafood, fruits, nonstarchy vegetables, nuts, and berries.

Dining with cavemen: The Paleolithic diet

I wasn't there, but I think I can safely say that rarely, if ever, did cavemen eat croissants. You know why? It's because early humans were hunter-gatherers, eating what they could hunt — and gather.

They ate what their bodies were designed to eat — lean meats, fresh fruits, and nonstarchy vegetables. There was no agriculture, so there were no farm animals or crops. That means no gluten.

You may be thinking that with some scary (and hairy) exceptions, today's humans don't really resemble cavemen, so this stuff isn't relevant — but you'd be mistaken. DNA evidence shows that genetically, humans have hardly changed at all in the last 40,000 years.

Because the hunter-gatherers I'm talking about lived in the Paleolithic era, their diet is cleverly called the *Paleolithic diet*, which follows these basic guidelines:

  ✔ **Lean meat, fish, and seafood:** *Lean* meat is key in the Paleolithic diet. Back in the day, the slow, plump porkers that people eat today just weren't on the hunting grounds. Their animals were lean, mean, fighting machines — as were the hunters who ate them.

I admit that a good wooly mammoth steak is hard to find these days. But lots of lean meats are available at any store — you may even want to experiment with lean game meat like alligator, buffalo, ostrich, kangaroo, and rattlesnake.

✔ **Fruits and nonstarchy vegetables:** There are lots of great fruits you can eat, including apples, figs, kiwis, mangos, cherries, and avocados. Just about any vegetable is a good bet (except for starchy ones like potatoes, yams, and sweet potatoes). Artichokes, cucumber, broccoli, cabbage, spinach, and mushrooms offer lots of nutritional value.

✔ **Nuts and seeds:** Not only are these accepted on the Paleolithic diet, but they're a great source of monounsaturated fats, which tend to lower cholesterol and decrease the risk of heart disease. Nuts and seeds include almonds, cashews, Macadamia nuts, pecans, pistachios, pumpkin seeds, sesame seeds, and sunflower seeds.

✔ **No cereal grains:** Grains weren't part of the diet until about 10,000 years ago. That's *yesterday,* evolutionarily speaking. Interestingly, when grains were introduced, health problems began to increase. While there's no scientific evidence to make a correlation, it's interesting to note that the average height of humans decreased, and people had more infectious diseases than their ancestors, more childhood mortality, and shorter lifespans. They had more osteoporosis, rickets, and other bone-mineral disorders, as well as vitamin and mineral deficiencies that caused diseases like scurvy, beriberi, pellagra, and iron-deficiency anemia.

✔ **No legumes:** Off-limit legumes include all beans, peas, peanuts, and soybeans.

✔ **No dairy:** It's pretty easy to see why cavemen didn't do milk. First, picture them catching a wild boar — what then? It begs the question, "How many cavemen does it take to *milk* a wild boar?" If you're worried that you're not going to get enough calcium if you cut out dairy, load up on broccoli, cabbage, and celery. Some of the best sources of calcium come from greens, like beet greens, kale, and mustard greens.

✔ **No processed foods:** (Of course.)

As a general rule, you can probably simplify the Paleolithic approach to: If humans made it, don't eat it.

You have to choose a lifestyle that you're comfortable with, that satisfies *and* nourishes you — and that may be a modified version of this diet. But overall, this approach offers complete nutrition, it's comprised of foods that are low glycemic-load, and best of all, it's gluten-free.

Find your own balance. Everyone is different — maybe you don't want or need that much protein. Maybe you're a vegetarian and choose to get your protein from other sources. The approach I outline here is simply a starting point to give you an idea of a healthful way to be gluten-free. For more information, you can discuss the diet with your doctor or dietitian.

You can find lots of detailed information about the Paleolithic diet by doing a quick Internet search. One of my favorite sites is www.thepaleodiet.com.

Comparing caveman-style to low-carb diets

Diet trends come and go faster than celebrity engagements. Within a matter of weeks, the absolutely-guaranteed-to-make-you-lose-20-pounds-in-20-minutes diet is replaced with an approach that doesn't even remotely resemble it. So how can they all be right? They can't.

And I want to point out that although the caveman approach I outline in this chapter can help you with weight management, my objective isn't to talk about weight loss; it's to talk about achieving optimal health through nutrition — and that just happens to involve a gluten-free diet.

You're probably gathering by now (that's a pun, in case you missed it) that the hunter-gatherer approach is low-carb. But it's not like some of the other no-carb or low-carb diets. Here are the important distinctions:

✔ **This isn't a low-carb or no-carb lifestyle.** It's a *good* carb lifestyle.

✔ **Eliminating carbs as some diets recommend cuts out foods like fruits and vegetables.** That means you're missing out on important vitamins, minerals, fiber, antioxidants, and other nutrients.

✔ **Some of the low-carb diets suggest eating high-fat foods like cheese, butter, and bacon.** These can cause cholesterol levels to skyrocket.

✔ **Most popular low-carb, high-fat diet plans don't make a distinction between good fats and bad fats.** Monounsaturated fats are good; saturated fats are mostly bad. Polyunsaturated fats are a little of each, depending on the ratio in which you eat them.

✔ **Most low-carb, high-fat diets don't talk about the dangers of salt.** People do need sodium in their diets to help regulate fluid balance, but if you get too much of it, sodium can cause high blood pressure, which can lead to heart disease and other health problems. It also messes with the body's ability to absorb calcium, which can eventually lead to bone loss and osteoporosis.

Even if you don't salt your food, you could be getting way too much salt in your diet. The sodium that's found naturally in foods like shellfish and some cheeses isn't usually a problem. But processed foods are often loaded with sodium in the form of flavor enhancers, thickeners, and preservatives. Even sodas often have sodium to help them maintain carbonation.

Differentiating between gluten-free and low-carb

People get confused because some of the low-carb diets tend to be gluten-free, or at least gluten-light, so they think gluten-free automatically means low-carb — but it doesn't work that way.

In fact, gluten-free can be very high-carb. Frequently when people give up gluten, they choose gluten-free replacements, like gluten-free breads, bagels, pastas, pizzas, cookies, and brownies. Not only are those things high-carb,

but they're basically empty calories, meaning they offer very little nutrition — but lots of calories.

Warning: The confusion between low-carb diets and the gluten-free diet can be a dangerous misconception. On many low-carb programs, small amounts of gluten are allowed back into the diet after the initial phases. For many people who need to be gluten-free, reintroducing gluten to the diet is never okay.

When you're counting carbs, you can easily see why you get more food for your carb count when you eat fruits and veggies than when you eat gluten. The average carbohydrate content of fruits is about 13 percent. For non-starchy vegetables, it's about 4 percent; and it's zero for lean meats, fish, and seafood. The carbohydrate content of cereal grains like wheat, though, averages a whopping 72 percent.

Reviewing the more healthful approach

I cover a lot of ground in this chapter — the glycemic index, glycemic load, the caveman diet, and clarifications on the low-carb/no-carb, good-carb/bad-carb controversies. If you're wondering what the heck I'm trying to get at, you're probably not alone.

It all boils down to this simple approach for a healthier gluten-free lifestyle:

- ✔ Keep it gluten-free, for sure. I don't want you to get so lost in this approach that you forget the whole point!

- ✔ Watch the carbs, making sure the carbs you're eating are good carbs like fruits and vegetables.

- ✔ Try to stick to low-glycemic-load foods, which raise your blood sugar levels gradually.

- ✔ Make sure the foods you eat offer nutritional value. Stay away from foods that are basically empty calories.

- ✔ A Paleolithic approach — eating seafood, lean meats, fruits, and non-starchy vegetables — is extremely healthful. Modify the diet to meet your personal preferences and needs.

Good food is food that goes bad quickly. That means fresh produce and other foods without many preservatives.

Being Healthy, Stealthy, and Wise

Writing and reading about nutritious foods is one thing, but actually *eating* them is another. What about the person who thinks broccoli is as palatable as dandelions (don't try this comparison at home; the dandelions in your yard may be poisonous)?

Some people want the nutrients that good foods offer, but they (or the people they're feeding) don't like the taste (or texture, consistency, color, density, or idea) of nutritious foods. Don't worry. You don't have to love Brussels sprouts to eat well. You just have to be creative about how you hide nutrient-rich foods in your meals. Most of the time, people don't even notice. Here are a few ideas for being stealthy, healthy, and wise:

- Hide fruits and even veggies in a smoothie by cutting them into small pieces and blending them in.
- Sneak broccoli, zucchini, and other veggies into lasagne or pasta sauce.
- Use a few tablespoons (or the amount recommended on the packaging) of protein powder to pack a punch in a shake or smoothie.
- Use kefir instead of milk, yogurt, or sour cream. Smoothies are the easiest way to enjoy kefir — just mix it with berries and blend.

Kefir is a supernutritious, gluten-free fermented drink that tastes like and has a consistency similar to yogurt. With live, active cultures, kefir is a *prebiotic* and *probiotic*. These are foods that promote the growth of good bacteria in the intestinal tract. You can find kefir near the milk and yogurt at most health food stores, and sometimes it's in the refrigerated health food section of grocery stores.

Kefir is easily digested; it cleans the intestines and provides beneficial yeast, vitamins and minerals, and complete proteins. Even if you're lactose intolerant, you can usually tolerate kefir because the yeast and bacteria contain lactase, which "eats up" the lactose that's left after culturing.

Avoiding nutritional pitfalls on the gluten-free diet

People often ask whether nutritional deficiencies arise as a result of being gluten-free. The answer is maybe yes, and maybe no.

If you choose the healthful approach to gluten-free living that I outline in this chapter, you shouldn't need to worry about nutritional deficiencies. You'll be healthier than most people who eat gluten.

If, however, you eat a gluten-free diet that's mostly gluten-free "replacement" foods like breads, pizzas, pastas, cookies, brownies, and cakes — and if your "vegetables" consist of rice, corn, potatoes, and the tomatoes in the pasta sauce — then you may have some nutritional concerns.

When adopting a gluten-free lifestyle, people tend to turn to starchy stand-bys, like rice, corn, and potatoes. You gravitate toward these foods partly *because* they're starchy, sort of like the bread, pasta, and bagels you were accustomed to eating when you ate gluten. Ironically, the same foods that you crave because they fill you up and give you that satiated feeling also make you hungrier. I talk more about this in the "Losing weight on the gluten-free diet" section.

Unfortunately, rice, corn, potatoes, and other starchy foods don't offer much in the way of nutrition — especially when you look at all the calories you get. Not much nutritional bang for the caloric buck, so to speak.

Other foods offer that fill-me-up satisfaction, many of which provide far more nutritional value and diversity than rice, corn, potatoes, or wheat. They include

- Amaranth
- Buckwheat
- Mesquite
- Millet
- Montina (Indian ricegrass)
- Quinoa
- Sorghum
- Teff

These alternative grains offer complete protein, fiber, and lots of vitamins and minerals. (If you want to read more about the nutritional value of these wheat alternatives, check out Chapter 4.)

The most common concerns focusing on nutrient deficiencies in the gluten-free diet revolve around folate or folic acid, iron, fiber, and B vitamins. The B vitamins specifically lacking in some gluten-free flours include vitamin B1 (thiamin), B2 (riboflavin), and B3 (niacin). Choosing the healthier approach I discuss is the best way to make up for any nutritional deficiencies. Supplements may work, too, but make sure they don't contain any gluten, and consult your doctor first.

Deficiencies in B-complex vitamins and iron may occur because when people were still a glutenivore, they were eating lots of flour, which is usually enriched and fortified with iron, riboflavin, niacin, and thiamine. Gluten-free flours aren't enriched.

Getting the fiber you need on a gluten-free diet

Fiber is important for lots of reasons. The most well-known benefit is that it helps keep the gastrointestinal plumbing — ya know, poo-poo, doo-doo, number two, caca — moving smoothly, and that's good for the whole gastrointestinal tract. Fiber can help reduce cholesterol and lower your chance of heart disease and cancer.

When people give up gluten and their diets consist mostly of gluten-free flours like rice and potato or tapioca flours, they're sometimes at risk of having too little fiber in their diets. If you're going to use flours, try to incorporate flax meal, Montina, chickpea, and amaranth flours into your cooking. They have much more fiber than white or even brown rice.

The most healthful diet that ensures you an adequate intake of fiber is the approach that most closely resembles the diet your ancestors ate, which is high in fruits and nonstarchy vegetables. Some good food choices include apples, kiwis, bananas, avocados, tomatoes, cabbage, broccoli, spinach, and Brussels sprouts.

The whole truth (and nothing but) about whole grains

If you're gonna do grains, the goal is whole. A grain has three parts: the germ, the endosperm, and the bran. Whole-grain foods contain all three parts:

- **Germ:** This is the part of the grain that a new plant sprouts from, and it's where you can find a lot of niacin, thiamin, riboflavin, vitamin E, magnesium, phosphorus, iron, and zinc. It also has a little protein and some fat.

- **Endosperm:** The kernel of the grain, the endosperm is the bulk of the seed. Because the seed stores its energy in the endosperm, it has most of the protein and carbohydrates, as well as some vitamins and minerals.

- **Bran:** The outer layer of the seed, the bran contains most of the grain's nutrients. It's a rich source of niacin, thiamin, riboflavin, magnesium, phosphorus, iron, and zinc. This is where most of the fiber is, too.

Chewing the fat with mega omegas

Saying "fat is bad" is like saying politicians are honest. Some are — some aren't — but you sure can't label them all the same. Fats are the same way — some are good, and some are bad. The saturated kind, like you find in fatty meats and cheeses, are bad, at least in excess. So are the trans fats you find in hydrogenated oils. Most people know these fats increase the bad cholesterol and can contribute to heart attacks and strokes.

Some fats are good, though — like mono- and polyunsaturated fats. Omega-3 fatty acids — like the ones in fish like wild salmon, whitefish, tilapia, catfish, flounder, and mahi mahi — are super-beneficial. Not only do they keep the arteries clear, but they also affect your *neurotransmitters* — the chemical messengers in your brain — reducing depression and improving your moods.

Refined grains have been stripped of their bran and germ layers during processing, so all that's left is the endosperm. They contain some protein and fat, and there may be some fiber and nutritional value left, but most of the good stuff gets tossed out during the refining process — like the proverbial baby with the bath water.

The individual components of whole grain — vitamins, minerals, fiber, and other nutrients — work together to help protect against chronic diseases such as diabetes, heart disease, and certain cancers. Grain components are *synergistic,* meaning that each individual component is important but the value of the whole grain is greater than the sum of its parts.

Quinoa, buckwheat, and some of the other alternative grains I talk about in Chapter 4 are whole grains, and they provide all the value that makes whole grains so nutritious.

Refined grains usually have nutrients added back in, but they're not as nutritious as a whole-grain product would be, and they lack the fiber that whole grain provides. (If the food were really nutritious, why would it need to be fortified?)

Fruits have almost twice as much fiber as whole grains, and nonstarchy vegetables have about eight times more fiber. To maximize your fill of fiber, be sure to eat the peel.

Winning the Weight Wars

The gluten-free diet is paradoxical — if you're too heavy, it's likely to help you lose weight. If you're too thin, it's likely to help you gain it. I know, even the miracle pills on TV don't claim to swing both ways, helping you lose *or* gain weight. But trust me . . . it's true!

Losing weight on the gluten-free diet

If you're fighting the battle of the bulge, you're obviously not alone. In today's world of globesity, whether you're part of the Boomer Generation or Generation Y doesn't matter: The majority of the population, regardless of age, is Generation XL.

The good news is that the gluten-free diet may be the key to losing and maintaining a healthy weight. Unfortunately, gorging on gluten-free brownies and cookies isn't part of this weight-loss plan; the key to weight control is that you adhere to a high-protein, low-glycemic-load, nutrient-dense diet (see "Dining with cavemen: The Paleolithic diet" and "Good Carbs, Bad Carbs: Tuning In to the Glycemic Index and Glycemic Load").

Battling hunger and cravings

Your blood-sugar levels affect hunger and cravings. Gluten-containing foods like bread, crackers, and pretzels are enemy number one. Those foods — and their gluten-free counterparts — cause a rapid rise in blood sugar, which sends signals to your body to produce insulin.

Insulin does its job and brings down your blood-sugar level, but it brings it so low that you get hungry and in fact crave more of the same kind of food that made it go up in the first place. Insulin also tells your body to store fat.

High insulin levels also inhibit the release of *serotonin,* a neurotransmitter in the brain that tells the body to stop eating.

On the other hand, when your body absorbs sugars slowly, as when you eat low-glycemic-load foods and foods high in protein, the rise in blood sugar is gradual, and so is its descent after insulin begins doing its job. The gentle decline in blood sugar means your cravings are less.

Making too much insulin causes you to store fat and stimulates the liver to make more cholesterol, increasing blood cholesterol levels. Excess insulin also inhibits the breakdown of fat that's already stored in your body, so even if you're working out like a fiend, losing those extra pounds is tough.

The power of protein

Protein is a strong ally in the battle of the bulge. It has a powerful *thermogenic* effect, meaning it revs up your metabolism and helps you burn calories. It also makes you feel fuller than fats or carbs do, so you tend to eat less than you would if your meal were mostly carbs and fats.

Protein also stimulates your pancreas to produce a hormone called *glucagon.* Glucagon's job is to raise your blood sugar and promote the mobilization of previously stored fat — so as you burn food reserves between meals, high levels of glucagon help that energy to be taken from those fat thighs or spare tire around your waist.

Gaining unwanted weight on the gluten-free diet

Lots of people gain weight when they go gluten-free, sometimes causing a weight problem that wasn't there before. This usually happens for two reasons:

✔ People who have a form of gluten intolerance often aren't absorbing all their nutrients — nor are they absorbing all their calories — before they embark on a gluten-free lifestyle. After they go gluten-free, their health begins to improve, and they're able to absorb nutrients — and calories — again. But they're usually still eating the same number of calories — often too many to maintain their pre-gluten-free figure.

✔ Some people gain weight because they're eating lots of rice, corn, and potatoes, which are high-glycemic-load foods that immediately turn to sugar. They may also be eating more than their fair share of gluten-free treats like cookies, brownies, and cakes in an effort to stave off feelings of deprivation.

If you've packed on a few unwanted pounds since going gluten-free, stick to a high-protein, low-glycemic-load approach, and you should have an easier time controlling your weight.

On the other hand, high-glycemic-load, carbohydrate-rich meals suppress glucagon secretion. That means the stuff that mobilizes stored fat — glucagon — isn't there, but the hormone that promotes storage — insulin — is. That's a one-two punch to the waistline.

If you've been boning up on protein, you may have heard that eating too much protein is bad for the bones. The idea is that extra protein can cause your body to get rid of calcium instead of absorbing it like your body's supposed to do (to make strong bones). Although too much protein can cause the calcium to leach from your bones (carbonated and caffeinated drinks can cause the same thing), you have to eat a lot of protein to make that happen: about 140 grams — the equivalent of a pound of chicken, fish, beef, or pork or two-and-a-half pounds of nuts — all in one day.

Gaining weight on the gluten-free diet

Some people who have suffered malabsorption as a result of being gluten sensitive or having celiac disease are underweight and actually need to pack on the pounds.

When these people go gluten-free, their gut usually heals quickly, and they begin to absorb nutrients and calories. Their weight is usually normalized quickly simply as a result of being gluten-free.

Sometimes when people go gluten-free, they inadvertently cut calories by cutting out things like bread and butter. If you're already underweight, you may need to supplement the healthful diet I outline in this chapter with high-calorie foods like nuts, avocados, tuna, and salmon.

Gaining an Athletic Advantage by Being Gluten-Free

Some athletes are afraid to go gluten-free because they're worried they won't get enough carbohydrates in their diets to sustain their intense energy needs. Carbs before, during, and after training or competition are essential to maintaining energy levels and speeding recovery after the event.

Not only is getting the carbs you need as an athlete possible, but being gluten-free can actually provide an athletic advantage. After all, you're not doing your carb-loading with pizza and spaghetti — those are relatively worthless nutritionally speaking. These foods also cause blood-sugar peaks and valleys because they're high-glycemic-load foods, as I discuss in "Good Carbs, Bad Carbs: Tuning In to the Glycemic Index and Glycemic Load."

The gluten-freeness of the diet doesn't deserve the credit in providing an athletic advantage; it's more the high-protein, low-glycemic-load approach (that happens to be gluten-free) that counts. This approach has several advantages for athletes:

- ✔ Enabling the body to gradually learn to use energy more efficiently from fat stores and to be less dependent on the food in its gut

- ✔ Minimizing the hypoglycemic effect that sudden, intense exercise can cause

- ✔ Increasing the free fatty acids in the bloodstream, enabling you to save muscle glycogen (used for energy) during exercise

- ✔ Maintaining stable blood-sugar levels during exercise, which is essential for the growth of muscle and strength, as well as for the flow of energy

Part II

Planning and Preparing: The Preludes to Cooking

The 5th Wave   By Rich Tennant

"Ooo, what's in there? Gluten-free eye of newt? I can barely tell the difference."

In this part . . .

I get you ready to cook your gluten-free meals. Hey, even if your idea of cooking is warming a frozen dinner (yes, frozen gluten-free meals are available!), you still need to plan what you're going to eat, buy it, and well, at least warm it up. Whether you cook to live or live to cook, meal planning, shopping, and preparing the food before you cook it present some unique considerations when you're gluten-free.

Here, I offer a nutritious approach to gluten-free eating so you can plan meals that are gluten-free and good for you. I help you create and maintain a gluten-free-friendly kitchen and offer recommendations for safely sharing the kitchen with gluten. Then it's off to the store, where I propose several options for where and how to buy gluten-free foods without breaking the bank. As the final prelude to cooking, I offer tips and techniques that are unique to gluten-free cooking, and I help you figure out how to make anything gluten-free, even without a recipe.

Chapter 7

Creating a Gluten-Free-Friendly Kitchen

*Y*our idea of cooking may involve only a can opener and a microwave. Or you may have kitchen gadgets no one else knows how to use, tote mystery ingredients home from faraway lands, and subscribe to magazines most people can't pronounce. No matter how you feel about cooking, you spend lots of time in the kitchen.

When you're gluten-free, the kitchen needs a little extra attention. Keeping yourself safely gluten-free isn't hard, but you need to keep some special considerations in mind, especially if your kitchen contains gluten.

Sharing the Kitchen with Gluten

When our kids were little and we'd take long road trips (parental torture chambers on wheels), my kids would screech, "Mommy, Kelsie's looking out my window!" to which Kelsie would quickly retort, gasping for air, "That's because Tyler's breathing my air! He took it all!" And the drama continued for hours (*whose* idea was this?).

Sometimes when I think of gluten in the kitchen, I envision the same scenario (flashbacks?): "Hey, wheat bread! Get outta here. This is gluten-free territory." "Just because they pay twice as much for you doesn't mean they like you more." "I think you spit a crumb on me! Now I'm contaminated!" Okay, now you know way too much about my issues and my fantasy world, so I'll get to the point.

Some people think that the only way to be 100 percent gluten-free is to make the entire household gluten-free (see Chapter 17 for the pros and cons of this). Not true. Sure, doing so makes things easier — menu planning and cooking are simpler, and if the whole house is gluten-free, you don't have to worry about possible mix-ups or contamination (and no feuding between the breads). But if you choose to share your kitchen with gluten, you'll be fine.

Here are some tips for sharing a kitchen with gluten:

- ✔ **Gluten-free comes first.** If you're making two varieties of a meal —grilled cheese sandwiches, for example — make the gluten-free one first. That way, the preparation surface, knives (always plural — see "The gob drop for spreadables" in this chapter), and pans stay uncontaminated. If you make the gluten-containing one first, you either have to wash the pan or griddle thoroughly before making the gluten-free sandwich or use an entirely separate pan.

- ✔ **Foil is your friend.** Using lots of aluminum foil makes your life easier. Cover cookie sheets with it, use it to separate different foods, and warm foods on foil rather than setting them directly on an oven rack. Foil is a great way to ensure your gluten-free foods aren't being contaminated.

- ✔ **Vacuum sealers save time.** You may find that you're making more home-made foods than you used to, like gluten-free breads, cookies, pizzas, and so on. Remember, homemade foods don't have preservatives in them (a good thing), so they go bad quickly (a bad thing). You can save time and money by making foods in larger quantities and then vacuum-sealing them so they stay fresh longer. Doing so is convenient, too, because you can vacuum seal individual servings and toss them in lunches or take them on the go.

- ✔ **Freeze it.** Again, homemade foods don't have preservatives, so they don't last as long. Freeze them, and then use them when you need to.

- ✔ **Use brightly colored labels.** Because you're likely to have some left-overs that are gluten-free and some that aren't, consider using brightly colored stickers or labels to stick on the storage containers so you can easily tell which leftovers are gluten-free. This is especially helpful if you have babysitters or other people in the house who may be likely to grab the wrong one.

Avoiding cross-contamination

When you're sharing a kitchen with gluten, gluten can contaminate (or *glutenate,* as I like to say) your food in several ways. Crumbs seem to throw themselves off gluten-containing breads and other foods, turning perfectly good gluten-free zones into danger zones in the blink of an eye.

Not only do crumbs fly, but preparation surfaces, pots, pans, grills, and utensils can contaminate food, too. You know those neat-freaks who drive everyone nuts because they're compulsive about cleaning? Take a hard look in the mirror and embrace the reality, because that's you now. Cleanliness isn't an option anymore; it's crucial to maintaining the purity of your gluten-free lifestyle.

Crumbs: Public enemy number one

If you think ants are your biggest problem in the kitchen, think again. The ants just go marching one by one (hurrah), and although certainly a nuisance, they don't hurt you even if you eat them. No, enemy number one in the gluten-free-friendly kitchen is the almighty crumb. Crumbs fly off bread like sparks in a fireworks display, and they're everywhere. I'm not pointing all the crumb-tossing blame at the gluten-containing kind of bread; in fact, quite the opposite. I won't name names, but between gluten-containing and gluten-free breads, everyone knows who the real winner is in the crumb-casting competition.

So here's the deal: When you work really hard to prepare a delicious gluten-free sandwich and then set it on the counter in a pile of gluten-containing crumbs, you are, literally, eating a gluten-containing sandwich, and your efforts to find, buy, and compile gluten-free makin's are all for naught. If you think a few crumbs don't matter, you're assigned to go read Chapters 2 and 5. Six times.

Even a few crumbs from gluten-containing breads or crackers can turn your gluten-free food into a toxic treat. Be diligent about cleaning crumbs, and remember the golden rule: When in doubt, leave it out. If you're not sure that your meal is uncontaminated, don't eat it.

So what about gluten-free crumbs? Do you have to be obsessive about wiping those up? Yes, if you're sharing your kitchen with gluten. Not for the sake of good hygiene as much as because you can't tell whether they're gluten-free by looking at them, so you never know for sure whether you're setting your sandwich in gluten or not. (And then you have to consider those annoying little marching ants.)

New rules for kitchen tools

You don't need to stock up on new pots, pans, tools, and utensils, but you do need to pay attention to how you use the ones you have. For the most part, if you clean your kitchen items well, you get the gluten off them. Nonstick surfaces that clean easily and thoroughly are especially safe.

The tale of two toasters

Have you ever looked inside a toaster or toaster oven? Of course you have. What do you see? Crumbs. Lots of crumbs. If you're sharing a kitchen with gluten, some of those crumbs are probably of the gluten-containing variety. That means your gluten-free bread has lost its "-free."

You have a few options in dealing with this dilemma. First, I recommend using a toaster oven instead of a toaster. For one thing, it's more versatile — you can actually bake things in a toaster oven, and when you want to heat a small quantity of something, it's very handy. But more importantly, you can remove the racks and wash them, and you have easy access to the crumb tray for cleaning. (Although if your toaster oven has a convection feature, remember to keep it turned off — otherwise the fan can blow flour and crumbs all over your gluten-free foods.)

Another option is to buy a second toaster or toaster oven if you can afford it. That's really the safest way to ensure you're not getting gluten crumbs on your gluten-free toast. If you don't have a second toaster or toaster oven, at least try to wipe the grills (while they're cool and the machine is unplugged) before toasting your gluten-free bread.

You can also buy toaster bags that you slide your toast or sandwich into before putting them in a toaster, toaster oven, or oven.

Keep in mind a couple of exceptions. I recommend having separate colanders and pasta servers if you're making both gluten-containing and gluten-free pastas in your kitchen. Clearly label one as being gluten-free only. Pasta tends to leave a residue that's sometimes tricky to get off. You don't want to drain gluten-free pasta in a colander that has remnants of the gluten-containing pasta on it. Same goes for the pasta servers.

I also suggest buying separate pots, pans, or utensils if you have a favorite item and it just doesn't clean well — a special crêpe pan, for instance. If you can see (or sense) that traces of gluten could remain there and you don't want to part with the pan to get one that cleans more thoroughly, just don't use it for your gluten-free cooking. I encourage you to mark your separate items well — one saying "gluten-free only" and the other saying "gluten" — so you don't get them mixed up.

Using a permanent marker may not be the latest trend in kitchen design, but it can save you from being unsure and may even spare you health-threatening mix-ups. A big, bold "GF ONLY" on your gluten-free utensils can reduce the chance of inadvertently contaminating your gluten-free foods by using the wrong kitchen items.

The gob drop for spreadables

The gob drop isn't a new teen fashion trend, dance move, or tasteless reference to body parts that have succumbed to gravity and an overzealous appetite. The gob drop is an action (and somewhat of an art), one that you need to master if you share your kitchen with gluten.

But first let me define my highly technical term *spreadables.* Spreadables are the foodstuffs you spread onto other foodstuffs. You know — mayonnaise, butter, margarine, jelly, peanut butter, honey (unless you buy the little squeezy bear), and other things usually falling into the condiment category. You can buy most of these condiments in squeeze bottles, but you should still learn the gob drop — you may want to buy spreadables in jars because of price or flavor (and squeezable peanut butter is just weird).

Most people dip their knives into containers, scooping out some of the spreadable, and then spread said spread onto their bread, cracker, tortilla, or other spreadee. Then they scoop a little more and continue the process. Each time the knife goes from a gluten-containing spreadee back in the spreadable, gluten crumbs get a free ride into the container, contaminating the entire tub or jar. And you know what they say about one bad apple.

That's why you need to do the gob drop. But first, toss out all the contaminated tubs and jars you have. Either keep all future tubs and jars gluten-free (by practicing the gob drop faithfully), or buy separate tubs, mark them clearly, and don't ever mix them up. For more on the damage even a small amount of gluten can do, see Chapter 2.

Here's how you do the gob drop to keep your spreads gluten-free:

1. **Use a knife to scoop out some of the spreadable.**

2. **Flick the spreadable onto the spreadee (see Figure 7-1).**

3. **Use the knife to continue with that process until you have enough of the spreadable on the spreadee.**

4. **You may then begin spreading.**

Admittedly, the gob drop takes practice. Flick too hard, and you miss the spreadee altogether. Don't flick hard enough, and it won't come off the knife. In dire situations, you may need a second knife to scrape the spreadable off knife number one.

Of course, you can use knife number one to spread, but you can't put a knife you've spread with back into the jar or tub. If you need more of the spreadable, you have to break out another knife.

People frequently ask, "Can I put the knife back into the spreadables if I used it to spread something onto gluten-free bread?" No. Because you'll not only end up with crumbs in the spreadables, which is gross, but you'll always wonder whether those crumbs are the gluten kind or the gluten-free kind. Resist the temptation.

Another frequently asked question is: "Do we have to do the gob drop if our entire household is gluten-free?" No (that's why this section falls under the "Sharing the Kitchen with Gluten" section), but ending up with tubs and jars full of crumbs is still really gross.

Don't touch knife to bread. Flick it.

Figure 7-1:
The gob
drop.

1.)   2.)

Gracious guests can lead to grief

Having too many cooks in the kitchen is bad enough, but when you're trying to keep your foods safely gluten-free and your visitors are especially "helpful," maintaining a gluten-free zone can be more than a tinge stressful. Sweet Aunt Mabel's gracious offer to help butter the bread can have you diving to protect your pristine (and well-marked) tub of margarine because you haven't yet taught her to properly execute the gob drop. And as you rescue the margarine and quickly try to decide whether teaching her the gob drop (and hovering over her so she doesn't make a mistake) would be easier than just buttering the bread yourself, Uncle Bob is getting ready to flip the burgers — and the buns — with the same spatula!

If your visitors are one-time or occasional guests, give them safe tasks to keep them busy and let them lend a hand — somewhere that won't put your gluten-free foods in peril. Have them pour the iced tea or set the table. But if they're frequent visitors, you probably need to invest the time to teach them the gob drop. Your spreadables are at risk! Your other options are to hide the tubs and jars and buy squeezables for their visit or to buy separate containers and clearly mark which ones are gluten-free.

Storing foods separately for convenience

For the most part, you don't need to have separate storage spaces for the gluten-containing and gluten-free foods unless you do so for convenience purposes. After all, simply reaching up to the gluten-free section of your pantry for a gluten-free flour mixture is easier than sorting through the shelves.

If you have kids on a gluten-free diet and others in the family still eat gluten — or if some people in the home have behavioral issues or learning disorders — then having separate storage areas can be a very good idea. For these gluten-free loved ones, it's easy to look in a pantry and be overwhelmed with all the things they can't eat, even if the things they can eat actually outnumber the things they can't.

By separating gluten-containing and gluten-free foods in the pantry, not only do you make quickly choosing from their safe shelves quite easy, but the number of things they can eat becomes more obvious to them. This can be a big psychological boost in what could otherwise be a daunting experience.

Consider marking gluten-free foods with a "GF" right when you get home from the store so the kids will have an easier time helping you put everything away in the right place.

Taking Inventory of the Pantry and Fridge

You want to have some basic ingredients and products specific to the gluten-free diet on hand. Admittedly, some of these items are a little pricier than their gluten-containing counterparts, and they're sometimes a little harder to find. In Chapter 8, I suggest where to buy them and how to save as much money as you can. But depending on how you cook (or don't), many of these items may become staples in your gluten-free-friendly kitchen.

Specialty ingredients to stock

Don't let this long list scare you. You don't need all these things; in fact, if you're not going to do any baking, you probably don't need any of them. If, however, you're planning to cook or bake gluten-free, consider having some of these ingredients on hand:

- **Arrowroot flour:** Higher in nutritional value than some other flours, arrowroot often takes the place of cornstarch.

- **Brown rice flour:** This flour still contains the bran, which makes it more nutritious than white rice flour. It has a slightly nutty taste.

- **Cornstarch:** You can use cornstarch for thickening or with other flours in baking mixtures.

- **Corn flour:** You can blend corn flour with other flours for baking, or you can mix it with cornmeal (ground corn) in cornbreads and other dishes.

- **Garbanzo/fava bean flour (or blend):** Don't let the names scare you; these are some of the best baking flours around today. They offer a great texture and extra nutritional value, and they don't taste like beans.

- **Gelatin powder (unflavored):** A lot of the gluten-free recipes now call for unflavored gelatin because it adds moisture and protein and it holds the ingredients together.

- **Guar gum:** You don't need both xanthan gum and guar gum, but you can use one in place of the other. Be aware that some people find guar gum to have a laxative effect.

- **Lecithin:** Lecithin is an *emulsifier,* which just means it helps ingredients blend together. Made from soy, lecithin improves aeration and the texture of baked gluten-free foods, and it makes the food a little more resistant to getting stale.

- **Potato starch flour:** This is not the same thing as potato flour (which tastes very much like potatoes). Potato starch is very fine, white flour. It doesn't have much flavor, so it doesn't distort the taste of your foods, but it improves the texture in baking mixes. You can use it as a thickener or with other flours in baking mixtures.

- **Sorghum (milo) flour:** This nutritious flour is making more and more of a mark in the gluten-free cooking world. Its relatively bland flavor makes it a versatile ingredient in gluten-free baking.

- **Soy flour:** These days, people use soy flour mostly in combination with other flours, if at all. It has a strong, distinctive flavor, which some people love but others definitely don't.

- **Sweet rice flour:** Some people get confused because sweet rice flour is made from *glutinous* rice, not to be confused with "glutenous" (which technically isn't a word, although I use it often). Glutinous just means *sticky.* Sweet rice flour cooks differently from white rice flour, and people use it most often for thickening sauces or soups.

- **Tapioca flour (or starch):** This is also called *cassava flour* or *manioc.* It's great because it gives gluten-free foods a little bit of a stretch or chew that's lacking in many foods that don't contain gluten.

✔ **White rice flour:** Long considered the basic ingredient in a gluten-free diet, white rice flour is being overshadowed by more nutritious flours and flours with better consistencies, like bean, brown rice, arrowroot, and sorghum. But white rice flour is, nevertheless, a staple in the gluten-free pantry. Its bland flavor doesn't distort the taste of baked goods, and it comes in different textures (fine through regular), which affect the consistency of foods.

✔ **Xanthan gum:** A must if you're baking gluten-free breads and other baked goods, xanthan gum helps prevent crumbling.

✔ **Yeast:** Dry, active yeast is an important ingredient for gluten-free breads and other foods that need to rise. Don't use the rapid-rise yeast unless the recipe suggests it. Fresh yeast is key.

✔ **Alternative grains:** These are the grains (they're not really all grains, but people call them that) I talk about — and espouse the virtues of — in Chapter 4. They're loaded with nutrients, and they're great to have on hand either as baking flours or as whole grains. Use whole grains to add flavor and texture, cook them as their own dish, or even add them to foods (see Chapter 9 to find out how to cook with these). Here are some alternative grains to check out:

- Amaranth
- Buckwheat
- Mesquite
- Millet
- Montina
- Quinoa
- Sorghum
- Teff

Grains — especially whole grains — have a lot of oil in them. Oil can turn rancid quickly, so when you buy whole grains and whole-grain flours, be sure to shop at stores where the turnover is high, and buy only what you plan to use within a few months. Refrigerate the flours and grains if you have the space, but pay close attention to the smell. Old flours and grains smell stale.

Mixes to have on hand

You should keep several types of gluten-free baking mixes on hand so you're always prepared. These mixes are not a compromise, nor are they (in my opinion) "cheating." They're so good that in many cases, I think the gluten-free variety would win a side-by-side taste comparison. Best of all, with very little work on your part, your house smells like you've been baking all day! (You can see Chapter 9 for more on baking with mixes.)

Some people complain about the cost of mixes, and I admit that they're a tad pricey. But if you add up the cost of the ingredients to make baked goods from scratch (have you priced xanthan gum lately?), factor in the batches that yield only inedible hand weights, and consider that your time is at least *somewhat* valuable, I think the price is well worth it.

Here are some of the mixes I suggest you keep handy:

- ✔ **All-purpose baking mix:** Several companies make various types of all-purpose baking mixes, and most are excellent. Some companies use the garbanzo/fava bean mixture, and some use mixtures of other gluten-free flours. Use these mixes for baking or as a coating for fried or baked foods (and flip to Chapter 9 for other foods that make great coatings).

- ✔ **Bread mixes:** Many different kinds of bread mixes are available today, most of which you can fix in a bread machine or can mix by hand and cook in the oven.

- ✔ **Brownies:** The brownie mixes today are absolutely amazing. Some come with chunks of chocolate, but if they don't, you can add your own.

- ✔ **Cakes:** Gluten-free cake mixes come in just about any flavor you want, and these days they're all incredibly moist, light, and tasty. With slight modifications that are almost always on the package, you can make your cakes into cupcakes.

- ✔ **Chebe:** Chebe is so unique that I couldn't figure out which heading to put it under — bread, all-purpose baking mix, or pizza — so it's on its own, and it's good enough to stand alone. You can make Chebe, which comes from manioc (tapioca), into bread rolls or sticks, pizza crust, or a variety of other foods. Truly, your creativity is the only limiting factor. New varieties of Chebe have recently appeared in the marketplace.

- ✔ **Cookies:** The gluten-free cookie mixes today are fantastic. They come in just about any flavor you can dream up, and they turn out better than anything you can get from a store. Of course you can tailor them to your tastes by adding chocolate chips or gluten-free candies.

- ✔ **Muffins:** You can make many different varieties of gluten-free muffins, including vanilla, blueberry, apple, and banana. You can also buy basic muffin mixes that you can make into any type of muffin you want.

- ✔ **Pancakes and waffles:** One mix makes both; just the proportions of ingredients change (and of course you need a waffle iron to make waffles).

- ✔ **Pie crusts:** In Chapter 9, I give you suggestions for making your own pie crusts from crushed cereal or cookies. But if you want something closer to the real deal, the mixes available for pie crusts are what you're looking for. These crusts are easy to make and delicious, and the mixes turn out a perfect crust every time.

- ✔ **Pizza dough:** Mixes to help you whip up a quick pizza crust are available. You just top the crust with your favorite toppings, and the pizza is as good as or better than anything other people deliver.

Keep in mind that most gluten-free foods, even many of those you buy commercially, don't have preservatives in them. That means that unlike a store-bought pastry that has a shelf life of seven millennia, your gluten-free foods should be refrigerated or even frozen.

Specialty pre-made products to consider

In addition to purchasing mixes that you can make at home, you can buy pre-made gluten-free products at natural foods stores, online, or even at some grocery stores (see Chapter 8 for more on shopping strategies). In fact, some of the natural foods stores are beginning to make their own gluten-free baked goods and are marketing them under a private label. I don't cover those products here because they're each specific to their own store.

In this section, I recommend pre-made gluten-free foods that you should keep on hand as staples for your pantry.

✔ **Bagels:** Believe it or not, gluten-free bagels are available, and most of them are great. They even come in different flavors. These bagels usually come frozen, but if not, stick them in the freezer. They're not always sliced, so you have to thaw them a little (remember, too long in a microwave makes them soggy and tough), cut them in half, and then toast them.

✔ **Bread:** It's true: Some stores are now selling freshly baked gluten-free breads (and other gluten-free baked goods) in their bakery sections. Unbelievable! If you're not lucky enough to live near one of those stores, you can buy pre-made gluten-free bread online, at natural foods stores, or in the specialty sections of some grocery stores. If the bread's not frozen when you buy it, put it in the freezer when you get home. Flavors of these breads are all over the board. Some breads are definitely better than others, so be prepared to experiment with a few varieties before you find one you like.

All gluten-free bread is best if you toast it first, even if you plan to eat it later (like in a lunch box).

✔ **Cereals:** Not too many big-company commercial cereals sold in "regular" grocery stores are gluten-free, other than the colored sugar flakes in a box. But peruse the aisles of a natural foods store or health food aisle of your grocery store, and you'll probably find lots of gluten-free cereals to choose from.

Aside from the obvious no-nos like wheat, the usual glutenizing culprit in cereal is malt or malt flavoring. Malt can be derived from corn, but it's usually from barley.

✔ **Cookies:** Gluten-free cookies are taking up more of the shelf space at natural foods stores and even specialty aisles of grocery stores. Most of them are excellent.

✔ **Crackers:** Not so long ago, gluten-free crackers were but a dream. Today they're not only a reality, but they're delicious. The type of cracker that's easiest to find at natural foods stores or specialty aisles of grocery stores is a rice cracker, marketed sometimes as a high-end specialty product and other times as an Asian cracker. Either way, they're crunchy and delicious. You can also buy nut crackers, corn crackers, and even Ritz-type crackers you can order online.

✔ **Donuts:** Yep. You can buy gluten-free donuts. They usually come frozen, and you just defrost them on a very low power for a few seconds until they're ready (or better yet, let them sit at room temperature for about half an hour).

✔ **Frozen dinners and sides:** If you're new to this lifestyle, you may not get how incredible this is, but those who have been doing this for a very long time are shocked and awed by the fact that they can actually buy frozen dinners and side dishes — good ones! — at natural foods stores, online, or even at some regular grocery stores.

✔ **Pasta:** Gluten-free pasta these days comes in all shapes, sizes, and flavors. Made from white rice, brown rice, corn, quinoa, potato, and blends of all the above, you can find lasagna, penne, spaghetti, angel hair, fettuccini, macaroni, and any other cut of pasta you're looking for. Best of all, long gone are the days when pasta turned to mush and you needed a spoon to eat your spaghetti. Today's gluten-free pastas have the same texture as regular pasta and sometimes offer far more nutritional value.

✔ **Pre-made pizza crusts:** These pizza crusts usually come frozen (if not, you want to freeze them when you get home). Just take them out of the freezer; add your favorite sauce, cheese, and toppings; and bake for 10 to 15 minutes, and you have the gluten-free population's number-one-most-missed food: pizza!

See? With all these specialty products available, you don't have to miss out on anything on the gluten-free diet. Except gluten, of course!

Chapter 8

Shopping Is Easier Than You Think

· ·

In This Chapter

▶ Developing strategies before you head to the store

▶ Figuring out what you want to buy

▶ Going places: Pick a store, any store

▶ Getting the most for your gluten-free dollar

· ·

After the doctor diagnosed my son Tyler with celiac disease, the first thing I did was go shopping. No, not the head-for-the-mall-because-I'm-shattered-and-surely-a-new-outfit-will-make-me-feel-better kind of shopping. I went grocery shopping. This *is* a book about food, ya know.

Now keep in mind that this was way back in the 1900s — 1991, to be exact. There was no Internet, I had no books, no source of information that I knew of at all. When I told the crotchety hospital dietitian that I needed dietary guidelines, she thought I meant *glucose-free.* And when I insisted I meant *gluten-free,* she said, "We haven't had that before," and dug out a tattered sheet of 7,456 things Tyler would never be able to eat again.

So off to the store we went, and I asked then-toddler Tyler what he wanted for a snack. This was, after all, *his* diet (I've since gone gluten-free, too). His eyes lit up, and he declared, "Crackers," so we skipped to the cracker aisle together and began to read labels.

Could it be? No, nope, not here — no "gluten" on the label anywhere! Yessssss! This was going to be easier than I thought.

First, I have to defend my intelligence, lest you think I have the I.Q. of sand. I was in shock — we were shopping truly just hours after the diagnosis — and I wasn't thinking clearly. Second, it's true: None of the cracker packages had "gluten" on the label (okay, that one's weak). My maybe-if-I-hope-hard-enough-it'll-be-true story just goes to show you that you're not alone if you've been a little — ahem — stymied by the process of shopping for gluten-free foods.

The good news is that finding gluten-free products really *is* easier than you may think, and thanks to new labeling laws and manufacturer awareness, it's getting easier all the time.

In this chapter, I start by helping you figure out what you want to buy. Then I offer some guidance on where to shop, how to shop, and — this is important — how to save money on gluten-free foods. You can find important shopping tips to save you time, money, frustration, and the embarrassment of having to tell a story like mine.

Knowing What You Want

One of the best things you can do to make shopping easier when you're enjoying a gluten-free lifestyle is to plan ahead. If you try to wing it, especially at first, you end up spending hours in the grocery store walking in circles, trying to figure out what to eat, what to buy, and *then* worrying whether the food's gluten-free.

Not only do planning meals ahead of time and making shopping lists save you time and headaches in the store, but these steps give you the peace of mind that the meals you're planning are, in fact, gluten-free. Heck, if you've read Chapter 6, they may even be ultranutritious.

Planning your meals

In my other life, when I'm a businesswoman and not an author, I follow the dictum "plan your work, and work your plan." Same thing goes for meals, although "plan your meals and eat 'em" isn't quite as catchy or clever.

Most people think planning meals sounds like a great idea, and they're able to pull it off once or twice. But for the most part, they're spontaneous and impulsive. They see something in the store that looks particularly appealing (and because they're usually starving while they're shopping, *everything* looks good), and they toss it in the cart. But planning meals helps you strategize before you head to the store.

When you're planning your meals, try not to think in terms of cutting out gluten, but instead think of how you can make substitutions. Think about the things you love to eat — with or without gluten — and build around those foods, making the substitutions you need to make to convert gluten-containing meals into gluten-free ones. (In Chapter 9 I explain how to make *anything* gluten-free with simple substitutions.)

I know sitting down and making a meal plan is tough, but it pays off in spades when you're at the store and you find your busy weekdays speeding by. You may find some of these tips helpful:

- ✔ **Have the whole family eat gluten-free.** Even if some members of your family are still gluten-eaters, make your life simpler by planning most, if not all, of the family meals to be gluten-free. This planning isn't hard if you follow the approach of eating meats, fruits, vegetables, and other natural foods (see Chapter 6 for more on this approach). And even if your meal includes things like pasta, the gluten-free varieties these days are so delicious that the entire family will love them — and may not even know the difference.

- ✔ **Plan a few days' menus at once.** Look through cookbooks (no, they don't have to be gluten-free ones) and at individual recipes for inspiration, keeping in mind the healthy guidelines I talk about in Chapter 6. Remember, the gluten-free diet is *not* all about rice, corn, and potatoes. In fact, the more variety, the better. Variety isn't just the spice of life; it's important from a nutritional standpoint.

- ✔ **Plan a marathon cooking day.** Maybe you designate Sundays to be your day in the kitchen. With the week's worth of meals already in mind, you can prepare several meals at once, saving yourself time cooking *and* cleaning up during the week.

- ✔ **Use foods that can do double-duty.** If you're planning to cook a large roasting chicken for dinner one night (I just happen to have a tasty recipe for one in Chapter 13), you can count on leftovers for chicken stir-fry the next night.

- ✔ **Plan meals you can cook in a slow cooker.** Slow cookers are great for complete one-course meals. And walking into a house that smells like you've been cooking all day is so nice!

Have the whole family help with menu planning. Nothing is more frustrating than spending a weekend planning, shopping, and cooking only to hear moans and groans about how what used to be someone's favorite food is now "gross." For that matter, enlist help with the cooking and cleanup, too.

Making lists

Your spontaneity is exactly what food manufacturers are banking on. They want you to be impulsive, and that's why they tempt you with the delicious-but-oh-so-bad-for-you high-profit-margin foods at the ends of aisles and checkout stands. (I talk more about store layout in the section titled "Navigating the Aisles" because you need to know the marketing secrets so you don't get sucked in.) How many times have you roamed the grocery store thinking of yummy, healthy meals to make for the week, only to get home with dozens of bags of groceries, unable to remember a single meal? Yeah, me, too.

At the risk of sounding a little elementary here, shopping lists are really helpful. Not only do they remind you of foods and ingredients you need, but they help prevent impulse shopping.

Keep a running list of what you're running low on or what you need to buy next time you're at the store. Make sure the list is handy for everyone in the family so no one whines that you "forgot" a favorite food (when you didn't even know that *was* a favorite food).

As you do your menu planning, add the ingredients you need for your week's worth of meals to the list. If you need to call manufacturers to find out whether some of the ingredients are gluten-free, now's the best time to do it (if the product's not sitting in front of you, you can usually find the manufacturer's phone number online). Don't wait till you're in the store, because you may find the company's customer service representatives have all gone home for the day. Oh, and don't forget to take the list with you (that's a note to myself, because I usually forget it)!

If you're a coupon-clipper, clip your coupons and refer to your grocery list and the store ads. Can you replace items on your list with ones that are on sale or that you have coupons for? You may even find that the coupons provide inspiration for meal-planning.

Don't forget the snacks! Whether your idea of a snack is ice cream or raisins, snacks are an important part of your day. When you're making your shopping list, encourage your family members to add their favorite snacks — preferably the healthy kind — so you don't have to hear, "There's nothing to eat in this house!"

Deciding What to Buy

Obviously, the most important considerations for figuring out what to buy are what do you like, what are you going to make, and is it gluten-free?

Keep in mind the two kinds of gluten-free foods: those that companies make as specialty items and those that are naturally gluten-free.

Checking out gluten-free specialty products

Gluten-free specialty items come from companies that specifically market some or all of their products to the wheat-free/gluten-free community. Most of the time, these products are foods — such as pasta, bread, crackers, cookies, and brownies — that would normally have gluten in them but have been formulated to be gluten-free. (See Chapter 7 for more on available specialty items.)

The specialty products are almost always labeled "gluten-free," so you don't have to question their safety as far as your dietary restrictions are concerned. The companies that make these products generally make several product lines and sell their foods by mail, online, or at specialty retailers. These days, "regular" grocery stores are starting to carry more of these specialty items.

Don't forget that wheat-free doesn't mean gluten-free. If you see a package labeled "wheat-free," the contents may still contain barley, rye, oats, or derivatives of those ingredients.

Remembering naturally gluten-free foods

Many people think the gluten-free lifestyle limits them to buying foods that say "gluten-free" on the label. This is *so* not true! Limiting yourself to those foods is ultrarestrictive, and it also means you're overlooking lots of foods that are inherently — or naturally — gluten-free, some of which are the most nutritious of all. These are foods that contain no gluten, although the distributor doesn't necessarily market them as such. They include the obvious players — meat, poultry, fish, seafood, fruits, vegetables, and nuts — but they also include some products that seem like they may have gluten in them but don't.

Many foods, including candies, chips, popcorn, deli foods, condiments, and spices, are inherently gluten-free. Even some commercial cereals are gluten-free but aren't labeled as such. (What? A cereal without malt flavoring?!)

Asian foods — like rice wraps, many Thai foods, and most fish or oyster sauces — are good examples of foods that are often inherently gluten-free (remember, though, that soy sauce usually has wheat in it). Mexican and other ethnic cuisines also offer a lot of naturally gluten-free foods.

 The best foods are those without a label: meat, seafood, produce, and so on. But many other foods are gluten-free and don't say so on the label. Read the list of ingredients, and if you don't see anything blatantly off-limits, call the manufacturer to confirm that the food is gluten-free. You'll be surprised at how often you find products that you can safely enjoy.

 If you wear reading glasses, bring them to the store. You have to do lots of label-reading, and you want to have your glasses handy so you can read all the ingredients.

Asking for opinions

The last thing you want to do is spend gobs of money on specialty items and expensive foods only to find that they taste more like cardboard than cake. Because gluten-free foods can be pricey, and because some are great and some are awful, asking around about gluten-free foods and getting opinions from others who've tried them is more important than ever. Of course, opinions vary, and what one person loves, another may hate, but opinions can be valuable, especially if you hear several of them. (You know what they say about opinions: They're like stomachs — everyone has one.)

If you want to hear opinions on products, you have a lot of options. Try some of these places:

- ✔ **Support groups:** If you attend support group meetings, ask the members whether they've ever tried a particular product or whether they have suggestions for, say, brownies. You can get lots of helpful ideas this way.

- ✔ **Listserv:** You can subscribe to e-mail lists (I go into detail about these in Chapter 5). Posting questions and comments about glucose-free products is a valuable part of belonging to these lists.

- ✔ **Online rating systems:** Some of the online shopping Web sites offer customer ratings. See how many stars a product has, and read the comments to help you decide whether you want to buy it.

- ✔ **Shoppers:** If you see people at a store buying a product you haven't tried before, ask whether they've tried it and what they like or don't like about it. At the same time, if you've tried a product and see someone looking at it, speak up. He or she will appreciate the input, I assure you.

- ✔ **Store staff:** Sometimes the store staff members are very knowledgeable about products. Ask them if they've tried a particular product and what they like or don't like about it.

Logging on to food blogs

You've probably heard of blogs, and maybe you've even tossed in your two cents. A blog is kind of like a real-time global conversation on the Internet. Short for *weblog,* a blog is a Web site where people can contribute opinions about a particular subject. The newest comments go on top, so you can have interactive conversations.

In this case, food blogs are becoming popular, and it's just a matter of time before gluten-free blogs are commonplace. Blogs can allow consumers to get the word out about stores that provide huge assortments of gluten-free products, specialty mixes that work and those that don't, restaurants that serve great gluten-free meals, recipe suggestions, and the name of the baker who takes the time to understand how to make the perfect gluten-free bread. Exchanging product information is all about the continuing evolution of consumer power, and communication tools like blogs will most likely have a tremendous influence on how people shop for gluten-free products in the future.

When you find products that you and your family love and have confirmed to be gluten-free, save the label or part of the packaging. Keep the labels in a binder and create divided sections such as "soup," "candy," or whatever sections you like. Then bring the binder with you to the store so you can quickly spot the items again and rest easy, knowing that you like the product and it is, in fact, gluten-free.

Deciding Where to Shop

So you know what meals you want to make, you have at least some idea of what foods you want to buy, and you may even have a list in hand. Where do you get all this stuff (some of which you've never heard of before)? Well, for most of your shopping needs, you can pick a store — any store — because you're not as limited as you may think.

"Regular" grocery stores

You can do most of your shopping at "regular" grocery stores. Yep — the kind you find on every corner in most cities. If you're surprised by this, don't be. Remember, I encourage you to eat mostly foods that are inherently gluten-free, and you can find those at your friendly neighborhood grocery store.

Obviously, these stores are more convenient and less expensive than specialty stores. But from a psychological standpoint, you have a couple of other, less-tangible reasons for shopping at a regular grocery store.

First, a gluten-free diet can seem restrictive and even daunting to some people, and some even find it to be somewhat isolating (hopefully not when they're finished with *this* book). Being forced to shop only at specialty stores or online confirms those feelings of isolation and despair. Being able to shop at "regular" stores and buy "regular" brands that everyone else is buying is really liberating for people who feel this way.

If you have kids on the gluten-free diet, considering the psychological impact of shopping at regular grocery stores is even more important. Kids want to be like all the other kids and eat brands (and junk foods) that all the other kids eat. And that's okay — feeling that way is perfectly normal. For most kids, fitting in ranks right up there with breathing.

Regular brands aside, many major grocery stores are starting to carry more gluten-free specialty items; some even have entire gluten-free sections. If you have some favorite specialty products that you want your local store to carry, don't hesitate to ask the manager whether the store can carry them. How often you get a positive response may surprise you, and the manager may be surprised at how much interest customers have in the gluten-free products.

You may also be pleased to know that many of the regular grocery chains have lists of the gluten-free products they carry, both name brand and generic. Some of the stores post the lists on their Web sites, and others offer the lists if you call their customer service numbers.

Natural foods stores

Most natural foods stores are well aware of the growing interest in gluten-free products, and they're stocking up to meet the increasing demand. You find all the meats and vegetables (usually organic) that are such a big part of the gluten-free diet, but you also find lots of gluten-free specialty items. Some natural foods stores even have dedicated gluten-free sections.

Because natural foods stores have become so popular, they've expanded their offerings and generally provide a huge array of exotic and gourmet health foods, supplements, and even cosmetics and household goods. Shopping at some of these places is more like being in a fun zone than a food zone.

Farmers' markets

Coming soon to a corner near you! Farmers' markets are popping up everywhere (not just next to farms), offering fresh produce, eggs, meat, fish, honey, nuts, and other (inherently gluten-free) items usually at prices far below those of most retailers. The foods are ripe, organic is the rule rather than the exception, and the generous samples that sellers pass out are enough to count as lunch.

You can also feel good knowing you're supporting local farmers and the environment: The food is usually grown without pesticides, and not having to ship the foods long distances uses less energy and gasoline.

Ethnic markets

You want a thrill? Go to an Asian market — the more authentic, the better — and check out all the stuff that's gluten-free. Don't forget the Thai and Indian aisles. Truly, the selection is amazing. Sauces, rice wraps, tapioca noodles, rice candies, things you've never heard of, and things that you may wonder about for years — all gluten-free. Of course, they're not labeled as such, but that's okay. If the label is in English, you can see for yourself that gluten isn't in many of the foods. Asians use very little wheat in their products.

Other ethnic cuisines may surprise and delight as well. Mexican is just one of the many other cultures that use lots of inherently gluten-free ingredients in their cooking. Explore new cultures without ever leaving your country and experience a thrill of the gluten-free variety.

Low-carb stores

Don't misunderstand me — low-carb does *not* mean gluten-free or even gluten-light. In fact, sometimes low-carb versions of a food have more gluten than their higher-carb counterparts. For a more-detailed explanation of why low-carb doesn't translate to gluten-free, check out Chapter 6 and see how they compare.

Low-carb stores are still popular, and they do have some foods that are safe on the gluten-free diet. You have to read the labels carefully.

Gluten-free retail stores

I'm not making this up. Once only a dream for those who have been gluten-free for a long time, gluten-free stores are finally a reality. Entire stores filled with gluten-free foods, books about being gluten-free, cookbooks, and other important resources are beginning to pop up, and I'm delighted to say they're thriving. You'll be seeing more and more of these, so keep your eyes open for a store opening near you.

Web sites and catalogs

You can do all your gluten-free shopping from the comfort of your favorite easy chair, any time day or night — you can even be in your wumfiest jammies, if you want. There are some great Web sites that specialize in selling gluten-free products, and within just a few minutes you can place your order. A couple of days later your shipment arrives at your doorstep — and you may be so excited to rip open that big box of gluten-free goodies, you feel like a kid at the holidays!

All the gluten-free specialty food manufacturers have Web sites, so if you know a specific brand you want to buy, you can go to the site and see what they have to offer (you can find the sites with a quick Google search). But here are a couple sites you can buy several different brands from:

✔ www.glutensolutions.com

✔ www.glutenfreemall.com

Some sites allow you to sort out other allergens, too, so you can narrow down the products that are, for instance, gluten-free, casein-free, corn-free, and soy-free. Some sites also provide customer rating systems. They give you an average customer rating and specific comments about a product. This type of a customer rating system is invaluable in helping you decide which products to buy.

If you don't have a computer, most companies offer a toll-free number, and some will send you a free catalog so you can order by phone or fax.

Navigating the Aisles

You thought grocery shopping was just a matter of steering the cart up and down the aisles, didn't you? And I bet you thought *you* were in control of your purchases, right? Actually, for decades now, grocery store psychologists have been studying ways to get people to spend more, and they've come up with subtle and subliminal ways to turn us all into Stepford Shoppers, falling victim to strategically placed temptations scattered about the store like land mines.

Copy a safe and forbidden ingredients list off the Internet (try the "Safe & Forbidden Gluten-Free Foods & Ingredients" list at www.celiac.com) and bring it with you to the store. You may need it when you're reading ingredients on product labels.

Perusing the perimeter

One of the best ways to avoid some of those glaring gluten temptations at the store is to shop the perimeter. Store layouts are predictable; produce, dairy, meat, and other staples are as far from the front door of the store as possible so that you have to walk past all the more expensive (and usually less nutritious) foods before you get to what you really want.

Planning impulsive purchases

High-powered grocery store psychologists have spent billions of retail-funded dollars on studies that finally concluded with a shocking revelation: Shoppers are impulsive. So the stores capitalize on your impulsivity by planning your impulsive purchases. "Planned impulsivity" may at first seem to be an oxymoron, but it's exactly what stores are creating when they strategize everything from where to place items to what music they play in the background.

Don't tell me you haven't fallen for the marketing. You're at the store for just a few items ("I'll just use a hand basket"), and you walk out with a cartload of things you didn't even know you wanted. You're captivated by flashing coupon dispensers, in-aisle displays, free samples, and heavily loaded end caps at the end of each aisle — all of which are there because the psychologists have done their homework. And don't forget the fact that your kids are the primary targets, as they tend to be quite influential when you make your impulsive purchases.

Rarely are these so-called *impulse* purchases directing you toward healthy foods, much less gluten-free ones. If you're having a hard time sticking to the diet, or if you find being tempted by the gluttonous gluten products out there to be daunting, be aware of the efforts to snare you at the stores, and have your guard up against impulsive gluten-containing purchases.

For the most part, the gluten-free items on your list are along the perimeter of the store. If your store has a good health food aisle, you may be able to find gluten-free pastas, mixes, cereals, bars, and other items. Your best bet in general, though, is to stick to the fruits, vegetables, meats, and dairy items — most of which are around the outsides. Just think of how much time you can save by not having to go through the cracker, cookie, and bread aisles!

Sorting through the health food aisle

At first, the health food aisles may seem to be the best bet for finding gluten-free foods. Not necessarily.

Health food aisles are full of product labels screaming "whole grain" or "multigrain." Lots of "healthy" foods are loaded with whole grains to provide fiber and nutrients, and although the gluten-free diet sometimes allows whole grains like brown rice, millet, or quinoa, for instance, most of the whole grains in those products contain gluten.

Health food sections do offer some benefits. The longer a food's ingredients list is, the less likely it is to be gluten-free, and health food aisles are good places to find items that have short ingredients lists. Read them carefully!

I'm excited to see that the major grocery stores are starting to carry a larger variety of gluten-free specialty products in their health food aisles. If your favorite grocery store carries gluten-free products, tell the manager how much you appreciate it and even make suggestions for products the store could carry that it doesn't. Chances are, store managers are "testing" the gluten-free products, and your feedback may be valuable in making sure the stores continue to carry them.

Living Gluten-Free — Affordably

One of the most common complaints I hear about the gluten-free diet is that it's more expensive — but it doesn't need to be. Yes, I understand that a loaf of regular bread is less than half the cost of a loaf of gluten-free bread. And the fact that gluten-free crackers and cookies are often smaller *and* twice the price of regular cookies isn't lost on me, either. And yes, I've paid more than my fair share in shipping expenses, too. But you have ways to save significant amounts of money when you're enjoying a gluten-free lifestyle. So before you take a second mortgage on your house to finance this diet, take note of these tips that can save you a bunch.

Scaling back on specialties

Most of the "extra expense" of the gluten-free diet is in the high cost of specialty items. I'm not suggesting you celebrate little Preston's birthday with store-bought rice crackers to save the expense of making a gluten-free cake. You need to have *some* specialty items on hand, and cakes or special-occasion treats are definitely among them.

But if you find you're spending way too much money to accommodate this diet, take a look at how many and what types of specialty items you buy. Breads, crackers, cookies, cakes, pizzas, pretzels, donuts — they're pricey, for sure. But you don't need them. You can substitute store-bought chips for a fraction of the cost of gluten-free pretzels. Even as high-priced as they are, candies and candy bars that you can get at any grocery store are far cheaper than specialty treats.

And really, most of the specialty items aren't good for you, anyway — they're high-calorie, high-glycemic-index foods (they raise your blood sugar quickly) that provide very little nutritional value. If you follow the more nutritious approach to gluten-free eating that I outline in Chapter 6, you find very little room for these expensive indulgences.

Some of the specialty items people buy are unnecessary. Gluten-free vanilla is a good example: All vanilla is gluten-free! You don't need to buy it as a specialty item.

Tax deductions for the gluten-free

Believe it or not, there's a tax-deduction available when you buy gluten-free food, but not everyone can take advantage of the deduction. You can deduct the *difference* in price between gluten-free products and "regular" food products. Here's an example using a loaf of bread:

Gluten-free bread:	$5.00
"Regular" bread:	$2.00
Difference in price:	$3.00

You can deduct the $3.00 difference. The cost of items you wouldn't normally need to buy, like xanthan gum, are completely deductible. Shipping costs are deductible, too. But to qualify, your unreimbursed medical expenses must exceed 7.5 percent of your adjusted gross income. That's a pretty tall order for most people. You also need a letter from your doctor saying that a gluten-free diet is medically necessary for you. All these expenses are reimbursable under a health care spending account of pretax income. Consult a tax advisor for more information.

Some specialty items may be important to have on hand. Pasta, some special-occasion treats, and maybe some bread or bagels, for instance. But in general, most people buy more specialty items than they need, and it definitely puts a burden on the budget.

Saving on shipping

If you do buy specialty items, you can find ways to save on shipping. For one, you can ask your local grocery or natural foods store to carry the product you want — that way the store pays for the shipping, not you.

If you're ordering online, order from a company that sells many different brands of products. That way, you pay one shipping charge for several different brands. Buying products onesey-twosey from individual manufacturers costs you a fortune in shipping.

Going generic

Don't assume that generics are off-limits on this diet. Most of the time, generic products are as clearly labeled as major brands, and sometimes a toll-free number is listed on the package so you can call to confirm whether the item is gluten-free. Usually generics are labeled as being "distributed by" a large grocery chain or distribution company. Dig a little — call toll-free information or go on the Internet to get a phone number for the large grocery chain or distribution company. Most of the time, you can find a customer service representative there who can help you find out more about the ingredients.

If the generics are a store brand, chances are good that you'll be able to get lots of information about the products. Some of the large grocery chains have lists of their gluten-free generics, and sometimes those lists are even available online. If you want more information about a store's generic products, call its toll-free number and ask to talk with the head of quality control or the nutrition department. I did this once and was pleased to hear from the lead nutritionist that the modified food starch in all of their generic products was derived from corn. That little bit of information was immensely helpful in realizing that even more generics than I'd known were gluten-free.

Eating nutritiously

Some people think that eating nutritious foods is more expensive. Not true. Fresh produce and meats do seem expensive — they are! But chips and other processed, blood-sugar-raising foods — which not only are worthless nutritionally speaking but also cause weight gain and make you hungrier — are a complete waste of money.

Developing good shopping habits

In addition to what I cover in this chapter, you can do lots of things that save you time and money when you shop. Here's a list to get you started:

✔ **Don't shop when you're hungry.** If you shop on an empty stomach, you're more vulnerable to falling victim to impulse purchases.

✔ **Bring a list.** Planning before you head for the grocery store keeps you focused on the healthy and gluten-free foods you need and makes you less likely to impulsively buy things you don't.

✔ **Stock up when you can.** Buying food in larger quantities is almost always cheaper if you can afford to do so and if you have somewhere to store the food. Remember that gluten-free foods often have a short shelf life, so if you're going to stock up on

pre-made products, make sure you have room in your freezer.

✔ **Consider co-ops.** Co-ops aren't in all parts of the country, but if you have one nearby, they're a great way to save money. The idea is that a group of people form a cooperative, buy food in bulk, and then offer the food to others to buy. Usually anyone can become a member for a small charge (nonmembers can buy, too, but usually for a surcharge). The focus is nearly always on healthy foods.

✔ **Join membership clubs.** Membership clubs are usually the big warehouse-type stores. One of the world's largest has recently begun carrying a large selection of gluten-free products. These stores are especially good if you want to buy in bulk, because most of their products are supersized.

- ✔ **Use coupons, flyers, rebates, and frequent-shopper programs.** Using coupons isn't just a fun way to annoy the people behind you. You can save hundreds of dollars a year by taking advantage of product incentives. Even if you're a less-than-enthusiastic coupon clipper, try to find a few to use each week, and don't forget to check the circulars that are at the front of the stores. They always list weekly specials, and they're usually for the meats and produce, which are gluten-free. If the store is out of an advertised special, ask for a rain check. You can get the sale price when the store has more of the product in stock.

- ✔ **Dare to compare.** Always look at the unit price of a product, not just the package price. Stores list unit prices on the price tags on the grocery shelves. The package price tells you only the cost of the entire item, whereas the unit price shows the cost per pound, ounce, and so on. This way, when you compare the price of one item to another, you're comparing apples-to-apples.

  If you don't have one already on your pocket protector, you may want to consider bringing a small (or large, if you're more the analytical type) calculator with you. Most stores offer cost-per-unit prices, but sometimes they mix up the units, so one item — take juice, for instance — will be in cost per ounce, while its competitor is in cost per box. If you have your handy-dandy calculator with you, you can make an accurate comparison and choose the best value.

- ✔ **Keep your eye on the scanner.** So you may have to forego the magazine that tells which celeb is giving birth to alien twins or how to lose all the weight you want in 23 seconds, but watching to make sure the price the scanner rings up is what you thought it would be is important. Stores do make mistakes. And a lot of times, believe it or not, those mistakes are not in your favor.

- ✔ **If possible, don't shop with your kids.** Yeah, they're adorable, but they're enemy number one when you're trying to resist the impulsive shopping that grocery stores are counting on. Kids are their primary targets. Notice where the sugary cereals are located — right at eye-level for an irresistible 5-year-old. Grocery stores are counting on your kids to lure you into impulsive purchases of high-profit-margin treats like cereals and snack foods.

- ✔ **Buy generics.** Lots of generic products are gluten-free. Some stores have lists of their gluten-free generics available at the customer service desk or on the Internet.

Buy nutritious foods, but buy only what you need. Most nutritious foods are also perishable, and if you don't use them within a few days, "fresh" produce isn't so fresh anymore.

Eating in

Eating out at restaurants or fast-food places eats through a budget in no time. Eating at home not only ensures that your meal is, in fact, gluten-free, but it also saves you money.

Sure, planning and preparing home-cooked meals takes time (I give some time-saving tips in Chapter 9), but the money you save and the peace of mind knowing your meals are nutritious and gluten-free are well worth it.

Using gluten-free mixes

The gluten-free mixes for baked goods like brownies, cakes, cookies, and breads may seem expensive, and they are. But compare them to the cost of buying several different types of specialty flours, xanthan gum (a must-have in gluten-free baking recipes), and other ingredients you need to make those homemade baked goods — then add on the cost of the failed attempts (you *will* have some failures), and suddenly the surefire-taste-delicious-and-always-turn-out-right mixes seem like a bargain.

Chapter 9

Cooking: Tips and Techniques

· ·

· ·

I have some unique cooking tips and techniques that can help in your gluten-free cooking adventures, and I cover them in this chapter. Those of you who know me or have watched me cook are smirking right now, because the truth of the matter is that I have a — ahem — *different* style of cooking, and you're probably wondering what I'm doing giving cooking tips. I don't want to point fingers, but my editors made me do it! Somehow, they didn't think "open bag of mix, approximate measurements, and improvise" would sit well with those of you who want to do real cooking.

Basically, I follow a few simple rules of cooking:

✔ Measuring is for patient people. I don't qualify.

✔ If a recipe calls for ¼ teaspoon of something, why bother?

✔ If a recipe calls for more than 12 ingredients, and if I have to go to a foreign country to purchase any of them, I don't bother.

✔ What's a sifter for?

✔ If you bake it in your oven, it *is* homemade. Therefore, by definition, using mixes qualifies as homemade cooking.

Don't get me wrong. I do cook — a lot. In fact, I love to cook. But I do it my way, and my measuring terms consist of *dollop, gob,* and *itsy bit,* and I use them interchangeably.

If you like the more technical approach, that's okay. The tips and techniques in this chapter apply to you whether you're my kind of cook or of the more scrupulous variety.

Creatively Gluten-Free: Improvising in the Kitchen

I believe that if you give a person a recipe, you feed him for a meal; teach him to make recipes gluten-free, and you feed him for a lifetime.

I have an enormous amount of respect and admiration for the Real Cookbook Authors out there, especially after writing the recipe section of this book. So if you love recipes, you may be delighted to know that this book includes 65 recipes and that there are dozens of excellent gluten-free cookbooks by Real Cookbook Authors.

But I also think finding out how to improvise and cook *anything* gluten-free has a lot of value. Sometimes that means taking a recipe for something that normally has gluten in it and modifying it to be gluten-free. Other times, that means throwing caution to the wind and doing without a recipe altogether.

No single ingredient is more important in gluten-free cooking than creativity. You may not always have ingredients on hand to make the gluten-free dish you want to make. You may not have a recipe handy for a meal you have in mind. You may think you have no way to convert your old favorite standby into a gluten-free goodie. Don't let any of those things stop you. Cooking gluten-free is actually easy if you improvise, explore alternatives, and stretch the boundaries of your creativity in the kitchen.

Adapting any dish to be gluten-free

Pop quiz: You're standing in line at the grocery store, mindlessly perusing the magazines offering valuable, up-to-date, star-struck gossip and surefire ways to lose all your belly fat in less than ten minutes, when the cover of your favorite cooking magazine catches your eye. It's a beautiful photo of (insert favorite food here), glistening with — agh! — Gluten! You:

A) Leave the store in tears, feeling sorry for yourself as you pathetically choke down a rice cake.

B) Buy the magazine as a reminder of a past life of gluten-gluttony.

C) Delight in knowing that because you or someone you love bought you this copy of *Living Gluten-Free For Dummies,* you can easily and confidently modify that recipe to be deliciously gluten-free.

The right answer is, of course, C. You can modify nearly any dish to be gluten-free. Some dishes are easier than others — baked goods are the toughest, so I deal with those last. You can go one of two ways when you're adapting a dish to be gluten-free: with a recipe or without.

Starting with a recipe

If you're following a recipe for something that's not gluten-free and you want to convert it, start by reviewing the list of ingredients the recipe calls for. Make a note of those that usually have gluten in them. Then, using the substitutions I suggest in this chapter or some of your own, substitute gluten-free ingredients as you need to.

For the most part, when you make substitutions, measurements convert equally — with the exception of flours, which I discuss in the section "Substituting gluten-free flours."

Don't have the right substitutions? Improvise. For instance, if a recipe calls for dredging something in flour before sautéing and you don't have any gluten-free flours, maybe you have a gluten-free mix that would work. Pancake mix, even muffin mix, can work quite well as a substitute for a flour coating.

Cooking without a recipe

If you're not using a recipe, creativity once again prevails. Say you want to make chicken nuggets. You certainly don't need a recipe for that; just slice some chicken and figure out what you want to coat it in before frying or baking. Put some of your favorite gluten-free barbecue potato chips in a plastic bag, and crunch them up. Now you have a coating!

At the risk of belaboring a point, you have to be creative. The substitution ideas in this chapter are just that — ideas. Coming up with substitutions that work for your convenience, preference, and budget is up to you.

Avoiding cross-contamination when cooking

After you've worked hard to create a delicious, gluten-free meal, you wouldn't go dust a bunch of wheat flour all over it, would you? Of course not. Yet sometimes the *way* you cook food can contaminate it as though you had done just that, and you may not be aware that your food is being contaminated.

Cooking gluten-containing foods at the same time as gluten-free ones is okay, but just be aware that cross-contamination during the cooking process is a very real consideration, and be careful not to glutenate (contaminate with gluten) your food inadvertently. Here are some things to watch out for:

- **Cooking utensils:** You can't flip a gluten-containing hamburger bun with a spatula and then flip a burger. Well, you can, but that burger is no longer gluten-free. Same thing goes for tossing the pasta and stirring the sauce. Use separate utensils while you're cooking, and keep track of which one is which.

✔ **Double-duty cooking surfaces:** If you're cooking gluten-containing and gluten-free foods on the same griddle, grills, or cookie sheets or in the same pans, you should cook the gluten-free version first. If that just doesn't work, you can use the same cooking surface for both versions, but be sure to find a clean spot for your gluten-free foods.

✔ **Frying oil:** When you fry breaded products in oil, bits of the breading or batter stay in the oil when you're finished frying. So if you fry gluten-containing foods in oil, don't use that same oil to fry your gluten-free foods. Either fry the gluten-free foods first or use completely separate pans and fresh oil for the gluten-free foods.

If you're cooking both glutenous and gluten-free foods in your fryer, you'll need to be extra diligent when you're cleaning it to make sure you get all the gluten out. If your fryer isn't easy to clean thoroughly, you may want to consider having separate fryers.

Using standby substitutions

To convert a recipe that usually contains gluten into one that's gluten-free, you need to make some simple substitutions. For the most part, with the exception of flours you use when making baked goods, the substitutions are simple — just swap one for the other. I cover flours for baked goods separately, later in this chapter.

✔ **Beer:** Some foods, especially deep-fried foods, may call for beer in the recipe. You can use either the gluten-free beers available online or try cider instead.

✔ **Binders:** A binder is just something that holds foodstuff together. Because gluten provides elasticity and stretch to baked goods, adding binders to foods that don't have gluten-containing flours in them is a good idea. Binders include xanthan gum, guar gum, gelatin powder (this is cool, too, because it adds protein and moisture), and eggs.

✔ **Breadcrumbs:** No-brainer here. Anyone who's ever eaten a piece of gluten-free bread (especially without toasting it) knows that breadcrumbs aren't hard to come by. You can buy gluten-free breadcrumbs from specialty stores or online, but if you can't or don't want to get those, consider using any gluten-free bread: Put the bread in a plastic bag and smoosh it into the size of crumbs you want. You can even toast the crumbs if you want added crunch or need dry breadcrumbs instead of fresh ones. Crushed cereals work well in place of breadcrumbs, too. Also consider using mashed potato flakes or quinoa flakes.

✓ **Bun:** Consider using a lettuce wrap, corn tortilla, or of course, gluten-free bread. Some good gluten-free buns are available online and at specialty shops.

✓ **Coatings:** If a recipe calls for some type of coating, you have several options. You can despair and not make the dish (Ha! Kidding!) or consider using any of the gluten-free flours I list later in this chapter, as well as any versatile gluten-free mix you have lying around, such as a mix for bread, muffins, or pancakes. Cornmeal or corn flour *(masa)* with seasonings mixed in adds an interesting texture, and crushed barbecue potato chips (gluten-free, of course) are one of my personal all-time favorites. You may also want to look into commercial brands of Cajun-style coatings, usually marketed as seafood seasonings (but shhhhhh . . . don't tell anyone . . . I use them on chicken!). Many of those are just cornmeal with some spices added.

✓ **"Cream of" soups:** Use chicken broth and sour cream or half-and-half. Remember to add the food the soup is a cream of — mushroom, celery, potato, and so on — to complete the soup.

✓ **Croutons:** Homemade croutons are actually very easy to make. Most recipes for croutons suggest you use stale bread, but I don't suggest you do that for gluten-free bread, because you'd probably end up with crumbled crouton crumbs instead. Cut fresh gluten-free bread into the size cubes you want and deep-fry them. After you drain and cool them, roll them in Parmesan cheese, spices, or any other flavoring you like. See Chapter 12 for a lower-fat version and other crouton substitutions.

✓ **Fillers:** *Filler* is a highly technical culinary term for something that fills stuff in. Yum. Generally not something you hope to see on a label, fillers aren't always a bad thing; they may be in meatloaf, for example, where the recipe often calls for breadcrumbs, crackers, and other filler-type materials to add, well, *filling*. Gluten-free bread or breadcrumbs are obvious substitutions here, but also consider leftover corn bread, mashed potato flakes, or even an unsweetened cereal that you've crushed up.

✓ **Flour:** Many recipes call for flour, usually to serve as a thickener (see the suggested thickeners in this list). Also consider using gluten-free flours such as rice flour, sweet rice flour (they're different), potato starch, sorghum flour, garbanzo/fava bean flour, and Montina (Indian ricegrass flour).

✓ **Flour tortillas:** The obvious substitution here is corn tortillas. Some new gluten-free flour tortillas are on the market now, and you can find recipes for homemade tortillas online or in cookbooks. Other wrap substitutions include rice wraps (found in Asian markets and featured in a few recipes in this book) or lettuce.

✓ **Pie crust:** One of the easiest ways to make a pie crust is to take your favorite cereal and smash it into tiny crumbs, add some butter (and sugar, if the cereal isn't sweet enough), and then press the mixture into the bottom of a pie pan. Some good gluten-free crackers and cookies work well the same way. Some pie crusts are supposed to be cooked before adding the pie filling, and others aren't. The fact that the crust is gluten-free doesn't change whether you need to cook the crust before filling the pie. Also check out some of the gluten-free pie crust mixes available on the Internet and at specialty stores.

✔ **"Special" sauce:** I've got news for ya, Jack. The secret's out: You can make their "special" sauce with just mayo and ketchup, both of which are gluten-free!

✔ **Soy sauce:** Most soy sauce has wheat in it (and the label clearly indicates wheat), but you can find brands that are wheat-free. (By the way, *tamari* — a thicker, Japanese soy sauce — is not always wheat-free, so check the label.) Either use a wheat-free soy sauce or try Bragg Liquid Aminos. You may also want to get adventurous and try an Asian sauce like fish sauce (careful — it's really fishy!) or oyster sauce.

✔ **Teriyaki:** Because most soy sauce has wheat in it, most teriyaki (which is made from soy sauce) does, too. A few brands of wheat-free teriyaki sauces are available, but don't be afraid to make your own (see my recipe in the "Making teriyaki sauce" sidebar).

✔ **Thickeners:** Many recipes call for flour as a thickener, but lots of alternatives are available. For sweet things, try using a dry pudding mix or gelatin. ClearJel works well with acidic ingredients (unlike cornstarch), tolerates high temperatures, and doesn't cause pie fillings to "weep" during storage. Arrowroot flour, agar, tapioca starch, and cornstarch are also excellent thickeners. So is sweet rice flour, which comes from sticky or glutinous rice (despite the name, it really is gluten-free). And remember that muffin or cake mix you have lying around. Not only do mixes thicken the recipe, but the sweet flavor is a pleasant surprise. You can find more information on using gluten-free thickeners in the section "Thickening with gluten-free starches and flours."

Making teriyaki sauce

Actually, the term *teriyaki* refers to a method of cooking, derived from the Japanese words *teri,* meaning *luster,* and *yaki,* meaning *grill* or *broil* (cleverly combined to form the word *teriyaki*). Traditional teriyaki dishes are marinated in the sauce and then grilled or broiled, creating a shiny *(teri)* glaze. Although you can substitute for it, the key ingredient in teriyaki sauce is *mirin,* a sweet Japanese rice wine for cooking.

✔ ½ cup soy sauce

✔ ½ cup mirin (***Note:*** If you don't have mirin, use ½ cup of sake and 1 tablespoon of sugar.)

✔ 3 tablespoons sugar

In a small saucepan, mix together the soy sauce, mirin, and sugar. Heat on low heat for about 3 minutes and then let the sauce cool. You can store teriyaki sauce in a clean bottle in the fridge.

Cooking with Wheat Alternatives

Most gluten-free cooking is pretty straightforward. You just substitute gluten-free ingredients for the gluten-containing ones, and for the most part, you're set. The process is a little different for baked goods, as I explain later in this chapter. But most gluten-free cooking isn't much different from "regular" cooking, especially if you follow the theme of this chapter and let your creative side take over.

Incorporating alternative gluten-free grains

Not only are the gluten-free grains and grain alternatives that I talk about in Chapter 4 ultranutritious, but they add unique flavors and textures to foods, too. For the most part, cooking them is just like cooking other grains, as you can see in Part III of this book and in cookbooks. But you need to know a few things to perfect the art of using alternative gluten-free grains.

When cooking gluten-free grains as whole grains (as opposed to using them as a flour in baked goods), you find these alternative grains cook like most whole grains — just toss them in boiling water, reduce the heat so the water simmers, and you're set. The grain-to-water proportion and cooking times are really the only things that vary. Table 8-1 has some approximations of amounts of liquids and cooking time; you can modify them to suit your preferences.

Table 8-1	Cooking Alternative Grains	
Gluten-Free Grain (1 Cup)	*Water or Chicken Broth*	*Cooking Time*
Amaranth	2½ cups	20 to 25 minutes
Brown rice (long or short grain)	3 cups	40 minutes
Buckwheat	2 cups	15 to 20 minutes
Corn (grits)	3 cups	5 to 10 minutes
Millet	3 cups	35 to 45 minutes
Quinoa	2 cups	15 to 20 minutes
Teff	2 cups	15 to 20 minutes
White rice	2 cups	15 minutes
Wild rice	4 cups	45 minutes

Quinoa, millet, teff, amaranth, buckwheat, and the other alternative grains are great additions to soups, stuffing, and other foods. Here are some places you can use alternative grains, whether you precook them or simply toss them in with the other ingredients:

- **Snacks:** Using a little oil in a pan, you can pop amaranth grains on the stove like popcorn and eat them seasoned or plain.

- **Soups:** Use buckwheat, quinoa, or millet in soups instead of rice or noodles. No need to cook the grains first; just add them to the soup as you're cooking it. Remember, they absorb the liquid and double in volume. Whole amaranth and teff are too small, and they may seem gritty in soups, although both work well to thicken soups if you use the flour form of them.

- **Stuffing:** Use the larger alternative grains such as cooked quinoa, millet, or buckwheat instead of breadcrumbs or croutons in stuffing. Season the stuffing to your taste and then stuff vegetables, poultry, or pork tenderloins.

Thickening with gluten-free starches and flours

People usually use starch-based thickeners such as cornstarch, arrowroot, and tapioca to thicken their sauces and gravies. Starch thickeners give food a transparent, glistening sheen, which looks great for pie fillings and in glazes, but the thickeners don't always look quite right in gravy or sauce, so knowing which ones to use is important.

 To thicken with gluten-free starches, mix the starch with an equal amount of cold liquid until it forms a paste. Then whisk the paste into the liquid you're trying to thicken. After you add the thickener to the liquid, cook it for at least 30 seconds or so to get rid of the starchy flavor. But be careful you don't overcook it — liquids that you thicken with these starches may get thin again if you cook them too long or at too high of a temperature.

Some of these flours have the advantage of working well with foods that are acidic. Acidic foods include canned or glazed fruits, citrus, tomatoes, and vinegar. Bananas, figs, avocados, and potatoes are examples of foods that aren't acidic (they're alkaline).

Take a look at your options for thickeners:

- **Arrowroot:** If you're looking for that shiny gloss for dessert sauces or glazes, arrowroot is a good bet. Use arrowroot if you're thickening an acidic liquid but not if you're using dairy products (it makes them slimy). Arrowroot has the most neutral taste of all the starch thickeners, so if you're worried that a thickener may change or mask the flavor of your dish, use arrowroot. You can freeze the sauces you make with arrowroot.

✔ **ClearJel:** This modified cornstarch works especially well for fruit pie fillings because it blends well with acidic ingredients, tolerates high temperatures, and doesn't cause pie fillings to "weep" during storage. It also doesn't begin thickening until the liquid begins to cool, which allows the heat to be more evenly distributed within the jar if you're canning.

✔ **Cornstarch:** Cornstarch is the best choice for thickening dairy-based sauces, but don't use it for acidic foods. Cornstarch isn't as shiny as tapioca or arrowroot. Don't use cornstarch if you're freezing the sauce, or the sauce will get spongy.

✔ **Potato starch:** Usually used to thicken soups and gravies, potato starch doesn't work well in liquids that you boil. Unlike cornstarch and some other grain-based foods, potato starch is a permitted ingredient for Passover.

Potato flour and potato starch flour are different. Potato flour is very heavy and tastes very much like potatoes. Potato starch flour is very fine, with a bland taste. It's great to mix with other flours for baking or to use as a thickener for soups or gravies.

✔ **Tapioca:** You can use pearl tapioca or tapioca granules to thicken puddings and pies, but they don't completely dissolve when you cook them, so you end up with tiny gelatinous balls. If you like the balls, you can also use instant tapioca to thicken soups, gravies, and stews. If you don't like them, you can get tapioca starch, which is already finely ground. Tapioca gives a glossy sheen and can tolerate prolonged cooking and freezing.

You can use any of the alternative grains to thicken sauces, gravies, stews, puddings — anything! Depending on what you're making, you can use whole grains or flours as a thickener. You probably want to use a flour instead of whole grain to thicken something like gravy, but whole grains add lots of nutrition and work well to thicken soups and stews.

When you're using these flours or starches as thickeners, substitution amounts are a little different. Instead of 1 tablespoon of all-purpose flour, use

✔ **Agar:** ½ tablespoon

✔ **Arrowroot:** 2 teaspoons

✔ **Cornstarch:** ½ tablespoon

✔ **Gelatin powder:** ½ tablespoon

✔ **Rice flour (brown or white):** 1 tablespoon

✔ **Sweet potato flour:** 1 tablespoon

Trying Your Hand at Gluten-Free Baking

I won't sugarcoat the situation: Baking is the trickiest type of gluten-free cooking you can try. But it's getting easier. Years ago, gluten-free baking produced brick-like breads and cakes that crumbled when you exposed them to air.

Gluten is what makes baked goods stretchy, elastic, and *doughy*. It also forms a support structure to hold the gases that expand and to help the bread rise and become fluffy. Without gluten, baked foods tend to either crumble excessively or be dense enough to double as a lethal weapon. Using xanthan gum and combining gluten-free flours are the keys to creating gluten-free baked goods that are just as good as the real deal.

Mixing it up with mixes

Swallowing your pride is a lot better than swallowing a dry wad doing its best to impersonate a cookie, don't you think? Sure, cooking from scratch is terrific, and these days, especially with the help of the Real Cookbook Authors, the success rate is high (certainly higher than it was when I started on my self-taught-gluten-free-baking-from-scratch adventures in the early 1990s).

But consider using some of the incredible gluten-free mixes now available for pancakes, cookies, cakes, breads, brownies, biscuits, pizza crust, pie crust, muffins, and just about anything else you can think of. Many of the mixes are so good these days that they rival even the best homemade gluten-containing foods. They're simple to make (have the kids help!) and fill the house with that June-Cleaver-lives-here smell of freshly baked treats.

Most of the mixes simply require an egg or egg substitute, water or milk, and oil. Many of the companies are aware of multiple food intolerances and offer casein-free, corn-free, soy-free, and other allergen-free products. You can keep it simple or jazz it up, adding your favorite ingredients and accommodating other allergies and intolerances. See Chapter 7 for a list of what kind of mixes you may want to have on hand.

The most common complaint I hear about mixes is that they're expensive — and they are. But when you consider that they're pretty much fail-proof, and when you add up the cost of some of the specialty gluten-free baking ingredients, like special flours and xanthan gum — and then you add on top of that the fact that sometimes when you bake gluten-free foods from scratch, you have some failures that you end up feeding to the dog — you realize that at $6.50 per cookie that didn't turn out, the *dog food* is expensive; the mix is a good deal.

Introducing xanthan gum: The star of the dough

Boasting unique properties that enhance the consistency of foods, xanthan gum is a key ingredient in successful gluten-free baking. Basically, it holds particles of foods together, and it's the component in salad dressings, gravies, sauces, and ice creams that gives those foods a creamy, rich, smooth texture. Xanthan gum has proven to work well in gluten-free foods, providing the stretch and elasticity that gluten usually offers.

Here's a guide for how much xanthan gum to use for each cup of gluten-free flour:

- **Breads:** 1 heaping teaspoon
- **Cakes:** ½ teaspoon
- **Cookies:** ¼ teaspoon
- **Muffins:** ¾ teaspoons
- **Pizza:** 2 teaspoons

I warn you, xanthan gum is pricey. Some people use guar gum instead, usually because it's cheaper. But be aware that guar gum is high in fiber content and can have a laxative effect.

When you're making gluten-free dough, use nonstick loaf pans, baking sheets, and pie pans; or be prepared to use lots of parchment paper, wax paper, or aluminum foil. Gluten-free dough is especially sticky.

Substituting gluten-free flours

Several gluten-free flours work well for baking. But they don't always work in a one-to-one trade. In other words, you can't just replace one cup of all-purpose or wheat flour with one cup of potato starch — at least not for the best results.

You should play around with these substitutions to find the flavors and consistencies you like best, but this list gives you a starting point for how you can use gluten-free flours.

Remember, each substitution is instead of *1 cup* of all-purpose flour (for those of you who aren't familiar with the highly technical culinary term *scant*, it simply means *loosely packed* or *barely*):

- **Amaranth flour:** 1 scant cup
- **Arrowroot flour:** 1 scant cup
- **Buckwheat flour:** ⅞ cup
- **Corn flour:** 1 cup
- **Cornmeal:** ¾ cup
- **Cornstarch:** ¾ cup
- **Garbanzo bean (chickpea) flour:** ¾ cup
- **Garbanzo/fava bean blend:** 1 scant cup
- **Mesquite flour:** 1 cup
- **Millet flour:** 1 cup
- **Montina (Indian ricegrass flour):** 1 cup
- **Potato flour:** ½ cup
- **Potato starch:** ¾ cup
- **Quinoa flour:** 1 cup
- **Rice flour (white or brown):** 1 scant cup
- **Sorghum:** 1 scant cup
- **Soy flour:** ¾ cup
- **Sweet potato flour:** 1 cup
- **Sweet rice flour (glutinous or sticky rice flour; *mochiko*):** ⅞ cup
- **Tapioca flour or starch:** 1 cup
- **Teff flour:** ⅞ cup

Making your own gluten-free flour mixtures

One of the things the Real Cookbook Authors discovered in the not-so-distant past is that if you mix a variety of flours together, they produce baked goods that have a better consistency and taste. Different combinations of gluten-free flour mixtures abound, and you can experiment to find your favorite.

If you're going to be doing a lot of baking, I suggest making up a large quantity of gluten-free flour mixture and storing it in a dark, dry place. That way you have it on hand when you want to bake. You can also buy many of these gluten-free flour mixtures pre-made.

A quick perusal of most gluten-free cookbooks or a visit to gluten-free recipe sites on the Internet can give you dozens of variations on these flour mixtures, but here are three of the most popular basic mixes. They can be used as a one-to-one substitution for all-purpose flour.

Bette Hagman's All-Purpose Gluten-Free Flour Mixture

- ✔ 2 parts white rice flour
- ✔ ⅓ part potato starch flour
- ✔ ⅓ part tapioca flour

You can use several other types of gluten-free flour mixtures, each with unique tastes and cooking properties. One of the more popular flour mixtures today has bean flour, which adds protein and texture. Here's a bean flour mixture:

Gluten-Free Bean Flour Mixture

- ✔ 1 part bean flour
- ✔ 1 part brown rice flour (or 1 part white rice flour)
- ✔ 1 part cornstarch
- ✔ 1 part tapioca starch
- ✔ ¾ parts sweet rice flour

Carol Fenster has also developed a gluten-free flour mixture using sorghum and corn flour (she suggests using a small coffee or spice grinder to make the corn flour out of white cornmeal).

Carol Fenster's Corn Flour Blend

- ✔ 1½ cups sorghum flour
- ✔ 1½ cups potato starch or cornstarch
- ✔ 1 cup tapioca flour
- ✔ ½ cup corn flour

Time-saving tips for the gluten-free cook

I know I tend to have a *PollyDanna* approach to the gluten-free lifestyle, but even I admit that being gluten-free sometimes *does* take more time and effort. That's why I thought you may appreciate some tips to save you time in your gluten-free cooking adventures.

✔ Make your gluten-free baking mixtures in advance, and double the recipe. Store them in large canisters in a cool, dry, dark place, and label them well (for example, "GF bread mix," "GF baking mix"). Remember, though, not to add the yeast until baking day. Fresh yeast comes in amber-colored, tightly sealed jars or individual packets to keep it as fresh as possible, which is best for baking.

✔ Make as much of the meal as possible gluten-free. If you have a blended family, with some members eating gluten and others eating gluten-free, making most of the meal without gluten is easier on you. This practice also makes the gluten-free member feel more included.

✔ Save your gluten-free mistakes or stale breads, because one bad batch is another meal. So the bread didn't rise, the cake crumbled, and the biscuits fell apart? Save the crumbs and use them for stuffings, casseroles, coatings, or breadcrumbs. (By the way, the easiest way to make fine crumbs is to put dry crumbs into a food processor or chopper.)

Baking bread the gluten-free way

Those who have attempted the sometimes taste-defying feat of experimenting with gluten-free breads know that at times the word *bread* is a euphemism for *brick* and the word *edible* is an overstatement. But never fear; help is here — whether you're a die-hard baker or a newbie in the kitchen, freshly baked, great-tasting, smell-the-kitchen-up, gluten-free bread is easier than ever to make.

Although some gluten-free breads do taste great these days, they still taste a little different from wheat-based breads. And why does that surprise people? That's like making an apple pie but using cherries instead of apples and being surprised that it doesn't have an apple flavor. Of course gluten-free bread doesn't taste exactly like wheat bread — it doesn't have *wheat* in it!

Gluten-free breads tend to look a little different, too. In spite of great strides to make them fluffier and airier, they're still a little denser and turn out best if you make them in smaller loaves. They also don't rise as much, so the tops are sometimes flat or even concave.

You *always* need to toast gluten-free bread. Toasting gives it a better consistency and makes it less likely to crumble. Gluten-free bread is great for grilled sandwiches because the butter and grilling process gives it a crispy texture and seals the bread so it doesn't crumble.

Here are a few general bread-making tips:

✔ All the ingredients that you use, except water, should be at room temperature.

✔ The water that you mix the yeast with must be lukewarm. Too hot, and you kill the yeast. Too cold, and you don't activate it. Also, you should dissolve the yeast in the water before adding it to the rest of the ingredients.

✔ Adding extra protein in the form of eggs, egg substitutes, dry milk solids, or cottage or ricotta cheese is important for helping the yeast work.

✔ Vinegar, usually cider vinegar, helps the yeast work and helps the flavor of the bread emerge. Sometimes recipes call for lemon juice or a dough enhancer instead. These ingredients also act as preservatives.

✔ You should use small loaf pans for gluten-free bread.

✔ Gluten-free bread tends to need to cook a little longer, so cover your loaf with foil for the last 15 minutes or so to keep it from burning.

✔ Wait until the bread has cooled to room temperature to slice it.

Given the choice of doing something by hand or using an efficient, easy-to-clean-made-for-the-job-tried-and-true tool to do it, I'm likely to opt for the tool. If you want to use a bread machine for your gluten-free breads, keep a few things in mind:

✔ Gluten-free bread needs only one kneading and one rising cycle. If you have a setting that allows you to do only one kneading and one rising, choose it.

✔ You really shouldn't share your bread machine with gluten-containing recipes. Getting all the residue off the beaters, pan, and other parts is nearly impossible.

✔ If you haven't bought a machine yet, buy one with strong paddles, a strong motor, and a strong fan.

✔ If your bread turns out soggy, take it out just a few minutes after baking, before the machine begins its "keep warm" cycle.

✔ Keep dry ingredients separate from wet ingredients, and add them in the order the bread machine manufacturer recommends. Whisk together wet ingredients before mixing them with the dry ingredients.

✔ A few minutes after the bread machine has started, use a rubber spatula to scrape the dough off the sides of the pan back into the dough.

If you're a glutton for punishment and choose to mix your dough by hand, keep these tips in mind:

- ✔ If you're following a recipe that calls for using a bread machine, double the amount of yeast and use a little more liquid (a couple of tablespoons).
- ✔ If you're following a recipe that calls for a bread machine and specifies that you use one teaspoon of unflavored gelatin, leave it out.

Part III

From Menus to Meals: Recipes for the Gluten-Free Gastronome

The 5th Wave   By Rich Tennant

"It's nearly a perfect meal. I've got 40% fat, 30% protein, 20% carbohydrates and 10% guilt for the 40% fat."

In this part . . .

1 give you gluten-free recipes. I feel compelled to come clean at this point and advise you that I'm not a Real Cookbook Author, nor do I pretend to be one on TV. But I *do* cook, and the recipes I'm giving you are actual recipes that I use (the measurements are estimates, but the publisher has a real, live professional tester, and she verified that the recipes actually work!). When I cook, not only do I *de-glutenize* old favorites, but I also embrace traditional ingredients and preparations from various cuisines that are inherently gluten-free. In this part, I bring you some of my favorite recipes — some simple, some sophisticated — but all easy-to-prepare.

Chapter 10

First Things First: Beginning with Breakfast

*W*hen most folks think of a typical breakfast, images of bagels, pancakes, muffins, toast, or granola often come to mind. So what are those of us on the gluten-free diet supposed to do? Dig in, that's what! Yep, you can enjoy delicious traditional breakfast foods that may at first seem to be off-limits on the gluten-free diet.

But don't be afraid to think beyond the traditional breakfast fare, too. Smoothies are delicious and nutritious, and chile rellenos casserole can spice up any morning — or afternoon, for that matter. Use this chapter as inspiration for exploring alternatives to the old standby breakfast routines. When you start to think outside the breakfast box, you may discover a whole new world of wholesome gluten-free options to start your day off right.

Getting Your Day Off to a Gluten-Free Start

If mornings are a tad chaotic at your house, taking the time to prepare a healthy, gluten-free breakfast may seem like a luxury you can't afford. But in reality, breakfast really is, as your mom probably told you, the most important meal of the day. Not only does breakfast help with weight management by revving up your metabolism first thing in the morning, but breakfast eaters also have more positive attitudes and perform better at work and school. Starting your day with a nutritious gluten-free breakfast has a positive impact on your entire day.

Breakfast is the first meal you eat after you wake up — after you've "fasted" for eight or more hours (hence the clever name for this meal: *break fast*). Your body is literally starved for nutrition and restoration to get going for the day ahead. Yet many people aren't hungry, or at least they think they aren't hungry — and most people are frantically rushing to get themselves or others out the door. Usually, what's sacrificed in this whirlwind of chaos is a healthy breakfast.

Grab 'n go starters

If you're limited on time, you still have plenty of nutritious gluten-free foods to choose from. The trick is to stock up on wholesome foods that are easy to eat and that you can take with you as you're running out the door. And the foods don't have to be traditional breakfast foods. Here are some suggestions:

- Cottage cheese (with or without fruit) in travel packaging
- Fresh or dried fruit or "fruit in a cup" products
- Gluten-free crackers with cheese slices
- Hard-boiled eggs (for extra flair, make them deviled)
- Homemade granola (like the upcoming "Gluten-Free Granola" recipe)
- Leftover gluten-free pizza
- Lowfat or nonfat yogurt

Trail mix is a fancy way to describe a mixture of nuts, dried fruit, and other bite-sized munchies, and it makes a great portable breakfast. Calling it trail mix gives the illusion that it's nutritious, even though some people work to dig out the chocolate chips! You can buy pre-made mixes, but be careful because some of the dried fruits (especially dates) are coated in oat flour, and some of the nuts have seasonings on them that may contain gluten. It's easy to make your own using your favorite gluten-free ingredients, which may include

✔ Nuts (like peanuts, almonds, and cashews)

✔ Dried fruit (like raisins, apricots, banana chips, and cranberries)

✔ Shaved coconut

✔ Chocolate chips or chunks

✔ Carob

If you know you'll be rushed in the morning, pack a breakfast-on-the-go meal the night before. Put trail mix, yogurt, an apple, and a small juice or water bottle in a brown paper bag and put it in the fridge. If you really want to embarrass your kids or spouse, decorate the bag with colorful hearts and doodles. And don't forget a spoon for the yogurt!

○ Gluten-Free Granola

Granola is a great take-it-with-you breakfast food, but oats are still the number-one most controversial is-it-gluten-free-or-isn't-it food, and for now they're still on the forbidden list. That means commercial granolas are a no-no. The good news is that gluten-free granola is delicious, nutritious, and a cinch to make the night before. In this recipe, I call for roasted peanuts, but feel free to substitute any 1-cup combination of soy nuts, sunflower seeds, or almonds. Likewise, dried apricots, dates, and bananas work well in place of the raisins and dried cranberries.

Preparation time: *30 minutes*

Cooking time: *2 hours*

Yield: *12 servings*

2 cups puffed rice cereal	*½ cup light corn syrup*
2 cups puffed corn cereal	*½ cup honey*
1 cup Perky's Nutty Rice cereal	*¼ cup vegetable oil*
1 cup Kashi Cranberry Sunshine cereal	*½ cup raisins*
1 cup roasted peanuts	*½ cup dried cranberries*
2 teaspoons vanilla extract	*Nonstick spray*

1 Preheat the oven to 250 degrees.

2 In a large bowl, combine the puffed rice cereal, puffed corn cereal, Perky's Nutty Rice cereal, Kashi Cranberry Sunshine cereal, and peanuts.

3 In a small saucepan, heat the vanilla extract, light corn syrup, honey, and oil over medium heat (it just needs to get warm so it flows more easily; don't overheat it). Stir the mixture occasionally as it heats.

4 Pour the warm honey mixture over the dry ingredients, making sure it all gets mixed up.

5 Place the mixture on large baking sheets that you've coated with nonstick spray. Bake the granola for 2 hours, stirring every 15 minutes to keep the mixture from sticking.

6 Carefully add the raisins and cranberries to the hot granola, folding them into the mixture so they're well mixed. Let the granola cool to room temperature, and serve.

Tip: *Homemade granola tends to go stale quickly. Extend the life of your homemade granola by using a vacuum-packing system to seal and store several individual-sized servings. Too late? If your granola has already gone stale, use it to make granola bars (see recipe in Chapter 15).*

Per serving: *Calories 288 (From Fat 98); Fat 11g (Saturated 1g); Cholesterol 0mg; Sodium 91mg; Carbohydrate 46g (Dietary Fiber 3g); Protein 5g.*

Power-start your gluten-free day with protein

Protein really does pack a nutritional punch, regulating blood-sugar levels and providing lots of time-released energy throughout the day. By starting your day with a meal high in protein, you're giving yourself a nutritional boost that can carry you for hours.

Not only does protein provide sustained energy, but it helps you lose weight. Protein stimulates the secretion of *glucagon,* a hormone that tells your body to mobilize fat and begin breaking it down. This reduces fat stores and, ultimately, your waistline.

Fortunately, high-protein foods are plentiful in the gluten-free diet. In fact, many of the foods found on "traditional" breakfast menus that aren't gluten-free, such as bagels and pancakes, actually offer very little in the way of protein. In contrast, many foods that are inherently gluten-free, such as eggs and meats, are very high in protein.

From a gluten-free standpoint, whether your protein is from plant or animal sources really doesn't matter. Eggs are an obvious source of protein for breakfast (see the following section for recipe ideas using eggs), but you can incorporate plenty of other protein sources into your first meal of the day:

- ✔ Canadian bacon or ham slices
- ✔ Dairy products (lowfat milk, cheese, and yogurt)
- ✔ Lean sirloin or steak strips
- ✔ Nuts
- ✔ Protein shakes and smoothies (you can find recipe ideas under "Smoothies for Starters")
- ✔ Turkey slices

The Incredible, Edible Egg

Eggs offer more value than many people realize. They're extremely nutritious, containing all the essential amino acids and countless vitamins and antioxidants. They're also convenient, inexpensive, easy to prepare, and easy to chew. They rarely cause allergic reactions, and they play important roles in a variety of recipes.

Have you ever wondered how to tell whether your eggs are raw or hard-boiled? Simply take 'em for a spin. A hard-boiled one spins freely, and a raw one doesn't. This happens because the hard-boiled one is solid, so everything spins in one direction all at once. The raw egg sloshes around and doesn't allow a fast spinning motion.

Eggs in a Bread Basket

This is a fun way to serve eggs and toast, especially if you have kids in the house. Because gluten-free breads tend to be smaller than other breads, you may want to put two slices side by side, cutting shapes in the touching edges to create the cut-out area that the egg goes into.

Preparation time: 5 minutes

Cooking time: 5 minutes

Yield: 4 servings

4 slices gluten-free bread	4 tablespoons margarine	4 eggs

1 Heat a griddle or large nonstick frying pan over medium-high heat. While the pan is heating, butter both sides of each piece of bread.

2 In the center of each bread slice, cut out a circle about the size of an egg. You can use a knife to cut the circle, or use a cookie cutter to make cute shapes.

3 Make sure the pan or griddle is hot enough that if you put a drop of water on it, the water sizzles. When the pan or griddle is hot, put all the bread — slices and cutouts — on the pan or griddle to fry.

4 When the bottom side of the bread is golden brown, after about 2 minutes, flip each slice and cutout.

5 Crack an egg into the hole in the center of each slice of bread. You may find you have too much egg and that it covers the bread. That's okay.

6 When the second side of bread is golden brown, after about 2 minutes, flip it over again to cook the egg on the other side. Cook the egg until it's the firmness you enjoy, and serve the "eggs in a basket" with the cooked cutouts as decorative additions.

Vary It! If you'd like to cut out a lot of the cholesterol, toss the yolks and simply make this recipe with the whites.

Per serving: Calories 318 (From Fat 205); Fat 23g (Saturated 5g); Cholesterol 213mg; Sodium 196mg; Carbohydrate 21g (Dietary Fiber 1g); Protein 7g.

Breakfast Quiche

"Real men" may not eat quiche, but gluten-free people can — with a few modifications, of course. The beauty of this dish is that with a few tricks, it's incredibly easy . . . and with a little creativity, it can be exceptionally nutritious. This dish is great as a vegetarian dish — just leave the meat out and add extra veggies.

Preparation time: *15 minutes*

Cooking time: *45 minutes*

Yield: *4 servings*

3 cups frozen hash browns, thawed	⅓ cup diced onion
⅓ cup melted butter	1 cup grated Swiss cheese
Nonstick spray	¼ cup grated cheddar cheese
5 eggs	¼ cup grated Monterey Jack cheese
¾ cup milk	2 teaspoons chopped fresh basil
1 cup cooked diced ham	Salt and pepper to taste

1 Preheat the oven to 325 degrees.

2 To prepare the crust, mix the hash browns and butter carefully, making sure the potatoes don't turn to mush.

3 Spray a 9-inch pie plate or quiche pan with nonstick spray. Press the potato-butter mixture evenly on the bottom and sides of the pan.

4 In a large mixing bowl, beat the eggs with an electric mixer for 2 minutes on low speed. Add the milk, ham, onion, Swiss, cheddar, Monterey Jack, basil, and salt and pepper. Stir until they're well mixed.

5 Pour the egg mixture into the crust, and bake it for 45 minutes. To test whether the quiche is done, insert a knife in the center. If it comes out clean, the quiche is ready.

Tip : *To add nutritional value and flavor, add any cut up veggies and meats you like to this recipe.*

Per serving: *Calories 585 (From Fat 392); Fat 44g (Saturated 23g); Cholesterol 368mg; Sodium 808mg; Carbohydrate 22g (Dietary Fiber 1g); Protein 29g.*

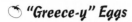

"Greece-y" Eggs

If you're in a Mediterranean-morning mood, try these "Greece-y" eggs, which include sun-dried tomatoes, olives, and feta cheese. Actually not greasy at all, these are an especially lowfat version of Greek eggs because they use only the egg whites. To see how to separate whites from yolks, check out Figure 10-1.

Tools: *Food processor, 4-inch ramekin or stovetop-safe bowl*

Preparation time: *10 minutes*

Cooking time: *15 minutes*

Yield: *2 servings*

Olive oil spray

½ cup egg whites (from about 4 to 5 eggs)

3 tablespoons sun-dried tomatoes (I prefer the hydrated kind, not packed in oil)

¼ cup fresh basil leaves, packed in the measuring cup

4 pitted Kalamata olives

½ teaspoon minced garlic (about 1 clove)

2 tablespoons crumbled feta cheese

2 slices toasted gluten-free bread

1 Spray a 4-inch ramekin (a small casserole dish) or bowl with olive oil spray. Place the ramekin in a large pot, and then add water to the pot until the water level comes halfway up the sides of the dish.

2 Place the pot over high heat, and add the egg whites to the ramekin. As soon as the water boils, turn the heat to low and cover the pot. Set the timer for 15 minutes.

3 While the eggs are cooking, combine the tomatoes, basil, olives, and garlic in a small food processor. Pulse the ingredients until they're finely minced. Stir in the feta cheese.

4 When the 15-minute timer goes off, check the eggs. Cook the eggs until the center is no longer runny. When the eggs are done, carefully remove the ramekin from the hot, simmering water.

5 Toast the bread. Spread two tablespoons of the basil-tomato-cheese mixture on each piece of toast.

6 Loosen the eggs from the dish with a knife and plop them onto the toast. Each piece of toast should get half the eggs. Add the remaining basil-tomato-cheese mixture on top of the eggs and serve.

Per serving: *Calories 241 (From Fat 99); Fat 11g (Saturated 2g); Cholesterol 8mg; Sodium 443mg; Carbohydrate 25g (Dietary Fiber 2g); Protein 10g.*

3 WAYS TO SEPARATE AN EGG

1. CRACK THE EGG IN HALF, OVER A BOWL... ..AND PASS THE YOLK FROM 1 SHELL TO THE OTHER, ALLOWING THE WHITE TO GRADUALLY FALL INTO THE BOWL BELOW.

2. CRACK THE EGG AND BREAK THE EGG INTO YOUR CUPPED HAND HELD OVER A BOWL. GENTLY, RELAX FINGERS, AL-LOWING THE WHITE TO SPILL THROUGH INTO THE BOWL BELOW.

3. USE AN EGG SEPARATOR! PLACE IT OVER A SMALL BOWL OR GLASS. CRACK THE EGG OPEN AND LET IT FALL INTO THE CENTER.

THE WHITE WILL SLIP THROUGH THE SLOTS AND THE YOLK WILL STAY IN THE SEPARATOR.

Figure 10-1:
Separating
eggs.

Smoothies for Starters

Smoothies are a great way to start the day. These thick, smooth drinks use a foundation of fruit or fruit juice, milk, and yogurt or ice cream. No need for any fancy equipment — any blender, immersion hand-blender, or even a shaker cup will work. Not only are smoothies delicious and easy to whip up, but sneaking lots of nutritious things into them without anyone knowing is easy. Creamy, rich, refreshing, and energizing, smoothies suit any taste and any mood. The only thing limiting your options is your creativity.

If you have bananas lying around that are a little too brown for your taste, or strawberries that are getting a tad too mushy, toss them in a smoothie. Bananas and other fruits, especially when at the tail end of being aestheti-cally acceptable, sweeten up smoothies and add loads of nutritional value.

Be creative in your attempts at stealth health. Here's a starter list to give you some ideas of things you can slip into smoothies to enhance the nutritional value. You can find all these ingredients at most health food stores:

✔ **Protein powder:** Literally hundreds of types of protein powders are on the market— low-carb, low-cal, high-carb, high-cal, and everything in between. They're usually derived from whey, egg, soy, and rice, and they come in both flavored and unflavored varieties.

✔ **Spirulina:** For centuries, people across the world have been eating spirulina, a blue-green algae purported to be ultra-rich in vitamins and minerals, with claims of nutritional and medicinal benefits.

✔ **"Greens":** Sometimes called *superfoods,* greens come in the form of a powder and are specialized plants that provide a full spectrum of naturally occurring, absorbable vitamins, minerals, antioxidants, amino acids, fatty acids, fiber, and other beneficial nutrients.

✔ **Flaxseed meal or flax seeds:** Flax is rich in protein but is most notable for its addition of essential fatty acids and fiber to the diet. (You may also want to note that it's a potent laxative, so beware!)

✔ **Omega-3, -6, and -9 essential fatty acid oils:** Although these offer the same type of essential fatty oil that flax adds, some people prefer the oils to the meal or seed, especially for smoothies.

✔ **Instant breakfast powders:** This is a quick way to add some nutrients and flavor to a smoothie. Check the flavors to make sure the one you're using is gluten-free; some are, but some aren't.

And of course, the all-time winner for perking up your smoothie with nutritional value, color, and overall goodness goes to ripe fruits and veggies.

☕ Simple, Stylin' Smoothie

This is the foundation smoothie from which all other smoothies are born: simple, delicious, and just waiting for you to enhance it with nutritious ingredients and a creative style all your own. This smoothie combines the sweetness of bananas and honey with the slight tartness of strawberry yogurt.

Tools: *Blender*

Preparation time: *4 minutes*

Yield: *3 cups*

½ cup milk	*2 ripe bananas*	*¼ cup ice cubes*
1 cup strawberry yogurt	*1 teaspoon honey*	

1 Put all the ingredients in a blender.

2 Mix until smooth.

Vary It! *Remember, you can make a smoothie countless ways — be creative, and use ingredients you have on hand, especially those that are a little too ripe to eat plain. Play with the portion sizes and types of ingredients you use to get the taste and nutritional value that suits you. The only fruit that doesn't work well is citrus.*

Per serving: Calories 141 (From Fat 18); Fat 2g (Saturated 1g); Cholesterol 9mg; Sodium 41mg; Carbohydrate 29g (Dietary Fiber 2g); Protein 4g. based on three-1 cup servings.

🍎 *Chocolate Peanut Butter Smoothie*

Fruit and berry smoothies are delicious and nutritious, for sure. But if you're in the mood for something with a little more substance — and, well, a few more calories — the chocolate peanut butter smoothie is for you. Go ahead — live a little, and whip it up!

Tools: *Blender*

Preparation time: *4 minutes*

Yield: *2 cups*

1 cup chocolate ice cream	*2 tablespoons peanut butter*	*¼ cup ice cubes*
¼ cup milk	*1 ripe banana*	

1 Put all the ingredients in a blender.

2 Mix until smooth.

Vary It! *I call for chocolate ice cream in this recipe because, well, everything is better with chocolate. But feel free to switch things up in the ice cream department. Almost any flavor works, but vanilla is sure to please (and I'd think about staying away from strawberry or mint).*

Per serving: Calories 311 (From Fat 148); Fat 16g (Saturated 7g); Cholesterol 26mg; Sodium 140mg; Carbohydrate 38g (Dietary Fiber 4g); Protein 8g. Based on 2 servings.

Wake Up and Smell the Coffee Cake: Hot Breakfast Ideas

Ah . . . few things get a morning off to a better start than waking up to the smell of freshly baked muffins or coffee cake. Think you have to do without that experience on the gluten-free diet? No, my gluten-free friends. This section proves that opportunities abound for the ooey, gooey breakfast foods that you may have feared were a thing of the past.

Many of the recipes for baked goods and quick breads call for a gluten-free flour mixture. You can either buy a baking mix or create your own. I've put together a list of recommended baking mixtures and a recipe for how to make your own in Chapter 9.

☞ Coffee Cake

I wonder why it's called coffee cake when there's no coffee in it. Well anyway, coffee or no coffee, this cake is sure to get the family out of bed and down to the breakfast table in a hurry. And no wonder — if they're like me, they're probably just after the cinnamon-sugar streusel topping!

Preparation time: *10 minutes*

Cooking time: *25 minutes*

Yield: *4 servings*

¼ cup canola oil	1½ teaspoons xanthan gum	2 tablespoons gluten-free flour mixture
2 eggs, beaten	1 cup sugar	
½ cup milk	2 teaspoons baking powder	2 teaspoons cinnamon
1½ cups gluten-free flour mixture	Nonstick spray	3 tablespoons melted butter
	½ cup brown sugar	

1 Preheat the oven to 375 degrees.

2 In a large mixing bowl, combine the oil, eggs, and milk.

3 Sift together the 1½ cups flour mixture, xanthan gum, sugar, and baking powder. Add these dry ingredients to the egg mixture, and mix well.

4 Spray a 9-inch square pan with nonstick spray, and pour in the batter.

5 In a small bowl, create the streusel topping by mixing together the brown sugar, 2 tablespoons flour mixture, cinnamon, and butter. Pour the topping mixture over the cake batter.

6 Bake the cake for 25 minutes. To see whether the cake's done, insert a toothpick in the center of the cake. If the toothpick comes out clean, the cake's ready.

Per serving: Calories 785 (From Fat 243); Fat 27g (Saturated 8g); Cholesterol 133mg; Sodium 260mg; Carbohydrate 131g (Dietary Fiber 3g); Protein 9g.

Pancakes

Whether you call them hotcakes, griddle cakes, flapjacks, flannel cakes, or johnnycakes, pancakes have been cherished as a favorite breakfast staple for centuries. You can also use this batter to make waffles — just follow the cooking instructions that came with your waffle iron. Dress up your waffles and pancakes by adding sliced bananas or chocolate chips to the batter, or top them with fresh fruit or whipped topping. Personally, I think the best thing about pancakes and waffles is that they soak up lots and lots of syrup.

Preparation time: *10 minutes*

Cooking time: *5 minutes per pancake*

Yield: *8 servings*

Nonstick spray	*1 teaspoon xanthan gum*	*2 eggs, beaten*
1 cup gluten-free flour mixture	*1 teaspoon baking powder*	*2 tablespoons vegetable oil*
	2 teaspoons vanilla	*1 cup milk*

1 Heat a griddle or frying pan over medium heat. To see whether the pan is at the right temperature, let a drop of water fall in the pan — if the water sizzles immediately and moves around, the pan's hot enough. Spray the pan lightly with nonstick spray.

2 In a medium mixing bowl, combine the flour mixture, xanthan gum, and baking powder. Add the vanilla, eggs, oil, and milk. Stir the batter until moistened, using a whisk to remove lumps.

3 Use a large spoon to drop about ⅓ cup batter onto the hot griddle or pan (to make mouse pancakes, drop one large spoonful of batter, and use two smaller ones for ears).

4 Bubbles should begin to form in about 3 minutes. When they do, lift a pancake slightly with a spatula to see whether the underside is golden brown. If it is, flip the pancake over. This time you won't see bubbles to know when the pancake is browning, so you'll have to check occasionally. Usually the pancake takes 2 to 3 minutes to become golden brown on the second side.

Tip: *Try using "melted" berries for a healthy syrup option. Put fresh or frozen whole strawberries or blueberries in a saucepan with a little sugar, mash the berries slightly, and add a tiny bit of water. Heat the mixture slowly until the sugar dissolves in the juice.*

Per serving: *Calories 141 (From Fat 55); Fat 6g (Saturated 1g); Cholesterol 57mg; Sodium 82mg; Carbohydrate 18g (Dietary Fiber 1g); Protein 4g.*

Crêpes

The word *crêpe* is French for *pancake* and is derived from *crêper,* meaning "to crisp." Basically thin, crisp pancakes, crêpes are most delightful when filled with a variety of stuffings or smothered in garnishes or syrups. Although creating crêpe batter is simple, actually cooking crêpes can take a little practice. The technique starts with a good pan. You can buy pans made specifically for crêpes, but you really don't need one. Any flat-bottomed nonstick skillet between seven and eight inches in diameter will do. Make sure it's nonstick and shallow and has sloping sides.

Tools: *Crêpe pan or flat-bottomed nonstick skillet*

Preparation time: *10 minutes*

Cooking time: *20 minutes*

Yield: *4 servings*

1 cup gluten-free flour mixture	*¼ teaspoon salt*
½ teaspoon xanthan gum	*2 tablespoons melted butter*
2 eggs, beaten	*Nonstick spray*
1 cup milk	

1 In a large mixing bowl, whisk together the flour mixture, xanthan gum, and eggs. Gradually add the milk, stirring to combine.

2 Add the salt and the butter; beat the mixture until it's smooth. The thickness should be about that of cream. If it's too thick or runny, add a bit of flour or milk until you achieve the desired consistency.

3 Heat a pan over medium-high heat. To see whether the pan is at the right temperature, sprinkle a drop of water on it. If the water bounces around, the pan is hot enough. Spray the pan liberally with nonstick spray.

4 Pour just enough batter in the pan to be able to make a thin coating on the bottom of the pan. For an 8-inch crêpe pan, use ¼ cup batter. Lift the pan off the burner and quickly tilt the pan so the batter sloshes from side-to-side, thinly covering the entire bottom.

5 Return the pan to the burner. When the crêpe is light brown on the bottom and the top of the crêpe is firm, after about 1 minute, gently loosen it with a spatula and flip it. Start checking the bottom of the crêpe when the sides become crispy and slightly loosen themselves from the pan. When both sides are light brown (the second side browns more quickly than the first), your crêpes are ready!

Tip: *Figuring out how to make crêpes is a matter of trial and error, and pan temperature is important. The batter should cook as soon as it touches the pan but shouldn't sizzle. If your crêpes are thick or bubbly, turn down the heat or lift the pan off the burner for a while. If they stick or aren't browning or setting, turn up the heat or return the pan to the burner.*

Vary It! *Dress to impress. Without toppings and fillings, crêpes are just — well, just thin, crispy pancakes. The fun — and the way to really impress your guests — is with the fillings and toppings. The key is, once again, creativity. You can either spread some filling on a crêpe and roll it up, or spread the filling and cover it with another crêpe, sandwich-style. You can make as many layers as you like, and even alternate fillings. Here are some ideas to get you started that also work well with pancakes and waffles:*

- ✔ *Peaches 'n cream:* *Combine fresh, sliced peaches with cream cheese, sour cream, whipped cream, and brown sugar.*

- ✔ *Banana sundae:* *Not exactly on the Weight Watchers menu, this indulgence calls for using sliced bananas as a filling and then topping the crêpes with your favorite ice cream and sauce (caramel, butterscotch, chocolate, hot fudge, and so on). Top it off with whipped cream or even banana liqueur.*

- ✔ *Strawberry style:* *In a hurry? Mix a little strawberry jam with ricotta or cream cheese. You may want to sweeten it up a tad with a dash of sugar or sugar substitute — and if you're feeling really wild and crazy, top the crêpe with fresh strawberries.*

- ✔ *Ready-to-spread toppings:* *Even quicker ideas for toppings include applesauce, powdered sugar, whipped cream, and nondairy whipped topping.*

Per serving: *Calories 266 (From Fat 97); Fat 11g (Saturated 6g); Cholesterol 130mg; Sodium 212mg; Carbohydrate 35g (Dietary Fiber 1g); Protein 8g.*

Crêpes suzette

The most famous crêpe dish throughout the world seems to be crêpes suzette, often prepared in restaurants in full view of the guests. Served hot with a sauce of sugar, orange juice, and Grand Marnier, crêpes suzette are usually topped with brandy and ignited for the pyro pleasure of everyone. In fact, the flames are all for show, because flaming the brandy doesn't change the flavor of the dish in any way. (My super-cautious editor insists that I warn you about the dangers of preparing flaming dishes, as the flame can be difficult to see and still be present after you think it's extinguished. Now I have, and now you know.)

↻ *Versatile Blueberry Muffins*

Nothing makes you feel more like June Cleaver than to call your kids to a breakfast of freshly baked muffins. You have lots of room for creativity here — hence the name *versatile* muffins.

Preparation time: *15 minutes*

Cooking time: *20 minutes*

Yield: *6 servings*

1 cup gluten-free flour mixture	2 teaspoons vanilla
¼ teaspoon xanthan gum	2 eggs, beaten
4 tablespoons sugar	1½ tablespoons vegetable oil
1 teaspoon baking powder	2 teaspoons milk
½ teaspoon cinnamon	½ cup blueberries

1 Preheat the oven to 350 degrees.

2 In a large bowl, combine the flour mixture, xanthan gum, sugar, baking powder, and cinnamon. Add the vanilla, eggs, oil, and milk. Stir until all the batter is moistened (use a whisk to remove lumps). Fold in the blueberries.

3 Pour the batter into a muffin tin lined with paper muffin cups.

4 Bake the muffins for 20 to 25 minutes. Check for doneness by inserting a toothpick in the center of a muffin. If the toothpick comes out without batter on it (it may have blueberries on it), the muffins are done.

Vary It! *Instead of blueberries, consider using applesauce (I like chunks of apples, too), bananas, or other fruits. Toss in a dash of cinnamon, too.*

Per serving: *Calories 192 (From Fat 51); Fat 6g (Saturated 1g); Cholesterol 71mg; Sodium 88mg; Carbohydrate 31g (Dietary Fiber 1g); Protein 4g.*

🍑 French Toast

French toast makes me think of easy elegance. It's ridiculously easy to make but some-how boasts an air of sophistication, especially if you serve it with powdered sugar and strawberries. Don't forget the syrup!

Preparation time: *5 minutes*

Cooking time: *6 minutes per slice*

Yield: *6 servings*

4 eggs	*2 tablespoons butter*
¼ cup milk	*6 slices gluten-free bread*
¼ teaspoon cinnamon (optional)	

1 In a medium bowl, combine the eggs, milk, and cinnamon (if desired). Beat the mixture with a whisk or fork until well blended.

2 Melt the butter in a large frying pan or griddle over medium heat.

3 Dip each slice of bread in the egg mixture, coating the bread well on both sides.

4 Place the bread on the hot griddle or in the pan. Cook the bread until it's golden brown on both sides, about 3 minutes per side.

5 Serve the French toast warm. You can top the toast with syrup, powdered sugar, and/or sliced strawberries — get creative.

Per serving: *Calories 232 (From Fat 125); Fat 14g (Saturated 4g); Cholesterol 153mg; Sodium 48mg; Carbohydrate 21g (Dietary Fiber 1g); Protein 6g.*

Dinner for Breakfast, Anyone?

Whether freshly prepared in the morning or left over from the night before, sometimes the best breakfast is dinner — after all, who says dinner has to be eaten after a certain hour?

☺ Chile Rellenos Casserole

Whether for breakfast, lunch, or dinner, chile rellenos are a great gluten-free meal that couldn't be much easier to make. When you eat these for breakfast, you're sure to have an *olé* kind of day. Serve these rellenos with warm corn tortillas and salsa, topped with guacamole for a creamy, flavorful touch (see Chapter 11 for my guacamole recipe).

Preparation time: *10 minutes*

Cooking time: *25 minutes*

Yield: *8 servings*

Nonstick spray	*1 pound colby cheese, grated*
6 eggs	*1 pound Monterey Jack cheese, grated*
Salt and pepper to taste	*2 8-ounce cans whole green chilies*

1 Preheat the oven to 350 degrees. Spray a 9- by 13-inch casserole dish with nonstick spray.

2 Separate the egg whites from the yolks. With an electric mixer on medium speed, whip the whites in a medium bowl until they're stiff. In a small bowl, beat the yolks with a fork or a whisk until they're smooth. Fold the yolks into the whites. Add salt and pepper.

3 Combine the colby and Monterey Jack cheeses.

4 Spread about ⅓ of the egg mixture in the bottom of the dish.

5 Split open the chilies. Layer the chilies on top of the egg mixture. Spread a layer of cheese on top. Continue layering — egg, chilies, cheese — until you've used all the ingredients. You should end up with about three layers of each ingredient, finishing with the egg mixture.

6 Bake the chile rellenos for 25 minutes or until golden brown.

Per serving: *Calories 377 (From Fat 224); Fat 25g (Saturated 14g); Cholesterol 222mg; Sodium 795mg; Carbohydrate 4g (Dietary Fiber 1g); Protein 33g.*

Chapter 11

Appetizers with Attitude

In This Chapter

▶ Making snack attack finger foods

▶ Digging in with dips

▶ Wrapping it up

Appetizers, by definition, whet people's appetites — you know, make 'em hungry. (Am I the only one who sees some irony in filling up on yummy starters in order to make you hungrier?)

Every great get-together begins with great-tasting appetizers, whether you're at a casual gathering of friends and family or an elegant soirée among socialites. Not only do appetizers whet the appetite, but they whet the imagination, setting the stage for the meal yet to come.

But appetizer anticipation can quickly turn to disappointment for someone on the gluten-free diet, as more often than not, appetizers, by definition, seem to be big globs of gluten. And the party planner perusing most appetizer recipes finds that appetizers are likely to contain flour, breading, or myriad other gluten-containing ingredients, striking fear into hosts and hostesses everywhere: What can I serve that's impressive and gluten-free?

If you find yourself paralyzed with appetizer anxiety, never fear: Gluten-free appetizers are here! Just don't blame me if everyone's too full for the main course.

Fashioning Finger-Lickin'-Good Finger Foods

People love to eat with their fingers. And as long as you're wearing jeans so you can wipe your hands off, what's the harm in dining with your digits? In this section, I bring you some of my favorite recipes that help get the party started with fun finger foods.

➔ "It's-Not-Chex" Party Mix

Chex Party Mix is always a fiesta favorite, but unfortunately, Chex has gluten in it (and in rare occasions, so does Worcestershire sauce). Let that stop you from enjoying one of the best snack foods on the planet? I think not! With some simple substitutions, you can transform party mix into a gluten-free version of its sister snack, and no one may ever know the difference. **Warning:** Party mix is extremely addictive.

Preparation time: *10 minutes*

Cooking time: *1 hour*

Yield: *12 servings*

6 tablespoons margarine	½ teaspoon onion powder
2 tablespoons Worcestershire sauce	4 cups Health Valley Corn Crunch-Ems! cereal
¾ teaspoon garlic powder	
1½ teaspoons seasoned salt	4 cups Health Valley Rice Crunch-Ems! cereal

1 Heat the oven to 250 degrees. Melt the margarine in a large roasting pan in the oven.

2 Remove the pan from the oven, and stir the Worcestershire sauce, garlic powder, seasoned salt, and onion powder into the margarine. Gradually stir in the corn and rice cereals until they're evenly coated with the margarine-seasonings mixture.

3 Return the pan to the oven. Bake the mix for 1 hour, stirring every 15 minutes.

4 Spread the mix on paper towels to cool. Store it in an airtight container.

Vary It! *Add pretzels, mixed nuts, or raisins to your party mix. You can find gluten-free pretzels by Glutano or Ener-G online or where gluten-free foods are available.*

Per serving: *Calories 127 (From Fat 51); Fat 6g (Saturated 1g); Cholesterol 0mg; Sodium 261mg; Carbohydrate 18g (Dietary Fiber 1g); Protein 3g.*

⟳ Spicy Corn Fritters

This delicious dish uses polenta. Once considered a peasant food (like its cousin corn grits), polenta is an Italian cornmeal mush that's becoming quite trendy. You can find polenta at most grocery stores, and it often comes in a round plastic tube. For this appetizer, the polenta adds more than just flavor — it actually holds the corn balls together.

Preparation time: *15 minutes*

Cooking time: *25 minutes*

Yield: *4 servings*

1 cup canned corn	*3 tablespoons chopped fresh cilantro*
2 fresh red chilies, seeded and finely chopped	*2 eggs, beaten*
1 teaspoon minced garlic (about 2 cloves)	*½ cup pre-made polenta (about 4 ounces)*
10 kaffir lime leaves, finely chopped (found in Thai sections of Asian markets)	*¼ cup finely sliced green beans*
	½ cup peanut oil (for frying)

1 Put the corn, chilies, garlic, lime leaves, cilantro, eggs, polenta, and green beans into a large bowl; mix them thoroughly. Use your hands to form balls about the size of golf balls. Set them on a plate.

2 Heat the peanut oil in a wok, skillet, or deep fryer to a high heat. You'll know the oil is hot enough when you add a small drop of water into the oil and it pops. (Be careful, though. More than a drop, and it may pop and burn you.)

3 Turning the fritters occasionally, cook them in the oil until they're brown and crispy on the outside (about 7 minutes). Remove the fritters from the wok, skillet, or deep fryer with a slotted spoon, and let them drain on paper towels.

Per serving: Calories 294 (From Fat 149); Fat 17g (Saturated 3g); Cholesterol 106mg; Sodium 226mg; Carbohydrate 28g (Dietary Fiber 4g); Protein 7g.

Spicy Buffalo Wings

No, Jessica, buffaloes don't have wings. These are actually chicken wings, named *Buffalo* for the city in New York where they originated in 1964. Remember to serve them with celery sticks and ranch dressing.

Preparation time: *5 minutes*

Cooking time: *10 minutes*

Yield: *2 dozen wings*

1½ cups gluten-free flour mixture	*½ cup honey*
2 teaspoons seasoned salt, divided	*2 tablespoons molasses*
24 chicken wings	*3 tablespoons ketchup*
Oil for frying	*3 tablespoons Cholula or your favorite hot sauce*
½ cup red wine vinegar	

1 Put the flour mixture and 1 teaspoon of the seasoned salt in a gallon-sized plastic bag, and shake the bag to mix them. Add the wings (about five at a time) and shake the bag to coat them well.

2 Heat the oil over medium-high heat in a heavy skillet. Fry the wings in about 2 inches of hot oil for approximately 5 minutes, until they're crispy on the outside. Break a wing open and make sure the meat inside isn't pink. Drain the wings on paper towels.

3 Prepare the sauce by mixing the remaining teaspoon of seasoned salt, red wine vinegar, honey, molasses, ketchup, and hot sauce together in a medium bowl.

4 Dip the cooked wings in the mixture to coat them with the sauce.

Tip: *For an easier recipe, use commercial wing or hot sauces. Simply coat and cook the wings as indicated in steps 1 and 2 and then coat the wings with sauce as indicated in step 4.*

Per serving: *Calories 176 (From Fat 102); Fat 11g (Saturated 2g); Cholesterol 29mg; Sodium 178mg; Carbohydrate 9g (Dietary Fiber 0g); Protein 9g.*

Helpful hints if you're relying on frying

Inarguably not one of the healthier modes of cooking, frying is, nonetheless, a common cooking method, especially for many appetizers. Here are some important tips that may help you create the perfect crunch:

✔ **Use oil you designate for gluten-free foods.** If you're preparing gluten-containing foods and gluten-free ones, make sure you either cook the gluten-free foods first or change the oil in between. Breadings and batters can contaminate the oil, turning your gluten-free goodie into an unwitting source of wheat.

✔ **Choose the right oil.** Some oils, like olive and sesame oil, aren't meant to be heated to the very high temperatures deep frying requires. Corn, canola, and peanut oils are some of the best deep-frying oils, because they have a high smoking point. Find an oil that matches the flavor profile of the food you're cooking and turn down the heat if your oil begins to smoke, which indicates the oil is degrading. Degrading oil can affect the flavor of the food.

✔ **Don't overload the basket.** If you're impatient like I am, you may be tempted to "hurry" the cooking process by cooking as much as you can at once. Overloading the basket can result in uneven cooking and may even cause the food to absorb extra oil.

✔ **Filter and clean often.** If the oil gets smoky or has debris in it, dump it out and start with new oil. Clean your fry pot regularly.

Once you've finished frying or deep frying your favorite gluten-free goodies, you need to figure out what to do with the used cooking oil. You can't just dump it down the drain; that's not only bad for the environment, but it's bound to clog the pipes. After the oil has completely cooled, pour it into a coffee can or other empty can or jar with a lid. Seal the lid tightly and throw it in the trash. Keep empty cans and lids on hand to use for getting rid of used cooking grease.

Some restaurants have grease bins where they keep used grease, and it's later recycled. If you do a lot of frying and have a lot of grease to get rid of, you may want to ask permission to use a local restaurant's recycling bin.

Digging into Dips and Dippers

Whether you're dipping veggies, chips, or fried foods, a few good dips go a long way, and you can vary your repertoire of basic recipes to create exciting gluten-free graze-ables. Although many dips are inherently gluten-free, others require just a few tweaks here and there to make them safe for anyone avoiding gluten.

Double-dipping is *not* allowed, especially if some of the guests are eating gluten-containing foods. After people have dunked gobs of gluten into the dip, it's no longer gluten-free.

By the way, dips aren't just for dipping. Use them as fillings for hollowed veggies or halved hard-boiled eggs, or spread them on quesadillas. Or put them on crêpes (you can find a recipe in Chapter 10) or corn tortillas — you can roll the filling into a wrap and then eat the whole thing as a tasty picnic snack or slice it into stylish roll-ups.

Artichoke and Spinach Dip

You won't find this one in *Dieting For Dummies,* but it is gluten-free! Use this cheesy dip with corn tortilla chips, rice crackers, veggies, or deep-fried potato skins. Or if you have a favorite gluten-free bread, slice it thinly, toast it, and spread the artichoke and spinach dip on top.

Preparation time: *10 minutes*

Cooking time: *25 minutes*

Yield: *12 servings*

8-ounce package cream cheese	*½ cup grated Romano cheese*
¼ cup mayonnaise	*¼ cup grated mozzarella cheese*
½ teaspoon minced garlic (about 1 clove)	*14-ounce jar artichoke hearts, drained and chopped*
1 teaspoon fresh basil	
Salt and pepper to taste	*½ cup spinach, drained and chopped*
½ cup shredded Parmesan cheese	*Nonstick spray*

1 Preheat the oven to 350 degrees. Let the cream cheese warm to room temperature.

2 In a large bowl, cream together the cream cheese, mayonnaise, garlic, basil, and salt and pepper. Setting aside a few teaspoons of each cheese to use as a topping, add the Parmesan, Romano, and mozzarella cheeses. Mix until everything is well blended.

3 Add the artichoke hearts and spinach, and mix again.

4 Spray a one-quart ovenproof serving dish with nonstick spray, pour in the dip, and top it with the cheese you set aside in step 2.

5 Bake the dip for about 25 minutes or until the top begins to brown and the cheese melts.

Per serving: *Calories 139 (From Fat 111); Fat 12g (Saturated 6g); Cholesterol 30mg; Sodium 292mg; Carbohydrate 3g (Dietary Fiber 0g); Protein 5g.*

○ *Guacamole*

Guacamole is an avocado-based dip that originated in Mexico. Most guacamole recipes start with fresh, peeled avocados and add lime (or lemon) juice, tomatoes, onions, cilantro, garlic, and spices. The lime juice actually keeps the guacamole from turning brown when you expose it to the air. Leaving the avocado pit in the guacamole until just before you serve it also decreases browning. For this guacamole, feel free to kick it up a notch with your favorite hot sauce.

Preparation time: *15 minutes*

Yield: *6 servings*

2 ripe avocados	*4 tablespoons lime juice*
1 small-to-medium ripe tomato, diced	*2 teaspoons chopped cilantro*
½ small red onion, chopped	*2 teaspoons Worcestershire sauce*
½ teaspoon finely cut jalapeño pepper	*Salt and pepper to taste*

1 Peel the avocados, remove the flesh from the pits, and cube the avocado flesh. Save the pits. See Figure 11-1 if you're not sure how to remove the pit from an avocado.

2 In a medium bowl, combine the avocado flesh, tomato, onion, jalapeño, lime juice, cilantro, Worcestershire sauce, and salt and pepper.

3 Mix all the ingredients well, keeping the guacamole lumpy. Place the avocado pit in the dip and remove the pit just before serving.

Per serving: *Calories 104 (From Fat 76); Fat 8g (Saturated 2g); Cholesterol 0mg; Sodium 117mg; Carbohydrate 8g (Dietary Fiber 5g); Protein 2g.*

Figure 11-1: Pitting an avocado.

How to Pit and Peel an Avocado

Slice avocado in half lengthwise and pull apart.

Firmly strike the pit with a chef's knife.

Lift the pit out with a gentle twist of the knife.

GENTLY scoop out the meat with a spoon.

Chop or slice according to your recipe.

Becoming an avocado aficionado

Avocados are one of nature's prepackaged wonder foods. Most people think they're a vegetable, but they're actually a fruit. Loaded with potassium (60 percent more than bananas!) and the good-for-you monounsaturated fat, avocados are sodium- and cholesterol-free. Here are some other avocado factoids:

✔ California grows 95 percent of the United States' avocados, and most of those (60 percent) grow in San Diego County (where I live!).

✔ One California avocado tree can produce about 120 avocados each year. That's about 60 pounds of fruit.

✔ California avocados grow year-round.

✔ In Latin America, people wrap avocados and give them as wedding gifts.

✔ Some people claim avocados are an aphrodisiac.

🍅 Mango Salsa

Salsas come in endless forms and flavors. Fresh mango salsa is versatile and easy to make. You can serve it as a dip or use it to dress up main courses, putting it over grilled pork, chicken, or salmon. You can also use it to make fish tacos — just spoon this salsa over cooked fish and wrap the mixture in a corn tortilla.

Preparation time: *20 minutes*

Yield: *6 servings*

1 ripe mango, peeled, pitted, and diced (about 1 cup)

½ medium red onion, finely chopped

1 jalapeño pepper, minced

1 large tomato, diced

¼ cup fresh cilantro, chopped

4 tablespoons fresh lime juice

Salt and pepper to taste

1 Combine the mango, onion, jalapeño, tomato, cilantro, lime juice, and salt and pepper in a bowl; mix them until well-blended. Don't mix so hard that you mash the mango — the salsa should contain chunks.

2 Chill the salsa for an hour or more to blend all the flavors.

Tip: *Check out Figure 11-2 to see how to dice a mango. With that big seed in the middle, they aren't easy to work with.*

Per serving: *Calories 35 (From Fat 2); Fat 0g (Saturated 0g); Cholesterol 0mg; Sodium 101mg; Carbohydrate 9g (Dietary Fiber 1g); Protein 1g.*

How to Cut a Mango

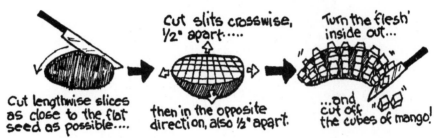

Figure 11-2:
Cutting a
mango.

Cut lengthwise slices as close to the flat seed as possible....

cut slits crosswise, 1/2" apart.....

then in the opposite direction, also 1/2" apart.

Turn the flesh inside out...

...and cut off the cubes of mango!

🍅 Homemade Tortilla Chips

Corn tortilla chips, or *totopos* in Spanish, are great for scooping up salsas or dips. You can sprinkle them with a little grated cheese, or *queso seco* (dry Mexican cheese), and serve them with other dishes, such as soups. Start with corn tortillas that are a few days old; fresh tortillas don't crisp as well when you fry them.

Preparation time: *15 minutes*

Cooking time: *15 minutes*

Yield: *48 chips*

8 corn tortillas   Oil for frying   Salt

1 Cut each corn tortilla into six triangular wedges.

2 Pour the oil into a large, heavy frying pan (or deep fryer) so at least ½ inch of oil covers the bottom. You want enough oil in the pan so that both sides of the tortilla can cook at the same time. Place the pan over medium-high heat.

3 Test the oil temperature by putting one tortilla wedge into the oil. If it bubbles and floats, the oil is hot enough. If not, discard that wedge and wait for the oil to heat some more.

4 Fry the tortilla wedges until golden brown (just a few moments). Use a slotted spoon or tongs to remove them from the oil, and drain the chips on paper towels.

5 Sprinkle the tortilla wedges with salt.

Vary It! *To make lower-fat tortilla chips, bake fresh corn tortillas at 400 degrees for 8 to 10 minutes or until they're crispy. You can cut the tortillas into triangles before baking or break them into chips afterward.*

Per serving: *Calories 99 (From Fat 48); Fat 5g (Saturated 0g); Cholesterol 0mg; Sodium 0mg; Carbohydrate 12g (Dietary Fiber 1g); Protein 2g. based on 8 servings.*

Simple but sexy spreads

The difference between a dip and a spread is consistency. A dip is creamier, so even a fragile dipper can withstand the pressure of a good dig through a dip. On the other hand, you usually serve a spread with spreading knives and put it on crackers, tortillas, or quesadillas.

Today, several widely available varieties of rice, corn, and nut crackers make the perfect crackers for spreads. Consider using these ideas to impress your guests but still have plenty of time left to enjoy your own party:

✔ **Jalapeño cream cheese:** Put a block of cream cheese on a serving platter. Top it with jalapeño jelly (you can usually find this in the same aisle as all other jellies and jams). It's not too hot, but this jelly adds a slightly spicy, semisweet topping to the cream cheese.

✔ **Brown sugar on baked brie:** Place a wedge or round of brie cheese on an ovenproof serving platter. Top the cheese with a layer (about ¼-inch thick) of light brown sugar. Bake at 350 degrees for 8 minutes or until the inside of the cheese appears to be soft.

✔ **Crab cream cheese brick:** Set a brick of cream cheese on a serving platter. Drain a can of crab meat and spread the meat evenly over the top of the cream cheese. Drizzle a tasty, spicy sauce over the top (make a cool design if you feel so inclined).

✔ **Hummus:** Hummus is made from garbanzo beans/chickpeas and is flavored with seasonings such as garlic and spices. Traditional hummus contains *tahini*, a sesame seed paste. Usually available at any grocery store, hummus' consistency is actually right in between a spread and a dip, so it works well for either.

Going Wild with Wraps

As one of today's most popular food trends, wraps offer never-ending possibilities for gluten-free dishes, many of which make great appetizers or main dishes. The only limits to what you can make into a wrap are your creativity and your sense of adventure. Use corn tortillas, crêpes, rice wraps, or lettuce for your wrapper, and then let your imagination run wild as you concoct clever, flavorful fillings based on which wrapper you're using. (Check out Chapter 10 for a gluten-free crêpe recipe.)

A word of advice, though: You may want to skip the wraps on a first date or when you have the boss over for dinner. They're delicious, no doubt, but you may not make your best impression: A serving of these finger foods usually turns into a fistful.

If you're having trouble figuring out what to put in your wraps, I give you some recipes to impress all your guests in the following sections. But here are some ideas to get you started:

- **Caesar salad wrap:** Actually, any salad works well in a wrap. Of course, using a lettuce wrapper is a bit redundant, and it really just looks like you're searching for an excuse to eat your salad with your hands. Go for the corn tortilla.

- **Fajita:** Fajitas are basically a Mexican blend of marinated meat and sautéed onions and peppers wrapped in a tortilla. Feel free to get creative, though, and use any meat or veggie combination you like. You generally serve the meat and veggies together and serve the tortillas separately so guests can wrap them up themselves.

- **Fish wraps:** In Southern California, we call these "fish tacos." Taco, wrap — either way you wrap it, you have a corn tortilla holding a bunch of cooked fish inside. Add some of that "Mango Salsa" from the recipe in this chapter, and you've got yourself a gourmet meal!

- **Leftovers wrap:** Seriously, every fridge on the planet has something in it that you can make into a wrap. Go with it. Mix. Blend. Be wild and crazy, and clean out the refrigerator at the same time.

- **Pulled pork wrap:** You can use a barbecue sauce, salsa, or flavored mayonnaise to add more flavor to this wrap. I use either a corn tortilla or a lettuce wrap for this.

- **Quesadilla:** A quesadilla is simply a folded tortilla — corn, for the gluten-free crowd — with melted cheese inside.

- **Spicy Southwest wrap:** If you're looking for a little zap in your wrap, spice it up with a Southwest flair. Wrap up any burrito or enchilada filling with lettuce or a corn tortilla.

Rice rolls

Rice rolls are a great type of wrap. Available in Asian markets, rice paper wrappers come from a paste of ground rice and water, which people stamp into rounds and dry. When you moisten pieces of rice paper, the brittle sheets become flexible, which makes rice paper perfect for wraps. Rice paper wrappers can be tricky to use, but they're well worth it after you've gotten the hang of working with them.

Pre-made wrappers and bottled dipping sauces are readily available in Asian markets and the Asian section of most supermarkets. The secrets to making great rice rolls are to use the freshest ingredients, to moisten the rice paper wrappers until they're pliable but not too wet, and to roll the bundles tightly. Here are some tips and tricks:

1. **Soak 'em.**

   To make the rice paper wrappers pliable for folding, you need to soak them one at a time for about 4 to 5 seconds until they're soft. Although some people simply use hot water for soaking, others believe the key to making a rice wrap that's pliable but doesn't fall apart is in the mixture. If hot water makes your wrapper fall apart, try this for your soaking mixture:

   > 2 cups warm water

   > 2 tablespoons sugar

   > ¼ cup cider vinegar

2. **Drain the wrappers on a flat surface.**

   You can use your hands to take the wrappers out of the water and lay them flat on a cutting board or plate. Don't put them on top of each other, though, or they'll stick together and you'll never get them apart. Pat them dry. Handling rice paper wrappers can be tough, because they tend to stick to themselves. Be patient. With a few attempts, you can get the hang of handling them.

3. **Layer the ingredients in the wrapper.**

   Folding rice paper wrappers can be tricky: If they're not sticking to themselves, the wrappers seem to be ripping in all the wrong places. To avoid ripping, don't overfill the softened wrappers. The easiest way to prevent tearing is to layer the filling mixture.

4. **Fold with finesse.**

   Check out Figure 11-3 to see how to fold these wraps.

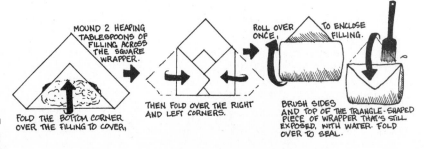

Figure 11-3:
Rolling and
folding rice
paper rolls.

TIP

To give your rice wraps an extra fancy look, garnish them with a few sprigs of chives or sprouts coming out one end of each roll.

Vietnamese Rice Wraps, or Summer Rolls (Goi Cuon)

Get on a summer roll. Goi cuon (pronounced *goy koong*) is a fresh counterpart to the spring roll, which is fried. Summer rolls are delicious, nutritious, and gluten-free. You can make them with the rice paper wraps I talk about in the preceding section and fill them with raw veggies, such as romaine lettuce, carrots, cucumber, Maui onions, bean sprouts, radish sprouts, alfalfa sprouts, mint, and basil. Some people add shiitake mushrooms and tofu. The meat inside these rolls can be cooked chicken, pork, shrimp, fish, or fish cake.

Preparation time: *30 minutes*

Yield: *1 roll*

1 sheet of rice-paper wrapper

2 peeled and cooked shrimp, cut lengthwise and sliced

3 pieces washed and dried romaine (center rib removed) or Boston lettuce, torn to about the size of a deck of cards

3 fresh mint leaves

1 tablespoon radish sprouts

1 tablespoon bean sprouts

2 tablespoons rice vermicelli, soaked in warm water until soft

5 very thin slices of cooked pork

1 Soak a single rice wrapper in hot water or in a soaking mixture (see the numbered steps at the beginning of the "Rice rolls" section) for 4 to 5 seconds. Drain the wrapper on a flat surface and pat it dry.

2 Layer the ingredients in the rice wrapper. For instance, lay down the shrimp and then follow that with the lettuce, mint, radish and bean sprouts, vermicelli, and pork.

3 Fold the right side of the wrapper toward the center, and then fold the short ends over the filling. Roll the wrapper gently — but firmly and tightly — toward the left until you've formed a neat, oblong bundle. Slice each roll in half at a slight diagonal.

Vary It! *For a vegetarian summer roll, substitute tofu for the shrimp and pork.*

Tip: *This recipe makes one wrap. If you're going to make several wraps at once, you may want to gather the ingredients and separate them into bowls. You can refrigerate the ingredients for up to three hours before putting the wraps together.*

Per serving: *Calories 153 (From Fat 25); Fat 3g (Saturated 1g); Cholesterol 82mg; Sodium 118mg; Carbohydrate 18g (Dietary Fiber 1g); Protein 17g.*

Pork Spring Rolls

Although many spring rolls use a wheat-based wrapper, using rice wrappers works great and makes a gluten-free version of this delicious treat. Because you fry spring rolls, they're not quite as healthful as the fresh summer rolls, but they're definitely delicious.

Preparation time: *30 minutes*

Cooking time: *10 minutes*

Yield: *8 servings*

8 rice paper wrappers

¼ pound ground pork, cooked and drained

1 cup cabbage, shredded

3 carrots, shredded

½ cup onion, diced

1 teaspoon minced garlic (about 2 cloves)

1 teaspoon minced fresh ginger

Salt and pepper to taste

Corn oil for frying

1 Soak the rice wrappers, one at a time, in hot water or in a soaking mixture (see the numbered steps at the beginning of the "Rice rolls" section) for 4 to 5 seconds. Drain the wrappers on a flat surface and pat them dry.

2 In a large bowl, combine the pork, cabbage, carrots, onion, garlic, ginger, and salt and pepper.

3 Drop about 2 tablespoons of the mixture into a softened wrapper. Fold the right side of the wrapper toward the center. Fold the short ends over the filling. Roll the wrapper gently — but firmly and tightly — toward the left until you've formed a neat, oblong bundle. Place the rolls seam-side down onto wax or parchment paper until you're ready to cook them.

4 Heat the corn oil in a skillet over high heat to about 350 degrees. To test the oil's temperature, dip a corner of a roll into it. If the oil bubbles, it's ready. Fry the rolls two at a time in very hot oil until they're golden brown, about 4 minutes.

5 Drain the cooked rolls on paper towels.

Tip: *You can freeze these rolls and save them for later. To reheat, bake them in a 375-degree oven until they're warm, about 10 minutes.*

Tip: *If the rice wrapper tears while you're preparing a roll, don't start all over again. Just use a second wrapper over the first one. You'll end up with a thicker skin, which you may prefer, anyway.*

Per serving: *Calories 262 (From Fat 139); Fat 16g (Saturated 4g); Cholesterol 38mg; Sodium 172mg; Carbohydrate 21g (Dietary Fiber 3g); Protein 13g.*

Exploring lettuce wraps

One of the coolest things about lettuce wraps — besides the cool, crisp palate-cleansing wrap itself — is the versatility they offer gluten-free diners. You can stuff lettuce wraps with any kind of meat, seafood, poultry, veggie, and cheese combinations, or you can use pre-made stuffings such as kung pao chicken, fajita filling, jambalaya, shrimp or egg salad, or well, anything.

Here are a few things to keep in mind so your lettuce wraps can make an even bigger hit:

- ✓ **Use large, pliable leaves.** Consider iceberg, red lettuce, and radicchio leaves or large spinach leaves. Core the lettuce and soak it in ice water for a couple of hours to help you get the leaves off the head without tearing them.

- ✓ **Dry the lettuce before serving.** After you've removed the leaves, let them drain individually, and then put them on a towel in the fridge for a couple of hours to make them crisp.

- ✓ **Serve the lettuce chilled.** For one thing, cold lettuce leaves make a great contrast to the warm innards you fill them with. For another, they hold together better when they're chilled, and they tend to collapse into limp, lifeless leaves when they're warm.

- ✓ **Use a variety of colors, textures, and flavors in the filling.** The filling should include bold flavors and lots of varying texture and colors. Consider using flavorful ingredients like mustards, yogurt, plum sauce, hoisin sauce, and sesame oil in your fillings. When you're trying to decide what to serve, don't forget to check out your stash of leftovers. They can usually inspire and delight you.

- ✓ **Make the fillings and sauces ahead of time.** Fillings are usually served chilled, so make them in advance and give yourself time to refrigerate them.

- ✓ **Let your guests assemble their own wraps.** People love to fill their own lettuce wraps, so put the lettuce leaves and fillings where everyone can reach them, and say, "Lettuce dig in!"

Asian Pork Lettuce Wraps

The variety of lettuce wraps you can make is endless. This recipe follows one of the most basic approaches to lettuce wraps, featuring ground pork and an array of Asian flavors. You can also substitute minced or ground chicken for the pork. Serve the wraps with individual containers of peanut sauce or any type of gluten-free Asian dipping sauce.

Preparation time: *15 minutes*

Cooking time: *2 minutes*

Yield: *6 servings*

2 cups cooked ground pork	¼ cup shredded carrots
3 tablespoons rice vinegar	1 cup cooked rice vermicelli
2 tablespoons gluten-free soy sauce	Salt and pepper to taste
2 teaspoons sesame oil	8 to 10 chilled lettuce leaves
¼ cup chopped green onions	

1 In a medium glass bowl, combine the cooked ground pork, rice vinegar, soy sauce, sesame oil, green onions, carrots, and rice vermicelli. Season the ingredients with salt and pepper and mix them well.

2 Cover the mixture and heat it in the microwave oven on high for about 2 minutes, until the mixture is warm.

3 Serve the pork mixture in a serving bowl with a large serving spoon. On a separate platter, arrange a stack of chilled lettuce leaves. (See the list under "Exploring lettuce wraps" to make the most of your lettuce wraps.) Let people fill their own wraps.

Per serving: *Calories 193 (From Fat 103); Fat 11g (Saturated 4g); Cholesterol 44mg; Sodium 446mg; Carbohydrate 8g (Dietary Fiber 1g); Protein 13g.*

Chapter 12

Sensational Soups, Salads, and Sides

In This Chapter

▶ Getting bowled over by soups

▶ Finding a fresh perspective on salads

▶ Stimulating your sides

Soups, salads, and side dishes can be just as important as the main meal itself. In fact, they can be the meal itself. But many soups are thickened with flour, salads are often dressed up and topped off with gluten-laden goodies, and sides are sometimes seasoned with sauces that make them off-limits to people enjoying a gluten-free lifestyle.

So should you just forget about creamy chowders, crunchy croutons, and rich, thick sauces or seasonings on your favorite side dishes? Are you stuck with boring salads of just lettuce and tomatoes? I don't think so. Are you limited to the old gluten-free standbys of rice, corn, and potatoes? No way. Stick with me, and you can be whipping up some scrumptious accompaniments to rival — or even serve as — the main course.

Sipping Soups and Chowing Down on Chowders

Soup has been a versatile and important part of the diet since people invented waterproof containers about 5,000 years ago. Soups can be hot, cold, thick, thin, creamy, chunky, elegant, or simple. You can create them from leftover food, cutting costs and helping to clear the fridge. Soups are comforting, satisfying, and nutritious.

But commercial soups often contain flour, pasta, or other ingredients that make them taboo. Fortunately, great-tasting gluten-free soups are easy to make, and even creamy chowders and noodle-based soups are a breeze. And when you make soups yourself, they're generally more wholesome and you get to choose what goes in them, so you're bound to love them even more.

New England Clam Chowder

Many clam chowder recipes call for flour to thicken them, but not this one. Remember a few key ingredients that go in a really good clam chowder. First, it's all about the clams; although some connoisseurs may be able to tell the difference, for the most part, it doesn't matter what kind you use — as long as they're fresh, and as long as you either use large ones or lots of them. Next is the cream: Personally, my belly bulges just thinking about heavy cream, but for this recipe, it's worth it — besides, milk may curdle. And finally, the fish stock: Some people use water for the base, but pre-made fish stock adds a ton of flavor to this incredible chowder, so that's what I choose to use. If you can't find fish stock, you can make your own with equal parts of clam juice and chicken stock.

Preparation time: *30 minutes*

Cooking time: *45 minutes*

Yield: *8 servings*

3 cups fish stock	*¼ pound sliced bacon, cut in 1-inch pieces*
1 cup dry white wine	*2 medium onions, chopped*
½ teaspoon dried thyme	*1½ pounds of red potatoes, peeled and diced*
1 bay leaf	*2 cups heavy cream*
½ teaspoon dried parsley	*Pepper to taste*
8 pounds of fresh, cleaned clams (still in the shell)	

1 In a large pot, simmer the stock and the wine over medium heat. Add the thyme, bay leaf, and parsley. Add the clams, cover the soup, and cook it until the clams open (about 8 minutes for smaller clams and up to 15 minutes for large clams).

2 Remove the clams from the pot, take the clams out of the shells, and set the clams aside.

3 In the large pot, cook the bacon until the pieces begin to get crispy. Remove the pieces with a slotted spoon and set them aside. Discard all the fat except a teaspoon or so.

4 Add the onion to the bacon fat, turn the heat to low, and cook the onions till they're soft but not brown (about 15 minutes).

5 In that same large pot, add the strained cooking liquid and the potatoes. Simmer the soup gently until the potatoes are cooked through — about another 20 minutes or so.

6 Add the clams, bacon, and cream to the soup, and add pepper to taste.

Tip: *To clean the clams, let them sit in fresh water for a few hours. Or you can rinse them in a few changes of fresh water, letting them sit in the water a few minutes between changes.*

Vary It! *You've probably seen restaurants serve clam chowder in bread bowls and figured those days are gone now that you're gluten-free. Well, try this: Heat your oven to 425 degrees and mix up a batch of Chebe bread (see the Introduction for information on Chebe). Using ovenproof bowls as molds, press a layer of Chebe about ½-inch thick into each bowl. Bake the bowls until the bread is golden brown, about 20 minutes. Peel the bread out of the bowl-mold and pour clam chowder into your bread bowl. See? You can have your bowl and eat it, too.*

Per serving: *Calories 412 (From Fat 238); Fat 27g (Saturated 15g); Cholesterol 132mg; Sodium 316mg; Carbohydrate 18g (Dietary Fiber 2g); Protein 24g.*

Is chicken soup really nature's remedy for the cold and flu?

More than half of the chicken soup sales in the United States take place during the cold and flu season. That's because many people believe that chicken soup has healing properties. Physician Moses Maimonides first proposed using chicken soup as a cold and asthma remedy in the 12th century, and scientists have studied the therapeutic properties of chicken soup extensively in recent decades. These studies indicate that scientific evidence supports this belief.

Most people agree that chicken soup has some positive effect on cold and flu symptoms, though they disagree on why. Some say the steam helps clear up congestion. Others say the blend of nutrients and vitamins in chicken soup slows the activity of certain white blood cells, reducing the pain and swelling that occurs when these cells fight infection; this temporarily relieves common cold and flu symptoms. And still others claim that the spices in the soup — garlic and pepper, for instance — thin the mucus and make breathing easier. Nearly all doctors agree that increasing fluid intake by eating the soup also relieves congestion.

Whether chicken soup is really the cure for what ails ya, chicken soup is delicious — and easy to make. Start from scratch, or use a premade chicken stock and add your favorite ingredients, like chunks of chicken, veggies, rice, and gluten-free noodles.

Faux Pho — Thai-Namese Shrimp and Chicken Soup

This soup is my simplified version of a traditional Vietnamese noodle soup called pho. ("Faux pho" is supposed to be a play on words, except the real pronunciation of that Vietnamese word is *fuh*. But it's my dumb little joke and I'm sticking to it, so bear with me.) Today the soup is a worldwide favorite, with many variations. My version has a Thai influence, with the fish sauce, ginger, and curry, but the rice noodles make it Vietnamese. Hence the name I've given it: "Thai-Namese."

Tools: *Dutch oven*

Preparation time: *15 minutes*

Cooking time: *20 minutes*

Yield: *4 servings*

4 cups chicken stock	*½ pound skinless boneless chicken breasts, cut in 1-inch-square pieces*
8 ounces bottled clam juice	*1 cup trimmed snow peas*
2 tablespoons fish sauce	*½ cup fresh lime juice*
2 teaspoons minced garlic (about 4 cloves)	*2 tablespoons sugar*
2 teaspoons minced fresh ginger	*2 tablespoons sliced green onion tops*
¾ teaspoon red curry paste	*2 tablespoons chopped fresh cilantro*
8 ounces mushrooms, sliced	*13.5-ounce can light coconut milk*
1 pound large shrimp, peeled and deveined	*4 cups cooked rice noodles (slightly firm)*

1 Combine the chicken stock, clam juice, fish sauce, garlic, ginger, and red curry paste together in a large Dutch oven, stirring the ingredients with a whisk. Add the mushrooms, and bring the mixture to a boil over medium heat.

2 Reduce the heat and simmer the soup for 5 minutes. Add the shrimp, chicken, and snow peas, and bring the soup to a boil. Cover the soup, reduce the heat, and simmer it for 5 minutes.

3 Stir in the lime juice, sugar, green onion tops, cilantro, and coconut milk. Cook the soup for 4 minutes or until it's thoroughly heated. Add the cooked rice noodles.

Tip: Figure 12-1 shows you how to peel and devein shrimp.

Per serving: *Calories 462 (From Fat 102); Fat 11g (Saturated 5g); Cholesterol 206mg; Sodium 2,094mg; Carbohydrate 57g (Dietary Fiber 2g); Protein 35g.*

Make no bones about it

The origin of the expression to "make no bones about it" actually has to do with soup. Today it means to speak frankly and directly — to have no difficulty or hesitation in saying what you want to say. But when a version of the phrase appeared in 1459, the author was making an analogy to soups that didn't have any bones in them; diners wouldn't hesitate to swallow the soup, because they wouldn't have to eat around the bones.

Cleaning and Deveining Shrimp

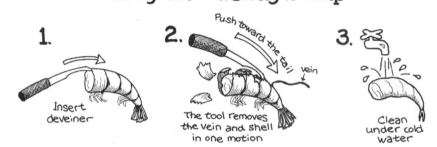

Figure 12-1: Prepping your shrimp.

 Many Thai ingredients are inherently gluten-free, although you do need to check the labels, especially in Americanized products. Fish sauce is a good example. Traditional fish sauce comes from fermented, salt-cured fish, and most fish sauce is just that — fish. But you may occasionally find a label that shows added wheat. Remember, you always need to read labels. Even the authentic Asian products have English labels if they've been imported to the U.S.

Making Strides with Salads and Sides

Most people know that plain green salads are gluten-free — and of course, you can have steamed or boiled vegetables — but even hard-core veggie fans get tired of those things pretty quickly. In this section, I show you ways to dress up delicious and nutritious veggie salads and help you make fast salad meals a snap.

But another kind of salad falls somewhere between a salad and a side. This is the kind without any lettuce-like substances at all; instead, it features potatoes, pasta, rice, and other alternative salad makin's. Potato salad, for instance: Is it a side or a salad? You think about that while I show you some ways to snazz up your salads — sides — whatever.

Serving salads with green, leafy stuff

Veggie salads are a great way to combine interesting grains, fruits, vegetables, and meats in one dish. As a side or a complete meal, salads are nutritious and delicious, and they're especially great on a hot, summer day, when they make for a cool, quick dinner (without making you resort to cereal and milk).

Most of these salads start with a basic bed of greens or a variety of lettuce types. Prewashed bagged greens make these salads even simpler, but of course you can use any type of lettuce you want. Remember that the darker the lettuce, the more nutritious it probably is.

From there, the options are endless. Here are a few of my personal favorites:

- **Caesar Salad:** Start with romaine lettuce and add Caesar dressing. You can buy it or use the easy recipe in this chapter. Remember to add freshly grated Parmesan cheese.
- **Cool as a Cucumber Salad:** In a medium-sized bowl, mix finely chopped cucumber (peeled and seeded) with plain yogurt, onion powder, lemon juice, and black pepper. Put it over a bed of greens and top it with diced tomatoes.
- **Grilled Garlic Chicken Salad:** In a small bowl, mix ¾ cup Italian salad dressing with 2 teaspoons minced garlic and a dash of crushed red pepper flakes. Add sliced red bell pepper and sliced mushrooms to the dressing, and toss them so they're well-coated. Fish the peppers and mushrooms out of the dressing, setting the remaining dressing aside, and grill the peppers and mushrooms as you grill your chicken. Place salad greens on plates and add the grilled vegetables and chicken. Drizzle the remaining dressing on top.
- **Thai Beef Salad:** Start with a bed of greens and add ¼ cup mint leaves (torn into large pieces), half a cucumber (peeled and sliced), several thinly sliced pieces of grilled flank steak, 2 tablespoons chopped peanuts, and lime wedges (for garnish). Top the salad with an Asian salad dressing like the one I give later in this chapter.

⟳ **Tomato and Basil Salad:** Over a bed of greens, add sliced beefsteak tomatoes topped with torn pieces of a large, fresh basil leaf. If you'd like, add a slice of mozzarella. Then drizzle the salad with a balsamic vinaigrette dressing.

⟳ **Warm Beet Salad:** In a large saucepan, cook some green beans in boiling water until they're tender, about 8 minutes. Add a 16-ounce can of sliced beets (drained), and cook them over medium heat until they're heated through. Drain the beans and the beets. Meanwhile, in a screw-top glass jar, combine about 3 tablespoons orange juice, 3 tablespoons extra-virgin olive oil, 1 tablespoon balsamic vinegar, 2 teaspoons minced garlic, and a dash of white pepper. Shake the dressing well. Lay out some mixed greens, place the beans and beets on top of them, and coat the veggies with the dressing.

Dressing it up with dressings

Lots of commercially available salad dressings are gluten-free. People used to think that most salad dressings were off-limits for those on a gluten-free diet, but that was because they thought vinegar wasn't allowed. Now that they know vinegar (with the exception of malt vinegar) is okay, store shelves are loaded with options. But if you'd prefer to make your own dressings — because you like to, because doing so saves money, or because the dressing has more wholesome ingredients that way — the recipes in this section should get you started in the right direction.

No time for recipes? Here are a few quick and easy dressings you can toss together for your salads:

↙ **Roasted Red Pepper Vinaigrette:** Mix chopped roasted red pepper with white wine vinegar, minced garlic, chopped flat-leaf parsley, extra-virgin olive oil, and salt and pepper.

↙ **Garbanzo Vinaigrette:** Mix coarsely mashed garbanzo beans (chickpeas) with sherry vinegar, minced shallots, chopped chives and parsley, extra-virgin olive oil, and salt and pepper.

↙ **Lemon Parmesan Dressing:** Mix fresh lemon juice and freshly grated Parmesan cheese with mayonnaise, minced garlic, extra-virgin olive oil, and salt and pepper.

↙ **Pesto Vinaigrette:** Mix pesto sauce with white wine vinegar, extra-virgin olive oil, and salt and pepper.

☜ *Asian Salad Dressing*

Most commercial Asian salad dressings use soy sauce, and nearly all of them contain wheat. Asian salad dressing is easy to make yourself, though, and to keep it gluten-free, just use any type of gluten-free soy sauce. This dressing can also double as a marinade for meats or tofu.

Preparation time: *5 minutes*

Yield: *8 servings*

½ cup rice vinegar	*1 teaspoon sesame oil*
¼ cup gluten-free soy sauce	*1 teaspoon toasted sesame seeds*
2 tablespoons water	*⅓ cup canola oil*

1 Combine the vinegar, soy sauce, water, sesame oil, and sesame seeds in a jar with a tight-fitting lid, and shake the mixture well.

2 Add the oil and shake again.

Per serving: *Calories 94 (From Fat 90); Fat 10g (Saturated 1g); Cholesterol 0mg; Sodium 460mg; Carbohydrate 0g (Dietary Fiber 0g); Protein 1g.*

Don't fear the fat on salads

Most people are well aware that smothering their salads in fatty salad dressings turns a healthy meal into a high-fat, diet-sabotaging indulgence. So they opt for fat-free salad dressings and figure they're making a healthy choice. But a study published by the *American Journal of Clinical Nutrition* shows that people may be compromising the nutritional value of their salads when they do that, because dietary fat is necessary for the absorption of nutrients from fruits and vegetables. In the study, people who ate salads with fat-free salad dressing absorbed far less of the helpful nutrients and vitamins from spinach, lettuce, tomatoes, and carrots than those who ate their salads with a salad dressing containing fat.

Keep in mind, though, that you don't have to get the fat from your dressing, and you don't have to eat all that much fat to help with the absorption of these important nutrients. Eating just a handful of nuts or a quarter of an avocado gives you plenty of dietary fat to help with absorption.

Caesar Salad Dressing

Everyone loves Caesar salad, and you can make it in a number of ways. The real chefs prepare it at the table, gently mixing one ingredient at a time. Not me. I cheat. I make it in a blender or small food processor, and it takes less than 5 minutes to prepare. I haven't had a complaint yet.

Tools: *Blender or food processor*

Preparation time: *5 minutes*

Yield: *8 servings*

1 egg

½ cup lemon juice

½ cup extra-virgin olive oil

2 teaspoons minced garlic (about 4 cloves)

2 tablespoons gluten-free Worcestershire sauce

¾ cup fresh Parmesan cheese

2-ounce can anchovies

1 teaspoon freshly ground pepper

1 Place the egg in a microwaveable dish and cover it with a paper towel. Heat the egg in the microwave on high for 10 seconds.

2 Combine the egg, lemon juice, olive oil, garlic, Worcestershire sauce, Parmesan, anchovies, and pepper in a blender or small food processor, and process the dressing until smooth. If it's too runny, add a little Parmesan cheese. If it's too thick, add a little more lemon juice or olive oil.

Per serving: Calories 186 (From Fat 154); Fat 17g (Saturated 4g); Cholesterol 39mg; Sodium 450mg; Carbohydrate 3g (Dietary Fiber 0g); Protein 6g.

Creamy Green Anchovy Salad Dressing

This dressing is one of my all-time favorites. You can make this vegetarian by leaving out the anchovies and adding a little salt instead. Add a little avocado to this for a creamy twist. Use it on your favorite salad or greens. Because the dressing is green and creamy, I especially like this on a colorful salad with lots of tomatoes; yellow, green, and red peppers; and avocados.

Tools: *Blender or food processor*

Preparation time: *5 minutes*

Yield: *8 servings*

2 cups mayonnaise	*2 teaspoons chopped fresh chives*
5 anchovy fillets, minced	*1 tablespoon rice vinegar*
1 chopped green onion	*2 teaspoons chopped fresh tarragon*
2 teaspoons fresh parsley	*2 teaspoons lemon juice*

1 Mix the mayonnaise, anchovies, green onion, parsley, chives, rice vinegar, tarragon, and lemon juice in a blender or food processor.

2 Process the mixture until the dressing is smooth. Refrigerate it until you're ready to serve.

Per serving: Calories 402 (From Fat 397); Fat 44g (Saturated 7g); Cholesterol 35mg; Sodium 406mg; Carbohydrate 2g (Dietary Fiber 0g); Protein 1g.

Finishing off your salad with some fixin's

Toss it in to mix it up. You can add lots of things to your salad to perk it up and provide more nutrition at the same time:

- ✔ **Beans and legumes:** Try green beans, kidney beans, black beans, or garbanzo beans (chickpeas). Not only do they add flavor, but they add lots of fiber, too.

- ✔ **Bok choy:** Oh boy — bok choy (Chinese white cabbage) is loaded with nutrients, and new shredded varieties are great on salads.

✔ **Cherry tomatoes:** Several varieties of cherry tomatoes are available, and they come in all different colors and shapes.

✔ **Crumbled bacon:** Of course, bacon adds some fat, but it also adds flavor.

✔ **Crumbled cheese:** Be creative, using cheeses like *queso seco* (Mexican dry cheese), *queso fresco* (fresh Mexican cheese), or freshly grated Romano or Parmesan.

✔ **Diced ham or turkey:** A little less fatty than bacon, these meats add protein and flavor to a salad.

✔ **Fruit:** Grapes, pineapple, melons, kiwi — a variety of fruits can liven up a salad.

✔ **Greens:** Iceberg lettuce is boring and relatively worthless nutritionally speaking. Consider radicchio, romaine, kale, spinach, arugula, and other greens to increase the vitamin, mineral, and fiber content — not to mention flavor.

✔ **Jicama:** Somewhere between an apple and a potato, jicama (pronounced *hee*-cuh-muh) adds crunch, flavor, and lots of fiber.

✔ **Mushrooms:** Buy them sliced to make preparing salads easier on yourself. They add lots of minerals and an interesting flavor.

✔ **Nuts:** Any kind of nut will do. They add nutrients, crunch, and flavor.

✔ **Olives:** If you use chopped olives, you can spread them around the salad and get just as much flavor without as many calories.

✔ **Onions:** Red onions and scallions are two of the most popular varieties to put on salads. Onions and other white vegetables add nutrients, too.

✔ **Radishes:** Not only do these add a zip to your salad, but they have potassium and vitamin C.

✔ **Raisins:** Also try similar toppings like dried cranberries.

✔ **Raw broccoli:** New packaged broccoli slaws make adding flavor and crunch easy. Broccoli is loaded with cancer-fighting nutrients and calcium.

✔ **Shredded cabbage:** In the same family as broccoli, cabbage contains nutrients that are important for cancer prevention.

✔ **Sprouts:** Loaded with fiber and nutrients, sprouts are a great addition to any salad. And they're easy to grow yourself. See the "Sprout 'em yourself" sidebar for tips on growing your own sprout garden.

Sprout 'em yourself

Sprouts are a great source of protein, fiber, and vitamins A, B, and C, and they're loaded with antioxidants. In fact, a study at John Hopkins University found that broccoli sprouts actually have higher levels of cancer-fighting compounds than fresh broccoli.

You don't even need a green thumb to grow sprouts — just a few basic starter items, and you can watch your sprout garden grow.

You can grow sprouts in soil, just like any other plant, but most people grow them in jars. For that, you need:

- A large jar
- Cheesecloth or nylon netting
- A rubber band
- 1 tablespoon sprout seeds (alfalfa, radish, mung bean, or buckwheat are good sprout starters), available at nurseries or online
- Water

Here's what you do:

1. **Put one tablespoon seeds into the jar, cover the seeds with water, and tighten the cheesecloth or nylon netting over the jar opening with a rubber band.**

   Let the seeds soak overnight.

2. **Drain the water from the jar through the cheesecloth. Leave the jar on a shelf, in a cupboard, or under the kitchen sink.**

   If you keep the jar in the dark, the sprouts grow white; if you expose the jar to light, the sprouts come out green.

3. **Rinse and drain the seeds once a day or more.**

   This step is the most important because the seeds need to be moist but not wet. If you don't rinse the seeds often enough, they may start to mold. If you notice a bad smell from your sprouting seeds, they're probably no good. Toss them and start over again.

In less than a week, the sprouts should be ready to eat. To harvest them, just use scissors to cut the edible sprouts away from the roots, leaving what you don't need. The rest keep growing, and you can use them later.

Getting creative with croutons

Okay, I don't know about you, but I have some pretty specific crouton criteria. After all, if you're going to indulge, you may as well do it right. Personally, my crouton criteria include crunch, flavor, and just a tinge of decadence. I mean, broccoli just doesn't cut it as a crouton for me; does it for you?

But croutons are usually made from bread and are therefore off-limits on the gluten-free diet. But don't worry — with a little creativity, you can make all sorts of different types of croutons. Try some of these ideas:

- **Barbecue potato chips:** Crush these up on your salad. These are a little lighter than a tortilla chip, but they work well, too.

- **Dehydrated veggies (and fruit):** Marinate the veggies in any marinade and then dehydrate them in a dehydrator. Zucchini, sweet potatoes, and even bananas work well (you can also buy pre-made banana chips).

- **Deep-fried veggies:** Take your favorite veggie — sweet potatoes work really well for this — and dredge them in any gluten-free flour mixture you have lying around. Deep-fry, and you have veggie croutons.

- **Gluten-free homemade croutons:** Use any gluten-free bread (stale bread works best), cut the bread into cubes, and deep-fry. Then coat them with Parmesan and seasonings. If you want a lower-fat version, put the cubes on a baking tray and drizzle olive oil over them. Season the bread with fresh herbs or seasoned salt and bake them in the oven.

- **Polenta:** Polenta is a boiled cornmeal mush that grocery stores usually sell in plastic tubes. Dice polenta into crouton-sized pieces and deep-fry it for a great salad topper.

- **Potato croutons:** Dice two potatoes and put the pieces on a baking tray coated with nonstick spray. Then drizzle the potatoes with oil and bake at 425 degrees for 30 minutes or until crisp and golden.

- **Potato skins:** Peel the innards out of potatoes and save the skins. Deep-fry and season the skins with seasoned salt.

- **Tortilla chips:** Take any kind of gluten-free tortilla chip (even the flavored kind) and crush them up.

Move Over, Mashed Potatoes: Considering New Sides

Some people think side dishes on the gluten-free diet are easy, and that's true to some extent. Rice, corn, and potatoes do serve as staple sides for most people new to the gluten-free lifestyle. But I say, "Move over, mashed potatoes," to make way for more provocative sides featuring more interesting players, such as quinoa, millet, and beans.

One of my favorite alternative grains is quinoa (pronounced *keen*-wa). Called an ancient food because it was one of three staple foods of early South American civilization, quinoa was then — and still is — known as the Mother Grain. Boasting nearly 20 percent protein in some varieties, quinoa has more protein than any other grain. And it's a complete protein, with a good balance of all the essential amino acids. It's also high in fiber, vitamins, and minerals. I use it in recipes for couscous (in place of couscous), tabbouleh, or just about any other grain. See Chapter 9 for more on preparing quinoa.

☜ *Lemon Quinoa Crunch*

Crunchy, colorful, tangy, and nutritious, you can serve this dish at room temperature or cold (I prefer cold). This food makes a great stand-alone side or salad substitute. In fact, because quinoa contains all the amino acids your body can't produce on its own, this grain can be the main dish. You may want to double the recipe, because the leftovers are fantastic — this dish gets better each day as the flavors infuse the grain.

Tools: *Fine sieve*

Preparation time: *15 minutes*

Yield: *6 servings*

¼ cup lime juice	¾ cup peeled, seeded, and diced cucumber
¼ teaspoon white pepper	¾ cup seeded and diced tomato
¼ teaspoon freshly ground black pepper	¾ cup sliced red bell pepper
¼ cup sliced marinated jalapeño pepper	¼ cup sliced yellow bell pepper
¼ teaspoon coarse salt	¼ cup sliced green onions, white part only
¼ cup olive oil	¼ cup chopped Italian parsley
3 cups water	¼ cup chopped fresh mint
1½ cups quinoa	Salt and pepper to taste

1 Make a vinaigrette by whisking together the lime juice, white pepper, black pepper, jalapeño, coarse salt, and olive oil. Set the mixture aside.

2 Place the quinoa in a fine sieve and wash it under running water, rubbing it with your hands for a few minutes. Drain the water out.

3 In a large pot, combine the water and quinoa. Bring the mixture to a boil, lower the heat, and simmer it uncovered for about 10 to 15 minutes, or until the quinoa is barely tender. Don't overcook it. Strain the quinoa, drain it thoroughly, and let it cool. Don't rinse it.

4 Mix the quinoa in with the cucumber, tomato, red bell pepper, yellow bell pepper, green onions, parsley, mint, and vinaigrette. Add a little salt and pepper to taste (you don't need much, because this dish has plenty of flavor). Serve it at room temperature or cold.

Per serving: Calories 260 (From Fat 105); Fat 12g (Saturated 2g); Cholesterol 0mg; Sodium 240mg; Carbohydrate 34g (Dietary Fiber 4g); Protein 7g.

◌ Rice Salad with Red Peppers, Garbanzo Beans, and Feta

This dish is loaded with flavor. It's already nutritious, but to add nutrients, try using brown rice instead of white.

Preparation time: *15 minutes*

Resting time: *1 hour*

Yield: *6 servings*

½ cup lemon juice

2 teaspoons minced garlic (about 4 cloves)

¼ cup extra-virgin olive oil

Salt and pepper to taste

3 cups cooked rice, cooled to room temperature

15-ounce can garbanzo beans (chickpeas), drained

1 cup finely diced feta cheese

½ cup chopped fresh parsley

¼ cup chopped fresh dill

4 green onions, washed, ends removed, thinly sliced

½ cup roasted red peppers

1 Make the dressing by whisking together the lemon juice, garlic, olive oil, and salt and pepper.

2 In a large serving bowl, combine the rice, garbanzo beans, feta cheese, parsley, dill, green onions, and red peppers.

3 Pour the dressing over the rice mixture and mix well. Let it sit at least an hour before serving. Serve at room temperature or cold.

Per serving: Calories 308 (From Fat 137); Fat 15g (Saturated 5g); Cholesterol 22mg; Sodium 561mg; Carbohydrate 35g (Dietary Fiber 3g); Protein 8g.

Latin American Marinated Seafood (Ceviche)

Ceviche poses an imponderable question — is it cooked or not? *Ceviche,* sometimes spelled *seviche,* is a delicious Latin American seafood dish that people prepare by using an ancient method of "cooking" that uses the acid from citrus juice instead of heat. The acid actually changes the protein structure in the fish, and you can watch the fish turn from translucent pink to opaque white. Ceviche is usually a mixture of chunks of raw fish, lemon and/or lime juice, chopped onion, minced garlic, and chile peppers. The fish cooks in the citrus while flavors blend into a spectacular dish that you can serve as an appetizer or even an entree.

Preparation time: *15 minutes*

Refrigeration time: *6 hours*

Yield: *8 servings*

2 pounds fresh red snapper fillets, cut into 1/2 inch pieces	*1 teaspoon of salt*
¼ cup purple onion, finely diced	*2 teaspoons chopped fresh cilantro*
1 cup fresh peeled, seeded, and chopped tomatoes	*Dash Tabasco sauce*
	Dash cumin
1 serrano chile, seeded and finely diced	*½ cup freshly squeezed lime juice*
	½ cup freshly squeezed lemon juice

1 Place the fish, onion, tomatoes, chile pepper, salt, cilantro, Tabasco, and cumin in a glass or ceramic dish.

2 Cover the mixture with the lemon and lime juice, and let it sit covered in the fridge for at least 6 hours.

3 Stir it frequently, making sure the citrus covers all the fish.

4 Serve the ceviche with heated tortillas and avocado slices or with tortilla chips for dipping.

Tip: You can use shrimp, scallops, or squid instead of or in addition to the fish. You can also use any type of fish you'd like — just make sure it's firm, like red snapper or cod.

Vary It! Get creative and add diced fruit like mangos, and serve the ceviche rolled in a fresh, warm corn tortilla with lettuce and a little salsa, or with chips for dipping.

Per serving: Calories 86 (From Fat 10); Fat 1g (Saturated 0g); Cholesterol 28mg; Sodium 244mg; Carbohydrate 3g (Dietary Fiber 0g); Protein 16g.

⏁ Sweet-Potato Potato Salad

You may have caught my comment about potatoes being an indulgence. But sweet pota-toes (as opposed to "regular" ones) are actually very nutritious. (By the way, sweet potatoes are not the same as yams; if you're in the U.S., you're probably technically eating sweet potatoes.) Try this simple and refreshing potato salad for a unique Southwestern twist on an old American favorite.

Preparation time: *15 minutes*

Cooking time: *20 minutes*

Refrigeration time: *2 hours*

Yield: *6 servings*

2 pounds sweet potatoes, peeled and cooked	2 tablespoons chopped cilantro
3 tablespoons canned chopped green chilies	Dash paprika
½ cup chopped red pepper	⅓ cup mayonnaise

1 Peel and dice the sweet potatoes. Steam them for 20 minutes, or until they're tender but not mushy.

2 In a large serving bowl, mix the sweet potatoes, green chilies, red pepper, cilantro, paprika, and mayonnaise. Chill the potato salad for at least 2 hours; serve it cold.

Per serving: *Calories 216 (From Fat 90); Fat 10g (Saturated 2g); Cholesterol 7mg; Sodium 112mg; Carbohydrate 30g (Dietary Fiber 3g); Protein 2g.*

Trying tater toppings

Baked potatoes are a staple side on the gluten-free diet. But seriously — do you think anyone ever gets a hankerin' for a plain ol' baked potato with nothing on it? No doubt, the spud needs some serious support from the wonderful world of toppings. After all, if you're going to indulge (yeah, I consider a potato an indulgence because it's a very high-glycemic-index food; you can read more about the glycemic index in Chapter 6), you may as well make it worth eating. Bottom line: An unadorned baked potato is, plain and simple, too plain and simple unless you dress it up. Try these toppers:

✔ Bacon or ham pieces

✔ Bragg Liquid Aminos or gluten-free soy sauce

✔ Broccoli tops

✔ Butter or margarine

✔ Caramelized onions

✔ Chili

✔ Chives

✔ Diced or shredded chicken

✔ Guacamole or avocado slices

✔ Jalapeño peppers

✔ Ranch salad dressing (or any of the dressings in this chapter)

✔ Salsa

✔ Shredded cheese

✔ Sour cream

✔ Steak or barbecue sauce

Chapter 13

Enticing Entrees

*H*ome-cooked dinners are one of life's great pleasures. But these days, many people are so busy that cooking homemade meals is a luxury; top that with the idea of working within the parameters of a gluten-free diet, and you may find yourself stuck in the rut of fixing the same three or four entrees each week.

Well, forget the boiled chicken and plain burger patties, my friends! You can make anything gluten-free, as long as you figure out how to make simple substitutions (really, check out Chapter 9).

Oh, and speaking of simple . . . keep in mind that I'm not into recipes with 24 ingredients (many of which I've never heard of) and lengthy instructions that include words in other languages. I'm all about being simple — at least in the kitchen — but I love to eat, and taste is something I don't scrimp on. So in this chapter, I share with you a few of my favorite-but-simple entrees, gluten-free style.

Making Poultry with Pizzazz

You may not realize just how versatile poultry really is. Not only do these birds soak up flavors from marinades and rubs, providing an array of flavors and taste experiences, but your fine (formerly feathered) friends in and of themselves are oozing with options. White meat or dark? Breast or thigh? Skin or no skin? Don't underestimate the significance of these choices — to people with a preference, white meat versus dark is an entirely different bird.

Fowl factoids

Chicken provides you with lots of great imponderables: Which came first, the chicken or the egg? Why did the chicken cross the road? Why does everything taste like chicken? Chicken also provides you with pretty interesting trivia. Chew on some of these chicken tidbits:

- The average American eats more than 81 pounds of chicken each year.

- More than half of all chicken entrees ordered in restaurants are for fried chicken (and are therefore not usually gluten-free).

- The average hen lays 255 eggs per year.

- Eating chicken with a fork is illegal in Gainesville, Georgia, the "Chicken Capital of the World."

- Chicken is safe to eat when the internal temperature reaches 180 degrees. The breasts are done at 170 degrees, and the thighs take the longest to cook. Remember, though, that meat continues to cook for a few minutes after you take it out of the oven or off the grill, so you may want to take it out about three to five degrees before it reaches your target temperature.

- The most common way to tell if poultry is done is by the color of the juice that comes out when you poke the chicken with a fork. Most people think that if the juices run clear, it's done; if they're pink, it's not. However, note that meat around the bones may be dark pink because of bone marrow. And purists point out that meat may remain pink due to certain cooking methods, so temperature is the only reliable way to know that the meat's done.

Chicken is a great source of protein as well as niacin, vitamins B-6 and B-12, vitamin D, iron, and zinc. Ounce for ounce, skinless chicken is one of the lowest-fat meats around. Although breast meat definitely has the lowest fat content, even skinless dark meat is comparatively low in fat, and most of the fat it does have is unsaturated — the good kind.

Dark meat is dark because birds use their leg and wing muscles more, so those muscles require more oxygen. *Myoglobin* is an iron-containing protein that transfers oxygen from the blood to the muscles, changing the color of the meat — and providing you with more iron.

Spicy Chinese Game Hens

Game hens give the appearance of being fancy and ultra-gourmet, but they're actually simple to prepare and fairly inexpensive. Marinating game hens enhances the flavor, but longer isn't necessarily better (see the "Merry marinades" sidebar). More than eight hours is overkill, because the flavor doesn't really improve at that point. Remember to marinate the hens in the refrigerator in a glass, ceramic, or stainless steel dish (not aluminum or iron).

You can usually find game hens in the frozen section next to the turkeys. They weigh about one to two pounds, so you can plan on half a hen per person. This recipe calls for hoisin sauce, oyster sauce, and Asian chile sauce; you can find them in the Asian food sections of grocery stores.

Preparation time: *15 minutes*

Refrigeration time: *30 minutes to 8 hours*

Cooking time: *20 minutes*

Yield: *8 servings*

1½ teaspoons minced garlic (about 3 cloves)	*¼ cup hoisin sauce*
3 tablespoons minced ginger	*¼ cup oyster sauce*
3 green onions, chopped	*3 tablespoons sesame oil*
¼ cup chopped cilantro	*1 tablespoon Asian chile sauce*
¾ cup orange juice	*4 game hens, cut in half*
¼ cup lemon juice	

1 Preheat the grill. If you're using a gas grill, heat it on high for 10 minutes, and then reduce the heat to medium.

2 In a small bowl, mix the garlic, ginger, green onions, cilantro, orange juice, lemon juice, hoisin sauce, oyster sauce, sesame oil, and chile sauce. Set aside ½ cup of this mixture for basting the hens; use the rest as a marinade in step 3.

3 Place the halved game hens in a shallow dish or a sealable plastic bag, and add the marinade. Refrigerate the hens for at least 30 minutes, and up to 8 hours, turning them occasionally.

4 Grill the game hens on a medium heat, not too close to the flame (or it could flame up and burn), for about 10 minutes on each side, until the internal temperature is 160 degrees or the juices run clear when you pierce the meat with a fork. Baste the hens with the marinade you set aside in step 2.

Vary It! *If you don't want to grill the hens, you can roast them in a 425-degree oven for 25 minutes.*

Tip: *To split game hens in half, use poultry shears to cut the hens through the breast and backbone (see Figure 13-1). Cut the backbone out and toss it, if you'd like.*

Per serving: *Calories 753 (From Fat 470); Fat 52g (Saturated 14g); Cholesterol 337mg; Sodium 365mg; Carbohydrate 9g (Dietary Fiber 1g); Protein 58g.*

Ginger: Good and good for you

Some people refer to ginger as a root, but it's actually a *rhizome,* an underground stem. One is depicted in the following figure. Most commonly in Indian and Asian dishes, it has a peppery, sweet flavor when it's fresh. When dried, it's actually got a bit of a spicy kick. Ginger is also a stimulant for the circulatory system, and some cultures consider it an aphrodisiac.

ginger root

Figure 13-1: Cutting a game hen in half.

Place the bird breast side up. Cut along the breast bone from cavity to neck end. Gently pry open.

Turn the hen over and cut along one side of the backbone, cutting the hen in half.

discard

Cut along the other side of the backbone to remove and discard.

Your Basic Roasted Chicken

Few dishes are easier, more delicious, and more nutritious than your basic roasted chicken. I like to stuff mine with any fresh herbs I happen to have growing in the kitchen or garden (doing so makes the kitchen smell great), but you can skip that step if you'd like. This dish is so good that you probably won't have any leftovers, but if you do, use them to add lots of flavor to just about anything: salads, chicken soup, enchiladas, or stir-fry.

Preparation time: *10 minutes*

Cooking time: *1 hour, 15 minutes*

Yield: *4 servings*

¼ cup chopped onion

⅓ cup lemon juice

1½ teaspoons minced garlic (about 3 cloves)

2 tablespoons fresh, chopped rosemary

Salt and pepper to taste

4 tablespoons olive oil

1 tablespoon sesame oil

1 large roasting chicken

1 Preheat the oven to 375 degrees.

2 In a small bowl, mix the onion, lemon juice, garlic, rosemary, salt and pepper, olive oil, and sesame oil.

3 Take the sack of giblets and the neck out of the chicken and discard (or save them for another recipe). Rinse the cavity out with cool water and pat dry.

4 Spoon about half the herb mixture into the inside of the chicken cavity. Use your hands to rub it around and coat the inside of the chicken. Rub the rest of the mixture on the outside of the chicken until the entire chicken is covered. Pat the chunks of onion and herbs from the mixture onto the chicken. Some of them will probably fall off while you're cooking, but that's okay.

5 Place the chicken in a roasting pan and cook it for about 1 hour and 15 minutes, until the breast meat reaches 170 degrees or the juices run clear when you pierce the skin with a fork.

Tip: *Save the drippings. Let them cool and scrape the fat off the top. Then pour the drippings into an ice tray and freeze them. You can use the cubes later for soup broth or seasonings.*

Per serving: *Calories 754 (From Fat 469); Fat 52g (Saturated 12g); Cholesterol 252mg; Sodium 337mg; Carbohydrate 4g (Dietary Fiber 1g); Protein 65g.*

Skinless or skinful? It's really not so sinful

The skinny on skin is that although people often think cooking chicken with the skin off is healthier, it actually isn't. Calorie-wise, the meat is the same whether you cook it with the skin on or off, and leaving it on actually helps the chicken retain moisture and intensifies its flavor. Of course, you can't *eat* the skin in this case. Just cook the chicken with it on and then — if you have the willpower — peel it off and throw it away. The good news? Chicken skin (unless seasoned or coated with gluten) is gluten-free, so if you're into indulgences, go for it!

Do you like (cooking) it low and slow or hot and heavy?

I'm talking about oven temperature and cooking time. Poultry preferences vary, and although some people like crispy, crunchy skin, others prefer a softer skin. How the skin turns out depends on how you cook the chicken. For a crunchy outside, cook the chicken at a very high oven temperature — 500 degrees works well. After about 20 minutes, turn the oven down to 350 degrees so the meat can finish cooking before the skin burns. If you go this route, start the cooking process with the breast side down so the legs and thighs get a head start cooking. About halfway through, turn the chicken over so the breast can brown. Lower oven temperatures don't make the outside crunchy, but the meat stays moist and tender.

Lemon Caper Chicken

I happen to love lemon, capers, and chicken, so this dish is definitely one of my favorites. It's easy to make, but it looks like you spent hours in the kitchen. The recipe calls for rice flour for dusting the chicken, but feel free to use any gluten-free flour or baking mix that you have lying around. (By the way, capers are a type of pickled flower bud — look for them near the pickles in the store.)

Preparation time: 20 minutes

Cooking time: 25 minutes

Yield: 4 servings

4 boneless skinless chicken breasts	¼ cup chicken broth
4 tablespoons olive oil, divided	½ cup dry sherry
¼ cup rice flour	¼ cup freshly squeezed lemon juice
Salt and pepper to taste	4 tablespoons capers, drained and rinsed
3 green onions, chopped	2 tablespoons unsalted butter
1 teaspoon minced garlic (about 2 cloves)	

1 Pound the chicken breasts to an even thickness — about ½ inch is good. If you don't have a meat tenderizer, you can use any other heavy, manageable object, like an iron skillet.

2 Put enough olive oil into a large skillet to coat the bottom of the pan. This will probably require about 2 tablespoons. Heat the oil over medium-high heat.

3 Dredge the chicken breasts in flour and season the chicken with salt and pepper.

4 Brown the chicken, about 3 minutes on each side. If your pan isn't big enough, you may need to do this in a couple of batches. Make sure you have enough oil in the pan at all times (you'll probably have to add another tablespoon of oil during cooking). Transfer the chicken to a warm serving platter and cover it with foil.

5 Clean the pan to get the residual flour out, or use a new skillet. Reduce the heat to low and add the rest of the olive oil to the skillet (you should have about 1 tablespoon left). Add the green onion, garlic, chicken broth, sherry, lemon juice, and capers. Turn the heat up to medium-high and simmer until the liquid has reduced to half (about 5 minutes).

6 Tilt the pan so the liquid pools on one side, and whisk in the butter until the sauce is smooth. Pour the sauce over the chicken breasts and serve immediately.

Per serving: *Calories 362 (From Fat 205); Fat 23g (Saturated 6g); Cholesterol 89mg; Sodium 529mg; Carbohydrate 11g (Dietary Fiber 1g); Protein 28g.*

Eating Meat

Yes, you can have your steak and eat it, too. And your pork and lamb and ostrich and buffalo and kangaroo. Even if you're trying to eat healthily, meat can be part of a well-balanced diet. Red meat does have a fair amount of fat, but it's also a great source of protein, vitamins, and minerals, and it has no carbohydrates. Just remember to eat it in moderation and to watch your portion size — a serving of meat is three ounces cooked (four ounces before cooking), about the size of a deck of cards.

Buying beef

If you've ever stood at the meat counter wondering whether you should buy a chuck, flank, round, rib, or sirloin, you're not alone. Adding to the confusion are different names for the same cuts and vague labels that confuse even the savviest of consumers. Thankfully, I have some basic guidelines to help you make sense of the age-old question, "Where's the beef?"

Beef grades

Prime, choice, and select grades of beef are descriptions of a cut's leanness and palatability and the age of the animal. *Select* cuts are leaner than *choice* cuts, and choice cuts are leaner than *prime* cuts. Select cuts look less marbled and aren't as tender or juicy as choice or prime cuts.

The aged meats you usually buy in fine restaurants are prime grades. You can find select and choice grades in the grocery store and in less expensive restaurants — but keep in mind that select cuts are the leanest. If you like the tenderness that comes with higher fat grades, you can learn to work around the leanness of certain cuts with the use of marinades and simple cooking techniques.

Beef cuts

Beef is available in many different cuts, including steaks, roasts, brisket, stew meat, and ground beef. Tender cuts come from the ribs and loin, while tougher cuts come from the rump and shoulder (see Figure 13-2). Table 13-1 shows how some of the cuts compare nutritionally. The cuts at the top of the list give you the most protein per gram of fat.

Figure 13-2:
Cuts of beef.

Table 13-1	Nutrition Content of Cuts of Beef (Raw)		
Cut Type (3 Ounces)	*Grams Protein*	*Grams Fat*	*Calories*
Round	25.6	8.1	183.6
Flank	22.4	10.6	192.1
Sirloin	23.6	13	219.3
Chuck	23.2	20.2	282.2
Short Loin	19.7	19.8	262.6
Corned Beef Brisket	15.4	16.1	213.3
Beef Brisket	21.3	24.2	309.4
Ribs	18.6	25.1	306.1

Steak and Peanut Pepper Pasta

In this amazing dish, crunchy, colorful veggies mixed with some of your favorite gluten-free pasta serve as a bed for thinly sliced steak covered in a spicy peanut sauce. Seriously, this is one of the most delicious, unique, and impressive (shhhh . . . it's really very easy) dishes I've ever made!

Tools: *Blender*

Preparation time: *25 minutes*

Refrigeration time: *2 hours*

Cooking time: *15 minutes*

Yield: *4 servings*

½ cup rice wine vinegar	*4 ounces fine gluten-free noodles*
½ cup olive oil	*1½ cups shredded cabbage*
4 tablespoons gluten-free soy sauce	*1½ cups bok choy*
4 tablespoons peanut butter	*1 cup spinach*
2 tablespoons chopped fresh cilantro	*1 cup carrots*
1 teaspoon minced garlic (about 2 cloves)	*½ cucumber, thinly sliced (for garnish)*
½ teaspoon crushed red pepper	*½ yellow summer squash, halved and thinly sliced (for garnish)*
1 pound lean top sirloin steak	*¼ cup chopped peanuts*

1 Preheat the grill or set the oven to broil. If you're using a gas grill, heat on high for 10 minutes, and then reduce the heat to medium-low. If you plan to broil the steak, move the oven rack so it's about 5 inches from the top of the oven.

2 Combine the vinegar, oil, soy sauce, peanut butter, cilantro, garlic, and red pepper in a blender. Cover and blend the dressing until it's well-mixed.

3 Trim the fat from the meat. Put the steak in a shallow dish and pour about one-third of the dressing from step 2 over the meat. Cover and marinate the meat in the refrigerator for 2 hours, turning occasionally. Chill the remaining dressing.

4 Drain the meat, throwing away the dressing it was marinating in. Grill or broil the steak until it's cooked the way you like it, turning once halfway through. This should take about 8 to 12 minutes, depending on the thickness of the meat and how you like your steak cooked.

5 Cook the noodles according to the package directions, making sure they're *al dente* (slightly firm and not overcooked). Drain them and set them aside.

6 While the meat is cooking, combine the noodles, cabbage, bok choy, spinach, and carrots in a medium-sized mixing bowl. Add about half of the remaining dressing to the pasta-veggie mixture and stir until it's well-mixed.

7 When the meat is done, slice it into thin slices across the grain. To assemble this dish, serve the pasta-veggie mixture on each person's plate. Put a few slices of meat on top of the noodle mixture. Garnish the dish with a few slices of cucumber and squash. Drizzle the remaining dressing mixture over each plate, and top with peanuts.

Tip: Instead of shredding the veggies myself, I buy a shredded broccoli-carrot-cabbage mixture. You can really use any veggies you want, as long as they're thinly shredded.

Per serving: Calories 573 (From Fat 333); Fat 37g (Saturated 7g); Cholesterol 64mg; Sodium 1,229mg; Carbohydrate 30g (Dietary Fiber 4g); Protein 33g.

Cooking with pork

Porky the pig's not so porky anymore. That's because farmers these days have changed their breeding and production methods to make the pork much leaner and healthier. In fact, if you cut all the fat off the edges and buy a lean piece of pork, it's about the same as chicken in terms of calories, cholesterol, and fat. To see where most of the cuts of pork come from, check out Figure 13-3.

Lean pork doesn't have fat to keep it moist, so it's especially important not to overcook it, or it'll get tough and dry. Pork should be cooked to about 155 or 160 degrees.

You should let meat stand for about 10 to 15 minutes before you carve it. This is called a *resting period,* and it allows the juices to be redistributed so your meat turns out moister. But the meat's temperature continues to rise about 5 to 10 degrees during this time, so you need to stop cooking a little early to allow for this rise in temperature.

Here are a few ways you can tell whether pork is done:

- ✔ **Use a thermometer.** Stick the thermometer into the thickest part of the cut. At 160 degrees, it's medium-done and safe to eat.

- ✔ **Prick it.** If you prick it with a fork, the juice that comes out should be clear, not pink.

- ✔ **Cut it open.** When you cut into the meat, it should be white. A little bit of pink is sometimes okay.

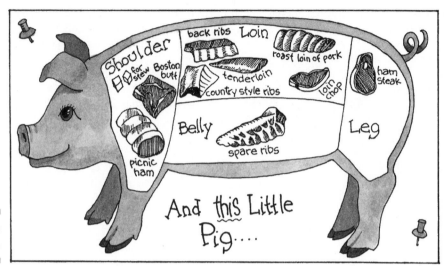

back ribs Loin
Shoulder
for stew Boston butt
roast loin of pork
tenderloin
country style ribs
loin chop
ham steak
Belly
Leg
spare ribs
picnic ham

And this Little Pig....

Figure 13-3:
Cuts of pork.

Shredded Pork

Occasionally, recipes for shredded pork call for flour. Flour certainly isn't necessary, as you can see from the recipe I use. This recipe is especially easy because you put everything in a slow cooker and leave it to simmer into a delicious meal. You may want to serve this with a side of gluten-free noodles, using some of the leftover sauce to drizzle over the pasta.

Tools: *Slow cooker, at least 2.5-quart capacity*

Preparation time: *15 minutes*

Cooking time: *4 to 5 hours*

Yield: *4 servings*

2 pounds boneless pork shoulder-blade roast	*2 teaspoons ground coriander*
1 cup chicken broth	*2 teaspoons ground cumin*
2 large onions, cut into quarters	*2 teaspoons dried, crushed oregano*
4 jalapeño peppers, sliced	*Salt and pepper to taste*
3 teaspoons minced garlic (about 6 cloves)	

1 Trim the fat from the pork. Place all the meat in the slow cooker, cutting the pork roast into pieces if it doesn't fit. Add the chicken broth, onions, jalapeño peppers, garlic, coriander, cumin, oregano, and salt and pepper.

2 Cover and cook the pork on the high-heat setting for 4 to 5 hours. Use a slotted spoon to get the meat out of the liquid; discard the liquid. When the meat cools, use two forks to shred it.

Tip: You can use shredded pork to make a variety of meals. Dress it up with condiments and extras such as sour cream, shredded lettuce, refried beans, olives, salsa, diced tomatoes, jalapeño peppers, spicy carrots, and guacamole, and use it for:

- ✔ *Burritos*
- ✔ *Enchiladas*
- ✔ *Fajitas*
- ✔ *Nachos*
- ✔ *Tacos*
- ✔ *Tostadas*
- ✔ *Quesadillas*
- ✔ *Sandwiches*
- ✔ *Salads*

Per serving: Calories 393 (From Fat 194); Fat 22g (Saturated 7g); Cholesterol 133mg; Sodium 510mg; Carbohydrate 9g (Dietary Fiber 3g); Protein 39g.

If you're watching your fat intake, pork tenderloin is a good choice. Nearly as low in saturated fat as chicken breast meat, it's one of the leanest meats available.

Merry marinades

Besides adding flavor, acidic marinades also tenderize foods. The enzymes in the acids break down the muscle and connective proteins in the meat, making the meat less tough. Here are some tips for marinating:

✔ Refrigerate meat to avoid the growth of harmful bacteria. The temperature at which you marinate doesn't affect the meat's tenderness. The enzymes break down proteins only at temperatures between 140 and 175 degrees, so leaving the meat at room temperature serves no purpose.

✔ Poultry and fish can turn to mush or become tough if you marinate them too long. Poultry does well when marinated up to four hours, and about 30 minutes is a good amount of time to marinate seafood.

✔ Natural tenderizers include pineapple, figs, papaya, kiwi, mango, honeydew, wine, citrus, vinegar, tomato, yogurt, and buttermilk.

✔ Be careful with what kind of container you use. Don't use aluminum containers — only glass, ceramic, stainless steel, or plastic. When you marinate in metals other than stainless steel, the metal and the acidic marinade produce a chemical reaction.

✔ Never reuse a marinade. If you're going to use some of the marinade for a sauce, take out the amount you need and set it aside before you marinate the meat or seafood. After you've marinated food in a marinade, throw the marinade away.

Diving into Seafood

Seafood has been an important source of protein and other nutrients in diets around the world since, well, since people started eating. Fish and shellfish usually contain significant amounts of zinc, which studies show is important for thinking and memory.

Although many recipes call for coatings and breadings or pasta sides that ruin seafood for us gluten-free types, you can easily modify the recipes so they're delicious and gluten-free.

People with dermatitis herpetiformis (see Chapter 3 for details on DH) sometimes need to eliminate iodine from their diets as well as gluten. Iodine is commonly found in shellfish, among other things.

Tequila-Lime Shrimp and Scallops

People usually eat this dish wrapped in flour tortillas — but my family doesn't. Substitute corn tortillas as a wrap, or spoon the shrimp and scallops over rice (I prefer brown rice over white) or your favorite gluten-free pasta.

Preparation time: *2 minutes*

Cooking time: *10 minutes*

Yield: *4 servings*

1 pound medium shrimp, cooked, peeled, and deveined	2 teaspoons minced garlic (about 4 cloves)
½ pound sea scallops	2 teaspoons hot sauce
¼ cup lime juice	½ teaspoon ground cumin
¼ cup lemon juice	½ teaspoon dried oregano
¼ cup chopped fresh cilantro	1 large onion, cut into thin wedges
2 tablespoons olive oil, divided	1 green bell pepper, cut into bite-sized strips
¼ cup tequila	1 red bell pepper, cut into bite-sized strips
	4 lime wedges (for garnish)

1 If your shrimp or scallops are frozen, thaw and rinse them. If the scallops are as large as an egg or larger, cut them in half and set them aside.

2 In a large glass, ceramic, or stainless steel mixing bowl, stir together the lime juice, lemon juice, cilantro, 1 tablespoon oil, tequila, garlic, hot sauce, cumin, and oregano. Add the shrimp and scallops.

3 In a large skillet over medium-high heat, cook the onion, green bell pepper, and red bell pepper in the remaining tablespoon of oil until they begin to get soft, about 4 minutes.

4 Add the shrimp-scallop mixture to the skillet, and bring everything to a boil. Cook and stir the mixture for about 3 minutes, until some of the liquid has burned off and the scallops are cooked.

5 Serve the seafood over rice, pasta, or in the wrap of your choice, and garnish it with lime wedges.

Per serving: *Calories 397 (From Fat 205); Fat 23g (Saturated 10g); Cholesterol 181mg; Sodium 499mg; Carbohydrate 12g (Dietary Fiber 2g); Protein 36g.*

Szechwan Scallops with Orange Peel

This simple Szechwan dish can impress anyone. If you're not a seafood lover, you can use chicken instead of scallops.

Preparation time: *1½ hours*

Refrigeration time: *1 hour*

Cooking time: *15 minutes*

Yield: *6 servings*

1 large orange

1 pound large scallops

2 tablespoons wheat-free soy sauce or Bragg Liquid Aminos

2 tablespoons dry sherry

5 green onions, cut into 1-inch pieces

½ cup sliced red pepper

1 teaspoon minced ginger

2½ teaspoons cornstarch

¾ teaspoon sugar

½ cup orange juice

¼ cup salad oil, divided

½ teaspoon (or to taste) crushed red pepper

1 Preheat the oven to 200 degrees.

2 Use a vegetable peeler or sharp knife to cut the peel from the orange in 1-inch-wide pieces, being careful not to cut into the white part of the peel. Cut the pieces into strips about 2 inches long, and put them on a small cookie sheet. Bake them in the 200-degree oven for about 30 minutes to dry them out.

3 In a medium bowl, mix the scallops, soy sauce (or Liquid Aminos), sherry, green onions, red pepper, and ginger. Cover and refrigerate the mixture for an hour or so.

4 In a small bowl, mix the cornstarch, sugar, and orange juice. Cover and refrigerate this mixture for about an hour.

5 When you're almost ready to serve the meal, heat half the oil (⅛ cup or 2 tablespoons) in a large skillet over medium heat. Stir-fry the orange peels until they're crisp and the edges are slightly browned, about 2 minutes. Drain the peels on paper towels.

6 Turn that same skillet to high. Use the remaining oil to stir-fry the scallop mixture until the scallops are cooked through, about 5 minutes. Stir the orange-juice mixture and then add it to the scallops, and stir-fry the mixture until the sauce is slightly thick and it coats the scallops.

7 Spoon the scallop mixture onto a serving platter, and sprinkle it with the orange peels. Add as much red pepper as you like to spice it up.

Per serving: Calories 191 (From Fat 91); Fat 10g (Saturated 1g); Cholesterol 37mg; Sodium 513mg; Carbohydrate 7g (Dietary Fiber 1g); Protein 16g.

Baked Lemon Mahi Mahi

This delicious fish dish is high in protein and low in fat and carbs. If you're not a fan of mahi mahi, you can use any other mild, white fish fillet. Serve it over brown rice for extra fiber and nutrients.

Preparation time: *10 minutes*

Cooking time: *30 minutes*

Yield: *8 servings*

Nonstick spray	*½ teaspoon freshly ground pepper*
8 boneless, skinned mahi mahi fillets	*¼ teaspoon paprika*
4 tablespoons lemon juice	*¼ cup chopped cilantro*
3 tablespoons melted butter	*8 orange slices*
½ teaspoon minced ginger	*20-ounce can crushed pineapple*
½ teaspoon minced garlic (about 1 clove)	

1 Preheat the oven to 375 degrees.

2 Using the nonstick spray, lightly grease two medium-sized baking dishes. Wash and pat dry the mahi mahi fillets, and lay them in a single layer in the baking dishes.

3 Mix the lemon juice, butter, ginger, garlic, pepper, paprika, and cilantro in a small bowl. Drizzle this lemon juice mixture over the fillets.

4 Place an orange slice over each fillet. Drain and discard about ¾ of the juice from the canned pineapple, and pour the crushed pineapple and remaining juice over the fillets.

5 Bake the fillets at 375 degrees for about 20 to 30 minutes, or until the fillets are opaque. Don't overcook.

Per serving: *Calories 265 (From Fat 51); Fat 6g (Saturated 3g); Cholesterol 161mg; Sodium 187mg; Carbohydrate 14g (Dietary Fiber 1g); Protein 38g.*

Exploring Vegetarian Entrees

Typically, the vegetarian diet relies heavily on pasta, breads, pilafs, various forms of wheat, and meat replacements — all of which are usually loaded with gluten. But plenty of dishes are naturally gluten-free and vegetarian or vegan; and you can easily convert plenty more. Best of all, these vegetarian dishes are so delicious that even die-hard carnivores love them.

⟳ Fresh Harvest Penne

This easy-to-prepare one-dish vegetarian meal is a great way to use fresh veggies you've grown or bought from a farmers' market. If you can't find gluten-free penne, use another type of gluten-free pasta. Several varieties are available, and all are delicious.

Preparation time: *30 minutes*

Cooking time: *30 minutes*

Yield: *8 servings*

16-ounce package gluten-free penne (or any cut) pasta

2 tablespoons olive oil

½ medium red onion, diced

¾ cup thickly sliced zucchini

¾ cup thickly sliced yellow squash

1 tablespoon minced garlic (about 6 cloves)

1 cup ½-inch eggplant cubes

2 medium tomatoes, diced

⅓ cup fresh basil, chopped

⅓ cup freshly grated Parmesan cheese

1 Cook the pasta as directed, being careful not to overcook it.

2 In a large frying pan, heat the olive oil over medium heat. Add the onion, zucchini, and squash to the frying pan, and sauté, stirring often, for about 5 minutes.

3 Add the garlic and eggplant to the pan, and continue stirring frequently.

4 When the eggplant begins to get soft, after about 5 minutes, reduce the heat to low and add the tomato. Continue stirring the mixture for 3 to 4 minutes.

5 Drain the pasta. In a large serving bowl, combine the pasta, vegetables, basil, and Parmesan cheese.

Per serving: Calories 252 (From Fat 51); Fat 6g (Saturated 1g); Cholesterol 3mg; Sodium 64mg; Carbohydrate 46g (Dietary Fiber 8g); Protein 6g.

 ## Vegan Lasagne

This dish is easy to make and a hit with guests, who may never have a clue that what they're eating is gluten-free. Be sure to double the recipe and freeze a pan of lasagne for later. When you're ready, take it directly from the freezer to a 350-degree oven, and heat it for an hour and a half, uncovering it 15 minutes before it's done. This lasagne is even better the next day as leftovers! If you can't find the rice cheeses, you can substitute regular dairy cheeses for a vegetarian (but not vegan) lasagne.

Preparation time: *15 minutes*

Cooking time: *1 hour, 30 minutes*

Yield: *10 servings*

½ cup rice cream cheese	½ cup diced zucchini
½ cup rice mozzarella	¼ cup sliced black olives
½ cup rice Parmesan	¼ cup sliced mushrooms
2 24-ounce jars pasta sauce	¼ cup chopped onions
¼ cup fresh chopped basil	1 tablespoon Bragg Liquid Aminos
1 teaspoon onion powder	Nonstick spray
¼ teaspoon white pepper	10-ounce package of gluten-free lasagna noodles, uncooked
Sea salt to taste	
½ cup chopped spinach	

1 Preheat the oven to 350 degrees.

2 In a large mixing bowl, combine the rice cream cheese, mozzarella, and Parmesan. In a medium bowl, mix together the pasta sauce, basil, onion powder, pepper, and salt. Set aside both mixtures.

3 Heat a large skillet over medium-high heat. Cook the spinach, zucchini, olives, mushrooms, and onions in Bragg Liquid Aminos for 4 minutes or until the onions begin to soften. Don't overcook (remember, the veggies will still cook when the lasagne bakes). Set this mixture aside.

4 Spray a shallow 9- by 13-inch baking dish with nonstick spray. In the baking dish, layer the lasagne as follows:

Place one-third of the sauce on the bottom of the dish, followed by a layer of uncooked noodles (just enough to cover the sauce), half the cheese mixture, and half the vegetable mixture. Repeat this layering process with the another third of the sauce, another layer of noodles, most of the remaining cheese, and the rest of the vegetables. Finish with the last third of sauce on the top.

5 Top the lasagne with a thin layer of mozzarella and Parmesan.

6 Cover the lasagne with aluminum foil and bake it for 1 hour. Remove the foil and bake the lasagne 30 minutes longer or until its top is golden brown. Cool the lasagne for at least 15 minutes before cutting into it.

Tip : *Be creative and use whatever veggies and other "stuffing" ingredients you like.*

Tip: *If your sauce isn't flavorful enough, try adding a teaspoon of minced garlic.*

Per serving: *Calories 313 (From Fat 53); Fat 6g (Saturated 1g); Cholesterol 0mg; Sodium 1,002mg; Carbohydrate 51g (Dietary Fiber 3g); Protein 11g.*

Black Bean Veggie Burgers

Gluten-free veggie burgers are hard to find — so why not make your own? These are made from black beans, but you can use a combination of beans and even add grains like millet and buckwheat. Wrap one of these burgers in a lettuce bun, top it with salsa and guacamole, and you have a delicious, nutritious vegetarian meal.

Tools: *Food processor or blender*

Preparation time: *10 minutes*

Cooking time: *10 minutes*

Yield: *8 servings*

3 pounds cooked black beans, rinsed and drained	*¼ cup egg substitute*
	1 cup cooked quinoa
¼ cup diced onion	*2 tablespoons chopped cilantro*
½ cup diced red bell pepper	*2 tablespoons olive oil, divided*
1 teaspoon cayenne pepper	*8 crisp, cold lettuce leaves*
1 teaspoon cumin	*Salsa and guacamole (if desired)*

1 Put the beans, onion, bell pepper, cayenne, cumin, egg substitute, quinoa, and cilantro into a food processor or blender. Process the mixture until it has a consistency that you can mold into patties.

2 Shape the mixture into eight patties.

3 Heat 1 tablespoon of olive oil in a large skillet over medium heat. Add as many patties as will fit in the skillet, and fry them for two minutes per side, turning once. Add the remaining tablespoon of oil and cook the remaining patties.

4 Wrap each patty in a lettuce leaf, topping the burgers with salsa and guacamole.

Per serving: *Calories 303 (From Fat 43); Fat 5g (Saturated 1g); Cholesterol 0mg; Sodium 67mg; Carbohydrate 47g (Dietary Fiber 16g); Protein 19g.*

☺ Cheese Enchiladas

You have to be careful with enchiladas, because many store-bought or restaurant-prepared enchilada sauces have flour in them. You can dress up this quick and easy recipe with your favorite veggies, other types of cheese (my favorite is *queso seco*), salsas, sour cream, or meat (such as the shredded pork from the recipe earlier in this chapter).

Preparation time: *25 minutes*

Cooking time: *1 hour*

Yield: *6 servings*

2 cups grated cheddar cheese	*4 cups tomato sauce*
2 cups grated Monterey Jack cheese	*3 tablespoons chili powder*
1 teaspoon garlic powder	*1 teaspoon oregano*
3 teaspoons cumin, divided	*2 teaspoons hot sauce*
3 tablespoons cooking oil, divided	*Nonstick spray*
1 small white onion, finely minced	*12 corn tortillas*
2 teaspoons minced garlic (about 4 cloves)	*¼ cup sliced black olives*

1 Preheat the oven to 350 degrees.

2 Combine the cheddar, Monterey Jack, garlic powder, and 2 teaspoons of the cumin; set the mixture aside.

3 To make the enchilada sauce, heat 1 tablespoon of the cooking oil in a large skillet over medium-high heat. Add the minced onion and garlic, and sauté them until they're soft, about 4 minutes. Add the tomato sauce, chili powder, oregano, hot sauce, and the remaining teaspoon of cumin. Cover the sauce and simmer it for about 30 minutes.

4 When the sauce is finished, spray a 9- by 13-inch baking dish with nonstick spray, and then pour about ⅔ cup of the sauce into it. Set aside the remaining enchilada sauce for step 6.

5 In a small skillet, heat the remaining 2 tablespoons of cooking oil (or enough oil to generously cover the bottom of the pan) over medium-high heat.

6 Briefly dip one corn tortilla into the hot oil to soften it (about 5 seconds), making sure both sides get coated, and then dip it in the enchilada sauce, coating both sides. Lay the tortilla flat on a plate or cutting board, and put about ⅓ cup of the cheese mixture down the center of the tortilla (lengthwise). Roll up the tortilla, and put it seam-side down into the baking dish.

7 Repeat steps 5 and 6 for each enchilada, laying the enchiladas side by side in the baking dish. Pour the rest of the enchilada sauce over the rolled-up enchiladas, and sprinkle any remaining cheese mixture over them. Add the sliced black olives on top of the cheese.

8 Bake the enchiladas for 20 to 30 minutes, until the cheese is melted and bubbly.

__Per serving:__ Calories 548 (From Fat 306); Fat 34g (Saturated 16g); Cholesterol 73mg; Sodium 1,640mg; Carbohydrate 41g (Dietary Fiber 7g); Protein 25g.

Chapter 14

Pizza, Pasta, and Bread: Foods You Thought Were a Thing of the Past

In This Chapter

▶ Perfecting gluten-free pizza

▶ Making lotsa pasta you can eat

▶ Baking light and flavorful bread

*B*eing gluten-free doesn't mean you have to pine for pizza and balk at breads. In fact, some of the gluten-free versions of pizza and pasta — and yes, breads — are even better than the real deal.

Can you grind your own flours and press your own pasta? Sure, grind away! But you don't have to. These recipes are simple enough for a beginner to master, and they may even have those gluttons for gluten coming back for more.

Pizza with Pizzazz

When I first describe the gluten-free diet to people, they react with emotion somewhere between disdain and horror. Usually I'm still talking, chirping the praises of the gluten-free lifestyle, when they interrupt me, unable to hide the shock in their voices: "You mean you can't eat pizza?"

The good news is that you *can* eat pizza. Maybe not of the fast-food variety, but gluten-free pizza is delicious nonetheless. And you never have to tip a driver.

The passion for pizza goes way back

I know that Chicagoans and New Yorkers can argue for hours about who makes the best pizza. And I even know that some of them laugh at us Californians who have supposedly disgraced America's favorite food by topping it with froufrou toppings like feta cheese and sushi. But pizza has evolved over the centuries, and it was around long before Chicago and New York showed up on the map.

The credit for pizza really goes to ancient Middle Eastern cultures that made flat, unleavened bread in mud ovens. Pizza took the form you're most familiar with in Naples, Italy, where peasants in the Middle Ages made a seasoned flatbread and covered it with cheese.

The mass appeal of the tomato-mozzarella cheese combination is thanks to a Neapolitan baker named Rafaele Esposito. In 1889, Esposito made a special pizza for the visiting King Umberto I and Queen Margherita. He decorated the pizza to look like the Italian flag, with red tomatoes, white mozzarella cheese, and green basil leaves as toppings. The pizza was a hit, and of course, naming the pizza after the queen didn't hurt its popularity; Pizza Margherita is still an Italian favorite.

Crust: The pizza foundation

The secret of a good pizza isn't in the sauce; the sauce is really just squashed tomatoes with spices. It isn't in the toppings; those are just a euphemism for leftovers. No, the secret to any great pizza is undeniably in the crust.

I believe in using mixes or even pre-made crusts for my gluten-free pizzas, especially because these days they're so good. But this is the recipe section of this book, and my editors claim that simply saying "take pre-made pizza crust out of package" isn't good material. So I'm including the pizza crust recipe I'd use if no one had invented those great-tasting gluten-free mixes and pre-made crusts.

⏺ Basic Pizza Crust

I like to double or even triple the recipe for pizza crust and then freeze what I'm not going to use. I love being able to pull a crust out of the freezer, let it defrost for 10 minutes, top it, and pop it in the oven. Easy as pizza pie!

Tools: *Electric mixer or bread machine*

Preparation time: *30 minutes*

Rising time: *1 hour*

Cooking time: *25 minutes*

Yield: *One 17-inch or two 12-inch pizza crusts (8 servings)*

1 cup sorghum flour

1 cup tapioca flour

½ cup bean flour

½ cup rice flour

1 tablespoon xanthan gum

½ teaspoon salt

1 tablespoon active dry yeast

1 tablespoon sugar

⅓ teaspoon garlic salt

⅓ teaspoon oregano

1¼ cup warm milk

1 teaspoon cider vinegar

1 egg, beaten

2 tablespoons olive oil

A fistful of rice, bean, tapioca, or sorghum flour to keep the dough from sticking

1 In a large bowl, mix the sorghum flour, tapioca flour, bean flour, rice flour, xanthan gum, salt, yeast, sugar, garlic salt, and oregano. Then add the milk, vinegar, egg, and olive oil.

2 Use an electric mixer or bread machine to knead the mixture for about 3 minutes, until the dough is soft and thick. Roll the dough into a ball.

3 Sprinkle some rice, bean, tapioca, or sorghum flour on a cutting board, and put the dough ball on top. Use your hands or a rolling pin to flatten the dough to the thickness that you like your crust. Add as much flour as you need to keep the dough from sticking to the rolling pin and the cutting board.

4 Leave the dough in a warm place to rise for about 1 hour.

5 Preheat the oven to 425 degrees.

6 Spread the dough onto a nonstick pizza pan. The diameter of the pizza depends on how thick you make your crust. Use your fingers to pinch the edge and make a lip around the outside of the crust. Add the sauce and toppings to the crust, and bake the pizza at 425 degrees for 12 to 15 minutes or until the cheese is melted.

Per serving: Calories 263 (From Fat 59); Fat 7g (Saturated 2g); Cholesterol 32mg; Sodium 218mg; Carbohydrate 48g (Dietary Fiber 3g); Protein 7g.

Using a pizza stone

Nothing's worse than soggy pizza, and using a pizza stone is the best way to get a crispy crust. To use a pizza stone, heat it in a 425-degree oven for about an hour before you want to cook your pizza. Then coat the stone with cornmeal and transfer the crust to the stone (if you're following a recipe that calls for letting the crust rise, let it rise on a separate pan before moving it to the stone). Cook the crust on the stone, add the toppings, and cook the pizza again.

Important: Don't use oil on a pizza stone, because the high temperatures can cause the oil to catch on fire. *Equally as important:* If you cook gluten-containing pizzas and gluten-free pizzas, don't share stones; they can absorb the flour and contaminate your gluten-free pizza.

Pizza sauces

I'm gonna let you in on a couple of secrets. First, just about any commercial pizza sauce is gluten-free (of course, you still need to check the ingredients to be sure). Second, pizza sauce can be as simple as a little brushed-on olive oil or chile oil. But if you like to get fancy, and if you like to make your own, feel free. I offer a couple of simple recipes to get you started.

Use sauces and condiments you already have in your kitchen for sauces on your pizza: gluten-free teriyaki sauce, Cholula, Dijon mustard, hoisin sauce, taco sauce, ranch dressing, or barbecue sauce.

Tomato Herb Pizza Sauce

Traditionalists lean toward this type of a sauce, because, well, it's traditional.

Preparation time: 10 minutes

Cooking time: 15 minutes

Yield: Enough for one 12-inch pizza

2 tablespoons olive oil

1 teaspoon minced fresh garlic (about 2 cloves)

¼ cup finely chopped onion

2 cups chopped or diced tomatoes (including the juice)

1 teaspoon fresh oregano

2 tablespoons fresh minced basil

½ teaspoon salt

½ teaspoon black pepper

3 tablespoons tomato paste

1 In a medium saucepan, cook the onions and garlic in the olive oil over medium-high heat until they're tender (about 3 minutes).

2 Add the tomatoes, oregano, basil, salt, and pepper to the pan, and continue cooking the sauce over medium heat for a few more minutes.

3 Stir in the tomato paste. Simmer the sauce on low heat for about 10 minutes.

Per serving: Calories 48 (From Fat 32); Fat 4g (Saturated 1g); Cholesterol 0mg; Sodium 154mg; Carbohydrate 4g (Dietary Fiber 1g); Protein 1g.

○ *Alfredo Sauce*

This sauce is a great twist on an old favorite, and it makes a white pizza instead of a red one. It's basically the same type of cheesy, creamy Alfredo sauce you'd use on pasta — in fact, if you're feeling adventurous, feel free to use it on your pasta!

Preparation time: *10 minutes*

Cooking time: *5 minutes*

Yield: *Enough for one 12-inch pizza*

¼ cup butter	½ cup heavy cream
1½ teaspoons minced garlic (about 3 cloves)	¼ teaspoon salt
1 cup grated Parmesan cheese	¼ teaspoon pepper

1 Melt the butter in a medium saucepan over medium heat.

2 Add the garlic and sauté it for 2 or 3 minutes, stirring constantly. While you're sautéing, sprinkle a little salt on the garlic, which brings out some of the moisture and prevents burning.

3 Stir in the Parmesan, cream, salt, and pepper. Heat the sauce for about 5 minutes, stirring constantly.

4 Remove the saucepan from the heat. Let the sauce cool for 5 minutes before putting it on the pizza.

Per serving: *Calories 149 (From Fat 128); Fat 14g (Saturated 9g); Cholesterol 44mg; Sodium 266mg; Carbohydrate 1g (Dietary Fiber 0g); Protein 5g.*

MYOP (make your own pizza) parties

Rarely can an entire group agree on what should go on a pizza. So why not let everyone have exactly what he or she wants by turning the event into a party? That's what an MYOP party is all about. Here's how you do it:

1. **Make several batches of gluten-free pizza dough.**

2. **Roll up balls that, when flattened, will each be the right size for an individual-sized pizza (the balls should be about the size of a baseball).**

3. **Put out toppings — lots of them — in separate serving bowls.**

   Put sauce in one, different types of cheeses in others, pepperoni in another, mushrooms, pineapple, anchovies (yum!) in others, and so on.

4. **Give each guest a dough ball and let him or her roll it out to the desired thickness.**

   Have everyone mark the crust, using a toothpick, with his or her initials or something else that distinguishes one crust from another.

5. **Prebake the crusts and give them back to the rightful owners for sauce and toppings.**

6. **Bake the pizzas until the cheese has melted and the crust is golden brown.**

Of course, MYOP parties are about the messiest type of party you can throw, with flour and dough flying. And you always have the ubiquitous show-off who just has to prove he can toss the dough like the real pizza-makers do. Be prepared to clean up afterwards. Know also that these parties always incite friendly-but-competitive cases of "my pizza's gonna be better than yours." If you invite competitive friends, consider yourself forewarned!

Pizzas beyond cheese and pepperoni

For purists, adding anything to a pizza besides sauce and cheese is to sully a time-honored classic. For others, it's a chance to flaunt their creative or adventuresome sides. If you're a flaunter, read on.

Sauceless Inside-Out Seafood Pizza

Definitely not one for traditionalists, the "Sauceless Inside-Out Seafood Pizza" is an Italy-meets-Hawaii creation that offers seafood- and pizza-lovers the best of both worlds.

Preparation time: *15 minutes*

Cooking time: *10 minutes*

Yield: *8 servings (two 12-inch pizzas)*

2 12-inch pizza crusts (see the "Basic Pizza Crust" recipe)

1 cup crab meat

1 cup small cooked, peeled, deveined shrimp

½ cup crushed pineapple

½ cup sliced fresh mushrooms

3.8-ounce can sliced black olives, drained

¼ cup diced red bell pepper

1 cup shredded mozzarella cheese

1 cup shredded white cheddar cheese

1 Preheat the oven to 450 degrees.

2 Divide all the ingredients between the two pizzas. Spread ½ cup crab meat, ½ cup shrimp, ¼ cup pineapple, ¼ cup mushrooms, a handful of olives, and ⅛ cup red bell peppers evenly over each crust. Top each pizza with ½ cup mozzarella and ½ cup white cheddar.

3 Bake the pizzas at 450 degrees until the cheese is bubbly and starting to turn golden-brown. The pizzas should take between 10 and 15 minutes to cook.

Per serving: Calories 698 (From Fat 219); Fat 24g (Saturated 9g); Cholesterol 132mg; Sodium 803mg; Carbohydrate 100g (Dietary Fiber 7g); Protein 27g.

Pizza Pockets (Calzones)

When our kids were little, TV ads sang the praises of pizza pockets that looked like an Americanized version of a calzone — and looked, I might add, sinfully scrumptious and glutenous. But where there's a will, there's a way, and using the "Basic Pizza Crust" recipe earlier in this chapter, my kids and I created our own gluten-free version of this tasty junk-food meal and sang our own theme song. You can use any pizza dough recipe you'd like. Just make enough dough for two 12-inch pizzas (see Chapter 9 for ideas on which mixes to use). Calzones are great dipped in your favorite pasta sauce, and you know how kids love to dip!

Preparation time: *40 minutes*

Cooking time: *40 minutes*

Yield: *4 servings*

1 recipe "Basic Pizza Crust" dough, uncooked	*1 cup shredded mozzarella cheese*
About ¼ cup rice, sorghum, bean, or tapioca flour	*1 cup shredded Romano cheese*
Nonstick spray	*1 cup pepperoni slices*

1 Preheat the oven to 375 degrees.

2 Divide the dough into four equal parts, and roll each one into a ball. Cover the balls with a paper towel that you've dampened with warm water, and set the dough in a warm area for 20 minutes.

3 Spread some flour on a cutting board and on a rolling pin, and roll each dough ball flat so that it's about ¾-inch thick. Trim the edges so it's in an oval shape.

4 Line a baking sheet with aluminum foil, and spray it with nonstick spray. Put each of the ovals onto the lined baking sheet. Using your fingernail, a toothpick, or a knife, lightly draw a line across each oval, dividing it in half crosswise.

5 Put ¼ cup mozzarella, ¼ cup Romano, and ¼ cup pepperoni on one of the halves of each oval, leaving about ½ inch of dough along the edges.

6 Fold over the other half of the dough (the half with nothing on it) so it's lying on top of the filling. Using your fingers, gently crimp the edges of the dough together.

7 Bake all four pockets in the oven for 35 to 40 minutes, until they begin to turn golden brown, or until melted cheese begins to ooze out.

Per serving: *Calories 751 (From Fat 245); Fat 27g (Saturated 11g); Cholesterol 142mg; Sodium 1,352mg; Carbohydrate 99g (Dietary Fiber 6g); Protein 35g.*

🍅 Mexican Pizza

This version of Mexican pizza is vegetarian, but if you like meat, just add crumbled, cooked ground beef.

Preparation time: *20 minutes*

Cooking time: *25 minutes*

Yield: *6 servings*

2 12-inch pizza crusts (see the "Basic Pizza Crust" recipe)

16-ounce can refried beans

2 large green onions, thinly sliced

1 cup shredded cheddar cheese

1 cup shredded Monterey Jack cheese

½ cup sliced black olives, drained

4-ounce can diced green chilies

¼ cup sour cream

2 tablespoons fresh chopped cilantro

1 cup chopped fresh tomato

1 cup shredded lettuce

¼ cup sliced jalapeño peppers

1 cup salsa

1 Preheat the oven to 425 degrees.

2 Bake the crusts for 8 minutes, or until they just begin to turn golden brown.

3 Divide all the ingredients in half. Spread 8 ounces of refried beans on each crust. If it's too hard to spread, mix about 2 tablespoons of salsa into the beans to help thin it out a little.

4 On top of the beans, add one chopped green onion, ½ cup cheddar, ½ cup Monterey Jack, ¼ cup black olives, and 2 ounces green chilies on each pizza.

5 Bake the pizzas for 15 to 20 minutes or until the cheese begins to bubble.

6 Take the pizzas out of the oven and add ⅛ cup sour cream, 1 tablespoon cilantro, ½ cup tomato, ½ cup lettuce, ⅛ cup jalapeños, and ½ cup salsa to each pizza.

Per serving: *Calories 982 (From Fat 305); Fat 34g (Saturated 14g); Cholesterol 132mg; Sodium 1,338mg; Carbohydrate 147g (Dietary Fiber 14g); Protein 34g.*

No More Pining for Pasta

Whining about gluten-free pastas was once completely acceptable. They used to be gritty, heavy on the (insert flour flavor here) flavor, and they went from being *al dente* to all-mush in a millisecond.

But gluten-free pasta has come a long way, baby. In fact, even the most discerning pasta aficionados appreciate the taste, texture, variety of shapes and sizes, nutritional value, and cookability of today's gluten-free pastas.

Although these pastas are great with just a little olive oil or butter, you can also turn just about any pasta recipe into a great gluten-free dish simply by replacing traditional pasta with a gluten-free variety. Here are a few examples.

 *Three-Bean Pasta*

A colorful and delicious dish, the "Three-Bean Pasta" is best with the widest noodles you can find. If you can't find wide gluten-free pastas, break a lasagna noodle into ½-inch pieces. Each noodle should be as long as the width of the lasagna noodle.

Preparation time: *20 minutes*

Yield: *6 servings*

1 pound wide gluten-free noodles, uncooked	*½ cup chopped red bell pepper*
15-ounce can kidney beans, rinsed and drained	*3 tablespoons Dijon mustard*
15-ounce can chickpeas (garbanzo beans), rinsed and drained	*2 tablespoons olive oil*
	3 tablespoons red wine vinegar
1 cup fresh green beans, trimmed and rinsed	*3 tablespoons chopped fresh parsley*
½ cup chopped red onion	*1 tablespoon chopped fresh basil*

1 Cook the pasta according to the package directions, making sure it's *al dente* (slightly firm). Drain and rinse it under cold water.

2 In a large serving bowl, stir together the pasta, kidney beans, chickpeas, green beans, onion, red bell pepper, mustard, oil, vinegar, parsley, and basil. Toss the pasta to mix the ingredients.

Per serving: Calories 428 (From Fat 55); Fat 6g (Saturated 1g); Cholesterol 0mg; Sodium 336mg; Carbohydrate 76g (Dietary Fiber 7g); Protein 11g.

Sweet and Tangy Noodles with Peanuts (Pad Thai)

Cheating on this dish is way easier than making it from scratch. You can buy pad thai kits, complete with noodles and sauce, or at least use one of the prepared pad thai sauces available at most grocery stores and just about any Asian market. But if you're a purist and want to make the entire dish yourself, I tell you how here. Tamarind, which makes foods taste sour and is a natural preservative, is a critical ingredient in the sauce. Finding a replacement for tamarind is hard, so stock up if you plan to do much Thai cooking.

Tools: *Wok or large nonstick skillet*

Preparation time: *20 minutes*

Cooking time: *15 minutes*

Yield: *6 servings*

8 ounces rice stick noodles	*¼ cup fish sauce*
2 teaspoons tamarind concentrate	*¼ cup sugar*
5 teaspoons water	*¼ cup chopped chives*
2 teaspoons cooking oil	*¾ cup broken up roasted peanuts*
5 cloves garlic, finely chopped	*1 cup fresh cooked shrimp*
2 tablespoons chopped shallots	*1 egg, beaten*
½ cup diced firm tofu	*1 cup bean sprouts*

1 Soak the rice sticks according to the package directions so they're pliable but not mushy. Mix the tamarind concentrate and the water to make a tamarind juice, and set it aside for step 3.

2 Heat the cooking oil in a wok over medium-high heat. When the oil's hot, add the garlic, shallots, and tofu. Stirring constantly, cook them until the garlic and shallots begin to turn opaque, about 5 minutes.

3 Add the tamarind juice (from step 1), fish sauce, sugar, chives, and peanuts to the wok and stir-fry for 2 minutes to mix the ingredients. Add the shrimp and noodles, and stir-fry the mixture until the noodles are well coated with the sauce, about 2 minutes.

4 Scoop the noodle mixture to one side of the wok; slowly add the beaten egg to the other side, drizzling it into the hot wok to make a fine ribbon of cooked egg. Blend the egg and the noodle mixture together.

5 Add the sprouts, and cook the noodle dish for another 30 seconds or so.

Tip: You can add dried shrimp, available at most Asian markets, as a garnish. Another common garnish for pad thai uses ½ cup uncooked bean sprouts, ½ cup chopped chives, and ½ cup coarsely ground roasted peanuts marinated in a tablespoon of lime juice, a teaspoon of tamarind concentrate, 2½ teaspoons of water, and a tablespoon of fish sauce. Sprinkle the mixture on the cooked pad thai and place several lime segments and sliced cucumbers around the serving platter.

Per serving: *Calories 375 (From Fat 141); Fat 16g (Saturated 2g); Cholesterol 82mg; Sodium 1,574mg; Carbohydrate 45g (Dietary Fiber 3g); Protein 16g.*

Making Bread

Gluten-free bread has a reputation. And for years, it was well-deserved. But if any food deserves to win in the "most improved" category in the gluten-free foods' world, it's definitely bread. Thanks to some dedicated cookbook authors, bread has evolved from being, well, tasteless and brick-like to being light, doughy, and flavorful.

Best of all, the real cooks have done an incredible job of combining interesting, alternative flours that not only improve the flavor and texture but add nutrients as well. Now that gluten-free bread actually tastes good, it's superior in many ways to that gummy white "enriched" gluten-containing stuff that has more chemicals than a high school chemistry lab.

Although I'm admittedly not a Real Cookbook Author, and I'm really not patient enough to concoct complex baked goods that require a tender touch, I have experimented enough to come up with some simple bread recipes I share with you in this section. For some bread-making tips and tricks, check out Chapter 9.

Of course, if you'd rather not have to buy and measure all the recipe ingredients that go into bread, don't sweat it. Lots of excellent bread mixes are available. Just toss a mix in your bread machine, add a few ingredients, and turn it on.

"This is *bread?*"

I remember my first experience with gluten-free bread. In fact, I remember it vividly, like a bad nightmare that won't go away. My then-toddler son had recently been diagnosed with celiac disease, and I was more than just a little anxious about feeding him without poisoning him. This was, mind you, back in the 1900s — 1991, to be exact — and gluten-free products were scarce.

I was relieved and downright giddy to discover, in the bowels of a freezer box at what was then the only health food store within a 50-mile radius, a loaf of gluten-free bread. Screeching with delight, right there in the store, I pulled out a piece of the bread, chirping, "Tyler, you can *eat* this!" Before it made it out of the flimsy plastic bag, though, the bread-like substance began to crumble . . . and crumble some more. Somehow, I maintained my enthusiasm — albeit waning now — and lowered myself to my toddler son, eager to share with him the newfound treasure that was now nothing but a fistful of dry, tasteless crumbs. "Mommy," he said with sincere confusion, "this is *bread?*"

☺ Simple White Bread for Bread Machines

A simple white bread can go a long way. After all, everyone knows that bread is really just an instrument to allow you the pleasure of consuming an entire stick of butter without raising eyebrows. Simplify your life by using 3¼ cups of premixed gluten-free flour mixtures (I list some in Chapter 9) in place of the flours in this recipe and a bread machine to mix the dough and bake the bread. I like this particular recipe because the variety of flours enhances the taste, texture, and nutritional value.

Tools: *Bread machine*

Preparation time: *30 minutes*

Cooking time: *2 to 3.5 hours (depending on your bread machine)*

Yield: *6 servings (one 1½ pound loaf)*

½ cup tapioca flour	¼ cup canola oil
¼ cup millet flour	¼ cup honey
½ cup sorghum flour	2 cups warm milk
1 cup white rice flour	3 tablespoons butter
1 cup brown rice flour	1 teaspoon unflavored gelatin
1 egg	1 teaspoon salt
½ cup egg whites (about 4 or 5 egg whites)	1 tablespoon xanthan gum
1 tablespoon apple cider vinegar	1 tablespoon active dry yeast

1 Put the tapioca flour, millet flour, sorghum flour, white rice flour, brown rice flour, egg, egg whites, vinegar, oil, honey, milk, butter, gelatin, salt, xanthan gum, and yeast into the bread machine in the order recommended by the manufacturer. Make sure you add the yeast last, on top of all the other ingredients. Select the cycle for homemade breads. If your machine has the option of doing only one kneading and one rising cycle, choose that option (though letting the bread go through two kneadings doesn't hurt the bread).

2 After a few minutes of kneading, check on the dough. Scrape the flour off the sides of the tub and into the dough so it can mix thoroughly. Make sure the consistency is just a little thicker than a cake batter. If it's too thick, add more milk. If it's too runny, add a little rice flour.

3 When the bread is finished, let it cool for a few minutes and remove it from the pan.

Per serving: Calories 532 (From Fat 182); Fat 20g (Saturated 7g); Cholesterol 62mg; Sodium 487mg; Carbohydrate 79g (Dietary Fiber 4g); Protein 12g.

 *Flour Tortillas*

I prefer corn tortillas to flour ones, but some people yearn for flour tortillas. This recipe is actually really good!

Preparation time: *30 minutes*

Cooking time: *20 minutes*

Yield: *6 servings*

2 cups gluten-free flour mixture	1 teaspoon baking powder
2 teaspoons xanthan gum	2 tablespoons shortening
1 teaspoon sugar	1 cup warm water
1¼ teaspoon salt	

1 Heat a cast iron skillet or griddle over medium heat.

2 In a large mixing bowl, combine the flour mixture, xanthan gum, sugar, salt, and baking powder. Cut in the shortening using a pastry blender, fork, or two knives.

3 Add the warm water slowly, stirring after each addition, until the dough is smooth. Form it into balls about the size of tennis balls.

4 Put the dough between two sheets of wax paper. Using a rolling pin, flatten the dough balls, one at a time, until they're about ⅛-inch thick. They should be about 10 to 12 inches in diameter.

5 Remove the wax paper. Cook the tortillas on the hot iron skillet or griddle for about 45 seconds, until the cooked side has brown flecks; the tortilla may begin to bubble. Turn each tortilla once. The second side cooks quickly, in about 20 seconds. Peek underneath the tortilla to see whether it has brown flecks, a sign that it's done.

Per serving: Calories 175 (From Fat 47); Fat 5g (Saturated 1g); Cholesterol 0mg; Sodium 553mg; Carbohydrate 31g (Dietary Fiber 4g); Protein 4g.

Chapter 15

Getting Your Just Desserts

In This Chapter

▶ Delightfully decadent desserts

▶ Grab 'n go sweet stuff

▶ Sweets and treats for the health-minded

When you've cleared the main course, everyone eagerly anticipates one thing, and it's not doing the dishes. It is, of course, dessert. If you think the gluten-free lifestyle means having to deprive yourself of decadence and indulgence, this chapter surely proves you wrong.

Now if your idea of dessert is a bowl of sliced strawberries with raisins on top (for a splurge), that's cool. I've put together some healthful recipes in this chapter to satisfy your wholesome-and-healthy sweet tooth, as well as some recipes for delicious desserts that pack and travel well for when you're gluten-free and on the go. But if you're the more decadent type, you may be delighted to find recipes in this chapter for cakes, cookies, fudge, and other gluten-free indulgences.

Daring to Be Decadent: Gluten-Free Indulgences

Yes, you can have your cake and eat it, too. As long as it's gluten-free! I'm big into indulgences; I mean, if you're going to live it up from time to time, you may as well really satisfy that craving and get it out of your system. Plenty of gluten-free desserts can satisfy your cravings, but these first few recipes are wickedly wonderful.

Dessert is the course that comes after the main course — of course. And in most cultures, dessert is comprised of sweet, decadent foods. But in many cultures, dessert isn't sweet at all but is simply a course consisting of very strong flavors, like cheeses. The word comes from the Old French *desservir,* which means "to clear the table."

Flourless Chocolate Cake

One of the most incredible desserts on the planet, this flourless chocolate cake is rich, dense, moist, and surprisingly easy to prepare. It requires very few ingredients, none of which are specialty items. Prepare to be amazed.

Tools: *9-inch springform pan*

Preparation time: *30 minutes*

Cooking time: *50 minutes*

Yield: *8 servings*

Nonstick spray	*6 large eggs*
1 cup (2 sticks) unsalted butter	*1 cup sugar*
8-ounce bag semisweet chocolate chips (about 1½ cups)	

1 Preheat the oven to 275 degrees. Spray a 9-inch springform pan with nonstick spray. Don't know what a springform pan looks like? See Figure 15-1.

2 Put the butter and chocolate chips in a large microwaveable bowl. Microwave the chocolate and butter in 10-second intervals until they're melted, stirring after each interval.

3 Separate the egg whites and egg yolks, putting the yolks in a small bowl and the whites in another small bowl. Whisk the yolks into the chocolate-butter mixture.

4 Whisk the egg whites (or beat them on low speed) for 3 minutes, and add the sugar. Continue to beat or whisk the egg whites until they're stiff and glossy, about 3 minutes. Gently fold the egg white mixture into the chocolate mixture.

5 Pour the batter into the prepared pan, and smooth the top of the batter with a rubber spatula.

6 Bake the batter until the cake is set in the center — about 45 to 50 minutes. Let the cake cool for 15 minutes and remove it from the pan.

Tip: Cover the cake in powdered sugar or cocoa powder, or drizzle it with caramel sauce or chocolate sauce. If you're watching your calories (yeah, right!), you may want to cover it in raspberries instead.

Per serving: *Calories 489 (From Fat 315); Fat 35g (Saturated 20g); Cholesterol 221mg; Sodium 54mg; Carbohydrate 43g (Dietary Fiber 2g); Protein 6g.*

Figure 15-1:
The cylinder
of the pan
unlatches,
allowing the
bottom to be
removed.

⟳ *Oops-Proof Peanut Butter Fudge*

This incredible fudge is almost embarrassingly easy to make; it's oops-proof. The hardest part of this recipe is being patient enough to wait until it's cooled.

Preparation time: *10 minutes*

Refrigeration time: *2 hours*

Yield: *8 servings*

18 ounces peanut butter chips   *2 teaspoons vanilla*

14-ounce can sweetened condensed milk   *Pinch of salt*

1 Put the peanut butter chips into a medium-sized glass bowl, and add the condensed milk. Microwave the mixture on high for 3 minutes, making sure it doesn't bubble over.

2 Stir the mixture to make sure all the chips are melted and that the mixture's smooth. Add the vanilla and salt, and mix well.

3 Line a 10-inch square pan with wax paper, and pour in the fudge mixture. Refrigerate the fudge for 2 hours (if you can wait that long!). Cut it into 3-inch pieces.

Per serving: Calories 496 (From Fat 201); Fat 22g (Saturated 18g); Cholesterol 18mg; Sodium 218mg; Carbohydrate 57g (Dietary Fiber 3g); Protein 17g.

Crustless Cherry Cheesecake

Really, the best part of the cheesecake is the innards, anyway. This crustless cherry cheesecake is rich and decadent — the perfect indulgence.

Preparation time: *10 minutes*

Cooking time: *20 to 30 minutes*

Cooling time: *30 minutes*

Yield: *8 servings*

Nonstick spray	*1 teaspoon vanilla*
8-ounce package cream cheese, softened	*3 tablespoons gluten-free flour mixture*
½ cup sugar	*21-ounce can cherry pie filling*
2 eggs	*1 can whipped cream*
2 teaspoons lemon juice	*1 cup fresh cherries (for garnish)*

1 Preheat the oven to 350 degrees.

2 Lightly grease a 9- by 13-inch casserole dish with the nonstick spray.

3 Combine the cream cheese, sugar, eggs, lemon juice, vanilla, and gluten-free flour mixture. Pour this mixture into the casserole dish, and bake it at 350 degrees for 20 to 30 minutes. The cheesecake is done when a toothpick inserted in the center comes out clean.

4 After the cheesecake cools for at least 30 minutes, spread the cherry pie filling over the top. Then top it with whipped cream and garnish it with the fresh cherries.

Per serving: *Calories 284 (From Fat 111); Fat 12g (Saturated 7g); Cholesterol 89mg; Sodium 113mg; Carbohydrate 40g (Dietary Fiber 1g); Protein 5g.*

Making your own desserts

"Ooey Gooey Brownie-Cake-Cookie" — yum! Okay, I made that up. I really don't have a recipe to follow for a brownie-cake-cookie, but you *could* make one, which is the point of this. Really, I have two points:

✔ **Use mixes:** Literally dozens of companies make absolutely incredible mixes for gluten-free baked goods. Sure, using them is a little pricier than making stuff from scratch, but take it from someone who's made at least 436 cakes that didn't rise, 239 batches of brownies that I later served as fudged fudge, and 1,486 cookies that formed a large brick-like glob that I served as "bars": Mixes are tried, true, and — today, at least — absolutely delicious.

✔ **Be creative:** How my family and I dealt with last night's dessert fiasco is a great example of being creative. We made a cake, and although it did actually rise, it also stuck miserably to the Bundt pan. We eventually pulled all the cake from the pan in hundreds of pieces. I sprayed a pie pan with lots of nonstick spray and began to press the crumbs in. Then we realized we'd accidentally bought frosting that had gluten in it, but we *did* have leftover cookie dough. So we squished that, too, topped the cake crumbs with it, added some candy coated chocolate for color, and put the cookie and cake back in the oven for 10 minutes. We ended up with an ooey-gooey cake-cookie that actually tasted great!

Making Sweet Stuff to Pack 'n Snack On

Some desserts are just meant to be eaten at home. Ice cream, for instance, and flaming finales like bananas Foster and cherries jubilee. They're great if the get-together is at your house, but what if the party's somewhere else and the host asks you to bring dessert? What can you bring to picnics? What packs and travels well for a sweet treat in the kids' lunchboxes? What if you just want a quick grab 'n go indulgence? I'm glad you asked.

○ Chocolate Marshmallow Bars

Few sweet grab-n-go snacks have withstood the test of time like marshmallow bars. But most cereals used to make those bars have gluten in them, so they're usually off-limits. Try this simple variation using Cocoa Pebbles or any other gluten-free chocolate-flavored puffed rice cereal you can find.

Preparation time: *30 minutes*

Refrigeration time: *10 minutes*

Yield: *4 servings*

Nonstick spray

¼ cup margarine

10-ounce package marshmallows

5 cups gluten-free chocolate puffed rice cereal

1 Spray a 9- by 13-inch pan with lots of nonstick spray.

2 Put the margarine into a large saucepan and melt the margarine over low heat. Add the marshmallows, and stirring constantly, cook the mixture until the marshmallows are all melted and smooth. Remove the pan from the heat.

3 Add the cereal, and mix it well so all the cereal is coated with the marshmallow mixture.

4 Spread the warm mixture into the sprayed pan. Using wax paper or a spatula sprayed with nonstick spray, press the cereal mixture into an even layer.

5 Refrigerate the pan for 10 minutes, and then cut the mixture into squares. You can put the bars back into the fridge until they're as cold as you like them.

Per serving: Calories 519 (From Fat 122); Fat 14g (Saturated 4g); Cholesterol 0mg; Sodium 428mg; Carbohydrate 100g (Dietary Fiber 1g); Protein 3g.

♨ Sweet Peanut Butter- and Chocolate-Covered Cereal

These treats are sweet and crunchy, and they make a great on-the-go snack to satisfy your sweet tooth. Usually this recipe calls for puffed rice cereal squares like Chex, but Chex has gluten, so I use Health Valley's Rice Crunch-Ems! instead. I dare anyone to tell the difference!

Preparation time: *20 minutes*

Refrigeration time: *30 minutes*

Yield: *12 servings*

1 cup semisweet chocolate chips	13-ounce box of Rice Crunch-Ems! Cereal
1 cup peanut butter	1 tablespoon vanilla
½ cup margarine	2 cups powdered sugar

1 Combine the chocolate chips, peanut butter, and margarine in a medium-sized pan over medium-low heat. Stir the ingredients constantly until they're melted and well mixed.

2 Pour the cereal into a very large bowl. Drizzle the chocolate mixture over the cereal, and mix it well so all the cereal is coated.

3 Put the powdered sugar into a large plastic bag; add the cereal — a bagful at a time — and shake it to coat the cereal.

4 Spread out the mixture on wax paper, separating the chunks of cereal so they don't stick together in globs. Refrigerate the mixture for 30 minutes.

Per serving: Calories 458 (From Fat 207); Fat 23g (Saturated 6g); Cholesterol 0mg; Sodium 467mg; Carbohydrate 59g (Dietary Fiber 2g); Protein 8g.

☺ *Fruity Caramel Popcorn Balls*

In keeping with a cereal-makes-good-desserts theme, this recipe calls for any gluten-free fruit-flavored puffed rice cereal.

Preparation time: *20 minutes*

Yield: *12 servings*

3 cups fruit-flavored puffed rice cereal	*3 tablespoons butter*
1 cup popped plain popcorn	*3 tablespoons caramel ice cream topping*
½ cup peanuts	

1 In a large bowl, combine the cereal, popcorn, and peanuts.

2 In a small microwave-safe bowl, heat the butter and caramel topping on high for 1 minute, or until it's melted. Stir it until it's smooth.

3 Pour the caramel mixture over the cereal-popcorn-peanut mixture, and stir it well.

4 Spread the mixture on wax paper to cool. When it's cool enough to touch safely, mold it into balls the size of a tennis ball. Store the popcorn balls in an airtight container.

Per serving: *Calories 113 (From Fat 57); Fat 6g (Saturated 2g); Cholesterol 8mg; Sodium 105mg; Carbohydrate 13g (Dietary Fiber 1g); Protein 2g.*

↻ *Microwave Chocolate Chip Peanut Brittle*

Peanut brittle is a great on-the-go snack. Break it into small pieces and convince your-self that it's not going to sabotage your diet because the pieces are so small.

Preparation time: *20 minutes*

Cooling time: *1 hour*

Yield: *12 servings*

Nonstick spray	*1½ cups salted peanuts*
1 cup semisweet chocolate chips	*2 teaspoons butter*
1 cup sugar	*2 teaspoons vanilla*
½ cup light corn syrup	*1 teaspoon baking soda*

1 Spray two cookie sheets with nonstick spray. Spread ½ cup chocolate chips on each cookie sheet.

2 Put the sugar and corn syrup in a large microwaveable bowl. Cover the bowl with a paper towel, and microwave the mixture on high for 8 minutes. Stir the mixture, and then microwave it for 4 more minutes. Watch to make sure it doesn't bubble over.

3 Stir in the peanuts, and microwave for another 2 minutes. The mixture should be light brown in color.

4 Add the butter and vanilla, blending well. Microwave the mixture on high for another minute. The peanuts will be lightly browned. Add the baking soda and stir gently until the mixture is light and foamy.

5 Pour the mixture onto the cookie sheets over the chocolate chips. Let the mixture cool for an hour. When it's cool, break it into small pieces and store them in an airtight container.

Per serving: Calories 281 (From Fat 122); Fat 14g (Saturated 4g); Cholesterol 2mg; Sodium 201mg; Carbohydrate 40g (Dietary Fiber 2g); Protein 5g.

☼ Incredibly Easy Peanut Butter Cookies

By definition, a cookie can be any of a variety of handheld, flour-based sweet cakes, either crispy or soft. I break all the rules with this recipe, because there's no flour to be found. Best of all, the cookies are incredibly easy — they have only three ingredients!

Preparation time: *5 minutes*

Cooking time: *20 minutes*

Yield: *2 dozen*

2 eggs	*1 cup sugar*
1 cup chunky peanut butter	

1 Preheat the oven to 350 degrees.

2 Beat the eggs in a medium-sized bowl. Stir the peanut butter and sugar into the eggs.

3 Drop dollops of dough from a spoon onto the cookie sheet, about 2 inches apart. Use the back side of a fork to press them flat.

4 Bake the cookies for 10 to 12 minutes, or until the cookies spring back a little when you poke them.

Per serving: *Calories 203 (From Fat 106); Fat 12g (Saturated 3g); Cholesterol 35mg; Sodium 110mg; Carbohydrate 21g (Dietary Fiber 1g); Protein 6g.*

Zebra Meringues

These delicious meringue cookies are super easy to make, but they give the impression you spent hours in the kitchen.

Preparation time: *15 minutes*

Cooking time: *2 hours*

Yield: *40 meringues*

Nonstick spray	½ cup sugar
3 egg whites	1 teaspoon vanilla
⅛ teaspoon salt	1 cup chocolate chips
½ teaspoon cream of tartar	

1 Preheat the oven to 350 degrees. Lightly grease two cookie sheets with the nonstick spray.

2 Use an electric beater to beat the egg whites at high speed until they're foamy.

3 Add the salt and cream of tartar. Beat the whites until they form stiff peaks.

4 Add the sugar gradually while beating. Then add the vanilla, beating it in.

5 Using a wooden spatula, fold in the chocolate chips.

6 Use a teaspoon to drop the meringue batter onto the greased cookie sheets. Put them in the oven, and turn the oven off. Leave the cookies in the oven for about 2 hours.

Per serving: Calories 22 (From Fat 11); Fat 1g (Saturated 1g); Cholesterol 0mg; Sodium 12mg; Carbohydrate 3g (Dietary Fiber 0g); Protein 0g.

Being Sensible: Sweets for the Health-Conscious

"Healthy dessert." Isn't that an oxymoron? For the most part, desserts can be like land mines in the Battle of the Bulge and the Hunt for Health, sabotaging even your strongest attempts to eat well. Most of the recipes I've seen for healthful desserts usually just make a no-sweetener, no-fat, no-cal, no-carb, no-taste glob of textures that are more appealing to horses than humans.

But you *can* satisfy without sabotage and still keep the dessert gluten-free. In fact, some of the recipes I offer in this section are downright good for you, so you can enjoy them as part of a gluten-free, guilt-free, well-balanced diet.

Try sautéing fruits like apples, pears, or bananas over medium-high heat in sugar (or sucralose artificial sweetener, sold as Splenda) and water until they're a little bit caramelized. Doing so adds a caramel flavor without the fat of a caramel sauce.

⟳ Grilled Banana Split

You don't really have to grill the bananas, but they look cool with the grill marks, and warming them gives them a great texture.

Preparation time: *10 minutes*

Cooking time: *6 minutes*

Yield: *12 servings*

6 firm bananas, with peeling	*2 tablespoons light chocolate syrup*
3 tablespoons honey	*3 tablespoons fat-free whipped cream topping*
1 quart nonfat vanilla frozen yogurt	

1 Preheat the grill to medium-high heat.

2 Don't peel the bananas! Cut each one in half lengthwise and then again in half widthwise so you have four sections from each banana.

3 Brush honey on the flat sides of the bananas, and let them stand for about 5 minutes.

4 Put the flesh side of the bananas on the hot grill and cook them for about 3 minutes (until the bananas have grill marks). Turn them over and cook about 3 more minutes, until the peel begins to easily pull away. Make sure the bananas don't slip through the grate.

5 Arrange two sections of banana in each bowl, and top the bananas with frozen yogurt, a drizzle of chocolate syrup, and whipped cream.

Per serving: *Calories 141 (From Fat 1); Fat 0g (Saturated 0g); Cholesterol 1mg; Sodium 47mg; Carbohydrate 33g (Dietary Fiber 2); Protein 4g.*

☞ Blueberry Parfait

No need to peel, pit, core, dice, slice, or chop for these babies. They're easy, delicious, and loaded with nutritional value. Blueberries are higher in antioxidants than many other fruits and vegetables, and they're fat-free, low in calories, and high in fiber. Just one cup provides about 15 percent of your daily need for vitamin C. Fresh, frozen, canned, and dried blueberries are available all year long — but treat yourself to the sweet, fresh blueberries of summer for the best blueberries of all.

Preparation time: *30 minutes*

Freezing time: *2 hours*

Yield: *4 servings*

2 cups blueberries	*1 tablespoon lemon juice*
¼ cup sugar	*8 ounces nonfat plain yogurt*
2 tablespoons cornstarch	*2 cups sliced strawberries*
¼ cup cool water	

1 In a medium-sized saucepan, stir together the blueberries and sugar.

2 In a small bowl, mix the cornstarch and water together until the cornstarch dissolves.

3 Add the cornstarch-water mixture to the blueberries and sugar, and cook the blueberry mixture over medium heat until it begins to boil. Let it boil for 1 minute. Stir in the lemon juice, and let the blueberries cool.

4 Gently fold the yogurt into the cooled blueberry mixture so you don't crush the berries.

5 In four separate parfait glasses, layer some of the blueberry mixture, then some strawberries, and then the blueberry mixture again. Keep alternating layers until the glasses are full and you've used all the ingredients.

6 Freeze the parfaits for at least 2 hours. Take them out of the freezer 30 minutes before you plan to serve them.

Tip: *You can serve your favorite gluten-free cookies with these parfaits. Just before serving, when the parfait has softened a little, stick a cookie in the parfait.*

Per serving: *Calories 152 (From Fat 5); Fat 1g (Saturated 0g); Cholesterol 1mg; Sodium 39mg; Carbohydrate 37g (Dietary Fiber 4g); Protein 3g.*

⏾ Granola Bars

Most granola isn't gluten-free, so use a commercially available gluten-free granola or mix up a batch from the recipe I give you in Chapter 10. Turn your granola into a great gluten-free dessert with this one! This is a good way to use up your granola if it's beginning to go stale.

Preparation time: *30 minutes*

Cooking time: *30 to 35 minutes*

Cooling time: *1 hour*

Yield: *4 servings*

Nonstick spray	*1 egg, beaten*
2 cups granola	*⅓ cup honey*
1 cup chopped peanuts	*⅓ cup canola oil*
½ cup gluten-free flour mixture	*⅓ cup packed brown sugar*
½ cup raisins	*½ teaspoon ground cinnamon*

1 Preheat the oven to 325 degrees.

2 Line an 8-inch square pan with aluminum foil, and spray it with nonstick spray.

3 In a medium-sized mixing bowl, combine the granola, peanuts, flour mixture, and raisins. Stir in the egg, honey, oil, brown sugar, and cinnamon. Press the mixture evenly into the pan.

4 Bake the granola mixture for 30 to 35 minutes, or until it's lightly browned around the edges. Cool it for at least 1 hour.

5 Pull the foil out of the pan and flip the granola mixture upside down so you can peel off the aluminum foil. Cut the granola mixture into sixteen 2-inch squares.

Per serving: *Calories 810 (From Fat 387); Fat 43g (Saturated 5g); Cholesterol 53mg; Sodium 231mg; Carbohydrate 101g (Dietary Fiber 6g); Protein 15g.*

Satisfy your sweet tooth with fabulous fruit

Humans do love their sweets. If you give a baby a spoonful of ice cream and one of sour cream, you don't need a team of researchers and a multimillion-dollar, placebo-controlled, double-blind study to figure out which one will make him smile and which will make him grimace. Sure, people need glucose — that's the sugar that powers the body. But you can get enough of that from fruit, vegetables, and other foods. You also have the added benefit of getting vitamins, minerals, fiber, and antioxidants for far fewer calories than the "empty calories" you find in sugary foods. So satisfy your sweet tooth, but try to do it with foods that pack a nutritional punch. Here are some ideas:

✔ **Chocolate hazelnut spread fruit dip:** Warm up chocolate hazelnut spread a little and dip fresh fruit in it.

✔ **Grapes and French cream:** Combine about 1 cup fat-free sour cream, ½ cup powdered sugar, ½ cup sucralose artificial sweetener (Splenda), and a dash of vanilla. Mix the French cream with red, green, and black grapes.

✔ **Peaches 'n cream:** Put half of a peach or pear in a dish and add a small scoop of vanilla frozen yogurt. Put raspberries or strawberries on top.

✔ **Pudding:** If you use skim milk with a packaged pudding, it's pretty good for you. Serve it with bananas on top.

✔ **Strawberries and yogurt:** Slice strawberries and blend them with nonfat flavored yogurt. Top the mixture with artificial sweetener if you want a little extra sweetness.

✔ **Strawberry sweet and sour:** Dip fresh strawberries into fat-free sour cream and then into artificial sweetener or honey.

Remember: Fresh fruit is best for you when you store it properly. Don't refrigerate bananas and other tropical fruits. Melons don't need refrigeration until you cut them; store them in a separate bin, away from vegetables and meat.

Part IV

Living — and Loving — the Gluten-Free Lifestyle 24/7

The 5th Wave   By Rich Tennant

"I think you're overreacting, but yes, I'll find out if your opponents boxing gloves are gluten-free."

In this part . . .

I take a look at the social implications of living gluten-free, because getting out of the house is one of the most challenging practical aspects of living a gluten-free lifestyle. I give you the tools you need to enjoy eating at restaurants, traveling, and socializing — all while staying safely gluten-free — because your diet shouldn't ever stand in the way of your activities and adventures. I also discuss the unique emotional challenges that people face when embracing the gluten-free lifestyle and how to overcome those obstacles. Most of all, my goal in this part is to help you capture the essence of living — and *loving* — the gluten-free lifestyle.

Chapter 16

Getting Out and About: Eating Away from Home

In This Chapter

▶ Setting yourself up for success when eating out

▶ Preparing for restaurant adventures

▶ Packing it up — it's travel time!

▶ Going gluten-free on planes, trains, and automobiles (and ships)

*F*or some people, it isn't the gluten-free diet itself that presents the biggest challenge — it's getting out of the house. Even people who've been gluten-free for years sometimes feel uncomfortable about venturing away from home.

Most of this book focuses on reading labels, shopping and cooking, modifying recipes, keeping the kitchen gluten-free, and flicking the peanut butter off the knife so the knife doesn't get contaminated with crumbs. But what about when you eat out? There are no labels to read, you're limited to the selections others provide, and you have no idea whether they know how to do the gob drop (see Chapter 7). And for the most part, you have little control over how the cooks prepare the food.

Yet getting out is important. Life in a bubble is for oxygen molecules, not humans. Does venturing outside require extra effort on your part? Sure. Might you receive a meal contaminated with gluten? Yep. Are you going to pay $20 for a meal that would have cost $6 to make at home? Darned straight. Is it worth it? Absolutely.

The reality is that you can't always be at home in a crumb-free zone with pantries stocked with your gluten-free favorites and toaster ovens bearing the "GF" stamp of approval. Whether you're taking clients out for lunch, enjoying a romantic dinner for two at your favorite restaurant, traveling for business, or seeing the world for pleasure, you *will* be eating out. And unless you want to pout and starve, you need to know how to safely and comfortably accommodate your gluten-free lifestyle when you're away from home.

The Golden Rules of Going Out Gluten-Free

You just arrived at the social event of the year. You're energized, looking fabulous, and eager to spend a great evening with friends. And you're famished. You zero in on the buffet table, loaded with the most amazing spread you've seen in decades, and slowly you begin to realize that you can't eat anything within a 2.8-mile radius. Your mood plummets as fast as your panic rises, because you realize you're going to be there all night with nothing to eat.

What follows are some basic rules of going out gluten-free. These rules should prevent such a buzz-kill scenario, because there's no reason to let a little food (or lack thereof) ruin a good time. Armed with these practical and emotional guidelines, your social experiences can be as spectacular as ever.

Don't expect others to accommodate your diet

The office party is coming up in two months. Realizing food will obviously be there, you take the time to visit with the person planning the party, and you explain your dietary restrictions, right down to the sometimes somewhat-intricate details of the gluten-free diet. She's ranking high on the does-she-get-it scale, nodding in the appropriate places, even tossing in an "Oh, so you probably can't do the rolls, right?" Wow! She gets it! You're set, right? Don't bet your promotion on it. And whatever you do, don't expect it.

If she comes through and you see gluten-free goodies there (in which case you'll be tempted to fiercely guard them, elbowing guests away, defending your territory and hissing, "Those are for me! They're all I can eat!"), be gracious, thankful, and gush all over her (and don't hiss; it's really not becoming). She didn't have to make the effort to accommodate your diet, but she did.

Really, you shouldn't *expect* anyone to accommodate your gluten-free diet — I don't care who it is. Even those closest to you — those you love the most — are going to forget or make mistakes. This doesn't happen because they don't care — they (usually) do. Often, the lack of gluten-free goodies is just an oversight, or sometimes people think they understand the diet, but they missed some of the intricacies and what they think is gluten-free is floating in teriyaki.

Ask what's for dinner

Asking about the menu isn't rude. Well, sometimes it is. Like when you invite some people for dinner and they're trying to choose between that and another opportunity, so they respond, "Yeah, maybe. What's for dinner?" But that's another book (see *Responding to Rude Remarks For Dummies*). (Sorry, folks, I made that title up, so you're on your own for clever comebacks).

When you're gluten-free and attending a social function, asking what's for dinner won't earn you a spot on the social circuit blacklist. Of course, some ways of asking are ruder than others (see preceding paragraph), but I assume you have more tact than that and can simply say to the host or hostess, "I have a dietary restriction and was wondering if it would be okay to ask you about what you're serving so I can plan accordingly." Most of the time, people are receptive to sitting down with you, discussing the menu, even asking for your input, and accommodating your diet as best they can.

Fill 'er up before you go

Because you can't expect any gluten-free goodies you can eat at the party, filling up before you go is a good idea. That way you're not starved and fixated on food, and you can enjoy the party for what it's really all about, which is fun and friends.

The biggest problem with this rule is that if you get to the party and find lots of gluten-free goodies you can eat, you'll be so excited that you'll eat them all, even though you're not hungry. Beware of popping buttons.

BYOF: Bring your own food

I'm not suggesting that you walk into a formal soirée with bags of fast food under your arms, wafting the just-fried french fry smell among guests in tuxedos. No, that type of a grand entrance may not sit well with the host and hostess. The setting does, of course, determine the type of food you bring and how you bring it.

Don't worry that bringing your own food may offend the host. First, you can always discuss this option with him in advance. But if you don't, you can discreetly explain to him that you have a dietary restriction and rather than burden him with the details ("I know you've been busy getting ready for this party . . ."), you thought it would be easiest just to bring a few things for yourself to eat. Ask where you should put your things and whether serving yourself when you get hungry is appropriate.

Making smart choices at potlucks

Potlucks are tough because lots of cooks are in the kitchen. You have no idea what's in the dishes, and even those that look the safest could have seasonings or ingredients that turn a potluck surprise into party demise.

Your best bet at potlucks is to offer to bring something you happen to love — and that can fill you up and keep you happy throughout the party. So what if you're eating only the dish you brought? If anyone notices, you can explain. Chances are, though, people will be too busy loading up their own plates to check out what you have on yours.

Bite your tongue when they make a mistake

You sat down with the hostess, talked about her plans for the meal, and decided where she could make a few accommodations for you. You get to the party only to find croissants surrounded by phyllo-filled finger foods and breaded fried stuff. You:

A) Pout and starve.

B) Pout, starve, and yell at the hostess.

C) Pout, starve, scream rude things at the hostess, and pick the innards out of the phyllo-stuffed thingies (No! They're glutenated!).

D) None of the above. You enjoy the party and relax. You weren't hungry anyway, because you filled up before you came.

The correct answer, of course, should be D.

Enjoy the company

It doesn't matter whether you're at a nightclub, a festive party for 500, a restaurant enjoying an intimate dinner for two, a wedding, or a wake — social gatherings are not about the food. They're about the occasion, the atmosphere, the ambiance, the people you're with . . . oh, and did I mention that you don't have to clean up?

Now I'm not saying that social functions don't revolve around food. They do. Most societies use food as a focal point to draw people close during times of socialization and celebration. But don't lose sight of the celebration itself and the reason that people are gathering in the first place, because that's what social functions are about. (If you're invited to a bread-tasting party, ignore this paragraph — in that case, it is about the food.)

Dining Out: Restaurant Realities and Rewards

A great experience at a terrific restaurant is priceless. Good company, nice ambiance, respectful service, and delicious food synergize to create a multi-faceted experience that is far more than just a meal.

Being on a gluten-free diet shouldn't hold you back from going out. Sure, eating at restaurants involves some risk. You don't know for sure what ingredients are in your food, no matter how much you try to educate your server and chef. Kitchen and waiting staffs are busy and can (and do) make mistakes, and cross-contamination is always an issue. And by law, you will at least once in your gluten-free dining days receive a salad with croutons that you have to send back.

But with just a little extra effort, you can help ensure that your meal is safely gluten-free, and you can enjoy gluten-free dining as one of life's more pleasurable social experiences.

Here are some tips for eating out that can help make your gluten-free dining experiences the best they can be:

- ✔ **Be pleasant and grateful.** If you're demanding, you're going to put them on the defensive. When they accommodate your requests, be extremely grateful.

- ✔ **Give them just enough information.** Not too much, not too little. You may have to read the server to see whether he or she is really "getting" what you're saying.

- ✔ **Don't be afraid to ask for what you want.** You're paying for the meal, and you should be able to enjoy it knowing it's safe for you to eat.

- ✔ **Make it clear to the server and chef that this is a serious condition.** If you have to sound alarming, do so. One of the best ways to get their attention is to say, "It's kind of like an allergy to peanuts." You know it's not *really* like an allergy to peanuts, but it will get their attention.

- ✔ **Call ahead if you can.** Remember to avoid busy hours. See whether they can fax or e-mail you a menu. At the same time, you can fax or e-mail them a list of ingredients you can and can't have.

✔ **Know how foods are prepared.** The more you know about traditional preparation, the better decisions you can make when ordering.

✔ **Bring your own food.** Not only can you bring your own bread or crackers to snack on, but you can even bring food for them to cook for you. Remember to offer suggestions for how to keep your food from becoming contaminated by the rest of the food in the restaurant.

✔ **Send it back if it's not right.** Of course I'm not suggesting you be rude about this, but if they give you a salad with croutons on it, don't pick the croutons out and eat it. That's not safe! There's nothing wrong with politely saying, "Excuse me. I must have forgotten to mention that I can't have croutons on my salad. Do you mind bringing me a new one?" Everyone knows you mentioned it; you're just letting them off the hook.

Choosing the restaurant

Don't go to Sam's All-We-Serve-Is-Pizza pizza joint and whine that you can't eat anything. You're setting yourself up for frustration and disappointment if you choose restaurants that, by the very nature of their menu selections, aren't likely to have much (if anything) that's gluten-free.

Instead, go to restaurants that have large and diverse menu selections, or choose an ethnic restaurant that's likely to have more gluten-free foods. Happy gluten-free dining starts with choosing restaurants that are likely to have foods on the menu that are already gluten-free or that the kitchen staff can easily modify.

Good bets

With any restaurant you go to, you have to check ingredients in specific dishes. And of course, food preparation is an issue (are they using the same spatula to flip the burgers and the buns?). You can either ask the workers to make your food in an uncontaminated manner or you can opt to eat somewhere else. But as a general rule, the types of restaurants that are a good bet include

✔ **All-you-can-eat soup and salad:** Not only do these restaurants usually offer lots of items that are gluten-free, but they often have their ingredients handy so you can check soups and salad dressings to be sure. Sometimes the ingredients are actually posted on placards in front of the item. If not, ask a server or the manager whether there's a listing of ingredients. Some restaurants have notebooks with recipes for each item, and they're usually glad to let you take a look.

✔ **Barbecues:** Although you do have to check the sauces, many barbecues are good bets because they do traditional fare such as ribs, chicken, pork, corn on the cob, mashed potatoes, and potato salad.

✔ **Breakfast houses:** Be careful here — some breakfast places make the scrambled eggs with a boxed egg that has wheat flour mixed in (ick!). So ask for fresh eggs. You may also be able to get hash browns, fruit, yogurt, and lots of other good breakfast stuff.

✔ **Fast food:** Fast-food joints offer fries, shakes, salads, chili, and other foods that are often gluten-free. If you order a burger, make sure it's without a bun — even if you pluck it off, the bun contaminates your dinner. Many fast-food places offer a lettuce bun, even if they don't advertise that they do so. Several restaurants even have their nutritional information and ingredients posted online.

When you're getting fries, make sure they're not breaded or coated in anything, and ask what other things are fried in the same oil. You don't want to order fries that have been swimming with onion rings or something else that contaminates the oil with gluten.

✔ **Indian:** Many of the ingredients in Indian cooking are inherently gluten-free.

✔ **Mexican:** Mexican cooking includes many inherently gluten-free foods. Restaurants often guard their cooking secrets, but most Mexican recipes call for spices such as cumin, epazote, garlic, oregano, salt, and pepper. *Carnitas,* a traditional simmered pork dish served with corn tortillas, shredded lettuce, tomatoes, rice, and beans, is an example of a Mexican dish that's usually a safe bet. But as is the case with any meal, you need to make sure the kitchen staff doesn't add flour to the sauce, and of course, specify corn tortillas instead of flour if you get a choice.

✔ **Mongolian barbecue:** Mongolian barbecues are essentially choose-your-own stir-fry restaurants. Because you can make your own sauces and add your own ingredients, Mongolian barbecues tend to be a good bet for gluten-free dining. Be sure to have the cooks thoroughly clean the grill before cooking your meal. And tell them that you have food allergies so they can keep your food separate from your neighbor's teriyaki chicken.

✔ **Steak and seafood:** These restaurants are likely to have steaks or burgers, seafood, salads (hold the croutons), baked potatoes or rice, french fries, and ice cream for dessert.

✔ **Thai/Vietnamese:** What a treat to be able to go to a Thai or Vietnamese restaurant and eat noodles! Be careful — not all their noodles are gluten-free, but most of them are rice-based and are safe. The sauces they use, for the most part, are gluten-free, too.

You may notice lots of ethnic options on the "good bets" list. Many ethnic foods are naturally gluten-free. You need to figure out which ones you like, and of those foods, which are inherently gluten-free. Then you can choose a restaurant of that ethnicity and know what to order. Mexican, Thai, Vietnamese, and Indian cuisines are just a few that offer a huge selection of gluten-free foods. Do your homework to find out how the chefs prepare traditional fare, and then dig in.

Risky restaurants

You can definitely get gluten-free meals at some of these restaurants, but in general, restaurants that aren't going to be a good bet include

- ✓ **Bakeries:** I probably didn't need to point that out, did I?

- ✓ **Cajun:** You can get blackened fish and other gluten-free foods at Cajun restaurants, but be careful of contamination issues. For the most part, Cajun food is covered in breadings (sometimes they're just cornmeal and seasonings, and they may be okay). And many gumbos, étouffées, and other Cajun dishes are often flavored with a darkened roux, which is made from flour. Some foods that appear to be okay, such as shrimp, are often boiled in beer.

- ✓ **Chinese:** These restaurants use soy sauce in many, if not most of their dishes, and their soy sauce usually has gluten in it. You can bring your own soy sauce, but warn the cooks to be careful about contamination issues while they're preparing your food.

- ✓ **Italian:** Most Italian restaurants serve a lot of pasta, breads, and breaded items. You can, however, find restaurants that serve polenta, an Italian cornmeal classic, and of course you can eat the wonderful (crouton-free) salads.

- ✓ **Specialty coffee shops:** The trendy coffee shops you're familiar with offer foods and snacks, usually marketed as being wholesome or healthy. Unfortunately, what that usually means is that their muffins are bran muffins. For the most part, other than yogurt or fruit, coffee shops offer very little in the way of gluten-free snacks.

Calling ahead

Don't be afraid to call a restaurant ahead of time to talk about the menu and to figure out whether the chefs can accommodate your gluten-free diet. If possible, have someone fax or e-mail you a menu so you can see what the restaurant serves that's likely to be gluten-free, and then call back and discuss the ingredients with the head chef. You can also fax or e-mail the restaurant a list of the safe and forbidden ingredients. Sometimes restaurants are so accommodating that if you give them enough notice, they'll get special ingredients for your meal.

Call at the restaurant's slowest time of day (if you don't know when that is, ask them). If the restaurant serves lunch, you want to catch someone after the lunch rush and before the dinner crowd — probably around 2:30 or 3:00 p.m. If the restaurant serves dinner only, call earlier than that — more like 1:00 p.m. or so.

One of the best things about fast-food places is that they generally follow standardized guidelines, so one call to their corporate offices can answer your questions about dedicated fryers, ingredients, and even food preparation. Many chains also have Web sites that list their nutritional information and ingredients, and some even have a gluten-free menu online. If you eat at fast-food restaurants often, put the information into a small three-ring binder and keep it in your car. That way, when you're pulling into the drive-through of one of your favorite fast-food joints, you have a handy list of their gluten-free items.

Making smart menu choices

Set yourself up for success. Choose menu items that are likely to be gluten-free or that the kitchen staff can easily modify to be gluten-free. Obviously, breaded and fried items aren't going to be your best bets, although sometimes cooks can use the same meat, season it with spices, and grill it instead.

So, do you order the beer-battered fish? Not a good choice. The teriyaki pork stir-fry? Nope. Fried chicken? Probably not. Grilled chicken? There you go! Grilled fish? Steak? Sure! Of course, you still may need to ask a few questions, but at least you're on the right track.

Ordering is a four-step process:

1. **Find the foods on the menu that are already likely to be gluten-free or appear that they could easily be modified to be gluten-free.**

2. **Choose the item(s) you want.**

3. **Ask about ingredients and food preparation methods. I go into detail about this later in this chapter.**

4. **Make sure you've made your order clear and have offered suggestions for how to season and prepare your meal.**

Gluten-free menus

Close your eyes and imagine being at a beautiful restaurant with great company. The server chirps, "Hi, I'm Sarah. I'll be your server today. Would you like to see the gluten-free menu?" Okay, you can open your eyes now, because I know how hard it is to read this book with them closed. Besides, this isn't a dream. It's a reality!

Today, several restaurants, like PF Chang's and Outback Steakhouse, offer gluten-free menus — some of them are even online. You usually need to ask, though, so speak up and ask whether they have a gluten-free menu. You never know when your server may hand you one.

Do a bit of research on food preparation. The more you know about how foods are usually prepared, the easier ordering is. For instance, you should know that restaurants, especially Cajun restaurants, often boil seafood in beer. And the "crab" you find in sushi is usually a mixture of fish and wheat flour.

Talking with the staff: Ask and ye shall receive

My teenage kids hate being with me when I order food at a restaurant. All I have to do is hold up the menu and say to the server, "Could I ask you a question?" and my kids start fidgeting, rolling their eyes, mumbling, "Here we go . . ." But what's wrong with getting what you want when you're paying for your food? (Certainly, my kids don't hesitate to put in their short-order requests when I'm the chef!)

Don't be afraid to ask for what you want (even if your teenage kids are a tad intimidating). People ask for special considerations at restaurants all the time, even when they don't have dietary restrictions. If you feel that the server isn't getting it, ask to talk with the chef. Of course, be tactful about it. Asking for special considerations for your meal isn't rude — especially when your health depends on it.

Letting restaurant cards speak for you

Restaurant cards are small cards that explain the basics of the gluten-free dietary guidelines that you can give to a server or chef. You can make your own, download one from the Internet, or buy them from support groups and other entities. Basically, the card says something like this:

> I have a severe reaction to gluten and am on a strict gluten-free diet. Thank you for working with me to prepare a meal I can safely enjoy.

> I *cannot* eat wheat, rye, barley, or their derivatives. These include kamut, spelt, durum, semolina, bulgur, triticale, and malt. I also avoid oats. Foods and ingredients I need to avoid include croutons, bread, breadings, flour, soy sauce, orzo, buns and

rolls, brown rice syrup, and malt vinegar. I *can* eat rice, corn, potatoes, tapioca, soy, beans, amaranth, arrowroot, buckwheat, quinoa, millet, teff, and nut flours. I can also eat vinegar (except malt vinegar) and distilled alcohols.

> If you have any questions, please ask me. Thank you for working with me on this! Know that you have given me the opportunity to relax and enjoy my meal; I appreciate that very much.

If you make your own card, laminating it is a good idea, because it's likely to get covered in food when the chef handles it. I like to make up several of these cards and leave them behind with the chef for other patrons he or she may have in the future.

Yes, you really do need to talk to the server and maybe even the chef . . . and yes, you sometimes need to give them lots of detail. But for the most part, you should keep explanations as simple as possible and work your way into detail if you need to. You may be surprised at how little you need to say.

Of course, you've already chosen a restaurant that's likely to have gluten-free items and you've picked some items on the menu that look like they may be gluten-free or could be modified to be gluten-free. So at this point, you're ready to order. You may say something like this:

> **The Opener:** "I'm on a gluten-free diet and have some special considerations I'm hoping you can help me with."

You're likely to find that the staff is very receptive. I start right in with the words "gluten-free" because awareness is spreading, and these days when you explain that you need a gluten-free meal, your server is likely to respond with, "Oh, really? Do you have a gluten intolerance like celiac disease?" At this point, you feel like that server is your new very best friend, and you know your special order is in good hands. The kitchen crew will probably be on board, too. Today's chefs learn about the gluten-free diet in culinary schools, and they love to put their skills and knowledge to work to please a customer.

Assume, though, that the server doesn't seem to know anything about the gluten-free diet and simply shrugs his or her shoulders. At this point, the situation requires some explanation — but not too much. You don't want to overwhelm your server or relate your entire nine-year medical history. You do, however, need to get your server's attention.

> **The Alarm:** "I have a very severe reaction to gluten. Gluten is in wheat, rye, and barley, and I also avoid oats."

Notice the words "severe reaction." These are alarm words that in the restaurant owner's mind are a euphemism for "lawsuit waiting to happen." Not that you would sue — I hope you wouldn't. But ears perk up when you use the words, and that's a good thing. Restaurant workers and management then pay closer attention.

At this point, you can hand over your restaurant card or make specific suggestions for how the cooks could prepare the item you want to be gluten-free. Don't be afraid of over-stressing the importance of this and the details involved.

Remember to talk about how the staff prepares the food. If the food is grilled, you may want to say, "Could you please make sure that the part of the grill where you cook my food is clean and doesn't have crumbs from another meal? Also, could you please use a separate spatula to flip my burger?"

The do-they-get-it point system

When you talk to your server and/or chef, you can figure out how to read their responses and assign them do-they-get-it points. Your interactions with them throughout the ordering process and ensuing meal may depend on how many points they earn.

Listening attentively while you explain your dietary restrictions — 1 point

Saying, "I think I better bring the chef out to talk to you to make sure we get this right." — 1 point

Adding comments like, "Oh, you're gluten-free! Is that because you have celiac disease?" — 2 points

Commenting, "Sounds like a healthy way to eat!" — 1 point

Stopping you mid-sentence and saying, "Sounds like you'd like to see our gluten-free menu." — 2 points

Stopping you mid-sentence and saying, "Sounds like you'd like to try our freshly made gluten-free pizza, washed down with our home-brewed gluten-free beer, and topped off with our freshly baked gluten-free pastry selection for dessert." — 0 points (you're dreaming)

Staring at you as though you just ordered worms on your burger — -1 point

Giving you a quick, "Yeah, uh-huh, okay, next?" and turning to the person next to you — -1 point

Listening to your entire explanation and asking, "Okay, so then you want white bread instead of wheat?" — -1 point

Adding up the points:

-3 to -1: You should probably leave.

0: I hope you're not too hungry. You should either leave or realize you're going to have to work hard to make sure your meal is a safe one.

1 to 2: Probably a good bet. Bon appétit!

3 to 7: Hugs and kisses to the entire staff — and don't forget a big tip.

If the server just doesn't seem to be getting it or seems unwilling to work with you, ask to talk with the chef. This is not a big deal. People are so afraid to ask to talk to the chef, but chefs often love to mingle with the guests and are really interested in the gluten-free diet.

Having restaurants cook the food you bring

Many restaurants allow you to bring your own food into the restaurant, and they may warm it or even cook it for you. If you do this, be aware of how they normally cook their food, because you probably need to watch out for some contamination concerns.

For instance, most pizza places use convection ovens that blow the flour all around. If you bring a pizza crust and ask them to use their toppings and cook it, you have to be sure their toppings aren't contaminated (they often are), and then you have to make sure they wrap the pizza securely in aluminum foil before warming it in the oven — otherwise, your gluten-free pizza goes into a pizza oven that's blowing flour all over. Same goes for bringing a pre-made gluten-free pizza with you — make sure it's wrapped carefully before asking them to warm it in their ovens.

Pasta places often allow you to bring gluten-free pastas and cook them for you. Be sure to remind the workers to use a clean pot, clean water, clean utensils, and a clean colander before they make your gluten-free pasta.

I hope I'm not stating the obvious, but you probably should only ask the restaurant to prepare your food if you're actually buying some of theirs. A group of four, each of whom has brought his own meal in, won't win any popularity contests. But if one person in a group of four brings his meal, it's not usually a problem. Restaurants don't usually charge extra to warm or prepare meals you bring yourself, but you should ask to be sure.

You may want to think about getting toaster bags for toasting your bread when you're away from home. The bags are great for making sure your bread doesn't get contaminated when you're away from home. Just put your gluten-free bread in the bag, and anyone can put it in a toaster, toaster oven, or regular oven. Then just take your bread out, and you have perfectly uncontaminated gluten-free toast. The bags are washable and reusable, but you can just toss them when you're done.

Remembering the art of healthy tipping

I don't take tipping lightly, because when people accommodate your gluten-free diet and give you the peace of mind that helps you enjoy the multidimensional, multisensational experience of dining out, you should express your gratitude. If they've done it with an eager-to-please attitude, showing your appreciation is even more important.

The number of people going gluten-free is skyrocketing. Every server you talk to, every chef you inform, and every tip you leave will better the future for everyone going gluten-free today, tomorrow, and beyond.

The Incredible, Edible Journey: It's Travel Time!

Whether you're getting away for business or pleasure, nearly all people find themselves leaving home from time to time. You don't have to limit or, worse yet, give up traveling because you're on a gluten-free diet. In fact, you may actually find some countries to be more accommodating than you ever would've dreamed. For instance, when you order a burger at McDonald's in some parts of Sweden or Finland, they ask you whether you'd like that on a regular or gluten-free bun!

If you follow the "Golden Rules of Going Out Gluten-Free" that I outline earlier in this chapter, you'll be well-prepared for wherever your travels take you. And because traveling nearly always involves eating at restaurants, you should also pay particular attention to the advice in the preceding section on dining out. But to ensure a great gluten-free adventure, here are a few more things that you should know before you hit the road.

Knowing the boundaries when crossing the border

If you're traveling internationally, be aware of some special considerations. For instance, some countries won't allow you to bring food across the border. If that's the case, see whether you can send it ahead, or find out whether gluten-free products are available there, in which case you may not need to bring food with you.

Also be aware that different countries have different standards for what's allowed on the gluten-free diet. In Europe, for instance, manufacturers use an ingredient called Codex Alimentarius wheat starch, which has the gluten removed. Products that contain this ingredient are labeled gluten-free, but in the United States and Canada, that product isn't considered gluten-free.

Realize that your foods may be suspect in some countries. One time my family and I went to Mexico and brought some of our favorite gluten-free pancake mix. We didn't want to take the entire bag (we buy it in bulk), so we put some in a food storage zipper bag and tossed it in our carry-ons. Unfortunately for us, we didn't use much of it on our trip. Coming home through customs, our bags were searched, and the mysterious white powder was subject to — ahem — intense scrutiny.

Researching your destination

Do yourself a favor and spend some time researching the area before you go on your trip. You can always find grocery stores or markets, restaurants, and fast-food places, all of which will have at least some things you can eat. But you may do even better than that. Local support groups, Internet chat sites, and listservs may be able to steer you in the direction of gluten-free-friendly restaurants and stores, and researching what's typically available in the area can tell you how much food to bring and how much you can get while you're there. (A *listserv* is an e-mail list that allows people to post questions, answers, and other types of information targeted to a specific audience. You can find more information about the celiac listserv in Chapter 5.)

If, in doing your homework, you find health food stores or natural foods stores in the area of your destination, call ahead and ask what they carry in the way of gluten-free specialty items. You may be surprised to find they have a huge array. If not, ask whether they would consider stocking a few items for you, and let them know when you'll be arriving.

Sprechen zie gluten? Speaking gluten-free in other countries

Knowing some key words in the language of the country you're visiting is important. For instance, "flour" in Spanish is *harina*. But that can refer to corn flour or wheat flour, so you have to further distinguish what you're talking about by saying *harina de maiz* (corn flour) or *harina de trigo* (wheat flour). Learn the words for *gluten, with, without, no,* and *allergy.* Check out Table 16-1 for some key words in Spanish, French, and German.

Table 16-1	Terms for Explaining the Diet in Foreign Languages		
English Term	*Spanish*	*French*	*German*
I can	puedo	je peux	ich kann
I can't	no puedo	je ne peux pas	ich kann nicht
(to) eat	comer	manger	essen
gluten	gluten	gluten	gluten
wheat	trigo	blé	weizen
flour	harina	farine	mehl
corn	maiz	maïs	mais

(continued)

Table 16-1 *(continued)*

English Term	Spanish	French	German
with	con	avec	mit
without	sin	sans	ohne
yes	sí	oui	ja
no	no	non	nein
allergy	alergia	allergie	allergie

Restaurant cards that explain the gluten-free diet are available in different languages; a quick Internet search should turn those up. And you can also use translation software, like the Babel Fish translation at www.altavista.com and others you find on the Internet.

Choosing gluten-free-friendly accommodations

Where you stay can make your vacation a much more enjoyable experience. If possible, choose accommodations with a kitchen or kitchenette, like a condo or extended-stay hotel. Even a small fridge and microwave can make your trip a lot easier. That way, you can go to a local grocery store and stock up on some essentials, like fruit, milk, popcorn, deli meats, and snack items. If you have a full kitchen at your disposal, you can prepare your own meals if you want to, sparing yourself the worry of eating at restaurants — not to mention the expense.

If you don't have a kitchen, try to find accommodations that have a restaurant attached or that have several restaurants nearby. You can call the hotel restaurant in advance and have the staff fax or e-mail you the menu so you can discuss items you may be able to enjoy. Some restaurants may even work with you to accommodate your dietary needs during your stay.

If your accommodations are near several national restaurant chains, you can look up their Web sites and see whether they have menus online. You may even be surprised to find an online gluten-free menu.

Packing your own provisions

You may want to bring your kitchen in your suitcase (everything but the kitchen sink!). Depending on where you're going and for how long, your kitchen-in-a-suitcase may include some of the following items:

- ✔ Baking mixes (pancakes, cookies, cakes, brownies, bread)
- ✔ Bread slicer or serrated knife
- ✔ Cereals that may be hard to find
- ✔ Cookies
- ✔ Crackers and snack items that may be hard to find
- ✔ Pans to make the baked goods
- ✔ Pasta
- ✔ Pizza crusts (these sometimes need to be refrigerated)
- ✔ Sliced bread
- ✔ Toaster bags (see the tip under "Having restaurants cook the food you bring")
- ✔ Toaster or toaster oven

With any luck, the foods will survive the trip and you'll arrive fully prepared to enjoy your gluten-free stay.

If you don't want to lug the whole kitchen and pantry with you, consider sending your foods ahead. Either pack them up and send them in a box to your final destination or order them online and have them shipped to where you're going. Hotels and condominiums usually accept packages if you clearly mark the guest name and date of arrival on the box.

Getting there

Truly, getting there can be half the fun, and if you don't believe me, rent an old Chevy Chase "Vacation" DVD and see for yourself. Just don't expect model Christy Brinkley to be part of *your* getting-there plans.

Whether you're doing it by plane, train, automobile, or cruise ship, you need to consider the journey itself in your gluten-free plans.

Flying the friendly skies

First rule for flying: Bring food for yourself. You may find that airport food and what they serve on the airplane is limited in its gluten-free selections.

Airports do usually have fast-food restaurants, so if you know which fast foods are gluten-free, you can always go there if you want or need to. Some of the kiosks and cafés sell yogurt, fruit, and salads, and some airports have large restaurant chains where you can order as you would in any other restaurant.

Some airlines allow you to make a request for a gluten-free meal. If you do this, take food just in case. Sometimes you'll be served a meal that isn't remotely close to being gluten-free, and you want to be prepared for that. And many airlines are replacing their packets of peanuts with pretzels because so many people have peanut allergies. Sitting for hours on an airplane when you're starved, smelling everyone else's fresh, hot bread is pretty miserable. Sometimes, though, you'll be thrilled to find that they do accommodate the gluten-free diet. We were once served gluten-free rolls, individually packaged with the ingredients clearly labeled! To hear us cheer, you would have thought we had won the lottery.

Cruising the high seas

Cruise lines are extremely accommodating when it comes to dietary restrictions of any type. Most of the cruise lines I've looked into are very familiar with the gluten-free diet and even stock specialty items like gluten-free breads, pastas, cookies, and baked goods.

If you're planning a cruise, call ahead and ask to speak with the executive chef for the line you're going to be on. Discuss the gluten-free diet with him or her — if the chef isn't familiar with the diet, fax or e-mail the guidelines and follow up with a phone call to discuss the specifics of what you'll want while you're on board.

If for some reason you don't want to call ahead, you're probably still set. Most cruise lines offer healthy fare like fresh seafood, chicken, steaks, fruit, and vegetables. Have a talk with the chef when you're on board about contamination issues and special seasonings so he or she can make sure every meal's exceptional and gluten-free.

Taking the train

If you're taking the train somewhere, your best bet is to bring your own food. Rail lines usually don't have any restrictions about bringing your own food, so load up. The cafés on trains rarely have much that's gluten-free other than chips and maybe hot dogs (but usually they're pre-bunned); instead, the cafés usually serve packaged sandwiches, croissants, muffins, pastries, pizzas, and other oh-so-nutritious-and-not-even-close-to-being-gluten-free goodies. You don't want to derail your trip by starving the whole way.

Traveling near or far by car

Driving offers you the most flexibility, so it's often the easiest way to travel, at least in terms of accommodating your gluten-free diet. (The kids fighting and asking, "Are we almost there?" the entire way is another matter.)

No matter what country you're in, chances are you'll pass a McDonald's every 6.8 seconds, and even if you're spared the golden arches scenery, you can always find restaurants of some kind along the way.

Chapter 17

Raising Happy, Healthy, Gluten-Free Kids

It's one thing when adults need or choose to adopt a gluten-free lifestyle. It's an entirely different ballgame when your kids need to be gluten-free. Believe me, I know. I'm the mom(my) (I'll *never* let go of that!) of a happy, healthy, gluten-free kid.

Our son Tyler was almost 2 when he was diagnosed with celiac disease. That was back in 1991. (If you care to read our entire story, you can find it in Chapter 1.)

The abridged version is that he was sick, but the doctors didn't think so. They kept telling us nothing was wrong, even though he had severe diarrhea, his belly was growing distended, he was growing listless and lethargic, and his personality was changing before our very eyes.

Four pediatricians; a pediatric gastroenterologist; preliminary diagnoses of cystic fibrosis, cancer, or a blood disease; thousands of diarrhea diapers; and nearly one year later, we heard the bittersweet words that changed our lives forever: "Your son has celiac disease." We were shocked, panicked, mad, sad, glad, confused, frustrated, and terrified to feed our own child. And that was all within the first 2.4 seconds of hearing those words.

I've loaded this chapter with information to help you deal with your roller-coaster emotions, the practicalities of having kids on the gluten-free diet, and the psychological impact this may have on your family; I even give you a glimpse into the wonderful world of Terrific Teens who are avoiding gluten.

Before I dive in, I feel compelled to give away the most important message of all (so much for teasing you into reading the whole chapter!): Getting the diagnosis is a *good* thing in your child's life and yours. If you're having trouble believing me, read on.

Forging through the Feelings

Everything's different when your child's the one on the gluten-free diet: The feelings you feel, the way you communicate about the diet, the resentment you feel toward parents who don't have to make special accommodations just to feed their child, the preparations you make to go anywhere, the way you shop, the foods you buy, the school lunches, the resentment toward other parents (oops, that must be a biggie).

If you're a parent — or someone who loves a child as a parent would — and your child has to (for health or behavioral reasons) adopt a strict, gluten-free diet, then your emotions probably resemble a sine wave. You know: up one minute, crashing the next, as in Figure 17-1. It seems like just when you're feeling great about the diet, the lifestyle, and all the benefits that go along with it, you find out the kids had a birthday party at school, and your child was the only one without a cupcake. Your emotions go from flying high to a terminal-velocity free fall.

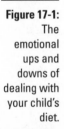

Figure 17-1:
The emotional ups and downs of dealing with your child's diet.

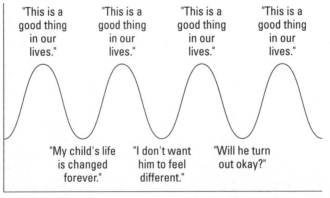

I talk in Chapter 18 about the emotional obstacles you may face when you switch to a gluten-free lifestyle. To quantify what the change feels like when your *kid* has to go gluten-free, as opposed to you, take the magnitude of those emotions, multiply by 100, square that, and add an exponential factor of infinity, and you'll be close.

In addition to the emotions I talk about in Chapter 18, you face other worries — nagging concerns that distress you because your child's most affected. See whether some of these strike a familiar chord.

"My child's life is changed forever"

Yep. That's true. And forever seems like a really long time, doesn't it? What happened to those visions you have for your children — the perfect life, where things are easy and magical? Well, for one thing, that's not reality.

Reaching out

I've always been acutely aware that Tyler may not *want* to be the poster boy for celiac disease, so I let him decide how involved he wants to be in my activities. For the most part, because being gluten-free has never been a big deal to him, he's opted to sit on the sidelines and let me chirp, perk, and sing the praises of the gluten-free lifestyle on my own.

One day, a few months after a local TV station had interviewed Tyler, a woman who'd attended one of our R.O.C.K. (Raising Our Celiac Kids) parties approached my son (for more about R.O.C.K., check out www.celiackids.com). I watched with curiosity and felt somewhat protective and guarded as this stranger took one of his hands in both of hers in what seemed like an affectionate gesture. "Tyler, you have changed my life," she said.

Then 13 years old, he said nothing and shot an anxious glance my way, looking for guidance, but I was as bewildered as he was. She began to get tears in her eyes as she continued. "I'm 65 years old. Three months ago, I was sick as could be. I'd

been to dozens of doctors and had a list of symptoms a mile long — everyone thought I was crazy. I even had to quit my job because I was so sick. I truly wanted to die. Then I saw you on TV talking about celiac disease. I insisted on being tested and tested positive. I've been gluten-free ever since and feel absolutely wonderful." With that, she gave him a bear hug, and he shot me a glance that I couldn't read.

I've learned not to embarrass my kids (well, sometimes I do it intentionally, but that's another matter), so I said nothing, and Tyler went about his business. Several minutes later, Tyler approached me with a beaming smile. "Mom, now I know why you do this! It feels really good to help other people!"

He has since decided that he's blessed to have celiac disease, because it has provided him with an opportunity to reach out and help others — an act that even at his young age he realizes is more satisfying for him than for those he's helping. Quite a perspective for a teenage boy, if I may indulge in a brief mommy brag!

People forget to dream about the hardships their kids will face and how they'll handle the difficulties in their lives. Yet how your children handle adversity is one of the most important lessons your children will ever learn. This is a chance for them to find out at an early age how to turn adversity into advantage.

Furthermore, what you may initially see as difficulty may actually be a good thing in your child's life (and yours). See the "Focusing on the good stuff" section for more information.

"I don't want her to feel different"

You envision your kids' lives as being smooth and painless, and part of that means fitting in. But kids are different in many ways, and although I'm not downplaying the importance of food and the part it plays in everything people do, your kids' differences are okay.

Kids are all different — some kids have blond hair, others have red; some prefer baseball to ballet; some are in wheelchairs, and others wear glasses. To pine away for her conformity is to send a signal that something about being different in this (gluten-free) way is *bad.* The last thing you want to do is send that message.

Parents worry that their kids won't fit in or won't be accepted because of their "different" diet, but kids can fit in regardless of what they're eating. Fitting in has much more to do with their attitude than anything else.

"Will he turn out okay?"

No, he'll be better-than-okay, because he's healthy! But I agonized over this same thing when Tyler was first diagnosed.

Oh, sure, friends and family told me, "It'll be okay," the way friends and family do in tough situations. But I felt they were just placating me — after all, what did they know? They hadn't even heard of celiac disease before I explained the diagnosis. And to be honest, I didn't care much at that time about what adults thought of the situation — I wanted desperately to hear it from a kid: "I turned out just fine!"

The truth is, being gluten-free has never been a big deal for my son. We started giving Tyler control of his diet from day one, which I believe is crucial. We've always maintained an optimistic yet realistic approach, with Tyler and his (non-celiac-but-oh-so-supportive) sister Kelsie being our guiding lights in terms of inspiration and positive attitudes. So rest easy, parents. Your kids will, in fact, be just fine. And so will you.

"This is harder for me than it is for her"

If you love a child the way a parent does (even if you're not the actual parent, but are, nonetheless, as emotionally entwined as a parent is), then you can comprehend the this-hurts-me-more-than-it-hurts-you Pain Amplification Phenomenon (PAP). Seeing a bloody knee or a broken heart truly causes pain — palpable pain — for the grown-ups who love that child.

Those of you who are agonizing over the fact that your child has been diagnosed with a condition that requires a strict, lifelong, gluten-free diet may have trouble accepting this idea at first, but believe me: Dealing with the diagnosis is harder for you than it is for your child.

Your dreams for your child's future make you think having to be gluten-free is hard on her — you envision her skipping merrily down the road of life, not tripping over *food,* for goodness' sake. But kids don't have visions for the future like that. To a kid, a vision of her future may take her to the next baseball game or her next allowance; it's far more nearsighted than your vision for her.

In most cases, kids are resilient. They accept what life dishes out, and they make the best of it. I think grown-ups should take note.

A kid's perspective

I'd love for Tyler to write a few words telling you how celiac disease is no big deal in his life, because it's really not. Tyler's actually quite an inspiration with an awesome perspective on this. For my first book, *Kids with Celiac Disease,* he wrote chapter one, "What It's Like to Be a Kid with Celiac Disease." But that was before he turned into a teenager and discovered he isn't supposed to want to do everything his parents ask.

My son would tell you that he thinks more about other stuff in his life — like friends, school, sports, and family — than about gluten. He knows the importance of being 100 percent gluten-free and

doesn't cheat. He's in control of what he eats and makes sure when he's away from home that he has access to gluten-free food (although much to my chagrin, that often consists of a candy bar or chips).

In spreading the gospel of gluten-free for all these years, I've had the opportunity to meet with hundreds, if not thousands, of gluten-free kids. With only a handful of exceptions, nearly every one has been upbeat, optimistic, and downright inspiring. So even if you don't take it from Tyler (channeling through me), take it from all the others: Gluten-free kids ROCK!

If you don't believe that this diagnosis is harder on you than it is on your child, go up to a kid and ask what he thinks about in his life, and take notes. He'll mention things like "baseball," "my best friend Sarah," "riding my horse," "recess," or any other number of answers. Go ahead — interview ten other kids. I'm reasonably certain you won't find any who answer "my diet." It's just really not a priority — nor should it be.

Focusing on the good stuff

Being gluten-free may be a good thing in your child's (and your) life for a lot of reasons. I encourage you to make your own personal list to pull out when you find yourself feeling frustrated or depressed. Here are a few to get you started:

- ✔ **Your child has the key to better health.** Most people who have celiac disease or gluten sensitivity never know what's wrong with them. They don't know that a dietary modification would fully restore their health, so they continue to eat the very foods that make them sick.

- ✔ **Your child will be less likely to develop associated conditions.** Your child has the advantage of being diagnosed early and going gluten-free at an early age. That means his or her chances of developing associated conditions (see Chapter 2) are far lower than for someone diagnosed after years of being sick with gluten sensitivity or celiac disease.

- ✔ **Chances are, she'll learn to be tolerant of others' sensitivities.** In fact, she may be more tolerant in general.

- ✔ **He may have the opportunity to help someone else who has gluten sensitivity or celiac disease.** Remember, if 1,000 kids attend your child's school, about ten of them may have celiac disease — and even more may have a form of gluten sensitivity. This awareness and opportunity to spread this knowledge is an opportunity to help improve other people's lives.

- ✔ **If your child has other dietary issues, like diabetes, controlling them will be easier on the gluten-free diet.** This is partly true because your child is more aware of her diet and more in control of what she's eating. But it's also true because, if done properly, the gluten-free diet can be extremely nutritious. Using diabetes as an example, if you avoid most of the high-glycemic-index foods (like the delicious gluten-free goodies available today!) and stick to more of a Paleolithic approach (I go into detail about this in Chapter 6), controlling blood-sugar levels can be far easier than if your child were on a "regular" diet.

- ✔ **If your child has behavioral issues in addition to gluten sensitivity or celiac disease, chances are, they'll improve.** Sometimes, behavioral issues are symptoms of gluten sensitivity or celiac disease, so ADD/ADHD-type behaviors or the inability to concentrate may subside or even completely go away when your child goes gluten-free.

I'm glad to be gluten-free because . . .

Sometimes before my talks, especially if a lot of kids are attending, I take the kids aside and do a little "Rappin' with Danna" session, in which we talk about their feelings about the gluten-free lifestyle. Usually I ask them to finish this sentence: "I'm glad to be gluten-free because . . ." They come up with the most inspirational stuff! Although most of the young ones talk about the yummy gluten-free brownies and cookies they get to eat, others are blatantly honest with responses like "because I don't have to eat my mom's gross casseroles anymore." For fun, ask your gluten-free kid to finish the sentence. I think you'll be delighted with the response you get (unless you make really gross casseroles!).

Talking to Your Kids about Being Gluten-Free

Whether your child is 18 months or 18 years old, now's the time to talk, and the entire family needs to be included. How you do this depends on your style, your intra-family relationships, and your child's ability to understand the intricacies of the subject matter. Talking to your kids is step one in making sure they develop healthy attitudes and habits.

Including the whole family

Even if your entire family doesn't choose to go gluten-free, having a gluten-free kid in the house affects everyone. All the family members need to know about your child's condition, the diet, and how to handle a variety of situations that may arise.

I'm not suggesting that you organize an extended family reunion and include fifth cousins thrice removed. But you do need to include your immediate family in some type of discussion. Don't think these talks need to take place all at once; discussion is an ongoing process, and you'll be talking about the gluten-free lifestyle for months, if not years, to come.

Kids will be kids, and sibs will be sibs. Just because the brothers and sisters understand the diet doesn't mean they'll always be kind. You may hear the typical taunting — you know, the "I can eat this and you can't" type of stuff. Treat that teasing the same way you'd treat any other act that you don't approve of between siblings. Don't let your feelings of sadness that your child has this condition make you overreact to unkind gestures. Mean is mean, and you should respond to meanness consistently.

Startled siblings

So you're sitting down to have a family discussion about Cassidy's new gluten-free lifestyle, and before your very eyes, her sister, Mild-Mannered-Missy, turns into Bordering-on-Ballistic-Barbie. What's going on? You did your best to frame everything in a positive way. Why is she freaking out?

Don't be surprised if you see this type of reaction from the siblings in the family. Their being scared, confused, and even a tinge panicked is perfectly normal.

Siblings can be wondering all sorts of things: Is my sister sick? Is she going to die? Am I going to catch it? If she has to eat gross stuff, do I have to eat it too? (Correct answer is that *neither* of you has to eat gross stuff!) How come she gets special attention and I don't? What if she gets better stuff than I do? Why did this happen to our family? And, most importantly, will my friends think I'm weird because my sister eats different food?

Being aware that these reactions are typical can help you respond in a sympathetic, understanding way. Address the feelings you suspect the startled sibs are having, even if they're not able to articulate their anxieties, and encourage them to tell you why the situation scares them. Before you know it, everyone can relax and you'll have a more productive discussion.

Keeping the discussion upbeat

Everyone you talk to about the gluten-free lifestyle — and the conditions that require it — finds out how to feel about the gluten-free lifestyle from you. Is being gluten-free a bad thing in your life? A scary thing? Good thing? How you talk about it has a far greater impact than you may know.

If you call a family meeting and gather somberly, you're going to scare your kid right out of her jammies and cast an impression of doom and gloom. This conversation should be upbeat, lighthearted, and interactive — after all, becoming gluten-free is a good thing in everyone's life. If you can't remember why, go back to the preceding sections in this chapter or look at some of the thoughts in Chapter 19.

The most important person to stay upbeat around is your child. For the rest of her life, how she feels about being gluten-free depends on you and your attitudes. She doesn't know how to feel — this is all new to her (granted, it's new to you, too). Give her the advantage of starting off upbeat and optimistic. If she's like most kids, she'll take it from there and will provide amazing strength and inspiration.

Don't make a huge deal out of needing to be gluten-free. As huge as it may seem to you, chances are this isn't going to be a huge deal in your child's life . . . unless you make it one.

Little ears are listening

When you're talking to other grown-ups about your child's diet and condition, keep in mind that your kid may be tuning in to every word you're saying. Sure, he may seem distracted with toys or friends, and he may in fact be too busy to hear what you're saying. But kids have ears, and they know how to use 'em (unless, of course, you're asking them to do the dishes).

Are you apologizing for the complexity of the diet? That can make your child feel like a victim.

Are you complaining about the restrictions? That may make him feel like a burden. Are you feeling sorry for yourself? He'll feel guilty for encumbering you with the challenges this lifestyle may present.

I'm not saying don't vent — if you're frustrated, exhausted, or feeling overly burdened at the moment, that's fine, and having someone to confide in is therapeutic. Just make sure little ears aren't listening.

Explaining the new lifestyle

The level of detail you get into depends on your child's age, maturity, and ability to understand this type of thing. In a nutshell, you want to give her the "why" she's gluten-free (to feel better), the "what" (what gluten-free means), and the "what now" (what she can eat now that she's gluten-free), which is really most important, because that's what matters most to her.

Be patient, and don't try to rush explaining everything. Understanding and accepting may not happen all at once but will more likely be an ongoing process for all of you.

Focusing on the benefits

Chances are, your child has had health or behavioral issues that led to the need for a gluten-free diet, so start the discussion with something positive like, "You're going to feel *so* much better now that you're going to be eating gluten-free foods!"

Kids think in specifics. Drive the point home to them with something they can personally relate to, like, "You know how much your tummy's been hurting lately?" or "You know how hard it is for you to focus in class?" — "You won't have that anymore now that you're gluten-free!" Specifics can help children understand exactly *what's* going to be better on the gluten-free diet.

Then, a few weeks into the lifestyle, remember to point out to your kids how much better they feel, thanks to the yummy gluten-free foods they're eating.

Using big words and good explanations

Don't underestimate what your kids can grasp. When explaining the diet to your child, use the "big" words like gluten (spare them the carboxymethyl-cellulose, though, okay?). Even if your child has developmental or learning disabilities, use the proper terminology so that he can better communicate what he can and can't eat to others.

Of course, he's not going to understand at first (did *you?*). Give him examples he can understand — explain that "gluten is in lots of the foods we used to eat, like bread, cookies, and crackers," and then quickly let him know that *lots* of yummy things don't have gluten in them.

Offering gluten-free alternatives

Always focusing on what your child *can* have is important. Anytime you or your child asks about or points out a food that's off-limits, try to point out something equally as scrumptious that's gluten-free.

Of course, you're not going to say, "You can't have those cookies anymore, Trevor, but look here! You can eat all the broccoli your little heart desires!" That won't win you any parent points, nor will little Trevor be likely to buy into this new lifestyle with much zest. Instead, you can accomplish three things at once here:

- ✔ Reward your child for grasping the diet
- ✔ Offer an alternative
- ✔ Reinforce that he can eat it *because* it's gluten-free

A couple simple sentences do the trick: "You're right, Trevor, you can't eat those cookies. But you *can* have this candy bar, because it's gluten-free!"

Always be prepared to do the Treat Trade. When your child has a treat she wants to eat but can't because it has gluten, be ready to trade it for something equally as appealing — but of the gluten-free variety. Kids are relatively easily distracted, and if you have some delectable goodies waiting in the wings as a Treat Trade, you're sure to turn that frown upside down.

Reinforcing the idea that gluten makes your child feel icky

Help your child make the connection that gluten makes him feel bad. You should use this in a couple of situations — first, whenever you talk about gluten: "You're right, you can't eat that. It has gluten, and gluten makes you feel icky." This way, he learns to associate gluten with feeling bad — and that's a very good thing. To state all this scientifically, the desire to cheat is inversely proportional to the realization that gluten makes you sick, as shown in Figure 17-2. When you can chart something, it must be true, right?

Figure 17-2:
The desire to cheat decreases as kids realized that gluten makes them sick.

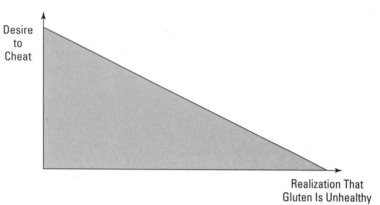

The other time you may want to point out the effects of gluten — and this is where a bit of prevarication comes in — is when your child doesn't feel good — for just about any reason. This works best for younger kids, usually about 6 and under. And it only works if you really don't know exactly what's making your child feel bad — a tummy ache, for instance. You may know full well that her discomfort has nothing to do with gluten, but seize the opportunity to say, "I'm sorry you don't feel well. We must have goofed, and you accidentally got some gluten. We'll have to be more careful next time."

The chances that she'll sneak gluten (or even want it, for that matter) are inversely proportional to the clarity of this association between gluten and not feeling well.

Chances are, your child is trying really hard to stick to the diet. Make sure your child doesn't feel like he's done something wrong by goofing. Point out that we all make mistakes and that gluten can be hidden in all sorts of things. It just means you have to be super careful in the future.

When kids who have celiac disease get tummy aches, you may jump to the conclusion that they feel sick because they got gluten, and you find yourself agonizing over what the culprit may have been. But remember, kids get tummy aches! They can be caused by all kinds of different things, but for the most part, they're a normal part of growing up. It's important to be diligent about the diet and, when you see a gluten reaction, to figure out what caused it. But sometimes tummy aches and other types of gastrointestinal distress are just normal parts of being a kid.

Handling your child's reaction

You can't predict how your child will respond when you first start talking to him about his new gluten-free lifestyle. His reaction will depend on how you present the diet, his age, maturity, level of understanding, ability to express his feelings, and of course, his personality.

You probably realize that if he shows anger, hostility, or other "negative" emotions, you should be soothing, understanding, and supportive — those parental responses are natural.

Don't think, though, that the initial "upset" reaction is going to stick. It's most likely a fleeting response that, as time passes and your child becomes accustomed to the new lifestyle, will evolve into a more positive outlook. Continue to remind him of the benefits he can look forward to now that his body is getting healthy by eating gluten-free foods.

Be prepared for little or no response. Appearing to be indifferent or apathetic is not unusual for kids. Don't read too deeply and assume this reaction is a "cover" for deep, disturbing thoughts — chances are, it's an honest response to a somewhat confusing issue or a reaction to something that truly doesn't seem to matter much at the time.

Helping your kids talk to others about the diet

Your kids need to learn to talk to other people — both adults and other kids — about their gluten-free lifestyle. They'll be doing it for the rest of their lives, and there's no time to start like the present. Of course, exactly what they say and how they communicate it will depend on their age, personality, style, who they're talking to, and how comfortable they are talking about this type of thing.

Explaining what they can and can't have

Teach your child a phrase to use, even if he's too young to know what it means. Use something comprehensive that he can repeat to adults.

For instance, teach him to say, "I can't eat gluten. That means I don't eat wheat, rye, barley, malt, and oats." I know that definition isn't technically correct (malt *is* from barley, and oats are gluten-free but sometimes contaminated), but it tells adults what they need to know.

Maybe that one's too cumbersome; but if your child can handle it, go with it. If not, find one that's more age-appropriate or one that suits your child's personality. The idea behind the memorized "sound bite" is that it covers a lot of bases with a relatively easy couple of sentences.

Of course, the more children can add, the better. If your child can explain to people exactly what she can and can't eat, that's terrific — and if she can add the fact that gluten makes her feel bad, that's better yet. Before long, your child will figure out what works best for her.

Teach your kid to be open and conversant about being gluten-free. I'm not suggesting you and your child walk into a room, grab a microphone, clear your throats, and begin proselytizing about the gluten-free lifestyle (even though that's what I do!). Nor do you want your child to feel he's entitled to have people accommodate his diet. But informing people (especially those who may be involved in feeding him) is important, and you can do this in a friendly, informative manner. You may find that your child becomes an effective awareness-spreading advocate before you know it.

Some kids feel more comfortable simplifying their explanation to something people can understand more easily, like, "I'm allergic to gluten," or even "I'm allergic to wheat." Even though that explanation's not technically correct, sometimes it's easier. Just make sure your kids know the *real* facts so they don't get confused later on.

Teaching kids to say "no thanks"

No matter how well your child communicates the fact that he can't eat gluten, some people will, usually with the best of intentions, offer him something with gluten.

This can be really confusing to your child, especially if the sweet-slipping-someone happens to be a loved one who folds a cookie into your child's hand and says with a conspiratorial just-between-you-and-me wink, "Don't tell Mommy and Daddy." Yikes! What's a gluten-free kid to do?

Explain to your child how and why this type of a situation may come up, and most importantly, how to handle it. Sometimes saying "no thanks" or "I appreciate it, but I can't eat that" is easy for a child. Other times, it's easier and more conciliatory just to accept the treat and not eat it.

Even if your friends and family won't be offering him gluten, someone out there will. You can spare your child disappointment and confusion if you help her deal with this type of situation before it comes up (and remember to bring gluten-free treats with you to the mall at the holidays so you can do the Treat Trade in case you're accosted by well-intentioned elves!).

Deciding Whether the Whole Family Should Be Gluten-Free

Many people assume that because one child is gluten-free, the entire family should adopt the lifestyle. After all, wouldn't it be cruel to be feasting on donuts while your gluten-free child is choking down rice cakes? Yeah, it would.

But having the entire family go gluten-free isn't always the right answer, either. You really have to weigh both sides of the issue and consider the practical and psychological issues.

The pros

Here are some advantages if everyone goes gluten-free:

- ✔ **You make only one version of each meal.** Rather than making a gluten-free version and a "regular" version of some dishes at mealtime, you can make just one gluten-free version and be done with it.

- ✔ **You shop only for gluten-free foods.** You can skip the bread and cracker aisles altogether.

- ✔ **There's no risk of contamination in the kitchen.** You also don't have to learn the gob drop (check out Chapter 7).

- ✔ **Your child doesn't feel different.** It's okay to be different, but it's also nice to feel the same, especially when it comes to being family.

- ✔ **The pantry is filled with "safe" foods.** You don't have to worry that you or your child accidentally grabs a gluten-laden snack, because you don't have any.

- ✔ **Your child isn't tempted to cheat.** At least not at home.

The cons

I'm trying to offer both sides here, but if you sense that the cons list is a little weightier than the pros list, you're right. Ultimately, in my opinion, the cons outweigh the pros of having the entire family go gluten-free:

- ✔ **A gluten-free world is not reality.** Your child needs to understand that the rest of the world eats gluten. They're not doing it to make him feel bad; they're not doing it to ostracize him; there are no malicious or evil intentions. What better environment to learn that important lesson than in a loving, supportive home?

✔ **Your child doesn't find out how to make food choices.** Knowing how to choose which foods he can eat and which he can't is important for your child. If the pantry's free of "no-nos," he doesn't need to decide. He may become complacent about mindlessly grabbing food without giving a thought to whether it's gluten-free.

✔ **It can create resentment among other family members.** Siblings — even parents — can be a little bitter about having to give up bread and bagels if they don't have a health condition that requires it. They can direct that resentment toward your gluten-free child, and that sets up an unhealthy family dynamic.

✔ **Your child isn't tempted to cheat.** Although this may sound like more of a pro than a con (it's really both), I believe that teaching your child to resist the temptation (especially because gluten is practically every-where) is better than never tempting him or her.

✔ **Eating a lot of specialty foods can be more expensive.** I'm not advocat-ing eating *lots* of specialty foods, but if you do, I think you'll agree that you'd rather save the $5 loaf of bread for your gluten-free child.

Middle ground

Sometimes a compromise is the best solution. See whether these ideas work for your family:

✔ **Make most meals gluten-free.** If you can make the majority of your meals gluten-free and still please everyone without using up your worth-their-weight-in-gold gluten-free specialty items, do so. This can make cooking and preparation easier, and everyone will be able to enjoy the same meals.

✔ **Buy gluten-free condiments and staples.** Using gluten-free salad dress-ings, soy sauce, and other staple or condiment-type items makes life a lot easier on you — and you don't have to make separate stir-fries just because one of them has the gluten kind of soy sauce on it.

✔ **Enjoy the delicious gluten-free baked goods.** Most of the mixes these days for cookies, cakes, brownies, and other baked goods are as good as the real deal. They're a little more expensive, maybe, but cost aside, you really have no reason to make separate batches of these things. Make one batch of the gluten-free kind and let the entire family enjoy.

How do gluten-free kids feel when others eat gluten around them?

I've asked dozens of kids this question: "Does it make you feel bad when other people eat gluten around you?" Admittedly, I've heard the occasional pauses or hesitations — maybe even a thoughtful consideration and a "sometimes" here and there. But nearly all the kids I've asked — including my own — have said *no*. It doesn't bother them. They like their food, and if you do the diet right, they should! The food tastes good!

Now I have to tell you that it used to break my heart when my son was about 4 years old and he would ask to *smell* the "real" pizza. I'd ask him why he wanted to do that — assuming, of course, that he was pining away for some, wishing he could eat it, and getting as close to consumption as he could without actually chewing. But he matter-of-factly answered, "I'm just curious."

Giving Your Child Control of the Diet

If your child doesn't take control of his diet, the diet will control him. No matter how young he is, he needs to learn from day one to make decisions about what he can and can't eat — and how important it is not to cheat, no matter how tempted he is.

From a psychological standpoint, it's important that the gluten-free diet doesn't take front-and-center-stage in your child's life — and that means she should be thinking of other things most of the time. But when it comes time to eat, she needs to realize how important it is that she makes good choices. Food is something she needs to pay close attention to.

A wise proverb says, "Give a man a fish, and you feed him for a day. Teach him to fish, and you feed him for a lifetime." You need to teach your kids to choose foods they can eat for a lifetime. Giving your child control of the diet also creates bonuses for everyone:

- ✔ **Your child has confidence.** He knows that even if you're not there, he's able to eat safely because he can make healthy food choices.

- ✔ **You can relax.** You know that even if you're not there, your child is prepared to make good food choices. And if you are there, you don't have to be doing all the decision-making.

- ✔ **Your child is learning the importance of healthful eating.** How many kids read food labels or give even a first thought (much less a second) to what they're putting in their mouths? Your child is learning to be conscious of nutrition at an early age, which is a valuable lifelong lesson.

Working together to make good choices

When I say to give your child control, I'm not suggesting you let her make all the decisions by herself — like everything else in life, children need a little guidance, especially at first. You can do lots of things together to help kids learn how to make good food choices.

- **Read labels together.** Even if your child is too young to read, pretend. Hold the ingredients label where you can both see it, and go through the ingredients out loud, one by one (just like when you're tired and reading them bedtime stories, you can skip the superfluous stuff). Point to the words, and when you come to pertinent ones, like *wheat,* remind them, "Nope. This one has gluten in it." And then, because you're well-conditioned to quickly point to the alternative, follow up with, "Let's try *this* one," and grab something you know is gluten-free.

- **Make a game out of it.** When you're reading labels or talking about foods, see who can decide which one is gluten-free (or not) first. (Note to those of you competitive types: Let 'em win a few.)

- **Have your child call manufacturers.** (This works best if your child is old enough to talk.) After she's seen you do it a few times, let your child make the calls. Sometimes being on another extension so you can take over is a good idea.

- **Have your child plan the menu.** Not only does this give him a chance to practice figuring out what's gluten-free and what isn't, but you know he'll actually eat everything he's served. So what if his menu consists of french fries, rice, candy bars, and gluten-free macaroni and cheese? Go with it. Remember, for that meal at least, he's in control.

- **Have your child pack his lunch.** If it's not perfectly nutritionally balanced, make some suggestions and see whether he'll add the nutritious stuff you want. If not, go with it. It won't kill him to have one bad meal — but it will let him know he can choose foods that are gluten-free (and yummy!).

- **Let your child cook.** Kids *love* to cook, even though it usually ends up being far more work than if they don't help. Figuring out how to cook at an early age is important for all kids, especially for those who will be requiring some specially prepared foods for the rest of their lives.

Trusting kids when you're not there

Letting g-g-g-g-go is one of the hardest things parents ever do; yet it's your job as a parent. On a daily basis, you're preparing your children for life so you can eventually set them free. If you do your job well, you can rest easy knowing they have all the tools they need to make decisions that'll lead to safe, happy, healthy lives.

The idea behind giving your kids control of their diet is that they need to know how to feed themselves, because you won't always be there. You don't have much of a problem giving them control of certain things — going potty by themselves, washing their hands, and using the VCR. But when it comes to choosing foods — and those foods could make them really sick — trusting that they'll make safe choices is hard!

You'll know when the time is right and when you can actually relax knowing they're making safe food choices. It'll most likely be way before you expect it and maybe way before *you're* ready.

Your children are going to make mistakes. Mistakes won't kill or permanently harm them, and with any luck, it'll cause some discomfort so they realize the importance of being more attentive.

Hitting the Road with the Gluten-Free Gang

Living life in a bubble is for helium molecules. Your child's life shouldn't be restricted just because he's on a restricted diet!

Really, getting out and about with gluten-free kids isn't much different from the way adults do it: You still follow the "Golden Rules of Going Out," tips for travel are the same, and ordering at restaurants isn't much different, except you may be ordering from a kids' menu instead of an adult one. I cover all these things in detail in Chapter 16, so for the most part, if you master the general ideas of that chapter, you'll do great getting out and about with the kids.

I do have a few suggestions that are specific to getting out with gluten-free kids:

- **Let your child order for himself.** At first this may be cumbersome, because he's likely to order chicken nuggets or spaghetti, assuming it's the gluten-free kind he eats at home. Don't worry about taking a long time or bothering the server. Figuring out how to order at a restaurant is really important for your child, and actually doing it is an important part of the learning process.

- **Don't be shy.** Some kids are mortified when adults "make a scene" (I call it "asking a question") at a restaurant. All I have to do is say, "Could I ask you about this menu item . . ." and the eyes start rolling, the "Oh boy, here she goes" comments start spewing forth, and I have, my children accuse me, scarred them for life. Ignore your kids and ask anyway. If they won't, you need to.

- **Consider bringing dessert for your child.** You can't assume the desserts at a restaurant are gluten-free, so just in case they don't have any, either bring your own or go somewhere else for dessert.

Leaving Your Gluten-Free Kids in the Care of Others

Leaving your kids with other people is scary enough, even when your kids don't have dietary limitations that can make them sick. But trusting someone else to safely feed your gluten-free child? Yikes! Letting go of a little parental control can be frightening, but spending time apart is an important part of growing up for both kids and parents.

Trusting your kids with friends, family, and sitters

The most important thing you can do to ensure your kids will be in good hands from a gluten-free standpoint is to educate the people caring for your child.

You may want to check out Chapter 16 to find out how to talk with others and how to assess whether they really "get it." If you suspect they don't fully understand the diet, work harder to make sure they do or find a new caretaker.

When you leave your kid in someone else's care, try to bring or leave prepared food as often as you can, and clearly mark on containers that the food is gluten-free. That prevents any mix-up between your child's food and someone else's.

Sending your children to school

Because they're away at school for several hours at a time, day after day, sending your gluten-free kids to school is one of the biggest challenges you face. Here are some tips:

- ✔ **Educate your teachers, nurse, nutritionist, and principal.** In fact, educate as much of the staff as possible. Not only will the staff be better prepared to deal with your child and his diet, but chances are, they have other kids at the school who need to be gluten-free and don't know it yet. You may have an enormous positive impact on those kids as well!

- ✔ **Give the teacher a stash of treats for your child.** Nothing's worse than finding out at the end of the day that it was Ashley's birthday and your daughter ate nothing while the other kids smeared cupcakes all over their faces. Bring bags of Halloween-sized candy packages that the teacher can store in a special place for your child in case of a surprise party or an event that involves treats.

✔ **Be aware of craft time.** Play-Doh has gluten in it, and although kids aren't *supposed* to be eating it, show me one kid who can resist. I know I couldn't! Other crafts involve gluten-containing cereals, and those activities often become a matter of "one for the necklace, one for me . . . one for the necklace, one for me." Make sure your teacher and your child are paying attention at craft time.

✔ **Work with the nutrition department.** Teachers or principals can help you find contact information. Buying lunch even once a week may be a big deal to your child. Most nutrition departments are willing to work with you to find ways your child can eat at least one meal each week. There's something cool about standing in that line.

✔ **Beware of the Eating Exchange.** Swapping food in school lunches is very serious business. Kids get right down to it, swapping egg salad for PB&J or bananas for cookies (*not* a fair trade). Talk to your child about how important not trading food is — even if someone else's food looks okay, it may not be (not to mention the fact that your kid's just going to give away those $4 cookies you bought). Ask the lunchtime supervisors to be on the lookout and make sure your child doesn't participate in the Eating Exchange.

Party time!

Parties are supposed to be all about fun! But to parents, parties sometimes seem like they're all about food. Apparently there's a new law that requires all children's parties to be held at pizza places with dancing animals on a stage. For a mere $15 per child, parents can host a party that lasts all of about an hour, stuffs the kids with pizza and cake, and scares the little ones who are smart enough to realize that bears shouldn't be playing guitars. So what about that pizza and cake? Do you let party time turn to pouty time? Nope. Try some of these ideas:

✔ **Make sure your child eats before he goes.** If he's full, he won't be thinking about food, and it won't be as big of a deal.

✔ **If you know the only food served will have gluten, bring your own.** If possible, bring something close to what they're serving — gluten-free pizza, for instance (be careful — the ovens at pizza places blow the flour all around, so cover it carefully if you're going to have them warm it).

✔ **If the party is at a restaurant that may have gluten-free food available, ask the host ahead of time whether you can order separately.** This isn't the least bit rude, and your host will probably be happy to help you with the details.

✔ **If it's your child's party, serve gluten-free foods.** This may sound like a no-brainer, but it's not. *Don't*, however, try to serve gluten-free pizza or something else that may cause that one kid (you know which one I'm talking about) to spit it five feet and ask, "What *is* this?" Serve hot dogs or hamburgers, and maybe do sundaes that kids can build themselves for dessert.

For a manual that thoroughly covers everything — snack and lunch ideas, talking with school staff, managing craft time, and dealing with bullies — I suggest you read *Kids with Celiac Disease: A Family Guide to Raising Happy, Healthy, Gluten-Free Children,* by yours truly. You can also find information on your legal rights regarding school lunches at public schools or at other schools that receive public funding.

Guiding Your Gluten-Free Teens

You can't push a teen any more than you can push a rope. By the time your kids are teenagers, the best you can do is hope that you've laid a good foundation and are still able to guide them in the direction you think they should go.

If your teen is newly diagnosed, the teen years can be a scary time for them. They're already going through many changes, and adopting a gluten-free lifestyle is one change that they may think will cast them way beyond being different and into the realm of being downright freaky.

If your teen has been diagnosed, even if that diagnosis happened years ago, you may see your child evolve from one who was very accepting and easygoing about the diet into one who fights it a little and may even cheat from time to time.

All these responses are normal, if *any* definition of the word "normal" applies to teenagers. You should handle these reactions with patience, understanding, and communication on both sides.

Noticing changing symptoms

Now you see 'em, now you don't; sometimes kids' symptoms seem to do a disappearing act during their teenage years — it's usually referred to as a *honeymoon period.* For some, the symptoms do go away — at least temporarily. At this point, they may be tempted to devour a pizza. They think that because they don't feel symptoms, they'll be okay. Not true! In fact, the whole thing is just an illusion (like some of the other things that take place during the teenage years!). Although your kids may not *feel* the effects, the gluten still does damage.

For others, the symptoms don't really go away but evolve into those traits more characteristic in adults — headaches, fatigue, and depression, for example. These teens, too, sometimes think their symptoms have disappeared, because what they used to associate with eating gluten — diarrhea, for instance — is no longer their typical reaction. They may not realize the headaches they get, or other symptoms, are also signs of their gluten intolerance.

Understanding why teens may cheat on the diet

I cover the topic of cheating and being tempted to cheat on the gluten-free diet in Chapter 18. But teens are a different animal, and they sometimes cheat or want to cheat for different reasons. Really, by the time kids become teens, parents really can't stop them from putting something in their mouths. But knowing why they want to cheat so you can be sympathetic and have an open discussion with them may help.

No longer is their desire simply a matter of "I want it, so I think I'll eat it." With teens, they may want to eat gluten because of

- ✔ **Peer pressure:** At no time in their lives is peer pressure greater than when kids are teenagers. Even if their friends aren't pushing them to eat gluten (they don't usually do that), your teen may just *want* to be like everyone else and be tempted to cheat on the diet.

  Kids love to proclaim how they want to be unique, but they really don't want to be different, and this diet may make them feel different. Don't be surprised if your teen orders a burger with a bun just to be like his buds.

- ✔ **Rebellion:** Your teen may be tempted to eat gluten as a way of being rebellious. Even if she doesn't tell you about the incident, she may subconsciously be exerting her control. Sort of an "I'll show you who's in control" type of behavior.

- ✔ **Curiosity:** A child who's curious about what gluten tastes like may actually have more restraint than a curious teen. Even if your teen's been diligent about following the diet for years, he's most likely to succumb in the teenage years.

- ✔ **Weight control:** Many teens figure out that if they eat gluten, they aren't absorbing all the available calories. Sadly, some intentionally cheat on the diet in an effort to lose weight.

Watch for signs of eating disorders in your kids. Sometimes they become obsessed with their restrictions and take them too far — or they use gluten as a means of losing weight. Address this issue immediately, as eating disorders are extremely serious issues.

So what do you do about your cheatin' teen? The best you can do is to have a two-way conversation. Try to find out why she cheated and what the consequences were, if she felt any. Educate her about what's happening to her body and remind her that even if she doesn't *feel* the effects of gluten, she's still doing tremendous harm to her body.

Helping teens after they move out

One of the hardest things for teens to handle, especially if they're new to the gluten-free lifestyle, is moving out. Being on their own actually isn't quite as tough as if they move into college dorms, where a meal plan and a lack of transportation can limit them to the food in the dining halls. In either case, make sure your child fully understands the diet and can choose foods that are healthy and gluten-free.

If your child lives on campus and has to eat in dining halls, have him contact the dining services office or the food service manager to discuss his dietary needs. Many of the available foods will already be gluten-free — and many won't. He may need to bring his own soy sauce, for instance, or otherwise modify what he's eating.

Having access to a fridge and even a full kitchen is helpful. Work with housing or residential services to make sure he has access at least to a microwave and refrigerator so he can store foods he buys at the store. Student lounges at dorms often have a microwave and/or fridge that students have access to if they can't have one in their room. Coming up with snacks and menus that he can make in the microwave (even gluten-free pasta!) is relatively easy.

Check the dorm policies before buying a mini-refrigerator or microwave. Some dorms that allow these appliances have size and power restrictions.

Care packages are sometimes the next-best thing to being there. Think about sending some gluten-free goodies in time for midterms or finals, or better yet, just to remind them you love 'em.

Chapter 18

Beating the Blues: Overcoming Emotional Obstacles

· ·

In This Chapter

▶ Identifying feelings that don't feel so good

▶ Confronting denial

▶ Dealing with mistakes

▶ Looking at the big picture

▶ Staying on track

· ·

*M*aybe I'm just not looking hard enough, but I haven't seen many best-sellers at the bookstore with titles like *How to Cope with Extreme Good Fortune.*

No, you really need help only when you're facing challenges. And some people feel that the gluten-free lifestyle is one big buncha challenges. Some of that has to do with why they're going gluten-free in the first place.

People who embark on a gluten-free lifestyle do so for one of a few reasons:

✔ **It sounds like fun!** Scrutinizing labels, deciphering code words, translating legal disclaimers provided by manufacturers' customer service reps, dodging carefully hidden sources of gluten . . . and best of all, no beer or pizza! (This group includes authors of the bestseller *How to Bring Yourself Down When You're Just Too Happy.*)

✔ **They think they should.** They haven't been diagnosed with any medical conditions, or if they have been tested, their tests came back negative. But they suspect they'd feel better on a gluten-free diet, or they believe the lifestyle is healthier. Or maybe they just want to support a loved one who's going gluten-free.

✔ **They have to.** They've been diagnosed with a medical condition that requires it.

Guess which groups have the easiest time from a psychological perspective. Bingo! When you choose to do something, you're starting off with a huge emotional advantage. Not only are you mentally prepared for the challenge, but you're welcoming the changes to come.

On the other hand, when someone tells you that you have to do something (those of you in group three), you're likely to have a harder time with it. (Think back to your childhood when you were just getting ready to voluntarily clean your room and just then your mom yelled, "Don't forget to clean your room!" Talk about a motivation-vacuum.) Toss in the unique social and practical challenges that arise when you're living a gluten-free lifestyle, and some people find themselves dealing with all sorts of complex emotional issues.

Okay, okay, so some people have accused me of being overly optimistic when it comes to espousing the virtues of a gluten-free lifestyle. And I do, from my very core, believe it's the greatest dietary lifestyle on the planet. But I'm not unrealistic — don't forget, I've been there, done that. I've been living this lifestyle for a very long time, and believe me, I've encountered my share of emotional challenges, as most people do when they adopt a strict gluten-free lifestyle. The idea is to find out how to identify those challenges and obstacles and overcome them.

The key thing to remember is this: Deal with it; don't dwell on it. You can be mad, sad, uncomfortable, ticked off, and out-of-your-head ready to scream with frustration. That's okay. All those reactions and emotions, and the others I talk about in this chapter, are perfectly normal when someone has told you to change your entire life. But getting mired in the negativity and difficulty of it all is easy, in which case these feelings may begin to consume you. Allow yourself to experience the tough emotions, and then move on.

In this chapter I discuss a bunch of different ways you can break out of the negativity and see things in a more positive light. Yes, for some people this is a difficult transition in life . . . but ultimately, you'll be better for it.

Recognizing Common Emotional Struggles

The reasons living gluten-free can be difficult from an emotional standpoint are vast:

- ✔ **Social activities revolve around food.** Now, because you don't eat gluten, you may feel isolated, or you may be afraid to participate in these social functions because you think you won't be able to eat anything. (If you're struggling with eating away from home, check out Chapter 16.)

- **People you love don't get it.** In Chapter 16, I talk about how to discuss the lifestyle with others. But sometimes, no matter how much you say or don't say, some people, many of whom are your closest buddies, just don't get it.

- **People may think you're crazy.** When you try to explain this to some people, or when they watch you stumble through one of your first experiences ordering at a restaurant, they may think you're outlandishly high-maintenance, that you're picky, that you have an eating disorder, or that you're crazy.

- **They call it "comfort food" for a reason.** Weight-management lectures aside, for better or for worse, many people find eating to be a stress-reliever. When your food options are limited, eating can be disconcerting and can create anxiety.

- **Some people don't do well with change of any type.** For those people, something that involves changing their entire lifestyle can be really disruptive.

- **You're losing control in your life.** You're hereby "sentenced" to a life of dietary restrictions. Wow. How's that for taking control away? You've been eating since you were a baby and choosing your own foods not long after that, and now someone's going to tell you what you can and can't eat? It's tough sometimes.

- **It seems so permanent.** Oh, wait. That's because it is. And that doesn't help someone feeling "put upon" by their restrictions.

- **You feel like you're on an island.** If you do, you'd better hope it's a big island, because millions of people are going gluten-free. But I digress. The gluten-free lifestyle seems isolating to some people; they even feel ostracized. If you're feeling like that, read on, because this part of the book should help you realize that you have control over those feelings and that you don't have to be isolated or feel like you're alone in this.

In this section, I talk about some of the common emotions people experience when they hear they have to go gluten-free. You may notice that these issues people face look a lot like reactions you may see in people who've experienced a trauma. That's not so surprising, because for some people, being told they need to change their entire way of eating *can* be traumatic and stressful.

Sheer shock and panic

If you've ever seen a teenage girl who can't find her cell phone, you've seen panic. For some people, changing to a gluten-free lifestyle is even worse than that.

On one hand, it all seems so sudden. You're in the doctor's office talking about your bowel movements or lack thereof, and the next thing you know, you're branded with a condition you've probably never heard of that will change the way you eat for the rest of your life. Yet in some ways, it's not sudden at all. Chances are, you've been having health issues for years. And now it has a name. And a treatment. Both of which can stun you.

Huh? That's about all you can think or say. You're numb — you're in shock. The good news (let's see, there's got to be some good news here — okay, here it is) is that by definition, you get this shocked feeling only once. (Have you ever tried to figuratively shock someone twice with the same news? Few people are that gullible.)

Have you ever had fingers that were so cold they were nearly frozen? They're kind of numb at that point, aren't they? But when they begin to thaw, they throb and feel like you've just run them through a wood chipper. That's kind of how you feel when sheer shock turns to pure panic. That's when the reality of the words "diet for life" begins to sink in, and you start to panic. What will you eat? How will you do it? Where will you find special foods? Can you do it?

Rest assured that these feelings are normal, and they do pass. You will figure out what you can eat, and your panic will subside as you become more comfortable with the diet, which begins on day one. The learning curve is steeper for some than others, but you *will* learn, and the panic will wear off.

Anger and frustration

The shock and panic have subsided, and you're beginning to feel more comfortable with what you can and can't eat. But something's eating at you. You realize you're miffed. Peeved. Fightin' mad and agonizingly frustrated!

It doesn't matter who or what you're mad at — some people in this situation are mad at their parents for giving them a "defective" gene; others are mad at themselves for passing the gene on to their kids; some are mad at their partner for not being more understanding; most are mad at the major cereal manufacturers who feel it's a Universal Cereal Manufacturer's Law that they must put malt flavoring in every cereal they make; and a few take it out on God for "thinking up" this crazy condition.

Bottom line is, you're fumin' mad, and it's stressing you out. Anger is a healthy emotion, and learning to deal with it is one of the most valuable lessons you can learn in life. Taking your anger out on those closest to you is tempting, especially if they're adding to the frustration by being less-than-understanding about your new lifestyle. If you need help dealing with the anger, reach out. But don't lash out, especially at the people closest to you, because they're not to blame, and they can be immensely supportive when you need it most.

Grief and despair

Are you grieving? Do you feel like you've lost your best friend? In a way, you may have. Food, your control over what you eat, and even the simple act of putting food into your mouth can sooth you and bring you comfort. When you're forced to give up your favorite foods (if they weren't your favorites before, they will be after you give them up!), the change can make you feel sad and melancholy. Furthermore, some people feel they're the only ones who have this problem, which can intensify feelings of isolation or loneliness.

If your child is going gluten-free, those feelings of grief can magnify. You dream that your children's lives will be carefree and ideal; having to deal with dietary restrictions that prevent them from eating what seem to be staples in a child's diet isn't usually part of your plan.

Some people reach a point of desperation or despair. They find the diet to be cumbersome and difficult, and they keep making mistakes. Then they figure if they can't do this right, they may as well not do it at all, and they give up.

Grief and despair are normal emotions, but don't give in to them. You will get over your feelings of sadness and loneliness, and this lifestyle doesn't have to be in the least bit isolating or depriving. As for doing it right, give it your very best effort — truly 100 percent — and you will get it. Dealing with a mistake from time to time is better than giving up and not trying at all.

Loss and deprivation

You may feel a couple kinds of loss when someone tells you that you have to go gluten-free. You obviously lose your favorite foods — and what about the social situations that seem to go hand-in-hand with them? You miss pizza and beer during Monday Night Football or Grandma's famous oatmeal-raisin cookies that everyone dives for before they remember to hug Grandma hello. And what about the great appetizers, all of which are heavily skewed toward the gluten-containing variety, during the dice game Bunco? (Okay, I'll stop with the reminders now.)

Many of your favorite foods, at least in the form you know them, are a thing of the past. At first the social situations may not seem the same without them — and they aren't just the same. They're the same but different, and that's okay. Remember when you attend these events that they're not really about the food — they're about the socialization. Also remember to bring yourself foods that you love — and follow the golden rules of going out gluten-free that I cover in Chapter 16.

Another kind of loss people feel is a loss of convenience. These days, food is prewashed, precut, prepeeled, precooked, prepackaged, pre-resealed, and practically pre-eaten and premetabolized into tummy fat before you ever get it home from the store. Convenience foods come as a complete snack or meal, in various combinations to please any palate. Yes, these foods are convenient — and sometimes, when you pluck them from the aisles of the produce section, they're even good for you and gluten-free. But many of them, for you, are a thing of the past.

So for many people, it's true: There is a loss of convenience. Your days of calling for pizza delivery are behind you, at least until the big pizza companies begin offering gluten-free pizza (a girl can dream). No longer do you zip through a store mindlessly plucking products off the shelves because they look good or they're on sale.

Okay, so giving up gluten isn't as convenient — and you miss your old faves. I'll give you that — you can feel a sense of loss. But look what you've gained. Your health! The gluten-free diet is your key to better health, and that's priceless.

Sadness and depression

Occasionally, people get so overwhelmed with the whole concept of their medical condition and the gluten-free diet that they feel an impending doom, and they experience depression to one degree or another.

Realize that depression can be a symptom you experience if you eat gluten despite your intolerance. Could the depression be due to accidental (or intentional) gluten ingestion? Or is it a lingering emotional discomfort from the pre-diagnosis days? Some people, before they're diagnosed (and some even afterwards), are accused of "making up" their problems, or they're told the symptoms are all in their head. The accusations in and of themselves can be so hurtful and frustrating that they cause the person to go into a state of depression.

People with celiac disease have a higher incidence of depression, mania, seizures, and other neurological problems. I talk more about how gluten affects behavior in Chapter 2.

And you also feel, of course, the restrictions, grief, sense of loss, anger, and other emotions I discuss in this chapter. All of those can lead to depression.

Unfortunately, depression caused by illness can result in a vicious cycle. The physical symptoms lead to suffering and depression, and then the depression makes the physical symptoms worse. Furthermore, depression can weaken the immune system and can affect your heart. Another reason to turn that frown upside down: People with depression are four times more likely to have a heart attack than those without.

If you're feeling depressed, make sure your diet is 100 percent gluten-free so you know that what you're feeling isn't a symptom of gluten ingestion. Also consider therapy of some type, whether it's confiding in friends or seeking professional help.

If you feel your case of the blues isn't serious and you want to try to work it out on your own, see whether these activities help:

- ✔ **Exercising:** When you exercise, your brain produces endorphins, and those chemicals create a natural high. Exercise also helps you get rid of stress hormones that build up in the body and wreak all sorts of physical and emotional havoc.

- ✔ **Eating well:** And that means, besides eating a healthy diet, staying strict about your gluten-free diet. Eating gluten exacerbates the physical and mental symptoms you may experience, and if you're gluten intolerant, gluten robs you of the important nutrients that are supposed to energize you and make you feel good. Stay away from the high-glycemic-index foods I talk about in Chapter 6, because those mess with your blood-sugar levels and affect your moods.

- ✔ **Avoiding alcohol:** Booze is bad news for people suffering from depression. Alcohol is a depressant, so by definition, it brings you down — it also interrupts your sleep patterns, which are important for feeling your best.

- ✔ **Relaxing (whether you want to or not):** It's hard sometimes, I know! But relaxation (even if you force it) is important to maintaining your mental health. Sometimes you may forget to take care of yourself, but doing so is crucial — otherwise you won't be able to help anyone.

- ✔ **Doing something nice for others:** You can find this next postulate under Danna's Second Law of Happiness: The amount of happiness you feel is directly proportional to the happiness you bring to others. Seriously, have you ever been down and done something nice for someone? Not feeling better when you make someone's day is practically impossible.

Dealing with Denial

It walks like a duck. It quacks like a duck. It even lays duck eggs. But you'd like to believe it's a golden retriever. As far as your personal health is concerned, maybe the flags are very, very red, pointing their little pointy flag-fingers at the glaring neon sign screaming, "Gluten-free's the way to be!" But you read, "Gluten-free? *I* sure don't need to be!" Denial comes in all sizes and shapes — some types affect you, other types affect those around you.

When you're the one in denial

When you hear you have to give up gluten for health reasons, deciding to run, not walk, to the nearest sand pit to start digging a hole for your head is quite common. It's called denial, and nearly everyone goes through it to one extent or another. Here are a few phases of denial, starting with the most immediate.

Right off the bat

Your doctor: You have (insert condition), and you need to eliminate all gluten from your diet beginning immediately.

You: Gluten? You mean like honey or sugar or something?

Your doctor: No, I mean like pizza, bread, and beer.

You: Surely you can't be serious.

Your doctor: I am serious, and don't call me Shirley.

Okay, so this is no time to joke, even if it is with classic lines from the movie *Airplane!* But the initial reaction is a common one: I can't have that condition; I've never even heard of it; I'm too fat to have that; I'm too old to have it; I'm too (insert adjective that will support your denial) to have that.

You can deny till the cows come home (where *were* they, anyway?), but that doesn't help your health any. What does help is getting on track as fast as you can, because you have improved health to look forward to.

Denial down the road

Another type of denial settles in after you've been gluten-free for a while and you're feeling great. In fact, you feel so good that you start to think maybe nothing was really wrong with you, and you can't really remember ever feeling all that bad.

Of course, this is about the time the reality of doing this for the rest of your life starts to set in, and you're tempted to cheat — but it's not cheating if you don't really need to be gluten-free now, is it? So begins the battle in your brain, where good and evil don't see eye to eye.

The good half of your brain is telling you, "Mmmmm, this is the yummiest gluten-free cracker I've ever had!" But the demon-in-denial side is saying, "No way am I sittin' through another football game eating rice cakes and drinkin' white wine while the other guys are plowin' through pizza and belchin' their beer. Besides, I don't have an intolerance . . . come on, just one piece of pizza . . ."

Step away from the pizza box. This is a period of ambivalence, in which you're hoping beyond hope that you don't really have to give up gluten and are "proving" it to yourself by ignoring red flags (and your conscience).

Acceptance

The biggest problem with denial is that it justifies eating gluten. When you have this epiphany "realizing" that you don't need to be gluten-free, it's tempting to run, not walk, to the nearest donut shop.

Resist the temptation. If you've been gluten-free for a while, then yes, you feel great, but that's because of the diet, not in spite of it. The danger in testing your little theory is that you may not have any reaction when you do, and then you're likely to jump to the obvious (by which I mean "desired") conclusion that you never needed to eliminate gluten in the first place.

If you're still not sure that you really should be gluten-free, here are some steps you can take that may clarify things for you a little bit:

- **Get properly tested.** Denial is one of the most compelling arguments in favor of proper testing. Check out Chapter 2 for more information about testing.

- **Realize that "negative" tests don't always mean you're free to become a glutton for gluten.** Allergy tests don't pick up celiac disease; celiac tests don't always pick up sensitivities. The tests have changed over the years, and maybe your tests were done long ago. You can also get false negatives — and problems with gluten can develop at any point, so just because you were negative once doesn't mean you'll be negative again. And finally, some people are negative on all the tests, yet their health improves dramatically on a gluten-free diet. Go figure.

- **Get another opinion.** If you're particularly stubborn, you may even want to get a third. Kind of like if Dad says no, ask Mom — but if they both say no, you may want to admit defeat.

- **Talk to others who've been there, done that.** Most people have gone through denial in one form or another. Talk to people who've been diagnosed with a condition that requires them to be gluten-free. They'll probably give you that smug smile with the yep-you've-got-a-classic-case-of-denial look on their faces, because they've been there before. You won't really need to hear much more.

- **Take notes.** Write down your symptoms, how you feel when you eat certain foods, and the symptoms of gluten sensitivity, celiac disease, or whatever condition you may have. Do you see a correlation? When you eat certain foods, do you notice that some of the symptoms you have are similar to some of the symptoms of the condition? Hmmmm . . .

When others are in denial

The most common type of denial that others exhibit occurs when they have all the symptoms themselves and refuse to admit it. Why is it so hard for relatives to believe they may have this? Problems with gluten, after all, run in the family, and lots of times family members have classic symptoms. Why is it so hard for friends? Gluten intolerance of one type or another is a common condition — yet often they say, "I don't have that." The bottom line is that they don't want to have it.

Conditions that require you to be gluten-free, such as celiac disease, have a unique common denominator: People don't always "buy" what you're telling them about your condition or the fact that a gluten-free diet may fully restore your health. They also don't always understand how strict you really need to be in sticking to the diet.

I've been accused on more than one occasion by more than one person of being neurotic about trying to avoid gluten. Doctors have told me I'm going "overboard" because I check the ingredients in a "tiny" pill. Loved ones have accused me of being obsessed about gluten and making sure food is gluten-free. And I'm guessing more than one waiter has muttered something about being high maintenance as he walked away.

I wish I had advice for how to handle the "others" in your life who don't believe you about your condition or won't accept that they, too, could have an intolerance to gluten. The best you can do is work hard to educate them. You have no way to force them into testing or trying the diet, which is sad — because those steps may dramatically improve their health.

Getting Back on Track When You're Feeling Derailed

So even I admit that some difficult emotional challenges arise when you go gluten-free. You may be making a monumental change in your lifestyle! But overcoming those challenges and getting back on track to enjoying life and all it has to offer — far beyond food — are important.

Regaining control

If you don't take control of this diet, the diet will control you. Part of the reason you sometimes feel out of control when you're told to go gluten-free is because you're afraid. Afraid of messing up. Afraid of believing inaccurate information. Afraid of letting go of your habits and favorite foods. Afraid you'll feel deprived. Afraid of being different. Afraid of trying new foods. Afraid of an entirely new lifestyle.

The only way to get beyond the fear is to try new things. Be creative — explore new foods — tantalize your taste buds with all the gluten-free goodies you can think of. Arm yourself with accurate information. Be prepared when you're out and about. Taking control of the diet — and giving your kids control of theirs — is key to living and loving the gluten-free lifestyle.

If you're finding that all your favorite comfort foods are now off-limits, realize that those old comfort foods were probably *dis*comfort foods that actually made you feel bad because they have gluten in them. Choose new favorites, but try to avoid the pitfall of undermining weight management efforts by turning to food for solace.

Getting beyond big words with heavy implications

Many people embarking upon a gluten-free lifestyle hear some pretty scary words being bandied around. Words like *disease, chronic, restrictions, lifelong, malabsorption, intestinal damage,* and *intolerance* are usually the catalysts for going gluten-free.

Although it's easy to be somewhat stunned by the heavy implications these words have, looking beyond them is important. Thinking more about the fact that your health will improve, you'll feel better, and you'll have more energy can help shift your perspective in a more optimistic direction.

Focusing on what you can eat

When the only food you can eat is gluten-free, every menu item begins to look like a croissant. Wanting what you can't have is the essence of human nature. Tell someone he can't juggle machetes, and he's likely to have a sudden urge to juggle machetes.

Believe me, I know how depriving this lifestyle can be. After all, for dinner my family is stuck with main courses like filet mignon, shrimp scampi, chicken Marsala, and seared ahi. Side dishes are scant with boring dishes like citrus quinoa, bean and feta salad, and saffron rice — and for dessert all we get are things like flan, tapioca pudding, chocolate (anything), ice cream, and crème brûlée. Depriving, indeed.

If you're feeling deprived, please don't let my sarcasm offend you. It's perfectly normal to feel like your selections are limited (they are limited but not limit*ing*) and to pine away for freshly baked sourdough. It's also normal to peruse a menu and feel like the only thing you can order is a side of fruit — or to stare at your pantry and see only saltines.

I like to use vegetarians as role models for how you can improve your perspective. They don't whine about the fact that they're missing out on greasy pork chops and flank steak. Quite the contrary: They revel in their diets, usually celebrating their meat-free lifestyle.

Focus on what you can eat, rather than what you can't. The list of things you can eat is a heckuva lot longer than the list of things you can't, and if you don't believe me, start writing, my friend. Make a list of all the things you can eat — let me know when you get that finished, wouldja?

One of the fastest ways to make a particular food take center stage in your life is to ban it, because it's human nature to want what you can't have. For many people, putting gluten on the no-can-do list makes them want it even more. So if you're feeling deprived, indulge yourself! Not with gluten, of course, but with your favorite gluten-free treat. A splurge from time to time can remind you of lots of delicious things you can eat and can help take your mind off the things you can't.

Are you a tad grumpy?
You may have dieter's depression.

People who are on a diet of any kind usually feel a "high" in the beginning, while they're still ultra-motivated and passionate about their commitment. But then, usually around the second or third week, something commonly called *dieter's depression* sets in, and making hard food choices becomes tougher. Dieters in this stage aren't much fun to be around. Usually, they're feeling resentful and emotionally deprived, especially if food was a source of comfort for them.

Also, low levels of the hormone serotonin can lead to depression, and the brain needs carbs to produce serotonin. Sometimes when people go gluten-free, they cut their carb level significantly and may become depressed as a result. If you think you may be falling into a dieter's depression, first make sure you're getting good carbs from fruits and veggies. If you find it too time-consuming or cumbersome to cook steamed garden favorites like broccoli and zucchini, you may want to opt for grab-n-go fruits and vegetables like apples, carrots, and sugar snap peas. All are excellent sources of good carbs and have other health benefits, too. Then finish reading this chapter, which can give you lots of tips for lifting your spirits and focusing on the positive.

Deflecting the temptation to be annoyed or offended

When it comes to your dietary restrictions, you will, most likely, encounter people who appear unconcerned, uninterested, thoughtless, and sometimes even downright rude. From time to time you may have hurt feelings and may even feel ostracized. (How's that for sugarcoating it?) Other times you'll find that people do care but forget to make accommodations or just don't "get it" and serve foods you can't eat.

Keep in mind that as you embark upon this new lifestyle, you're probably gaining an entirely new respect for food and a heightened awareness of what having dietary restrictions feels like. And you're probably much more aware of other people's restrictions and sensitivities.

Meanwhile, the rest of the world is unenlightened about the intricacies of the gluten-free lifestyle and may actually be "rude" enough to suggest you join them for dinner — at your (former) favorite pizza place.

Don't be annoyed or offended. People are busy and sometimes so focused on their own fast-paced lives that they can't possibly remember to accommo-date yours. Most of the time they're not being rude or thoughtless (okay, sometimes they are); they're just unaware. Be glad they asked you to dinner, and either bring something you can eat, order the salad, or suggest a differ-ent restaurant. Save the negative energy for something that really matters — like the kid next door who feels compelled to practice the drums at midnight.

Faking optimism

I'm not a fan of fake people. Fake people try to act like something they're not, usually in an attempt to impress others, and that is, for lack of a better term, kind of icky.

Faking optimism is an entirely different thing. It's when you pretend to your-self that you feel good about something that you really don't feel good about at all. Before you know it, you really do feel better about it. It's a really cool power our brains have!

Faking optimism is easier for some people than others, because everyone falls on different parts of the Optimism Spectrum to start with. There are the ohmy-gosh-those-are-the-most-incredibly-beautiful-mosquitos-on-the-planet types, and there are the I-find-her-chirpy-perky-optimism-downright-depressing types. Where you fall doesn't really matter; you, too, can fake optimism and have it affect your overall outlook in a positive way.

Avoiding "unpleasantry one-upmanship"

You know people who play this game: You almost mindlessly comment that you have a headache, and their quick comeback is, "You think *you've* got a headache? I had a migraine the other day that . . ." Yeah, you know the type. Always trying to one-up you in the you-think-*you've*-got-it-bad game. Well, in this game of what I call unpleasantry one-upmanship, you hold all the cards. If you've been sick with celiac disease and finally diagnosed, maybe your hand goes something

like this: "Yeah? Well, I have a *lifelong, chronic disease* and a *restricted* diet that prevents me from eating bread!" And then there's the trump card: diarrhea. Sure, you hold the winning hand, but don't play it. Playing this game forces you to focus on the negative and sucks you into a calamity competition that does you no good. Furthermore, people who play that game usually don't care about what you're saying; they're too busy choosing their next card.

Start by thinking of all the reasons the gluten-free lifestyle is a good thing in your life (check out Chapter 19 if you need some help). Maybe it makes you focus more on nutrition; maybe you're spending more time with the family eating home-cooked meals; maybe you're appreciating the improved health you're experiencing as a result of the diet; maybe you've helped someone else in the family discover the key to better health, too.

Make your list and convince (or remind) yourself that adopting this lifestyle is a wonderful thing in your life. Get excited about it — tell your friends and family how great you feel and why. Before you know it, you'll have convinced yourself and you won't be faking it anymore.

Spreading attitudes — they're contagious

Attitudes spread like germs through a preschool — and like germs, you can't see them, but if you catch the bad kind, they can make you feel pretty nasty.

Sometimes humans are like germs, silently spreading crummy attitudes to unwitting victims. If you're unhappy about having to adopt a gluten-free lifestyle and haven't found some of the tips in this chapter to help shake your anxiety, at least don't spread your misery around. Many people, if not most, aren't all that familiar with gluten, the gluten-free lifestyle, and the medical conditions that benefit from it. Chances are, you're the first person who's teaching them about it.

If you feel compelled to whine about the foods you miss or express excessive feelings of deprivation and despair, people will feel sad and sorry for your "misfortune." Do you really want their pity? Try instead to portray being gluten-free to others as a great lifestyle, a positive event in your life, and a healthful way to live so that others can feel that way, too.

You can grieve for the foods you can't eat anymore, or you can rejoice in your newfound health and strength.

Redefining Who You Are

If your doctor has diagnosed you with gluten sensitivity or celiac disease, you may feel different. You are different from other people — and that's okay. We're all different. Some have an interest in sports, others an aptitude for accounting. We readily acknowledge and accept that we're different in those types of things, but sometimes we don't like to be different with this diet. Your diet is different — but in the big picture, your restrictions are no different from those of people, such as vegans or people with peanut allergies, who have other diet restrictions.

Yes, you're different from other people — but you're not different from who you were before your diagnosis. Your lifestyle is different, but you're not.

So you're on a diet. That makes you unique?

You can't eat certain things. If you do, you have to deal with physical consequences. Your selections on a menu are limited, you have to be careful about what you eat when you're in social situations, and you can't always eat what everyone else is eating. Your diet is restricted, and it's a pain in the hiney! So what's so different about you? You sound like you're on a diet. That makes you unique? I think not!

You can go on a diet for lots of reasons. People usually think of going on diets to lose weight, but some are on special diets to gain weight (much to the chagrin of those trying to lose). Others are on special diets because they have high blood pressure, high cholesterol, heart disease, food allergies, diabetes, or autoimmune diseases like arthritis or multiple sclerosis. For health or ethical reasons, some people choose to avoid meat or foods that contain chemicals or hormones. Athletes in training often have special diets, and pregnant or lactating women sometimes choose to modify their diets to optimize their baby's health. Those of us on a gluten-free diet tend to think of it as being different from other diets — but in many ways, it's not different at all!

Sometimes people let their condition define who they are. Try not to do this. Is having this condition a disappointment? Maybe — maybe not (I hope after you finish this book you don't think so!). But okay, maybe you're bummed about it, and that's okay.

What you're not is a victim, a martyr, or a sick person. In fact, you're on the road to recovery and amazing health. Lots of people have some kind of adversity in their lives, and they deal with it — you can, too.

If you're having trouble dealing with the gluten-free lifestyle from an emotional or psychological standpoint, step back and take a look at the bigger picture. Why are you giving up gluten in the first place? Probably because each and every bite of gluten compromised your health.

Force yourself to remember that the gluten-free diet is key to your better health, and focus on the great thing you're doing for your body by being gluten-free. Here are a few more tips that may help you beat the blues:

- ✔ **Psych yourself up.** Change your perspective on why you eat, what you eat, and how you eat. Remember, you're supposed to eat to live, not the other way around.

- ✔ **Think outside the box.** Getting stuck in food ruts, eating the same basic meals day after day, week after week, is easy. Explore new foods, find new favorites, and be creative in finding new ways to tantalize your taste buds.

- ✔ **Remember, the diet gets easier with time.** If the gluten-free lifestyle seems difficult to you from an emotional or practical standpoint, realize that it gets easier over time. You will accept it and adapt to it and will hopefully learn to love it!

- ✔ **Seek out help.** Whether help comes from family members, support groups, friends, or counselors, sometimes others can help make the transition easier.

- ✔ **Avoid negative people and influences.** Basically, purge your life of the negative. If the gluten-free way of life is a struggle for you, the last thing you need is a malicious relative sabotaging your efforts.

- ✔ **Recommit yourself.** Sometimes you need to reaffirm your commitment by remembering why you're doing this.

Resisting the Temptation to Cheat

There are approximately 4.2 gazillion diets out there: lowfat, high-protein, low-carb, low-calorie, low-glycemic, and everything in between. The thing they all have in common is that people cheat on them. It's a fact. People cheat on diets.

But you can't cheat on this one, especially if you have celiac disease. No, not even a little. "Everything in moderation" and "a little won't hurt you" do not apply if you have gluten sensitivity or celiac disease.

Resisting the temptation to cheat starts with understanding why you want to cheat.

Realizing why you want to cheat

If you're spending a lot of time (or money on diet books) figuring out why you want to cheat on your diet, you're working too hard. There may be a lot of factors that play a part, but it all boils down to one reason, as far as I can tell: you *want* to. You *want* that cookie, pasta, or that bagel. After all, if you didn't want it, it wouldn't be a temptation.

There are lots of reasons you may want to eat the forbidden glutenous goods, and if you hope to resist the temptation, it's important to figure out what's driving your desire. Here are some of the more common triggers for temptation to cheat on the gluten-free diet:

- ✔ **It's just too good to resist.** I realize this isn't profound or worthy of landing me on any pop psych talk shows, but most people who indulge in a food not on their diet do so because it's just too yummy to say no.

- ✔ **Just this once.** Not a good plan. There's a slippery slope between "just this once" and a diet that's long-forgotten.

- ✔ **You want to fit in.** If everyone else were jumping off a cliff, would you? (Bungee jumpers aren't allowed to answer that.) Truthfully, other people probably aren't paying much attention to what you're eating, anyway. Social situations are about the company, the conversation, and the ambiance. Yeah, it's about the food, too, but people aren't paying attention to what *you're* eating.

- ✔ **It's a comfort food for you.** In difficult times, people sometimes have certain foods they turn to. If a gluten-containing goodie is your comfort food, a weak moment may send you straight to the food that you think will make you feel better — even though you know it won't.

- ✔ **It's a special occasion.** Try again. This excuse may work for other diets, but not this one. Eating even a little bit of gluten may turn your social affair into a dreaded nightmare. No occasion is worth compromising your health, and furthermore, special occasions are about the *occasion,* not the food.

✔ **You're bored by the diet.** If all you're eating is rice cakes and celery, I don't blame you. Live it up, get creative, and try new things. Use this book as a guide to figure out exactly what you *can* eat, and then challenge yourself to try something new. If you need a little inspiration, check out Chapter 9, which offers ideas for getting creative in the kitchen, and learning to make anything gluten-free.

✔ **A little won't hurt.** Yeah, it could. If you plan to use this as an excuse, you're assigned to read Chapters 2 and 3.

✔ **The diet's too hard.** Hey, this is a *For Dummies* book, remember? This book is supposed to make it really easy to figure out what you can and can't eat, and how to live (and love!) the lifestyle. Sometimes it's not easy to change your perspective, I'll give you that. But you *can* do it, and between your friends, family, books like this, and helpful resources listed in Chapter 5, you've got plenty of support.

✔ **Someone's sabotaging your diet.** People do this! In fact, it's common. Usually they're not aware that they're doing it, and they do it for all different reasons. Sometimes they do it because they're jealous that you're getting healthier than they are. Sometimes they do it because they don't "believe" you need to be on the diet (see the section called "When others are in denial," earlier in this chapter). Other times, people do it because they don't want to have to follow the clean-kitchen rules or don't want to have to put the effort into preparing gluten-free foods. Don't succumb to the sabotage efforts. Instead, try to find someone who seems particularly supportive of your gluten-free lifestyle, and ask for help. People *love* to help, and they get tremendous satisfaction out of lending a shoulder, an ear, or a hand.

✔ **I've already blown it so much, it doesn't matter anymore.** Not true. Today can be the first day of the rest of your gluten-free life.

Although these are powerful factors in enticing you to go for the gluten, overcoming the temptation is important. Sometimes the key to saying no is taking a look at the consequences.

You choose to cheat — or not — because you have full control over what you put in your mouth. When you cheat on the gluten-free diet, you're cheating yourself out of better health.

Assessing the consequences

One of the tough parts about looking at the consequences of your actions is that if they're not immediate and drastic, you sometimes feel that they don't matter. People who are dieting to lose weight often don't notice any consequences from a setback or two because they don't see the extra inches jump back onto their thighs when they eat a bowl of ice cream — and for that matter, they may never gain the weight back, because for them, a high-calorie indulgence from time to time may be okay.

If you have gluten sensitivity or celiac disease, though, the consequences can have serious adverse affects on your health, and if you cheat chronically, those effects can be cumulative. In fact, you could be setting yourself up to develop conditions like osteoporosis, lupus, thyroid disease, and lots of other conditions that I'm betting aren't worth that bagel. For some friendly reminders about how much damage you could be doing when you cheat, see Chapters 2 and 3.

Overcoming the temptation

After you realize why you want to cheat and you remind yourself of the consequences, you have to finalize the deal by just saying no. Here are a few things you can do to make this a little easier:

- ✔ **Indulge in your favorite gluten-free goodie.** If you're craving a brownie, eat it — the gluten-free kind, of course. Just about anything that has gluten in it has a gluten-free counterpart these days. If you'd rather just grab a (gluten-free) candy bar, that's cool, too. If you're tempted to eat something with gluten, try to find something else that will satisfy at least as much, but still keep you on track with your gluten-free lifestyle.

- ✔ **Reward yourself when you resist.** If you've been challenged by temptation and successfully overcome it, give yourself a treat. It doesn't have to be food — maybe you buy yourself something special or do something nice for yourself. Doing so can reinforce your strength and commitment to the lifestyle.

- ✔ **Simplify what you need to.** If the diet seems to cumbersome, maybe you're trying to do too much and need to go back to the basics. If your menu plans are overwhelming, cut something out so you don't have so much to think about. If you don't understand the diet, read parts of this book again, particularly Chapters 4 and 5. You may also want to seek out some of the resources in Chapter 5.

- ✔ **Make your lifestyle a priority.** This is about you — your health — your future. If you find this lifestyle too difficult because of your work commitments, think about changing your schedule. If you have negative people in your life who seem to sabotage your efforts, avoid them if you can. If something's not working in your life, change it. Being gluten-free is about more than a diet; it's about a lifestyle, and it should be a high priority.

Part V
The Part of Tens

The 5th Wave   By Rich Tennant

"This isn't some sort of fad diet, is it?"

In this part . . .

I summarize some of the many benefits of being gluten-free in Chapter 19. In Chapter 20, where I list tips to help you love the gluten-free lifestyle. If you're thinking you don't need or want to give up gluten, you may want to pay special attention to Chapter 21, where I list some of the lame excuses I've heard for not going gluten-free. If any of them sound familiar, you may want to do some soul-searching and reconsider your decision.

Chapter 19

Ten Benefits of Being Gluten-Free

In This Chapter

▶ Healing for people with celiac disease

▶ Preventing celiac disease

▶ Looking younger

▶ Managing your weight or menopausal symptoms

▶ Knowing what you're eating

*H*ow 'bout these for benefits: no more diarrhea, no more headaches, no more fatigue, no more depression, no more "irritable bowel syndrome" or "fibromyalgia"? (You can read more about how these conditions may benefit from a gluten-free diet in Chapter 2.) If you're going gluten-free because you have some form of gluten intolerance, I don't need to tell you how icky feeling icky feels — and the key to not feeling icky is being gluten-free. For you, the benefits are blatant.

But even if you have no medical reasons whatsoever for being gluten-free, the benefits of the gluten-free lifestyle are still vast. In fact, I could list way more than ten benefits of being gluten-free, but this is called the "Part of Tens," not the "Part of Tons," so I just give you the highlights.

You Know How to Improve Your Health

I always get way too excited and end up spilling the punch line halfway through a joke. Here I go again, giving you the very *best* benefit of being gluten-free right out of the gates: You, unlike many people, have the key to better health — a gluten-free diet.

This idea is especially true if you've been diagnosed with gluten sensitivity or celiac disease; most people who shouldn't eat gluten aren't so lucky. They don't know they have an intolerance to gluten, so they have no clue what's making them feel so bad. They try cutting out dairy or other potential allergens, and their surgeons try cutting out their gallbladders or various other innards, but nothing helps. You, on the other hand, know exactly what's making you sick — gluten — and you can eliminate it from your diet, enjoying fully restored health.

If You Have Problems with Gluten, Your Health Improves Right Away

If you have celiac disease, gluten damages your intestinal tract. The minute you go gluten-free, your body starts healing, you begin to absorb nutrients again, and before you know it, you're feeling so great that you can't even remember how bad you used to feel. Whether you've been sick for years, days, or never even seemed to feel any effects from gluten, your body can begin healing immediately, and that means your health can improve, too.

The Diet Can Be Super Healthful

You can do the gluten-free diet in several ways, and one of them is extremely healthful. It's an approach some people call the *caveman diet* or the *Paleolithic diet,* and it consists of eating meat, poultry, fish, seafood, fruits, vegetables, berries, nuts, ancient alternative "grains," and other foods that your body was designed to eat — all of which are naturally gluten-free. Follow this form of a gluten-free diet, and you may look and feel better, live longer, age more slowly, and have a nutritional edge over gluttons for gluten. You can find more information on this approach by doing a search on "Paleolithic diet" on any search engine (or by flipping to Chapter 6).

If You Don't Have Celiac Disease and You're Not Eating Gluten, You'll Never Develop It

You need three things to develop celiac disease: the genetic predisposition, an environmental trigger of some kind (a virus, surgery, trauma, pregnancy, or emotional distress, for instance), and a diet that includes gluten. If you're not eating gluten, you can't develop celiac disease!

You May Decrease the Chances of Developing Associated Autoimmune Diseases

Many autoimmune diseases go hand in hand, meaning that if you develop one, you're likely to develop another. If you have celiac disease and you continue to eat gluten, your chances of developing associated autoimmune diseases increase over time. Some studies have shown that the sooner you cut gluten out of your diet, the lower your risk of developing other conditions (to find out more about related conditions, see Chapter 2).

You May Be Turning Back the Clock

Is the gluten-free diet the holy grail for turning back the hands of time? Maybe, if you follow the principles of Dr. Nicholas Perricone, a dermatologist and adjunct professor of medicine at Michigan State University. He maintains that inflammation contributes to accelerated aging and that through diet (and supplements and creams), you can erase scars and wrinkles, increase the production of collagen and elastin, enjoy radiance and glow, and develop a dewy, supple appearance to your skin.

So how does the gluten-free diet fit into the picture of youth? Although Perricone doesn't actually pinpoint gluten as a culprit, he does say that wheat provokes an inflammatory response by quickly turning to sugar in the bloodstream. That inflammatory response causes your skin to age more quickly, and he maintains that avoiding foods like wheat may help reverse the aging process. You can find out more about the Perricone principles at www.nvperriconemd.com.

Symptoms of Menopause May Decrease

Some doctors think wheat-based foods may exacerbate symptoms of menopause, such as hot flashes, night sweats, headaches, fatigue, and mood swings. Eliminating these wheat-based products, especially foods that contain white refined flour, may reduce these symptoms.

Your Weight Can Be Easier to Manage

If you go gluten-free the nutritious way (see Chapter 6), you'll be eating high-protein, low-glycemic-index foods. Eating these types of foods stabilizes the "I'm hungry" and "I'm full" hormones, so you don't always feel hungry; it also causes your body to use the stored fat (read "love handles" or "saddlebags") as energy.

Sometimes when people go gluten-free, they seek out specialty gluten-free products like cookies, donuts, pizza crusts, breads, bagels, and pastas. These foods are fine in moderation, but they're not going to do you any favors when you're trying to squeeze into your skinny jeans. If you follow a naturally gluten-free diet, you'll help your body function the way it's supposed to, decrease your hunger pangs, and make managing your weight much easier.

You're More Aware of Nutrition

Now that you're gluten-free, you're way more knowledgeable about nutrition than most people. For one thing, you read labels. You know that processed foods usually have multisyllabic ingredients (with lots of *x*'s and *y*'s in them) that seem better suited to a pesticide than your plate. You, unlike the common Joe, know that malt usually comes from barley, maltodextrin doesn't contain malt, and glucose isn't the same as gluten (if you're thinking, "It isn't?" please read Chapter 3 before the pop quiz). Hopefully, you've even experienced the joys of quinoa, millet, and other alternative grains that many people have never heard of, and you know that they're nutritional powerhouses compared to the typical cereal grains.

Blood-Sugar Levels May Be More Stable

If you're doing the gluten-free diet the nutritious way that I outline in Chapter 6, then you're essentially eating low-glycemic-index foods that help stabilize your blood-sugar levels. High-glycemic-load foods found in lots of wheat-based products quickly turn to sugar in your bloodstream and cause your insulin levels to spike and then drop quickly. Energy levels and even moods can follow this yo-yo pattern, and not only is that unhealthy, but getting a rush of energy only to quickly crash and burn is no fun. A naturally gluten-free diet helps stabilize your blood-sugar levels and gives you sustained energy throughout the day. If you have diabetes, you can benefit greatly from this approach when you're trying to control your blood sugar.

Chapter 20

Ten Tips to Help You (or Your Child) Love the Gluten-Free Lifestyle

. . . .

. . . .

*T*he transition from gluten-gorger to "gluten-free is good for me" is harder for some people than others. Learning to live the lifestyle is one thing; learning to *love* it is sometimes quite another. Sometimes you're going along just fine with the gluten-free lifestyle, and for some reason life seems to turn into one big gluten-gala and resisting your gluten-glomming friends who seem to be taunting you with gluten galore becomes harder than ever.

Focus on What You Can Eat

Staring into a pantry and seeing nothing but gluten is really easy. Sometimes you may seem to find more gluten around you than oxygen molecules. It's true — gluten is everywhere — yet the reality is that the list of things you can eat is a lot longer than the list of things you can't. You just have to shift your thinking a tinge. Instead of thinking about the foods you can't have anymore, focus on the foods you can eat, and put a special emphasis on those that you especially enjoy. If you're feeling a little restricted or deprived, treat yourself to your favorite gluten-free indulgences. Try to think outside the box and explore foods you may not otherwise have tried, or figure out how to make your favorite glutenous meal into a gluten-freebie (Chapter 9 helps you get creative in the kitchen). Before you know it, you'll realize that the gluten-free lifestyle might have its restrictions, but it's definitely not restric*tive*.

Expand Your Culinary Horizons with Alternative Grains

There's a bold, gluten-free world out there filled with foods some people have never heard of; quinoa, amaranth, teff, millet, buckwheat, acai, kefir, and sorghum top the list of my faves. Don't underestimate your kids' willingness to try new foods, either. Even if they're reluctant to experiment at first, they usually make the leap and learn to broaden their horizons. Whether your palate is conditioned to enjoy bland and tasteless foods or foods exploding with flavor, you may find a whole new world of unique and sometimes exceptionally nutritious foods.

Enjoy an Ethnic Flare

Lots of cultures use naturally gluten-free ingredients in their cooking. Many Asian cuisines, including Thai, Vietnamese, and Korean, are often gluten-free, as are many Mexican and Indian dishes. Do some research on the Internet to find out what ingredients a particular culture uses, or explore cookbooks featuring recipes from around the world. You can figure out how to cook foods from those cultures or venture out to restaurants to enjoy a new taste experience gluten-free — globally!

Control the Diet

Whether you're 2 or 102, if you're going gluten-free, you need to take control of the diet. The diet can suddenly control things like what you eat, when and where you eat, with whom you eat, and even how you eat. But remember that you're in control. You decide what you're going to eat, when you're going to eat, and with whom. Planning ahead helps, and I talk about menu planning and shopping in Chapter 8. It's also important to make sure something's always available for you when you're hungry. I cover the golden rules of going out gluten-free in Chapter 16, because part of being in control of the diet is being able to get out and about and know that you're able to eat safely when you're not at home.

If your child's on the diet, start giving him or her control from day one, no matter how young he or she is. People usually way underestimate kids' abilities to understand the diet and why being strict about following it is so important. Check out Chapter 17 for more about raising happy, healthy, gluten-free kids.

Eat to Live, Don't Live to Eat

Your body is designed to use food as fuel, not as a comforter, pacifier, or partner-replacer. Sure, food has become a huge part of society and interpersonal relationships, and by definition, social functions all revolve around food. But that doesn't mean food *is* the social function, nor does that mean you have to eat the food that's there. Food tastes good, and having a full belly often feels good. But food serves a greater purpose, and you should treat it as fueler, not filler.

Remember: You're Different. So What?

People talk about wanting to be unique, and yet they cringe when they're afraid they appear out of step. The bottom line is that everyone is different, even when people try to look the same. If you're on the gluten-free diet, your bread may look a little different, and you may sometimes appear to be a tad high-maintenance at a restaurant. So what? Lots of people "customize" a menu. Vegetarians skip a huge portion of the buffet line. Some people don't like chicken; others don't do dairy; and some can die if they eat the wrong foods. Lots of people have "different" diets and lifestyles. Yours happens to be healthy, delicious, and the key to your better health.

Go Ahead — Enjoy a (Gluten-Free) Splurge

If you put too many restrictions on yourself in trying to maintain a healthy, gluten-free lifestyle, you may just find yourself getting bored and frustrated and feeling deprived. Give yourself a break. Indulge from time in time in your favorite gluten-free extravagance, whether it happens to be a sweet treat or a baked potato loaded with sour cream and butter. Finding and maintaining a good balance is an important part of any lifestyle.

Tune In to the Benefits

When you tune in and remind yourself of the benefits of being gluten-free (see Chapter 19), that step reinforces in your mind *why* you're living a gluten-free lifestyle. If you think it would be helpful to write down all the good things about being gluten-free, do it. Post the list on the fridge, if you want a daily reminder, or keep a list in a journal on your desk. Maybe you want to challenge yourself to add an item to the list each day or week. When you focus on the reasons being gluten-free is a good thing in your life, you can gain a new or renewed appreciation for the lifestyle itself.

Turn Away from Temptation

Avoid putting yourself in tempting situations when you can, saving your strength for when you have no choice in the matter. You're not doing yourself any favors if you surround yourself with tidbits of temptation, whether in the workplace, at home, or in social situations. You probably shouldn't take that job at the bakery. Don't think you're building character by holding a slice of pizza to your nose and taking a big whiff. And yeah, you may want to think twice about entering that pie-eating contest. There's enough gluten to go around in this world without setting yourself up for temptation and frustration.

Deal with It; Don't Dwell on It

If you're mad, sad, grief-stricken, confused, frustrated, agitated, and downright ticked off about having to live without gluten, that's okay. Lots of people experience those feelings, especially if they're forced to embark upon an entirely new — and sometimes very different — lifestyle. But deal with those feelings, and move on. Call on your friends, family, and support groups, share with them how you're feeling, and let them try to help you work through the feelings. If you need professional help, get it. Not wallowing in the negativity of your circumstances is important, or your thoughts may intensify and can even end up causing other physical and emotional problems.

Chapter 21

Ten Lame Excuses Not to Go Gluten-Free

. . . .

In This Chapter

▶ Hearing excuses, excuses

▶ Realizing excuses don't buy you good health

. . . .

I realize you may not want to give up pizza and bagels, much less beer. And I also realize that you're going to work really hard to justify why you don't need to. Some of the excuses I've heard for not going gluten-free are pretty creative — but I'm not buyin' em.

"I'm too fat to have celiac disease or gluten sensitivity."

This is one of the more understandable excuses, because most people associate gluten intolerance, celiac disease, and malabsorption in general with being skinny. But sometimes weight gain is a symptom as much as weight loss. In fact, because of the malabsorption that can result from gluten intolerance, your hormones — including the ones that make you store or use fat — can be way out of whack, wreaking all sorts of havoc on your body in many ways, including your weight. (And by the way — the gluten-free diet, if done as I recommend in Chapter 6, may actually help you manage your weight quite effectively.)

"I don't have the symptoms of gluten sensitivity or celiac disease."

More than 250 symptoms characterize gluten sensitivity and celiac disease, and I seriously wonder whether anyone can honestly claim to have none. Headaches? Fatigue? Joint pain? Gas? Bloating? Depression? Mouth ulcers?

Take a look at the list of symptoms in Chapter 2, and then remember that that's the short list. Some people with gluten sensitivity or celiac disease truly are asymptomatic (they have no apparent symptoms), but eating gluten causes them significant internal damage.

"I don't want to be deprived of important nutrients."

You mean all the nutrients you're getting from those bagels, pizzas, and beers? Trust me — your body will survive without those nutritional power-houses. In fact, if you have any form of gluten intolerance and you're still eating gluten, you're already depriving your body of important nutrients. Furthermore, the gluten-free diet can be extremely healthy, especially if you do it the way I recommend in Chapter 6. If you're still concerned about a lack of vitamins and minerals, you can take supplements — just make sure they're gluten-free.

"I don't want to give up (insert favorite gluten-containing food)."

Of course you don't want to give up your favorite foods, but not being tested and continuing to eat gluten won't make your problem, if you have one, go away. In fact, it'll get worse, and you may be setting yourself up to develop some nasty complications and associated conditions.

"My problem isn't with gluten. I just don't do well with pasta and beer."

Pinpointing a few foods that don't sit well with you is easy. What's hard is realizing that you may have a bigger issue that includes an intolerance to those foods — and many more. If you've targeted a few foods that you don't do well with and they happen to have gluten in them, consider the fact that gluten — not just those few foods — could be what's making you feel bad.

"Pizza makes me feel bad; I must have lactose intolerance."

Lots of people draw this kind of conclusion. They figure out that a particular food makes them ill, but they don't make the association between that food and gluten — usually because they've never heard of gluten. When pizza or pasta makes people feel bad, they often assume it's the lactose in the cheese or the tomatoes in the pasta sauce. You can also blame the bubbles in the beer, the sugar in the cookies, and the yeast in the bread. Of course, there's the possibility that you *are* lactose intolerant — but there's also the possibility that gluten may be the culprit.

"I have irritable bowel syndrome, and my doctor said diet doesn't affect it."

Irritable bowel syndrome (IBS) isn't a specific disease; it's a term for a group of symptoms — like gas, bloating, and diarrhea — that doctors use when none of the tests show a single underlying cause. All these symptoms are signs of gluten sensitivity and celiac disease. In fact, IBS is a common misdiagnosis for gluten sensitivity and celiac disease, as are fibromyalgia, chronic fatigue syndrome, gallbladder disease, migraines, and myriad other conditions — and in those cases, if they are due to gluten sensitivity or celiac disease, a gluten-free diet can help. Bottom line: If you aren't getting better, you may want to rethink your diagnosis.

"I had celiac disease as a kid, but I outgrew it."

In the 1950s and 1960s, physicians thought people outgrew celiac disease, so they often told patients to try eating gluten again as an adult, and if they didn't feel symptoms, to consider themselves "cured." Some people still believe that people can outgrow celiac disease, but now doctors know that no one outgrows celiac disease. Your symptoms may change — you may not even have any symptoms (or may not associate symptoms such as headaches and fatigue with gluten) — but if you had celiac disease at one time in your life, you have it forever and definitely need to be gluten-free for life.

"I was tested for celiac disease, and I was negative."

Once negative doesn't mean always negative. Celiac disease can develop at any point in your life, so even if you test negative once, you need to be tested again in the future if you're at risk for developing it or if you have symptoms. Furthermore, you can get false negatives if your testing is incomplete (not all the tests are done), if you're IgA-deficient (see Chapter 2 for more details), or if the tests were done or interpreted poorly.

"I don't have the genes for celiac disease."

You may still have a form of gluten intolerance. Some people test negative for gluten sensitivity and celiac disease, yet they still find they feel better on a gluten-free diet (which logically means that gluten makes them feel bad).

Index

NESS, CAREERS & PERSONAL FINANCE

0-7645-5307-0

0-7645-5331-3 *†

Also available:

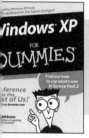

0-7645-4074-2

0-7645-3758-X

Also available:

- Accounting For Dummies †
  0-7645-5314-3
- Business Plans Kit For Dummies †
  0-7645-5365-8
- Cover Letters For Dummies
  0-7645-5224-4
- Frugal Living For Dummies
  0-7645-5403-4
- Leadership For Dummies
  0-7645-5176-0
- Managing For Dummies
  0-7645-1771-6

- Marketing For Dummies
  0-7645-5600-2
- Personal Finance For Dummies *
  0-7645-2590-5
- Project Management For Dummies
  0-7645-5283-X
- Resumes For Dummies †
  0-7645-5471-9
- Selling For Dummies
  0-7645-5363-1
- Small Business Kit For Dummies *†
  0-7645-5093-4

E & BUSINESS COMPUTER BASICS

- ACT! 6 For Dummies
  0-7645-2645-6
- iLife '04 All-in-One Desk Reference
  For Dummies
  0-7645-7347-0
- iPAQ For Dummies
  0-7645-6769-1
- Mac OS X Panther Timesaving
  Techniques For Dummies
  0-7645-5812-9
- Macs For Dummies
  0-7645-5656-8

- Microsoft Money 2004 For Dummies
  0-7645-4195-1
- Office 2003 All-in-One Desk Reference
  For Dummies
  0-7645-3883-7
- Outlook 2003 For Dummies
  0-7645-3759-8
- PCs For Dummies
  0-7645-4074-2
- TiVo For Dummies
  0-7645-6923-6
- Upgrading and Fixing PCs For Dummies
  0-7645-1665-5
- Windows XP Timesaving Techniques
  For Dummies
  0-7645-3748-2

D, HOME, GARDEN, HOBBIES, MUSIC & PETS

0-7645-5295-3

0-7645-5232-5

Also available:

- Bass Guitar For Dummies
  0-7645-2487-9
- Diabetes Cookbook For Dummies
  0-7645-5230-9
- Gardening For Dummies *
  0-7645-5130-2
- Guitar For Dummies
  0-7645-5106-X
- Holiday Decorating For Dummies
  0-7645-2570-0
- Home Improvement All-in-One
  For Dummies
  0-7645-5680-0

- Knitting For Dummies
  0-7645-5395-X
- Piano For Dummies
  0-7645-5105-1
- Puppies For Dummies
  0-7645-5255-4
- Scrapbooking For Dummies
  0-7645-7208-3
- Senior Dogs For Dummies
  0-7645-5818-8
- Singing For Dummies
  0-7645-2475-5
- 30-Minute Meals For Dummies
  0-7645-2589-1

ERNET & DIGITAL MEDIA

0-7645-1664-7

0-7645-6924-4

Also available:

- 2005 Online Shopping Directory
  For Dummies
  0-7645-7495-7
- CD & DVD Recording For Dummies
  0-7645-5956-7
- eBay For Dummies
  0-7645-5654-1
- Fighting Spam For Dummies
  0-7645-5965-6
- Genealogy Online For Dummies
  0-7645-5964-8
- Google For Dummies
  0-7645-4420-9

- Home Recording For Musicians
  For Dummies
  0-7645-1634-5
- The Internet For Dummies
  0-7645-4173-0
- iPod & iTunes For Dummies
  0-7645-7772-7
- Preventing Identity Theft For Dummies
  0-7645-7336-5
- Pro Tools All-in-One Desk Reference
  For Dummies
  0-7645-5714-9
- Roxio Easy Media Creator For Dummies
  0-7645-7131-1

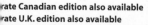

rate Canadian edition also available
rate U.K. edition also available

le wherever books are sold. For more information or to order direct: U.S. customers visit www.dummies.com or call 1-877-762-2974.
tomers visit www.wileyeurope.com or call 0800 243407. Canadian customers visit www.wiley.ca or call 1-800-567-4797.

SPORTS, FITNESS, PARENTING, RELIGION & SPIRITUALITY

0-7645-5146-9

0-7645-5418-2

Also available:
- Adoption For Dummies
  0-7645-5488-3
- Basketball For Dummies
  0-7645-5248-1
- The Bible For Dummies
  0-7645-5296-1
- Buddhism For Dummies
  0-7645-5359-3
- Catholicism For Dummies
  0-7645-5391-7
- Hockey For Dummies
  0-7645-5228-7

- Judaism For Dummies
  0-7645-5299-6
- Martial Arts For Dummies
  0-7645-5358-5
- Pilates For Dummies
  0-7645-5397-6
- Religion For Dummies
  0-7645-5264-3
- Teaching Kids to Read For Dumm
  0-7645-4043-2
- Weight Training For Dummies
  0-7645-5168-X
- Yoga For Dummies
  0-7645-5117-5

TRAVEL

0-7645-5438-7

0-7645-5453-0

Also available:
- Alaska For Dummies
  0-7645-1761-9
- Arizona For Dummies
  0-7645-6938-4
- Cancún and the Yucatán For Dummies
  0-7645-2437-2
- Cruise Vacations For Dummies
  0-7645-6941-4
- Europe For Dummies
  0-7645-5456-5
- Ireland For Dummies
  0-7645-5455-7

- Las Vegas For Dummies
  0-7645-5448-4
- London For Dummies
  0-7645-4277-X
- New York City For Dummies
  0-7645-6945-7
- Paris For Dummies
  0-7645-5494-8
- RV Vacations For Dummies
  0-7645-5443-3
- Walt Disney World & Orlando For Dum
  0-7645-6943-0

GRAPHICS, DESIGN & WEB DEVELOPMENT

0-7645-4345-8

0-7645-5589-8

Also available:
- Adobe Acrobat 6 PDF For Dummies
  0-7645-3760-1
- Building a Web Site For Dummies
  0-7645-7144-3
- Dreamweaver MX 2004 For Dummies
  0-7645-4342-3
- FrontPage 2003 For Dummies
  0-7645-3882-9
- HTML 4 For Dummies
  0-7645-1995-6
- Illustrator CS For Dummies
  0-7645-4084-X

- Macromedia Flash MX 2004 For Dum
  0-7645-4358-X
- Photoshop 7 All-in-One Desk
  Reference For Dummies
  0-7645-1667-1
- Photoshop CS Timesaving Technic
  For Dummies
  0-7645-6782-9
- PHP 5 For Dummies
  0-7645-4166-8
- PowerPoint 2003 For Dummies
  0-7645-3908-6
- QuarkXPress 6 For Dummies
  0-7645-2593-X

NETWORKING, SECURITY, PROGRAMMING & DATABASES

0-7645-6852-3

0-7645-5784-X

Also available:
- A+ Certification For Dummies
  0-7645-4187-0
- Access 2003 All-in-One Desk
  Reference For Dummies
  0-7645-3988-4
- Beginning Programming For Dummies
  0-7645-4997-9
- C For Dummies
  0-7645-7068-4
- Firewalls For Dummies
  0-7645-4048-3
- Home Networking For Dummies
  0-7645-42796

- Network Security For Dummies
  0-7645-1679-5
- Networking For Dummies
  0-7645-1677-9
- TCP/IP For Dummies
  0-7645-1760-0
- VBA For Dummies
  0-7645-3989-2
- Wireless All In-One Desk Reference
  For Dummies
  0-7645-7496-5
- Wireless Home Networking For Dum
  0-7645-3910-8

LTH & SELF-HELP

-7645-6820-5 *†

0-7645-2566-2

Also available:

- Alzheimer's For Dummies
  0-7645-3899-3
- Asthma For Dummies
  0-7645-4233-8
- Controlling Cholesterol For Dummies
  0-7645-5440-9
- Depression For Dummies
  0-7645-3900-0
- Dieting For Dummies
  0-7645-4149-8
- Fertility For Dummies
  0-7645-2549-2

- Fibromyalgia For Dummies
  0-7645-5441-7
- Improving Your Memory For Dummies
  0-7645-5435-2
- Pregnancy For Dummies †
  0-7645-4483-7
- Quitting Smoking For Dummies
  0-7645-2629-4
- Relationships For Dummies
  0-7645-5384-4
- Thyroid For Dummies
  0-7645-5385-2

CATION, HISTORY, REFERENCE & TEST PREPARATION

0-7645-5194-9

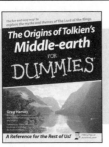

0-7645-4186-2

Also available:

- Algebra For Dummies
  0-7645-5325-9
- British History For Dummies
  0-7645-7021-8
- Calculus For Dummies
  0-7645-2498-4
- English Grammar For Dummies
  0-7645-5322-4
- Forensics For Dummies
  0-7645-5580-4
- The GMAT For Dummies
  0-7645-5251-1
- Inglés Para Dummies
  0-7645-5427-1

- Italian For Dummies
  0-7645-5196-5
- Latin For Dummies
  0-7645-5431-X
- Lewis & Clark For Dummies
  0-7645-2545-X
- Research Papers For Dummies
  0-7645-5426-3
- The SAT I For Dummies
  0-7645-7193-1
- Science Fair Projects For Dummies
  0-7645-5460-3
- U.S. History For Dummies
  0-7645-5249-X

Get smart @ dummies.com®

- **Find a full list of Dummies titles**
- **Look into loads of FREE on-site articles**
- **Sign up for FREE eTips e-mailed to you weekly**
- **See what other products carry the Dummies name**
- **Shop directly from the Dummies bookstore**
- **Enter to win new prizes every month!**

arate Canadian edition also available
arate U.K. edition also available

ble wherever books are sold. For more information or to order direct: U.S. customers visit www.dummies.com or call 1-877-762-2974.
stomers visit www.wileyeurope.com or call 0800 243407. Canadian customers visit www.wiley.ca or call 1-800-567-4797.